Rethinking Modernism

Edited by

Marianne Thormählen

First published 2003 by
PALGRAVE MACMILLAN
Houndmills, Basingstoke, Hampshire RG21 6XS and
175 Fifth Avenue, New York, N. Y. 10010
Companies and representatives throughout the world

PALGRAVE MACMILLAN is the global academic imprint of the Palgrave
Macmillan division of St. Martin's Press, LLC and of Palgrave Macmillan Ltd.
Macmillan® is a registered trademark in the United States, United Kingdom
and other countries. Palgrave is a registered trademark in the European
Union and other countries.

ISBN 1–4039–1180–0

This book is printed on paper suitable for recycling and made from fully
managed and sustained forest sources.

A catalogue record for this book is available from the British Library.

A catalog record for this book is available from the Library of Congress.

10   9   8   7   6   5   4   3   2   1
12   11   10   09   08   07   06   05   04   03

Graphic design and pre-press production by Alf Dahlberg/PAN EIDOS, Lund,
Sweden

Printed and bound in Great Britain by
Antony Rowe Ltd, Chippenham and Eastbourne

Rethinking Modernism

Also by Marianne Thormählen

'THE WASTE LAND': A Fragmentary Wholeness

ELIOT'S ANIMALS

ROCHESTER: The Poems in Context

T.S. ELIOT AT THE TURN OF THE CENTURY (*editor*)

THE BRONTËS AND RELIGION

Contents

Notes on Contributors

Derek Attridge is currently Leverhulme Research Professor in the Department of English and Related Literature, University of York, England. His chief specialities are James Joyce and prosody; but he has published widely on a number of subjects, including poststructuralist theory, and edited the 1992 Routledge edition of Jacques Derrida's *Acts of Literature*. His most recent book is a theoretical study entitled *The Singularity of Literature*, and he is completing a book on the fiction of J. M. Coetzee. His publications in the field of modernism include *Joyce Effects: On Language, Theory, and History*, Cambridge University Press 2000, and (as editor) *The Cambridge Companion to James Joyce*, Cambridge University Press 1990, and *Semicolonial Joyce*, Cambridge University Press 2000.

Michael Bell is Professor of English at the University of Warwick. His chief scholarly interests are nineteenth- and twentieth-century fiction, in Europe and Latin America as well as in Britain, and philosophy in relation to the novel. He is currently at work on a study of the *Bildungsroman*. Michael Bell's publications in the field of modernism include *The Context of English Literature: 1900–1930*, Methuen 1980; *D. H. Lawrence: Language and Being*, Cambridge University Press 1992; and *Literature, Modernism, and Myth: Belief and Responsibility in the Twentieth Century*, Cambridge University Press 1997. His most recent book is *Sentimentalism, Ethics and the Culture of Feeling*, Palgrave 2000.

Jewel Spears Brooker is Professor of English at Eckerd College, St Petersburg, Florida. Her main speciality is T. S. Eliot, but she has worked on other American writers as well, primarily Katherine Anne Porter, Denise Levertov, and Richard Wilbur. Her publications in the field of modernism include *Reading The Waste Land: Modernism and the Limits of Interpretation*, with Joseph Bentley as co-author, University of Massachusetts Press 1990; and *Mastery and Escape: T. S. Eliot and the Dialectic of Modernism*, University of Massachusetts Press 1994. Jewel Spears Brooker edited *The Placing of T. S. Eliot*, University of Missouri Press 1991, and *T. S. Eliot and Our Turning World*, Macmillan 2001.

Gunilla Florby is Professor of English Literature at the University of Gothenburg. Her main scholarly interests are Renaissance literature, especially drama, and Canadian fiction. She is just completing a study of George Chapman's Byron plays as a companion volume to her *The Painful Passage to Virtue: A Study of George Chapman's The Tragedy of Bussy D'Ambois and The Revenge of Bussy D'Ambois*, Lund Studies in English 1982, No. 61. Her most recent book is *The Margin Speaks: A Study of Margaret Laurence and Robert Kroetsch from a Post-Colonial Point of View*, Lund Studies in English 1997, No. 93.

Erik Hedling is Professor of Comparative Literature, especially Film Studies, at Lund University. In addition to his primary research field, he is interested in the interrelationships of the arts and has co-edited (with fellow Lundians Ulla-Britta Lagerroth and Hans Lund) *Interart Poetics: Essays on the Interrelationships of the Arts and Media*, Rodopi 1997, and (with Ulla-Britta Lagerroth) *Cultural Functions of Intermedial Exploration*, Rodopi 2002. His most recent book in English is *Lindsay Anderson: Maverick Film-Maker*, Cassell 1998.

Stefan Holander is an Assistant Professor of English at Finnmark University College, Norway. He is writing a dissertation on Wallace Stevens for Lund University.

Christopher Innes holds the Canada Research Chair in Performance and Culture, and has been Distinguished Research Professor at York University in Toronto since 1996. He began his academic publishing career with two books on German drama and has gone on to writing books about English-language drama, especially the avant-garde. His publications in the field of modernism include *Holy Theatre: Ritual and the Avant Garde*, Cambridge University Press 1981; *Modern British Drama: 1890-1990*, Cambridge University Press 1992; *Avant Garde Theatre: 1892–1992*, Routledge 1993; *British & American Twentieth Century Theatre: A Critical Guide to Archives*, Scolar Press 1999; and *Modern British Drama: The Twentieth Century*, Cambridge University Press 2002. Christopher Innes edited *The Cambridge Companion to Bernard Shaw*, Cambridge University Press 1998, and (with Frederick Marker) *Modernism in European Drama*, UTP 1998.

Edna Longley is a Professor of English at Queen's University, Belfast. Her chief research interests are modern poetry in Ireland and Britain and Irish cultural questions, interests featuring in her *The Living Stream: Literature and Revisionism in Ireland*, Bloodaxe 1994. Her publications in the field of modernism include *Louis MacNeice: A Study*, Faber & Faber 1989, and editions of the poetry and prose of Edward Thomas. She has edited a number of selections of modern writers as well as *The Bloodaxe Book of 20th Century Poetry from Britain and Ireland*, 2000. Edna Longley's most recent book is *Poetry & Posterity*, Bloodaxe 2000.

Lennart Nyberg is a Senior Lecturer in English Literature at Lund University. His main specialities are drama and twentieth-century poetry. He has published a book on twentieth-century productions of Shakespeare, *The Shakespearean Ideal: Shakespeare Production and the Modern Theatre in Britain*, Studia Anglistica Upsaliensa No. 66, 1988, and a Swedish translation of Emily Dickinson's poetry.

Claude Rawson is Maynard Mack Professor of English at Yale University. His main field is eighteenth-century literature, but he has published a number of essays and articles on twentieth-century poetry, among them studies of Wallace Stevens, Dylan Thomas, Philip Larkin, and John Ashbery. He was until recently Chairman of the Yale Boswell editions and serves on a number of editorial boards, among them that of *Modernism/Modernity*. Claude Rawson's most recent book is *God, Gulliver, and Genocide: Barbarism and the European Imagination 1492-1945*, Oxford University Press 2001.

Vincent B. Sherry is Professor of English at Villanova University, Pennsylvania. His research interests range over the twentieth century as a whole, and some of his studies trace developments over several decades up to the present time. He is currently working on a study of the First World War and literature, *The Great War and the Language of Modernism*, forthcoming from Oxford University Press in 2003. His publications in the field of modernism include *Ezra Pound, Wyndham Lewis, and Radical Modernism*, Oxford University Press 1993, and *James Joyce: ULYSSES*, Cambridge University Press 1995.

Stan Smith is Research Professor in Literary Studies at Nottingham Trent University. He is interested in literature from the late as well as the early twentieth century and has published essays on, among others, Ted Hughes and Seamus Heaney. Stan Smith is currently preparing a new book on Auden, to be called *Ruined Boys: W. H. Auden and the Lineage of Modernism*, an edition of Auden's *The Orators*, and a *Cambridge Companion* to Auden. His publications in the field of modernism include *W. H. Auden*, Blackwell 1985; *Edward Thomas*, Faber & Faber 1986; *W. B. Yeats: A Critical Introduction*, Macmillan 1990; and *The Origins of Modernism: Eliot, Pound, Yeats and the Rhetorics of Renewal*, Harvester Wheatsheaf 1994.

Lars-Håkan Svensson is Professor of Language and Culture at the University of Linköping. His main research interests are Renaissance poetry, particularly Daniel and Spenser, and twentieth-century literature, especially the modern novel in the English-speaking world and contemporary poetry in Ireland and America. The author of a study of Daniel's *Delia, Silent Art: Rhetorical and Thematic Patterns in Samuel Daniel's Delia*, Lund Studies in English 1980, No. 57, he is currently working on a book on Spenser.

Marianne Thormählen is Professor of English Literature at Lund University. Her chief research interests are Restoration literature, mid-nineteenth-century fiction, and early-twentieth-century poetry. Marianne Thormählen's publications in the field of modernism include *The Waste Land: A Fragmentary Wholeness*, Lund Studies in English 1978, No. 52; *Eliot's Animals*, Lund Studies in English 1984, No. 70; and (as editor) *T. S. Eliot at the Turn of the Century*, Lund Studies in English 1994, No. 86. Her most recent book is *The Brontës and Religion*, Cambridge University Press 1999.

David Trotter is King Edward VII Professor of English Literature at the University of Cambridge. His research interests include seventeenth- and eighteenth-century literature and culture; science, society, and the arts from the late nineteenth to the early twentieth century; and twentieth-century poetry in English. David Trotter's publications in the field of modernism include *The Making of the Reader: Language and Subjectivity in Modern American, English and Irish Poetry*, Macmillan 1984; *The English Novel in History 1895-1920*, Routledge 1994; and *Paranoid Modernism: Literary Experiment, Psychosis, and the Professionalization of English Society*, Oxford University Press 2001.

Acknowledgements

Acknowledgement is due to Faber and Faber Ltd for permission to quote from the poetry and prose of T. S. Eliot and Ezra Pound. The permissions issued by this publisher did not cover the American market, however, and the following US permissions have been gratefully received:

Excerpts from 'Burnt Norton' in *Four Quartets* by T. S. Eliot, copyright 1936 by Harcourt, Inc. and renewed 1964 by T. S. Eliot, reprinted by permission of the publisher; excerpts from 'East Coker' in *Four Quartets*, copyright 1940 by T. S. Eliot and renewed 1968 by Esme Valerie Eliot, reprinted by permission of Harcourt, Inc.; excerpts from 'Little Gidding' in *Four Quartets*, copyright 1942 by T. S. Eliot and renewed 1970 by Esme Valerie Eliot, reprinted by permission of Harcourt, Inc.; excerpt from 'The Function of Criticism' in *Selected Prose of T. S. Eliot*, copyright © 1975 by Valerie Eliot, reprinted by permission of Harcourt, Inc.; excerpt from *After Strange Gods: A Primer of Modern Heresy* by T. S. Eliot, copyright 1934 by Harcourt, Inc. and renewed 1962 by T. S. Eliot, reprinted by permission of the publisher; excerpts from *Inventions of the March Hare: Poems 1909–1917* by T. S. Eliot, text copyright © 1996 by Valerie Eliot, reprinted by permission of Harcourt, Inc.; excerpts from *The Use of Poetry and the Use of Criticism* (1933) by T. S. Eliot, reprinted by permission of Harvard University Press; excerpts from *To Criticize the Critic* by T. S. Eliot, copyright 1965 by T. S. Eliot, renewed © 1993 by Valerie Eliot, reprinted by permission of Farrar, Straus and Giroux, LLC; excerpts from *The Cantos of Ezra Pound*, copyright © 1934, 1937, 1940, 1948, 1959, 1962, 1963, 1966 and 1968 by Ezra Pound, used by permission of the New Directions Publishing Corporation; excerpts from *The Collected Early Poems of Ezra Pound*, copyright © 1926, 1935, 1954, 1965, 1967, 1976 by The Ezra Pound Literary Property Trust, used by permission of the New Directions Publishing Corporation; excerpt from *Selected Letters 1907–1941* by Ezra Pound, copyright © by Ezra Pound, used by permission of the New Directions Publishing Corporation.

Acknowledgement is also due to Faber and Faber Ltd for permission to quote from the works of W. H. Auden, Samuel Beckett, and Paul Muldoon; the latter also graciously granted personal permission to quote his poem 'Sushi' on pp. 172–3 of this book.

For permission to quote from the *Poems* of W. B. Yeats (ed. A. N. Jeffares, Macmillan 1989), acknowledgement is due to A. P. Watt Ltd on behalf of Michael B. Yeats. David Higham Associates granted permission to quote from the *Collected Poems* of Louis MacNeice (ed. E. R. Dodds, Faber and Faber 1966), and Houghton Mifflin Company gave permission to quote from Archibald MacLeish's 'Ars Poetica', the excerpt being taken from MacLeish's *Collected Poems 1917–1982*, © 1985 by The Estate of Archibald MacLeish, all rights reserved. The Society of Authors as the Literary Representative of the Estate of Virginia Woolf and Harcourt, Inc. (the latter with regard to US rights) generously granted free permission to quote from Virginia Woolf's *A Room of One's Own* (1928). The Literary Trustees of Walter de la Mare and the Society of Authors as their representative kindly granted permission to quote the poem 'The Listeners', on pp. 82–3 below, from de la Mare's *Collected Poems* (Faber and Faber 1979). Special thanks are due to Ms Lisa Dowdeswell at the Society of Authors, Ms Christine Smith at Harcourt, Inc., and Mr Dennis O. Palmore at New Directions for swift and courteous assistance over copyright matters.

Every effort has been made by the editor and publishers to secure permissions for all relevant works, and if any have been missed we will be happy to rectify the situation at the earliest opportunity.

Preface

Rethinking Modernism is the outcome of a research project funded by the former Swedish Council for Research in the Humanities and Social Sciences, now part of the joint Swedish Research Council. The aim of the project, which was called 'Elusive Modernism', was to explore the meaning and applicability of the term 'modernism' from a sceptical perspective. The designated general query was not so much 'what was modernism?' as 'was/ is modernism?'

In September 2000 the contributors to the present volume met for a three-day symposium in Lund, Sweden, to confront these issues together – both in the form of paper presentations and in the course of discussions. The latter included a panel debate some of whose highlights are incorporated in the introduction to this book. The contributors thus took the challenges with them into their respective areas of special competence and then brought their answers to Lund, to face and respond to one another's questions. In so doing, they cheerfully submitted to more far-reaching demands than most symposium participants ever encounter. Their loyalty to the project, and to their colleagues, ensured that the memory of the occasion remains an inspiration to everyone who attended. I am profoundly grateful to them all.

Special thanks are due to Professor Thomas Vargish, who served as editorial consultant and unofficial project monitor throughout. Tactful, astute, and humorous, Vargish proved an invaluable assistant, and the introduction is indebted to his summing-up of the symposium in several respects.

The Research Council was not only sole research financer but also main sponsor of the symposium. Two other organizations helped with the latter, however: I am grateful to the Royal Society of Letters in Lund (*Kungliga Humanistiska Vetenskapssamfundet*) and Lund University for helping me meet the costs of the arrangement. As an additional act of generosity, the Research Council made a substantial contribution to the cost of printing this volume, for which both the publisher and I are most grateful. The contributions of the Swedish participants called for visits to libraries in the United Kingdom and the United States, and again the Research Council ensured that such travel was possible. Among the libraries that helped produce this volume, the Bodleian Library and the English Faculty Library in Oxford and the Lund University Library lent especially extensive assistance.

Editing the volume was a much happier experience than such labours usually are, partly because all participants lightened the load by giving me prompt and skilful assistance at every stage and partly because I was able to finish my work on it in a setting which lends itself particularly well to thinking and rethinking of any kind. I am thankful to the Warden and Fellows of All Souls College, Oxford, for awarding me a blissful term as Visiting Fellow, in the course of which my own work on modernism and the Georgians gained new dimensions. A munificent grant from the Magn. Bergvall Foundation helped me make the most of my months in Oxford by covering the additional expenses that arose in consequence of going abroad for a term.

Throughout the production process, I was fortunate in being able to rely on the unfailing professionalism of graphic designer and pre-press producer Alf Dahlberg. As so often during our twenty years of collaboration on various book projects, his wit and good humour added a dimension of pleasure even to the most stressful phases of deadline-beating.

Finally, I wish to thank my daughter Åsa whose superb administrative skills ensured that I was able to enjoy hosting the symposium untroubled by organizational mishaps; my daughter Imke for scrutinizing my own manuscripts with her customary perspicacity; and my husband Axel for bearing the burdens of the project in more than one sense.

Lund in December 2002
Marianne Thormählen

Introduction

Marianne Thormählen

Anyone who performs a computer search on the term 'modernism [literature]' in a British or American research library will see more than three hundred book titles wander across the screen, a large proportion of them specifically related to early twentieth-century literature in English. No classifying concept has played a greater part in academic research on English poetry and fiction in the twentieth century. Many people have a stake in the term; for instance, following Harry Levin, scores of academics have written articles, essays, and book chapters entitled 'What Is/Was Modernism?'[1] Introductions to and readers in literary modernism began to appear in the 1970s, and a spate of expository works ensued. An academic generation after the appearance of Peter Faulkner's and Malcolm Bradbury/James McFarlane's pioneering guides, a 1999 Cambridge Companion testified to the entrenched status of the concept on the eve of the new millennium.[2]

In view of the term's dominance, it might seem perverse to ask whether there ever was such a thing as modernism in the first place; but some bold spirits have done so. One of them, John Harwood, has accused Academe of having 'invented' modernism: according to him, it is an academic fabrication which feeds a number of pseudo-scholars who spend their time picking at meaningless concepts, expressing their pointless findings in dull, jejune prose.[3] Before Harwood, Roger Shattuck created a fictional character who called the term 'modernism' 'a feather bed for critics and professors, an endlessly renewable pretext for scholars to hold conferences'.[4] These unkind definitions would have been easier to dismiss if they had not been barbed with some observations whose pertinence no student of academic literature on modernism can overlook. For example, Harwood rightly points out that virtually all authors on modernism start in a cautious and dutiful manner by saying something about the protean nature of the term and about there being more than one modernism, only to proceed, a few pages later, to employing the concept as if it were unambiguous and self-evident. Clearly there is an element of contradiction in this practice.

It all depends on how it is done, however, and to what end. Acknowledging the complexity of the term 'modernism' while going on to use it with patent ease does not, *per se*, invalidate the term itself. Indeed, those very

1

circumstances could be cited in its favour. After all, an implement with many functions can be extremely handy as long as every user is able to select the function adequate for his/her purpose and handle it appropriately; and around the mid-twentieth century, the swiftly expanding English Literature discipline felt the lack of such a multi-purpose tool as more and more interest was devoted to recent writing. In 1960, Graham Hough lamented that there was still no name for the revolution in English poetry which took place between 1910 and the Second World War.[5] A quarter of a century later, 'modernism' had filled that gap in such a decisive manner that many people had forgotten that a gap had existed, and relatively recently, too. If Academe did invent 'modernism', it did so in response to a need, and the swift acceptance of the term suggests that the need was answered.

In other words, the term 'modernism' was useful; it performed functions. Now that it is possible to survey the work it has done for a couple of decades, it is time to ask whether the outcome of its performance warrants its continued use: in short, it should be subjected to a roadworthiness test. While no one check-up would be likely to lead to the scrapping of such a powerful vehicle, there is reason to investigate the conditions on which it may stay on the road. It should also be possible to identify the circumstances which might, in due course, cause 'modernism' to join the other show-pieces in the museum of exhausted concepts – unless it manages to reinvent itself once more.

One reason for crediting the words 'modernism' and 'modernist' with the ability to perform such a reinvention is that they have done it before. Both were around long before their ready appropriation by Academe in the 1970s and 80s. Laura Riding and Robert Graves's *A Survey of Modernist Poetry* of 1927 – which dealt in part with poets whom later generations have come to regard as non-modernists – is usually cited as one of the earliest examples of their application to literature, but other men and women of letters used the words freely at the same time, and even before that time.[6] Multifariousness was a feature of the terms 'modernism' and 'modernist' from the start. That may be one of the reasons why they did not encourage the formation of a school among early-twentieth-century writers, quite apart from the fact that writers are naturally more apt to resist school-formation processes than academics. In the 1930s and 40s, some members of the educated public had no inhibitions about venting a certain weariness with 'modernist johnnies', not unlike the way 'postmodernist types' are dismissed today. It was thus in spite of a rather chequered history that 'modernism' proceeded to become a 'cheerword' in late-twentieth-century literary criticism,[7] and the fact of its having survived the strains inflicted by its association with a time that is passing from living memory suggests that it remains resilient.

The functions of the term 'modernism' as employed in present-day academic discourse are threefold and interrelated: periodizing, characterizing, and valorizing. None of them is clear-cut, but the first is the least problematic: the temporal core of modernism is located in the 1910s and 20s, 1922 being the *annus mirabilis* and the phrase 'the men of 1914' (usually referring to Ezra Pound, T. S. Eliot, Wyndham Lewis, and James Joyce) attaching a significant moment in time to some of the best-known exponents of modernism. The outside limits tend to be 1890 and 1940.[8]

By far the greatest amount of scholarly interest has been devoted to the second, characterizing, function. As the concept gained general currency, it acquired an accreted mass of partly overlapping characteristics among which the following have been given special emphasis in the relevant literature: a powerful attraction to formal experimentation and innovation;[9] logical ruptures and the linking of ostensibly incompatible phenomena; a deliberate cultivation of ambiguity, multi-facetedness, and associations; a preoccupation with disorder, crisis, randomness, and fragmentation; tautness and irony in the chosen modes of expression; an extreme valorization of art; a rejection of history as a chronological process; cultural pessimism; moral relativism and ambivalence towards philosophical idealism; rootedness in urban, even metropolitan, settings, including the anonymity of crowds and the consequences of technological developments; an interest in representations of sexuality; and explorations of different conceptions of reality and the self.[10]

Patterns and proportions within this assemblage of qualities are constantly being modified as the literature on modernism continues to proliferate. Such modification is naturally gradual, like most relocations of conceptual emphasis; but the third function embodies a disturbing element whose effects have become increasingly impossible to ignore: the tendency of the term 'modernism' to impart positive value to anything and anyone associated with it. While research on English literature is hardly a zero-sum game, the acquisition of favourable connotations by a categorizing term associated with a certain period naturally detracts from the lustre-generating potential of contemporaneous phenomena which are not seen to fall within its scope. And so it has been with modernism: for instance, the printed scholarly/critical works (books, articles, etc.) about the 'regular' modernists can be counted in six-digit numbers whereas the total scholarly/critical monograph literature on the Georgian poets would hardly fill three feet of bookcase space.

Such a discrepancy would not constitute grounds for reflection if it were obvious to any reasonably competent observer that the inferiority of the excluded matter warranted it; but in the face of the best work by, say, Edmund Blunden, W. H. Davies, Rupert Brooke, and James Elroy Flecker, such a stance seems hard to adopt. The enduring popularity of these poets not only among non-specialist readers (and after all, the preferences of the reading

public at large are part of the justification for such burgeoning academic specialities as crime and science fiction), but also among practising writers of
several generations, constitutes food for thought – at least among Eng.Lit.
professionals concerned about the legitimacy of their publicly funded pursuits.

There are other reasons for casting a cold eye on 'modernism' and all its
works. One is that what seemed innovative in the early twentieth century no
longer has the same capacity to surprise, let alone shock, always-already-aware
readers of the early twenty-first century, some hundred years after the onset of
'modernity'. Another, of course, is postmodernism, sometimes seen as a reaction to/against modernism and sometimes as its continuation by other
means. Postmodernism is now passing into history, which is not to say that it
will disappear but that what significance it possesses will not be that of a
paradigm which people feel obliged to position themselves in relation to. As
academics grapple with the consequences of that shift, a sceptical look at the
word itself, both with and without the post-, should be useful. For one thing,
one may wonder whether modernism will in some sense survive its successor.

Rethinking modernism is an undertaking that calls for massive effort on
the part of large numbers of scholars in a variety of fields, and the present
volume only raises a small number of questions in a limited area: that of early-
twentieth-century Anglo-American literature, including drama and film,
seen from the point of view of practising academics whose research necessi-
tates engagement with the modernism concept. Every contributor was asked
to address a topic which seemed to him or her to allow for the application of
a perspective that would be conducive to a re-examination of modernism,
regardless of whether the term itself figured prominently in the discussion.[11]

The outcome is a variegated compilation of essays which do not so much
explore a theme as exercise a set of conceptions. These conceptions are rooted
in engagement with the contention that a modestly proportioned body of
texts written by a small number of authors during a few decades at the beginning of the last century created a milieu – intellectual, artistic, psychological,
sociopolitical – which still, in the words of one of those authors, 'prevents us
everywhere'.

Vincent B. Sherry argues that the radical undermining of confidence in
the rational language of the 'liberal war' was one of the factors that made
modernist writing possible. David Trotter relates existential changes and
choices, chiefly with a bearing on T. E. Hulme and Wyndham Lewis, to the
evolution of the modernist will-to-abstraction. Lennart Nyberg looks at the
erasure of the imagination in modernism as a matter of relations rather than
essences, suggesting that Romanticism was an enduring presence in the twentieth century. Jewel Spears Brooker raises the question of the artist's moral

responsibility for his work, indicating that the aftermath of World War II, including the fate of Ezra Pound, caused T. S. Eliot to move away from modernist contentions concerning the supremacy of art over ethics. Marianne Thormählen maintains that the gulf between traditionalists and experimentalists in early-twentieth-century poetry is largely the creation of an academic posterity, hostile to what it has mistakenly regarded as the stale conventionalism of the Georgian poets. Claude Rawson revisits the modernist fascination with the primitive, investigating T. S. Eliot's meeting with Joseph Conrad's Kurtz in a discussion highlighting modern(ist) alienation. Lars-Håkan Svensson draws attention to Pound's and H. D.'s translations and appropriations of classical poetry as elements in the creation of poetic forms that were unique to modernism. Michael Bell explores the modernism concept in relation to the fiction of D. H. Lawrence, whose debatable 'modernist' status constitutes an instructive test case. Derek Attridge extends the referential range of 'modernism' by comparing *Ulysses* to Sigrid Undset's *Kristin Lavransdatter*, a very dissimilar novel which also appeared in 1922, finding artistic vigour and inventiveness in both. Edna Longley subjects conceptions of modernism to sharply sceptical scrutiny in the context of Irish writing and Irish nationalism throughout the twentieth century. Stan Smith surveys the vicissitudes of the terms 'modern', 'modernist', and 'modernism' from the 1920s to the 1940s, analysing T. S. Eliot's part – or rather parts – in their various manifestations. Christopher Innes explores the special and problematic relationship between the concept of modernism and early-twentieth-century theatre, with emphases on W. B. Yeats, T. S. Eliot, and Samuel Beckett. Erik Hedling shows that the use of the 'modernism' concept in film studies was closely associated with political factors at the time when film was establishing itself in Academe. Stefan Holander examines the respective basis, in relation to modernism, of some high-profile critiques of Wallace Stevens' poetry, finding not only divergences but also unexpected similarities. Finally, Gunilla Florby asks the question which no radical reconsideration of the modernism concept in the early twenty-first century can avoid, 'So what about postmodernism?', proceeding to answer it by means of pitting Linda Hutcheon against Fredric Jameson.

In addition to presenting the results of his or her own investigation, every scholar from whom an essay was commissioned accepted enrolment in a project expressly intended to challenge the 'modernism' concept. In the course of three days of intense discussion and debate, the term was subjected to the kind of scrutiny that has been known in other contexts as 'thinking the unthinkable' – in this case the possibility that the time has come to retire the concept of modernism, or even that there was no good reason to adopt it in the first place.

While these discussions brought out plenty of diverging nuances, constantly confirming the volatile character of the term 'modernism', there was agreement that the existence and continued application of the term remain justified. The only reason for attempting to outlaw a concept which has become so widely established would be that it has somehow been ethically contaminated, and no such case has been made. Events have taken place and words have formed around them; 'modernism' is such a word, and as long as it is carefully handled its uses outweigh its drawbacks. Like 'Renaissance' and 'Romanticism', it incorporates the acknowledgement of a major shift in epistemology and sensibility located around a certain point in time. While later generations cannot recreate the experience of the shock that such a loss of *terra firma* entailed, they – we – can salute it in accepting its legacy: affirming that we have not reached conclusion, refusing fixity in method and attitude, and recognizing that volatility can be seen as a sign of life, indeed of health.

Even so, a concept cannot be useful if it is allowed to mean anything and serve any purpose, and 'modernism' may be invested with a basic set of properties along the following lines: Applied to a limited period of time, approximately from 1910 to the early 1930s (with the partial exception of the theatre where modernist principles reached their highest and purest expression at a later date, in Beckett's plays), it denotes a high degree of awareness in relation to the epoch commonly referred to as 'modernity', with its revolutionary social changes and developments in science and technology. The word is applicable to certain literary/artistic phenomena which did not manifest themselves, or did not manifest themselves so patently and at such a universal level, during preceding periods and did not subsequently occupy positions of comparable dominance. It signals the presence/existence of certain clearly defined qualities, such as an experimental attitude towards the traditional forms of literary expression, a preparedness to challenge logic and order, and keen perceptiveness as regards the multiplicity of language.

The problem with the concept of modernism resides in what was referred to above as the third, valorizing, function. Being designated as 'modernist' has undoubtedly raised the prestige of a literary text or writer, a practice which has had two unfortunate consequences: works on which the label has not seemed to fit have been unfairly neglected, and the area of applicability has been stretched to (and sometimes beyond) the limit of meaningfulness – 'this work/author is so good/important that it/he/she must be an exponent of modernism, even if nothing specifically modernist leaps to the eye'. While 'modernism' is helpful when it comes to defining relationships, allowing us to establish differences as well as contiguity, it is simply not workable with regard to many of the twentieth-century works of literature and art whose survival testifies to their enduring appeal. The evolution of complementary terms and conceptual instruments which would be serviceable in scholarly engagement with such works must not be inhibited by the sheer viability of the term 'modernism'.

The concept of modernism may thus help present-day scholars to discriminate in constructive ways. However, they must be on their guard against allowing it to serve discriminatory, in the sense of derogatory or invalidating, purposes, and it is incumbent on them to ensure that their readers are apprised of the significance of the concept as employed in the particular context. 'Modernism' as used by present-day literary critics and scholars is an academic construct; and like all sound manufacturers and tradesmen, academics must accept responsibility for how their product works.

*

Rethinking modernism is a pursuit that must continue, assuming a multitude of shapes in conformity with the protean character of the elusive object itself. Among the most obvious omissions in the present volume are sustained engagement with the Continental roots of modernism, with the arts in general, and with science, philosophy, psychology, and sociology. A variety of temporal issues need to be addressed, too: when did 'the present' cease to be 'modern' and become merely 'contemporary'? Or is 'modernity' still where we are, and in that case, how justified is the comfortably backward-looking, historicizing perspective that the essays in this book employ? Related concepts in the other European languages should be considered alongside 'modernism' – *die Moderne* in German usage, the Hispanic *modernismo* which is closer to 'modernism' and yet not quite the same, and the French *modernité* which extends farther back into the nineteenth century than 'modernism' is normally allowed to do in an Anglo-American context. Considerations along those lines should incorporate continued examination of the functions of suffixes and prefixes (such as -ism, -ity, and post- in English). The bibliography that concludes this book defines ten special areas of enquiry for modernism scholarship; some are more recently established than others, their vigour and diversity suggesting a great deal of scope for further development. Continued efforts are required in most of them, though, and that will not be all: the peculiar dynamic that adheres to modernism, however defined, is a guarantee that they will be joined by others.

Notes

1 Levin's seminal lecture/essay was delivered and printed several times; see, for instance, Levin's *Refractions: Essays in Contemporary Literature* (Oxford: Oxford University Press, 1966).

2 Faulkner's *Modernism* appeared from Methuen in 1977, being followed in 1986 by a volume edited by him and called *A Modernist Reader: Modernism in England 1910–1930*, from B. T. Batsford (London). Malcolm Bradbury and James McFarlane (eds), *Modernism, 1890–1930*, a Pelican Guide to Literature volume which also takes non-English literature into account, appeared from Penguin in 1976 (Harmondsworth). *The Cambridge Companion to Modernism* (Cambridge: Cambridge University Press, 1999) was edited by Michael Levenson.

3 See ch. 1 in Harwood's *Eliot to Derrida: The Poverty of Interpretation* (London: Macmillan, 1995).

4 See the discussion of 'The Poverty of Modernism' in *The Innocent Eye* (New York: Farrar, Straus, Giroux, 1984), written for the conference that resulted in Monique Chefdor, Ricardo Quinones, and Albert Wachtel (eds), *Modernism: Challenges and Perspectives* (Urbana: University of Illinois Press, 1986).

5 In *Image and Experience*. See Faulkner, *Modernism*, p. ix. It is noteworthy that *The Pelican Guide to English Literature*, as late as 1961, did not mention modernism.

6 See, for instance, p. 78 below on Edwin Muir and Edith Sitwell's lecture 'Experiment in Poetry', *Tradition and Experiment in Present-Day Literature: Addresses Delivered at the City Literary Institute* (Oxford: Oxford University Press and Humphrey Milford, London, 1929), pp. 83, 87, 90, and 92–3.

7 Denis Donoghue has said that 'we continue to use [Modernism] as a swear-word or a cheer-word'; see *The Old Moderns: Essays on Literature and Theory* (New York: Alfred A. Knopf, 1994), p. ix.

8 Michael H. Levenson's *A Genealogy of Modernism* carries the subtitle *A Study of English Literary Doctrine 1908–1922* (Cambridge: Cambridge University Press, 1984). The commonest extended time-span is 1890–1930. The French connection is a factor of importance when it comes to determining the *terminus a quo*. In this regard, it is interesting to observe that Eliot, Pound, and others joined what was very much an Edwardian preoccupation; see Eric Homberger, 'Modernists and Edwardians', in Philip Glover (ed.), *Ezra Pound The London Years: 1908–1920* (New York: AMS Press, 1987), pp. 1–14.

9 The degree to which this particular element has come to be associated with the concept of modernism is suggested by the fact that a search on 'modernism' in the Bodleian OLIS catalogue proposes the 'narrower term' 'Literature, Experimental'.

10 This compilation was made on the basis of several works on modernism, among them Norman F. Cantor, *Twentieth-Century Culture: Modernism to Deconstruction* (New York etc.: Peter Lang, 1988), ch. 2, and Astradur Eysteinsson, *The Concept of Modernism* (Ithaca and London: Cornell University Press, 1990), ch. 2.

11 All contributors were free to choose the typographical representation of their 'modernism' – whether or not they wished to spell it with an upper-case initial letter or use quotation marks – as the variations in this book testify.

1

Liberal Measures: Language, Modernism, and the Great War

Vincent B. Sherry

The meaning the term *modernity* has acquired in its circulation through the scholarly discourses of the last two decades is now relatively certain. It refers us to the circumstances emergent in western history *circa* 1500. These are the nascent days of the Protestant Reformation, within Christendom, and, within civic tradition, of political Liberalism. These two influences join to forge what might be called, at least in the consensus understanding of our contemporaries, the main intellectual temper of modernity. It is drawn by John Rawls, for instance, in his *Political Liberalism*, which locates the historical origin of its subject in the Reformation and its immediate aftermath, when the need to achieve agreement between equal but opposing views is at once new and pressing. Out of these circumstances the theme words Rawls sounds are *Reason*, or the *reasonable*. These are taken to mean not so much an epistemological process, or not only that, but rather a whole social attitude, whose aspects he gathers under the heading of 'Public Reason'. Here an admitted diversity of competing needs and conflicting interests is addressed and appealed to a tonic and resolving power. This is a common sense that is also a 'sensis communis', where the better capacities of rational humanity operate, to communitarian benefit, through a reason equally practical and prudential.[1] Ideally said, to be sure. But expressive nonetheless of a recognizable norm, one against which departures and regressions are … well, departures, regressions. It is under the myth of *free* reason, working to the service and purpose of a *liberation* that is shared and reciprocated by other rational agents, that the main story of the *modern*, one primary meaning of the word, is told.

But modern*ism*? The sense the suffix adds cuts two ways, at least. As an *intensification*, 'ism' suggests some extreme instance of the primary quality here, thus of the liberal rationalism Rawls so representatively posits as its meaning. And in this sense 'modernism' would denominate accurately the activity to which it was in fact first applied. This was a movement specifically *religious*, occurring at the turn of the last century within the Catholic churches of England and France primarily, where a pressure identifiably or nominally liberal submitted scripture and dogma to rational, even sceptical analysis. [2] Alternatively, however, and in view of a more radical and elementary meaning of *modern*, which, as a word, derives from *hodie*, meaning 'these times', or, more accurately, '*recent* times': [3] here the 'ism' attached to 'modern' may represent the sense of a *particular moment* of history, an instant defined by a sense of itself as *separate*, all in all of residence in a present made inten*ser* by virtue of its self-conscious *difference* from what went before.

Now, it is pretty clear that if the literary production we know as modernist holds together at all, it hardly coheres as an extension of religious modernism: no triumph of the hyper-rational attitude, it is no more obviously a celebration of political liberalism. Whatever memory the marker preserved of this turn-of-the-century reference, when it entered wider currency as a term in literary history, it evidently settled, with the indiscriminate force of gravity, to label an energy once perceived and, long ago, even feared (from one vantage) as insurgent, counter-conventional. What convention literary modernism was sensed to counter is what interests me here. For the liberal rationalism that offers the historically grounded meaning of 'the modern' is the precedent and tradition to which literary modernism may be seen, at least in a sense worth entertaining here, to mark itself off from as its own exception; in its own separate, special, intenser present.

To test and develop this notion I turn our attentions to the moment in cultural time that stands perhaps as the most vivid instance of difference, of disruption, in the history of liberal modernity: the Great War of 1914–18. This event is cited by routine procedure as the watershed occurrence of the modern, when faith in the empirical Reason of science and its collateral belief in material Progress met its discredited end, among other things, in mass-technological warfare. Accordingly, it is to this spot of time that the activities of literary modernism are assigned by critics and historians to find their most representative, indeed exemplary, demonstrations. Yet these gestures of reference have tended to be made within world-cultural and world-historical frames and so have merged ever into perspectives really too epic to be credible. [4] If an historically responsible case is to be made for the existence and validity of a modernist literature, it is undertaken best, I propose, in a reading of the work emanating from and echoing back to war-time London – in a reading informed now, and here really for the first time, by a fully contextualized sense of the local and specific determinants on this writing, that is, of the really timely crisis of its intenser present. For it is in the political and intellectual culture of the English war in particular that we find the tradition of liberal modernity at its climax and climacteric, an upheaval which the writers of a specifically English modernism will distinguish themselves, first, by identifying, and then, by igniting to.

The *reasonableness* of the liberal war was a conceit deeply and revealingly paradoxical. The liberal government of Prime Minister Asquith and his Foreign Secretary Sir Edward Grey had inherited an ethic and method in matters of international relations from the nineteenth-century liberalism of Prime Minister Gladstone. This tradition consistently reiterated, variously in the policy documents of Gladstone's government and the *public* professions of Asquith's, the absolute and compelling need to *reason out*, on moral grounds, every foreign policy move, especially one involving military action The difficulty? Asquith and Grey were really Liberal Imperialists; they had entered a number of secret agreements and silent alliances to protect British interests in a global dominion they remained in support of. One of their pacts had bound them to France's side, itself bound to Russia, in the event of war with the Austro-Hungarian Empire. We know the rest of that story. What the British public did not know, and what the whole weight of the Gladstonian *ethos* worked to prevent the knowledge of, was the existence of those secret agreements. For an alliance system defied the idea of a moral rationale for war, taking away the freedom needed to make the 'correct' decision. It had been labelled 'that foul idol of our foreign policy' by John Bright, Gladstone's co-believer.[5] And so, in the days of early August 1914, the letter of those still secret agreements was being translated into the spirit of something quite different, since the Government was compelled, at least in public, to speak the language of ethical and prudential reasoning proper to a Gladstonian diplomacy. They found a serviceable cause in the case of Belgium, which Germany invaded on 2 August, but the fact that the decision had been taken several days earlier to go to war on France's side gave the lie to such pronunciations.

What this situation outlines then is a crisis in that language of rational morality that provided the standard and mainstay of liberal modernity, of Rawls's 'Idea of Public Reason'. A signal instance of the compromised character of this tradition comes in the address Foreign Secretary Grey delivered to Parliament on 3 August. Here the case being made for war is being offered in effect to the ethical deliberations of a freely reasoning and representative body.[6] Where its eloquent evangile takes up the case of Belgium, and uses it to appeal to the sensibility that will legitimate British involvement in a continental war, its moral logic seeks a sanction for military initiatives that are in fact already underway. The underlying and ramifying irony here reaches in its implications and consequences far beyond the now obvious hypocrisy of the performance. It strikes the keynote of the liberal war, of the language of the liberal war, which witnesses consistently a similar division between the public words of ethical rectitude, of prudential rationale, and some unkillable intimation that THIS IS NOT THE CASE.

An early instance of this division appears in the pages of two of the representative journals of political liberalism, the *Manchester Guardian* and the *Westminster Gazette*. The editorial of the *Guardian*, to begin with, holds true to the standard of Reason at Liberty, and protests openly that citizens and Parliament have not been given sufficient information, in this summary phrase, 'to form a *reasoned* judgment on the current of our policy.' The editor expatiates, in questions more than rhetorical: 'Is it *rational*? ... Can it be reconciled with any *reasonable* view of British policy? It cannot.'[7] Can*not*? Listen to this report of the speech, in the news leader of the same day, in the *Westminster Gazette*, beginning with this wholly credulous echoing of the Foreign Secretary's key words; of Grey's

> appeal to every man in the House to look into his heart and feeling and solve the question of our obligation for himself.
>
> From this Sir Edward Grey passed to the consideration of the present position of the French fleet in the Mediterranean which *evidently* sprang out of the plans for cooperation. The French fleet was in the Mediterranean *because of the feeling of confidence* between the two countries. *Hence it followed* that if a foreign fleet came down the channel we could not stand aside and see it attack the defenceless coast of France. *The House was brought to the conclusion* that we had a definite obligation to defend the coast of France from attack, and, generally speaking, it showed that it was prepared to support the government in taking action. France was *therefore* entitled to know and know at once that she could depend on British support in the event of an attack on her northern coast. There was a loud burst of cheering at this announcement.[8]

Complying entirely in this paraphrase with Grey's own rationalistic strata- gems, the report has reproduced that prosody of adventitious logic, paying special attention to insert those conjunctions that establish cause and rea- soned transition in the argument. Recasting its spell *à la lettre*, this writer makes explicit the persistent but insidious drive in Grey's address: to make reasonable what was, the *Guardian* editor was right in feeling, previously un- thinkable; to say with every appearance of rational seemliness what was, by the letter and ethic of liberal tradition, unspeakable. The dissonance goes to the one sound, the complex tonality, of reason-as-usual in the exceptional case. It features a language of analytical and ethical reasoning that is quite ostensibly *dubbed in*, imposed on a resistant circumstance, so that the rhetor- ical and hortative power of this rationalistic vocabulary increases – witness the density of logical connectives in this last passage – in nearly inverse ratio to the reason inherent in the case, or to one's confidence in that logic.

Instances of this sort of liberal double-speak could be repeated in lengthy series. For the sake of space, a single further citation to underline the division in the liberal sensibility at war, here to feature the compromised character and critical condition of its rationalistic language: the *two* accounts featured in the

Westminster Gazette, which was really the inside-track journal of the liberal party, in the week before the war. The recurring issue here involves the worthiness of a war fought on behalf of Servia, in alliance with Russia, a union usually regarded from the patronizing vantage of English liberal civility on the Slavs, who were regarded as irrationally backward, their local tribal feuds more or less of a piece with the atavisms of an older, baronial *mitteleuropa*. This is the line taken on 28 July, when the editorial finds 'The Serb … a man of primitive emotions and tastes, for whom town life seems to have little or no attraction … There are few towns in the country worthy of the name.' In a land in which the light of 'civilisation' is eclipsed, the commentator continues, 'the staple industries' are those benighted activities of 'pig-rearing' and elementary 'husbandry'.[9] Three days later, however, acting on the kind of information this unofficial yet privileged organ of the liberal party was often able to obtain, the feature piece redraws the portrait of the Servian national character in a pie ce of ethnographic conversion as stunning as it is unacknowledged. 'Posed gracefully before me', this writer opens, 'stands a typical Servian: the lines of Apollo flow easily round his robust figure. It is a good, honest, sun-scorched face', and if, as the writer concedes strategically about this people, 'their majority are illiterate', so too, the immediate appeal goes, 'they are quite intelligent'. Indeed, this unsavage nobility offers to the more civilized side of the hostilities now begun a *science* of war as advanced and *cerebral* as befits that ideological alliance, a virtual academy of 'artillery officers … well grounded in the *theoretical* branches of their work'.[10] The figure of fun liberal intellectuals have drawn in the Serb is exalted thus in accord with the liberal government's need to align the war with its own case and campaign of 'the war for civilisation', and the heavy pressure of that need goes so far here, in reconditioning that national type, as to rearrange its deities and tutelary spirits. Apollo has thrust out Caliban. And where those '*lines* of Apollo' settle now as a mask on the primitive visage, one sees the face of this new and unexpected ethnic hero recomposed in the name of the god not only of poetry, but of logic. The poetry of the case is already being written, and the spirit of reason prevails over the whole enterprise as its dubious muse.

That manoeuvres like these could be made with the impunity they seemed to presume is no doubt due to the fact that liberal interests formed the majority consciousness of these days. What defined the silent crisis of the party faithful, and of liberal modernity, became the voluble opportunity it provided for English modernism, then, within the crucial condition of this literary sensibility's relative distance or detachment from the attitudes of the centrist establishment. There are the two Anglo-*American* poets, after all, Eliot and Pound; there is *Virginia* Woolf, a woman even and still in 1918 *un*enfranchised. Their imaginative *ad*vantage would be drawn from an externality of political vantage. And so, as a lead into a reading of the modernist literature that kindles to the opportunities this off-angle position affords it, I want to look at the expressions of a sensibility similarly situated, one that turns out to offer a new route into an understanding of the timeliness, the real historical content and depth, of this early modernist literature.

This comes from a perspective drawn in the intellectual culture of war-time Cambridge. Here was an energy of dissent from the effort of the liberal war that finds its conscience, and its most indicative expression, in the activities there of the Union for the Democratic Control of Foreign Policy. Already in 1915 its leader, E. D. Morel, published a book, from the National Labour Press in Manchester, titled *Truth and the War*. It used his own insider vantage – he had been a liberal M.P., resigning his seat over the war issue – to expose the ruse of Asquith's and Grey's moralistic logic, revealing the really determining force of those previously secret agreements. Now, the activities of his Union, frowned upon by university officials, were tauntingly announced and advertised on the pages of the *Cambridge Magazine*, whose editors could animate to the awarenesses Morel and his people had made possible, usually in the joco-serious tone of the Undergraduate Wit. On 26 February 1916, for instance, in 'What the Public Wants, the Right Words in the Right Order', one Adelyne More is proposing a codification of rules to govern the new public speech, in a suitably mock-ironic format outlining its poetics and prosody. As a university advertisement this writer offers the services of undergraduate *logicians*, those young masters of the *logos*, to 'arrange other people's words'. The chief lesson these junior scribes will apply in stylizing even the efforts of 'Strong Silent Men' into grace and lucidity is one they have taken from their elders in political office, thus: 'All that is needed is to impress the general public with a sense of the dignity of *words properly arranged*.' Again: 'The trouble does not so much lie with the words themselves – they're all right: it's the *getting them in the right place* that bothers the man.' Nowadays, obviously, it is the sequence rather than the *con*sequence of words that is important, all in all the process of verbal argument and the artifices of logical thought rather than the conclusions or truths these protocols may attain. It is a formula that will allow the most outlandish notion to be countenanced, once dressed in proper grammar and syntax, and the likely market lies all too clearly in the political capital of London – an appeal this advertisement placards in the upper case. Thus, since '[s]pecial care is currently being given now to PATRIOTIC SUBJECTS', there is 'NO SUBJECT TOO DIFFICULT'. Indeed, arguments 'TO SUIT ALL CIRCUMSTANCES and ALL OPINIONS' will be cut to verbal order. [11]

But who is this Adelyne More? It is the pseudonym of an editor who had, occasionally, to *add a line more* to his fledgling journal. It is C. K. Ogden, friend and older contemporary of I. A. Richards. Their collaboration would include

The Meaning of Meaning, in 1924, a prelude to Richards's own critical book, *Science and Poetry*, in 1926, where he formulated the doctrine for which he is arguably most famous: that of the 'pseudo-statement'. This is a critical description and taxonomy of the language of verse, which discriminates between 'the intellectual stream' and 'the emotional stream'. What Richards's critical dictum is proposing most notably is that poetry works in the space between its verbal surface and depth, in particular in the discrepancy between an apparently rational grammar or syntax and what the words really mean and release as an energy of subtextual emotion or inference.[12] And what I want to suggest most centrally here is that the *crisis of liberal modernity* echoes in the critical perspective of Richards, who provides a framework for listening to the literature forming out of this fracture; to the literature of modern*ism*. For Richards, in the modernist poetry to which he is one of the first to respond, feels the power of poetry, not in the absence of a language of logic, but in the *fully present irrelevance* of reasonable speech, a perception that goes indeed to the deepest intimations of the meaning of recent history. It is of course only Eliot to whom Richards attends with any closeness, and never in a way that historicizes his particular version of pseudo-statement or draws its ingenuities into some internal and essential relation to the language of the liberal war. But that is the *explicit* connection of critical retrospect, and it is a linkage affirmed and strengthened with a reading of the modernist literature which he typifies.

The line the war draws through time is identified by all three of these writers in terms essentially the same as those we have used to define the crisis of liberal modernity. In *A Room of One's Own*, for instance, in the story of her recent sojourn in an Oxford college, Virginia Woolf attempts to account for the feelings of unease that a scene in collegiate life has stirred. The source of her disquiet lies, in a mildly Wordsworthian way, in the memory of an earlier visit, which she locates, lightly but decisively, some time *before* the war. What changed between 1913, say, and 1928 (or 1919) is told – subtly but unmistakably, elusively but urgently – in the tone of things. And here tonality locates itself specifically in the attitudes and practices of a sensibility she decorates with her most highly charged imagery, in her apprehension of that 'more profound, subtle, and subterranean glow which is the rich yellow flame of *rational intercourse*.' Equipped beforehand to savour the pleasures of its methods and consensus understandings, she is distressed instead in 'listening to the talk' to sense that 'something was lacking, something was different.' What? 'I had to think myself out of the room', the wrestling with her confusion begins, as, like Wordsworth, she returns to its origin in the former experience,

> back into the past, *before the war indeed*, and to set before my eyes the model of another luncheon party held in rooms not very far from these ... Nothing was

> changed; nothing was different save only – here I listened with all my ears not entirely to what was being said, but to the murmur or current behind it. Yes, that was it – the change was there. *Before the war* at a luncheon party like this people would have said precisely the same things but they would have sounded different, because in those days they were accompanied by a sort of humming noise, not articulate, but musical, exciting, which changed the value of the words themselves.[13]

Where once there was music in the rhythms of reasonable speech, it has lost its affective power. And that single but immense eventuality of the war may be taken to account now for all that is wrong, the offnote here in the undertone of things; in the institutional music of English intellectual life.

That Woolf will have exploited this dissonance to forge the sound of her own mature writing, in striking her specially modernist note, is a premise strengthened and affirmed by the advance and matching awarenesses of Pound and Eliot. Pound's own voluble commentary on the state of England at war comes in a now seldom referenced compendium of articles on the journalistic condition of the country, 'Studies in Contemporary Mentality', a twenty-part series he published through 1917 in *The New Age*. Here he draws an intellectual profile of an enislanded and, now, embattled *cultus*, whose dominant quality in duress proves indeed to be its *reasonableness*. He heckles it representatively, then, in this report on the wisdom of *The Quiver* [!]: 'Does the popular "common sense" consist in the huddling together of proverbial phrases, with incoherent deductions, contradictions, etc., leading yet to other proverbial phrases, giving the whole fabric a glamour of soundness?'.[14] The 'popular "common sense"' that Pound puts between the rebarbative marks of his own inverted commas here resonates in its critically diminished way to the 'sensis communis' of Rawls's Idea of Public Reason. This is a value invested in the rationalistic language of Liberalism in particular, and it is indeed in the venues of that partisan interest that Pound parses its grammar, scans a logic that is really only a prosody. In a sample whose mannerism he likens to the style of the flagship journal of literary liberalism, *The New Statesman*, he offers perhaps his most searching and revealing commentary on the linguistic music of this liberal war. 'And there, my dear Watson', he opens with a irony that will give away nothing in intensity of perception, 'we have it. I knew that if I searched long enough I should come upon some clue to this mystery. *The magnetism of this stupendous vacuity! The sweet reasonableness, the measured tone, the really utter undeniability of so much that one might read in this paper!* Prestigious, astounding!' Pound's savouring of the finenesses concludes thus, ironically, yes, but not completely dismissively: 'That is all there is to it. One might really learn to do it oneself.'[15]

The taunt Pound addresses here to his mimic gifts speaks from some intimation of the decaying strengths of his model and provocation, one that Eliot repeats, with his characteristically cannier capacity, in the first essay of is 1920 collection, *The Sacred Wood*. 'When a distinguished critic observed recently that "poetry is the most highly organized form of intellectual activity"... ',[16] Eliot motions in the first paragraph of an essay titled, with menacing irony, 'The Perfect Critic'. And Eliot continues, systematically and implacably unpacking a statement that was perfect, it turns out, only for his own purposes. He adduces it indeed as a type of 'verbal disease', [17] one that allows a sheer form of words, an apparent clarity merely, to replace concrete or verifiable truth. It is the Word, but not the World's Body, of Logical Positivism, and Eliot puts the more particular tradition it typifies to him within the resonating marks of his own rhetorical punctuation: ' "Liberal" ',[18] within inverted commas. Here the labelling and positioning indicate clearly the enfeebled condition of what until recently will have been a majority party in English cultural life, one to which this newcomer, rather in the manner of the classic agonist in another kind of 'Sacred Wood', the Nemi Grove of ancient Rome, could mount his own challenge for possession. There is a changing of the guard here, a moment of transition that is the instant of modernism.

The difference the war makes to the evolved consciousness of literary modernism may be indicated briefly here. It shows in the case of the two Anglo-American poets, most boldly, in the change of venue these new circumstances necessitated. It takes Pound into the unlikely genre of the prose fable, the four pieces he composed from late 1916-mid 1917, 'Anachronism at Chinon', 'Aux Étuves de Wiesbaden', 'Jodindranoth Mawhor's Occupation', and 'Our Tetrarchal Précieuse'.[19] This is a set of exercises unattended to by critics, who have not been in position to hear the background sound Pound is echoing here. For what this move into fictional prose allows Pound to do is to establish a ground rhythm of the logical and discursive, against which he plays his own critical difference – in the antic note we already hear in the outlandish titles of these pieces. A timely chord, one that sounds as well in the French exercises to which Pound set his American friend, early in 1917, to help to break a blockage of poetic composition Eliot had suffered for several years. Here grammatical rules had to be followed, but a semantic licence was enjoyed by *l'étranger*; mental discipline could combine with an ease about meaning. The exercise freed his voice, and in a tone echoing again to the circumstances that had probably blocked composition to begin with. For the rationality of a classic French syntax, with its apparatus of negative stipulation and logical restriction, is usually collapsing in these pieces into a near inanity of sheer sound: 'Ce n'est pas pour qu'on se dégoute / Ou gout d'égout de mon Ego / Qu'ai fait des vers de faits divers...' [20] The freeing effect of these liberties led Eliot then, again in Pound's company, through a study of the quatrain poems of Théophile Gautier, to a renewal of poetic activity, in his own quatrains, from 1917 to 1919. Pound also turned to foreign-language poetry, here the Latin text of Sextus Propertius, and in the form of creative translation opened novel opportunities for his own character-in-voice.

'Homage to Sextus Propertius' and the quatrain poems show a remarkable but little noticed consonance: in a phrase, that air of reasonable nonsense. Again and again the quatrain poems concoct this rhetorical fiction of sagacious highjinks, of sententious absurdity, using normative patterns of metre and syntax within the tautly strung rhythms of the quatrain line to create a form of reasoned meditation that dissolves constantly, however, into the imponderable, almost the unpronounceable:

> Polyphiloprogenitive
> The sapient sutlers of the Lord
> Drift across the window-panes.
> In the beginning was the Word.
>
> In the beginning was the Word.
> Superfetation of τὸ ἔν
> And at the mensual turn of time
> Produced enervate Origen. [21]

As Huck Finn once remarked: 'The statements was interesting, but tough' – and toughened here by the very appearance of reasonableness. Nor is quarter given on the verbal surface of 'Propertius':

> For Orpheus tamed the wild beasts –
>   and held up the Thracian river;
> And Cithaeron shook up the rocks by Thebes
>   and danced them into a bulwark at his pleasure,
> And you, O Polyphemus? Did harsh Galatea almost
> Turn to your dripping horses, because of a tune, under Aetna?
> We must look into the matter. [22]

'We must', indeed, 'look into the matter', but what do we see? Pound uses the logic of his own contemporary persona, the idiom and *logos* of his own present, to pretend that we all know the meaning of those obscure classical allusions that are the basic imaginative language of the poem. We do not; *he* does not; it is *as if* there were serious meaning here, but we cannot be sure what it is; we are left with a feeling of being at sea, but completely reasonably.

To reaffirm the present and immediate provocation of these new voices in the political and intellectual culture specific to the liberal war, we may consider a few well-chosen references within the verse itself. There is Pound's invocation, near the opening of the 'Homage' – a wording that represents nearly wholly an interpolation into the original Latin:

> Out-weariers of Apollo will, as we know,
> > continue their Martian generalities.
> We have kept our erasers in order. [23]

Apollo, the god of logic as well as poetry, was also invoked early in the liberal war, we recall from the pages of the *Westminster Gazette*, where he was appropriated to the unexpected service of the formerly backward, irrational, babbling Slav. So Pound's Apollo has been wearied or worn out, not by generals but by the gener*alities* of war – by political discourse, by statements that wear a hole in the language, in the *logos*, into the very logic of words. In that discourse the *Westminster Gazette* was indeed a tone-setter, and so it is no accident that the first of Eliot's quatrain poems, the earliest of his English pieces to hit the new sound, the previously unpublished 'Airs of Palestine No. 2', takes as its subject and target John Spender, *editor* of the *Westminster Gazette*. [24] And the Word we might have heard in the effort of that journal is sounded again as the opening line (it *is* the whole line) of 'Mr. Eliot's Sunday Morning Service', *'polyphiloprogenitive'*, a locution as astonishing, initially, as it is, on research, wholly circumscribed within a *liberal* frame of reference. Unlisted in the *OED*, and meaning (probably) 'loving multiple offspring', it occurs most notably in the final chapter of Matthew Arnold's *Culture and Anarchy*, 'Our *Liberal* Practicioners', as 'divine philoprogenitive*ness*', where it is placarded by Arnold to frame its original use, by Robert Buchanan, as a typifying instance of liberal *verbalism*, that is, a hollow and merely nominal knowledgeability. [25] And that is the sound Eliot is replicating, with the extra of his own *poly*syllabic, classical vocabulary, which includes *superfetation, enervate* (as an adjective), and *to en* (in Greek calligraphy). All of it adds up, if it adds up, to saying, quite fulsomely and with every apparent sign of sagacity, that nothing can be said.

This tonal conceit, I suggest, is the creative concept in the major modernist lyric I have cited here. It is the new voice of 1917. And it is the historicity of this voice, the new and timely element this poetic initiative represents, that accounts for the real density of significance here. It is a poetry of the end of liberal modernity; a verse of turning, of *difference*; of literary modern*ism*.

Woolf's turn appears most clearly on the pages of 'The Mark on the Wall', written in April 1917 as the first piece of literary composition she undertook since the completion in early 1914 of her first novel, *The Voyage Out*. Whereas this earlier work was conceived in 1908 within the narrative and linguistic conventions of Edwardian romance, against or beyond which it struggled unsuccessfully to voyage, the departure underway in the new work takes the war as its ordaining occasion. And in this next excerpt Woolf cites it, here in the shorthand description of the activities of 'novelists in future', in a wording that projects in effect the development of her own mature *oeuvre*. These are writers who will leave

> the description of reality more and more out of their stories, taking a knowledge
> of it for granted, as the Greeks did and Shakespeare perhaps – but these *generali-
> sations* are very worthless. The *military* sound of the word is enough. It recalls
> leading articles, cabinet ministers – a whole class of things indeed which as a child
> one thought the thing itself, the standard thing, the real thing, from which one
> could not depart save at the risk of nameless damnation.[26]

'Generalisations', the Pound sound-alike from the same year reminds us, present the new ideolect of total war, a context 'the military sound of the word' specifies clearly here. This is a usage echoed and specified to the meaningless language of official rationales; of policy documents and partisan briefs; of 'leading articles' and 'cabinet ministers'. Whereas the Anglo-American poets relate to this linguistic crisis strategically, with the opportunism of ex-colonials, it is fair to say that, for Woolf, a constellation of objects known and rituals remembered revolves around the words now ceasing to cohere. For Virginia *Stephen* had been born, as Sir Leslie Stephen's daughter, if not to the preferred gender, at least within the clerisy of cultural liberalism. So that the voiding of authority in the patrilogia stirs in the linguistic initiative it encourages as a most complex, difficult benefice. From the perspective of securities formerly maintained, a venture of this tradition-defying type leads to nothing less than 'nameless damnation', which is, indeed, the damnation of namelessness. And this is the nerve and courage I would fix to the initiatives stirring out of this moment for a writer who, because of her inwardness with that now broken tradition of liberal modernity, might be appraised as the foremost voice of literary modern*ism*.

So, the sound-alikes with the poets are already audible, now, if on the most obvious level, in the novel prosody of 'The Mark', to be marked already, say, in its opening gestures: '*If* that mark on the wall was made by a nail', the proposition overtures, then concludes, 'it can't have been for a picture, it must have been for a miniature – the miniature of a lady with white powdered curls, powder-dusted cheeks, and lips like red carnations. A fraud of course, for the people who had this house before us …'[27] We note the otherwise odd combination of opposite qualities: a syntax of seriously propositional reasoning coincides with an obviously fantastical construction of the object of attention, which, as 'a fraud of course', denominates equally the matter and the method of presentation. It is a keynote to the major linguistic inventions of the 1920s, which, in one summary description here, might be said to have evolved a prosody of the *mock*-logical, a grammar of the *pseudo*-propositional. A most typical instance occurs as the opening motion of her 1922 narrative, her first modern*ist* novel, *Jacob's Room*: "'So of course", wrote Betty Flanders, pressing her heels rather further in the sand, "there was nothing for it but to leave"'.[28] "'So of course"': the gesture of logical conclusion that opens this novel already includes a sense of its ending, the death in the Great War of Betty Flanders's son Jacob, an immanence projected from the beginning through a family name that goes to one of the most charged and valorized sites of that recent conflict. The one matter of narrative and logical course in the novel is the inevitability of an event otherwise, however, mainly *un*named in the story. The War is presented ever at the oblique angle of the extreme trope, or in moments of apparent chance evocation like a family name. What the verbal fabric of this novel traps again and again is the inadequacy of language to that salient fact, specifically of the rationalistic language it puts forward in so conspicuous and exposed a position here at its outset. And the ordinal force of that conceit is of course the pressure this unspeakable war has brought to bear on the older vocabulary and grammar of Reason; the *liberal* war. Demonstrations of this truth could be extended at length through *Jacob's Room* and *Mrs Dalloway* and *To the Lighthouse*. The implications of the practice are equally extensive. And it leaves behind a body of work that takes its place with Eliot's and Pound's (that otherwise odd accomplice) as a major statement of the end of liberal modernity; as a language, a literary language, of modernism.

Notes

1   John Rawls, *Political Liberalism* (The John Dewey Essays in Philosophy), (New York: Columbia University Press, 1993); see esp. pp. xxiv, xxvi–xxviii, xxx, 47–59, 212–27. See also the matching dates and identifications for 'the modern' in Jacques Barzun, *From Dawn to Decadence: 500 Years of Western Cultural Life: 1500 to the Present* (New York: Harper Collins, 2000), *passim*. One of the primary theme words for Barzun's 'modernity' is EMANCIPATION, an impulse he links originally with the Reformation and describes in terms of values similar to those invoked by Rawls.

2   Helpful accounts and analyses of these developments come from Clyde F. Crews, *English Catholic Modernism* (Notre Dame, IN: University of Notre Dame Press, 1984), and Lester Kurtz, *The Politics of Heresy: The Modernist Crisis in Roman Catholicism* (Berkeley: University of California Press, 1986).

3   Thus by Barzun, p. 125.

4   The major critical works on the literature of the Great War, Paul Fussell's *The Great War and Modern Memory* (New York: Oxford University Press, 1975) and Samuel

Hynes's *A War Imagined: The First World War and English Culture* (New York: Atheneum, 1991), pay no sustained or framed attention to modernism. Two recent studies, Alyson Booth's *Postcards from the Trenches: Negotiating the Space between Modernism and the First World War* (New York: Oxford University Press, 1996) and Trudi Tate's *Modernism, History, and the First World War* (Manchester: Manchester University Press, 1998), do not attempt to locate the meaning of the 'modernist' term in any specific sense, using it rather loosely to describe a literature identifiable beforehand, supposedly, as 'modernist'. The result is a sort of retrospective anachronism, whereby features supposedly assignable to modernism are simply reiterated. The lack of historical grounding is evident in the absence in both works of any clearly drawn picture of English political history, let alone the current and relative hegemony of the Liberal party.

5 The best treatments of this situation remain the ones referenced later in this essay in relation to the Union of the Democratic Control of Foreign Policy and its activities at Cambridge University: E. D. Morel, *Ten Years of Secret Diplomacy: An Unheeded Warning* (London: National Labour Press, 1915) and *Truth and the War* (London: National Labour Press, 1916).

6 The text of the speech was printed on 4 August by all the major dailies, with varying interpolations and commentaries, and reprinted in part throughout the war.

7 'Sir Edward Grey's Blunder', *Manchester Guardian*, 4 August 1914. Emphases added.

8 'A Dramatic Scene: The House and Sir Edward Grey's Statement: Logic of Events', *Westminster Gazette*, 4 August 1914, 10. Emphases added.

9 'The Peasant Nation', *Westminster Gazette*, 28 July 1914, 4.

10 'What Can Servia Do?', *Westminster Gazette*, 31 July 1914, 1. Emphasis added.

11 'What the Public Wants, The Right Words in the Right Order', by Adelyne More [C. K. Ogden], *Cambridge Magazine*, 26 February 1916.

12 I. A. Richards, *Science and Poetry* (New York: Norton, 1926), esp. 'The Poetic Experience', pp. 22–3, 34–5. The piece on Eliot is reprinted as an appendix in the second edition of *Principles of Literary Criticism* (New York: Harcourt Brace & World, 1928), pp. 289–95.

13 Virginia Woolf, *A Room of One's Own* (1928; rpt. New York: Harcourt Brace Jovanovich, 1989), p. 12. Emphases added.

14 Ezra Pound, 'Studies in Contemporary Mentality – The Beating Heart of the Magazine', *The New Age*, 11 October 1917, 506.

15 Ezra Pound, 'Studies in Contemporary Mentality: IV-*The Spectator*', *The New Age*, 6 September 1917, 406–7. Emphasis added.

16 T. S. Eliot, 'The Perfect Critic', in *The Sacred Wood* (1920; rpt. London: Methuen, 1976), p. 1.

17 *Ibid.*, p. 2.

18 *Ibid.*, p. 9.

19 'Jodindranoth Mawhor's Occupation', *Little Review* (May 1917), 12–18; 'An Anachronism at Chinon', *Little Review* (June 1917), 14–21; 'Aux Étuves de Wiesbaden', *Little Review* (July 1917), 12–16; 'Our Tetrarchal Précieuse (A Divigation from Jules Laforgue)', *Little Review* (July 1918), 3–12.

20 From 'Petit Epître' in T. S. Eliot, *Inventions of the March Hare: Poems 1909–1917*, ed. Christopher Ricks (London: Faber and Faber, 1996), p. 86.

21 T. S. Eliot, 'Mr. Eliot's Sunday Morning Service', *The Complete Poems and Plays* (London: Faber and Faber, 1969), p. 54.

22 Ezra Pound, 'Homage to Sextus Propertius', *Personae: The Collected Shorter Poems of*

Ezra Pound, ed. Lea Baechler and A. Walton Litz (New York: New Directions, 1990), p. 206.

23 Pound, 'Homage', p. 205.
24 Now published in *Inventions of the March Hare*, ed. Ricks, pp. 84–5.
25 Matthew Arnold, *Culture and Anarchy*, ed. John Dover Wilson (Cambridge: Cambridge University Press, 1969), p. 191.
26 Virginia Woolf, 'The Mark on the Wall', in *The Complete Shorter Fiction of Virginia Woolf*, ed. Susan Dick, 2d ed. (New York: Harcourt Brace Jovanovich, 1991), p. 86. Emphases added.
27 *Ibid.*, p. 83.
28 Virginia Woolf, *Jacob's Room* (1922; rpt. New York: Harcourt Brace & Company, 1950), p. 70.

2

Modernism, Anti-Mimesis, and the Professionalization of English Society

David Trotter

In the second of his two volumes of autobiography, *Rude Assignment* (1950), Wyndham Lewis tried to reconstruct the mood of the '*Blast* days', that heady period of Vorticist carnival brought rudely to an end, in his case, for a while at least, by the combined effects of gonorrhea and officer training. 'My literary contemporaries', he wrote, 'I looked upon as too bookish and not keeping pace with the visual revolution.' *The Enemy of the Stars*, the unperformable play published in the first issue of *Blast*, in July 1914, was his most rebarbative attempt to 'show them the way'. This punishing Vorticist programme had, however, one drawback. 'It became evident to me at once, ... when I started to write a novel, that words and syntax were not susceptible of transformation into abstract terms, to which process the visual arts lent themselves quite readily.' [1]

My subject is, as it were, the psychopathology of literary and artistic experiment. I want to examine, in a speculative fashion, the animus behind or within Lewis's utter determination to show his contemporaries the way. Lewis was not, of course, the only determined Modernist, though he may have been the *most* determined. I have written elsewhere about the potent will-to-literature evident in Eliot's commendation of Joyce's use of Homeric myth. The solution to literature's inadequacy in the face of the futility of the modern world, Eliot seemed to say, was *more* literature: the novel would render itself less 'novel', less abjectly the expression of an abject age, if it began to associate with epic. [2] To Lewis, by contrast, this was mere bookishness. What he had in mind was *less* literature in literature, not more. His aim was to import into literature that other version of the will-to-experiment which had already declared itself in the visual arts as a will-to-abstraction.

Such manoeuvres became Lewis's signature. It is not just that he notoriously trafficked between genres, and between media, as both William Blake and Dante Gabriel Rossetti had done before him, but that he sought to bring about change, and to theorize the necessity of change, by the strategic substitution, as circumstances appeared to demand, of one genre for another, one medium for another. *The Caliph's Design*, for instance, the pamphlet in which he renewed his bid for leadership of the English avant-garde, in October 1919, was just such a manoeuvre. Its subtitle is *Architects! Where is your Vortex?*. [3] Now it was architects who had to be shown the way. *The Caliph's Design* is the will-to-abstraction incarnate; it deserves recognition as a counterweight to Eliot's essays of the early 1920s, which are the will-to-literature incarnate. If we wish to see in it Lewis's signature, and thus an indication of one of the shapes English Modernism might have taken, or perhaps did take, then we will need to remain as alert as he was to the requirements of a career, which may include the strategic substitution of one genre or medium for another. *Rude Assignment* is, among other things, the first sociology of the 'Men of 1914'. [4]

Lewis will remain a glowering background presence in what follows. But my main focus is on the poet, philosopher, and art critic T. E. Hulme, who was killed in action in 1917, and whom Eliot was subsequently to hail as 'the forerunner of a new attitude of mind, which should be the twentieth-century mind, if the twentieth century is to have a mind of its own'. Hulme has now fallen into relative neglect; [5] but there can be little doubt about his prominence, as a critic and a trafficker between media, in the field of experiment which is my subject here. 'It was mainly as a theorist in the criticism of the fine arts', Lewis wrote in *Blasting and Bombardiering* (1937), his first volume of autobiography, 'that Hulme would have distinguished himself, had he lived.' He himself, he went on imperturbably, would undoubtedly have played Turner to Hulme's Ruskin. 'In England there was no-one else working in consonance with an "abstract" theory of art to the same extent as myself. Neither Gaudier nor Epstein would in the end have been "abstract" enough to satisfy the requirements of this obstinate abstractionist. He would have had to fall back on me.' [6] It is the *obstinacy* of Hulme's abstractionism, its animus, which seems to me, as it did to Lewis, its characteristic feature. [7] Why did Hulme, and Lewis after him, for a while, insist so often and so strongly on abstraction in everything?

In Hulme's career, as in Lewis's, the obstinacy took shape in or as a set of strategic substitutions, which we can begin to reconstruct with the help of Michael Levenson's meticulous account of the phases of his development as an intellectual. [8] The young Hulme had been much preoccupied with the growth of science, and its effect on moral and religious belief. By 1907, he had read, heard, and become acquainted with Henri Bergson, in whose distinction between 'intensive' and 'extensive' manifolds he found an antidote to materialism. In a series of lectures given at the end of 1911, he described the 'general idea' behind Bergson's work as the 'endeavour to prove that we seem inevitably to arrive at the mechanistic theory simply because the intellect, in dealing with a certain aspect of reality, distorts it in that direction'. Science provides an adequate account of matter by conceiving the world as a draught-board, and then establishing 'where the pieces are, and what moves they make'. But the understanding of life in its depth, in its interpenetrative entanglements, would require a different method, that of intuition. [9]

The metaphor of the draught- or chess-board, and of systematic thought as the perpetual rearrangement of counters on abstract plane, was one of which Hulme made frequent use in his early writings. [10] In 'Cinders', for example, a collection of notes begun in 1906 and intended as a 'personal philosophy', it defines the ways in which systematic thought of any kind imposes an abstract pattern on reality. 'The aim of science and of all thought is to reduce the complex and inevitably disconnected world of grit and cinders to a few ideal counters, which we can move about and so form an ungritlike picture of reality – one flattering to our sense of power over the world' (*CW* 11). [11]

As early as 1907, however, Hulme had begun to acknowledge the limitations of a Bergsonian perspective. The crucial impetus came from his growing admiration for the political and philosophical doctrines enunciated by Action Française, at that time the most effective focus of radical conservatism not only in France, but in Europe as a whole. Pierre Lasserre, literary editor of the movement's daily newspaper, had led the assault on the romantic sensibility in politics, philosophy, and literature; it was Lasserre whom Hulme consulted, in April 1911, when he began to suspect that Bergson might after all, horrible thought, have a bit of the Rousseau about him (*CW* 164-5). The result of this disillusionment was a series of essays on 'Tory philosophy' published in 1911 and 1912, and the stalwart defence of classicism for which he remains best known today. [12]

Hulme, however, did not stop at classicism, as Levenson has shown. He went on to demand a clean break not only from Rousseau's 'spilt religion', but from the whole tradition of Western thought, classical *and* romantic, since the Renaissance. His aim, from 1913 onwards, under the influence of the philosopher Edmund Husserl and the art-historian Wilhelm Worringer, was the emancipation of culture from anthropomorphism. 'Once Hulme saw *humanism* as the root of the problem', Levenson concludes, 'he ceased to regard the romantic/classical division as fundamental.' [13]

Levenson makes instructive use of Hulme's 'volatility' to demonstrate the degree of divergence between different emphases within Modernist 'doctrine'. [14] Hulme, we can now be sure, did indeed change his mind. But if we want to know *why* he changed it, we must, I believe, consider his doctrinal volatility in its performative dimension. For Hulme was, like Wyndham Lewis, a serial careerist. One of the points Lewis makes in *Rude Assignment* is that the freedom he had enjoyed in the pre-war years to pick and choose among specialisms was underwritten by an allowance from his mother. [15]

Hulme was in exactly the same position, except that *his* allowance came from a sympathetic aunt. [16] He, too, could pick and choose among marginally remunerative occupations. His Bergsonian incarnation required the role of poet and philosopher, his classicism that of political commentator, and his anti-humanism that of art-critic.

Hulme, furthermore, was as self-conscious as Lewis in his changes of career. He was fond of Nietzsche's comment that all philosophy is autobiography (*CW* 233), and inveterately cast his philosophical development in the form of 'personal confession' (126). And he liked the beginning and end of each phase of his career to be as emphatic as possible. Thus he stopped being a poet-philosopher by declaring his profound disappointment in a series of lectures Bergson gave at University College London in October 1911 (154-9), and by publishing his 'Complete Poetical Works' (all five of them) in the *New Age* in January 1912. The conversations he enjoyed with Worringer at the Berlin Congress of Aesthetics in the summer of 1913 had a similarly clarifying effect. 'Returning to England later in the year, he began a brief but impassioned career as an art critic.' [17]

Hulme, in short, like Lewis, thought in terms not only of doctrine in general, but of the particular role a particular set of ideas might require of him. Some roles simply did not 'take'. For example, he published his political commentaries under the pseudonym of 'Thomas Gratton', and one never feels that there is as much at stake in them as there is either in his defences of Bergson or in his propaganda on behalf of abstract art. Since in his maturity he never deviated from an orthodox Toryism, politics could not reveal him to himself, as Bergson had once done, as Epstein was to do. His primary interest was in techniques of persuasion. What is at issue in the writings about Bergson and Epstein, by contrast, is at once a set of ideas and a professional identity. There, Hulme had not only to expound a doctrine, but to perform it obstinately, to make it his life.

On the evening of 22 January 1914, Hulme and Lewis shared a lecture platform at Kensington Town Hall. Their topic was modern art. As Hulme began his lecture, in a barely intelligible murmur, Lewis, seated in the body of the hall, loudly informed the person next to him that you have to hold your head up when you speak in public. It was his turn next, and he, too, spoke in a barely intelligible murmur, addressing himself entirely to the piece of paper in front of him. [18]

Hulme's reinvention of himself as an art-critic was the product of two factors: a point of view, and a need to occupy himself. His reading of Worringer's *Abstraction and Empathy* (1908) provided him with the first of these. According to Worringer, the two fundamental urges to be found in the history of aesthetic styles correspond to different attitudes to experience. Empathy, he argued, is the product of a 'pantheistic relationship of confidence between man and the phenomena of the outside world'; the 'artistic volition' it has consistently nurtured in Graeco-Roman and modern Western art aims at the truths of 'organic life', or naturalism. Abstraction, by contrast, is the product of an 'inner unrest' provoked by the phenomena of the outside world, and 'finds its beauty in the life-denying inorganic, in the crystalline or, in general terms, in all abstract law and necessity'.[19] He thought that 'primitive' art, like that of the more developed cultures of India and Egypt, could only be understood through the urge it manifests, the urge to abstraction. Hulme incorporated Worringer's distinction between urges into the lecture he gave at Kensington Town Hall, 'Modern Art and its Philosophy', and put it to polemical use. He put forward the 're-emergence' of a geometrical art in the work of Epstein, Lewis, and others as proof of the re-emergence of the corresponding attitude towards the world, and the consequent 'break-up' of Renaissance humanism (*CW* 269).

Equally important for Hulme's reinvention of himself was the fact that 1913 was a good time to be an art-critic. The success of Roger Fry's two Post-Impressionist Exhibitions, in 1910 and 1912, had generated a flurry of avant-garde activity. There was now a market, of a kind, for abstract art, and therefore a need for expert assessment. Lewis, who in 1910 would have been more generally known as a writer than as an artist, took up his brush once again, in the aftermath of the first Post-Impressionist Exhibition, and with a vengeance. Within a year or so, his work was sustaining comparison with that of major figures in the continental avantgarde.[20] By the time Hulme stood up to speak at Kensington Town Hall, then, his position, as art-critic of the *New Age*, was an influential one. The week before, on 15 January 1914, he had reviewed the Grafton Group show at the Alpine Club, blessing Lewis, Nevinson, and Etchells, and blasting the 'mediocre stuff' shown by Fry and his followers. Eleven days later, Fry was still in shock. The 'Lewis group', he complained, had somehow 'got hold' of the *New Age* critic.[21]

At the private view for the first exhibition of the London Group at the Goupil Gallery, on 4 March 1914, Lewis, observing Hulme deep in discussion with Kate Lechmere in front of one of his own drawings, suspected the worst. Lechmere was currently his main source of income, as the money behind the Rebel Art Centure, and had been his lover. He now thought that he might be replaced in one capacity by Hulme's man Epstein, and in the other by Hulme himself (he was half-right). The item in front of which the discussion took place, which Lewis had told Lechmere to steer Hulme towards, was described in the catalogue as a drawing for sculpture, and it may well have been meant to compete with the small flenite figures by Epstein which Hulme was known to admire.[22]

Worringer described *Abstraction and Empathy* as a contribution to the 'psychology of style', and its crucial insistence is that all art should be assessed in terms of the 'psychic presuppositions' which give rise to it. At some places in his argument, the psychology of style tips over into a psychopathology of style. In 'primitive' cultures, he says, the urge to abstraction derives from an 'immense spiritual dread of space' which can be compared to agoraphobia, a 'pathological condition to which certain people are prone'. In more 'developed' cultures, a different problem makes itself felt, a dread of space which stands 'above' rather than 'before' cognition. The problem here, among the 'civilized peoples of the East', for example, has to do not with the emptiness of space but with the 'unfathomable entanglement of all the phenomena of life'. The urge it prompts is to rescue the object from its entanglement, from its 'arbitrariness', and thus construct for oneself 'a point of tranquillity and a refuge from appearances'. Abstraction alone will enable the artist to 'wrest' the object from its 'natural context', to 'purify' it of all its 'dependence upon life'. In abstraction, life has finally been 'effaced': 'here is law, here is necessity, while everywhere else the caprice of the organic reigns'.[23] In Worringer's understanding, abstraction, wherever and whenever it occurs, is both violent and compulsive. He stops short of attributing psychosis to the 'civilized peoples of the East', but not by much.

It seems to me that the account Worringer gives of abstraction's effacement of life provides another way to conceive the kind of behaviour which the early psychiatric nosologies and case-histories construed as 'monomaniacal' or 'paranoid'.[24] The history of modern ideas of 'delusional disorder' can be traced back at least as far as J. E. D. Esquirol's *Mental Maladies* (1838), which includes a graphic and highly influential section on 'monomania'.[25] Whatever its name, the disease has usually been thought to include, often in a relation of mutual dependence, delusions of grandeur and delusions of persecution. In many patients, paranoid symmetry adjusts the degree of fantasized grandeur to the degree of fantasized persecution. They hate me because I'm special; I'm special because they hate me. Of particular interest in the context of Modernism's will-to-abstraction are the analyses developed in turn-of-the-century psychiatry of paranoia's cognitive or epistemological dimension.

'The category of what is accidental and requires no motivation', Sigmund Freud observed in *The Psychopathology of Everyday Life* (1901), 'in which the normal person includes a part of his own psychical performances and parapraxes, is thus rejected by the paranoiac as far as the psychical manifestations of other people are concerned. Everything he observes in other people is full of significance, everything can be interpreted.'[26] In paranoia, meaning displaces event. There is no such thing as chance, as a causal sequence devoid of (malevolent) purpose. Sufferers from paranoia, Freud was to remark in a paper published in

1922, 'cannot regard anything in other people as indifferent'. [27] The paranoiac constructs an intricate but coherent parallel universe – a refuge against appearances, Worringer might have said – by acts of (over)interpretation. His or her rejection of the possibility that other people might remain indifferent, absorbed as they are in projects of their own, or in each other, is a rejection of that infinite entanglement of one phenomenon in another which constitutes the world as most people know it. Paranoia cannot abide entanglement.

An almost unbearably poignant aspect of Daniel Paul Schreber's *Memoirs of My Nervous Illness* (1903), the most vivid and influential record ever left by a psychotic patient, and one to which Freud devoted a famous essay, is his inability to shake off the conviction that there is no such thing as accident. By the end of 1895, Schreber explains, after five years of torture, the 'miracles' inflicted on him by a persecutory God had begun for the first time to assume a relatively 'harmless' character. An end to his suffering was in sight. Life, however, did not return to normal. 'As example I will only mention my cigar ash being thrown about on the table or on the piano, my mouth and my hands being soiled with food during meals, etc.' Being raped by cosmic rays was as nothing compared to these new persecutions which humiliatingly took the form of accident. When Schreber's mother and sister came to visit him, the cocoa he was drinking threw itself out of the mug. When he ate at the Director's table, plates broke in two of their own accord, without anyone having to drop them. Whenever he wanted to go to the lavatory, someone else always got there first. [28]

In 'Modern Art and its Philosophy', Hulme reproduced Worringer's terms, and at the same time his attribution of psychosis to 'primitive' peoples alone. Pure geometrical regularity, he said, gives a 'certain pleasure' to people 'troubled by the obscurity of outside appearance'. 'The geometrical line is something absolutely distinct from the messiness, the confusion, and the accidental details of existing things.' He went on to insist that such a 'condition of fear' is not a necessary prerequisite of the 'tendency to abstraction'; in the Indian and Byzantine cultures, the tendency takes an altogether different form (*CW* 274). This seems to me a defensive manoeuvre, on Hulme's part, as it is on Lewis's part, in the version of the hypothesis he put forward in the first issue of *Blast*. [29] Neither man was keen, for obvious reasons, to have abstraction associated with psychosis. But abstraction, in Worringer's account, fulfils more or less the same function as paranoia, in Freud's: to create a refuge from the unfathomable entanglement of all the phenomena of life, from the caprice of the organic.

Hulme may have felt a little defensive because the abstract art he championed was indeed both violent and compulsive in the fury with which it 'wrested' the object from its 'natural context'. At the London Group show, his attention was caught by David Bomberg's *In the Hold*, which masks its representational content with a grid consisting of sixty-four squares. [30] Bomberg had been introduced to this device by Walter Sickert, for whom it was a compositional aid in the transition from sketch to painting. In several major paintings of the pre-war period, the grid itself becomes at once focus and object. The 'outside scene', as Hulme explained with reference to *In the Hold*, becomes something else again in its 'passage' through the grid of squares. 'The square I might call K.Kt.6, for example, makes an interesting pattern. That the picture as a whole is entirely empty is, I suppose, on the theory I have just put forward, no defect' (*CW* 297). The metaphor of the chess-board which Hulme had once used to denounce scientific rationalism now enables him to demonstrate how the new art should be approached, how one might take pleasure in it. But he still felt a certain unease, it may be, at the brutality with which the new art abstracted its object from the natural world. Either that, or a lingering attachment to Bergson, prompted a final reservation about what he thought of as Bomberg's 'purely intellectual interest in shape' (*CW* 297).

In *Blasting & Bombardiering*, Lewis took pains to indicate the peculiar hybridity of the role in which Hulme ended up. Hulme, he observes, was an art-critic of a philosophical 'turn'. 'Although he has been called "a philosopher", he was not that, but a man specializing in aesthetic problems.' Lewis cannot quite make up his mind about the validity of the expertise engendered by that specialization. On the one hand, he adamantly maintains that Hulme's work should not be dismissed as the product of some bureaucratic programme for the training of experts in art-theory. 'His mind was sensitive and original, which is a better thing obviously than the routine equipment of the teaching profession.' On the other hand, Hulme's 'equipment' for the task did not seem altogether adequate. Hulme, Lewis points out, was 'a journalist with a flair for philosophy and art, not a philosopher. Of both these subjects he was profoundly ignorant, according to technician-standards.' And there is no mistaking the relish with which Lewis describes Hulme's discomfiture, in a debate about Kant, at the hands of a 'little university professional'. 'Hulme floundered like an ungainly fish, caught in a net of superior academic information.' [31] By Lewis's account, Hulme was both more and less than merely expert.

Jealousy and hatred apart, there is, I think, an important context for the equivocal feelings Lewis expressed about Hulme the art-critic. In Edwardian England, expertise was at once the most highly valued of all qualities and, in some quarters, a reliable object of contempt. What is at issue here, it may be, is the fundamental transformation of English society and culture, in the modern period, by expertise of one kind or another.

The most authoritative account of this transformation is that offered by the social and economic historian Harold Perkin. [32] Perkin has described in vivid detail the emergence during the nineteenth century of a professional or non-capitalist middle class, and the gradual definition of its methods and principles by the intellectuals who eagerly claimed membership of it. He argues that industrialization 'emancipated' not only the entrepreneur and the wage-earner, but the professional person as well, releasing him (and eventually her) from dependence on a handful of wealthy patrons. Unlike land and capital, the methods and principles which constitute professional identity do not belong to the few. Based on expertise, on human capital, professionalism potentially extends as far as there are human beings willing and able to invest human capital in the acquisition of expertise. By Perkin's account, its methods and principles can be said to have achieved something close to dominance in English society by around 1880.

Perkin's emphasis on the transforming effect of the emergence of a professional class has two advantages for the cultural historian. In the first place, it enables us to envisage social conflict within as well as between classes: a difference of outlook which distinguishes not only the doctor from the mill-owner, but the shop-steward from the panel-beater. In the second place, it draws attention to the very specific problem of identity which afflicts those whose capital is symbolic through and through: those who only have their own integrity and an esoteric knowledge guaranteed by certificate to sell, rather than muscle, or the possession of land, or existing wealth.

Might that specific 'problem' of identity develop in some cases into a specific madness? One the curious side-effects of the professionalization which transformed psychiatric theory and practice during the final decades of the nineteenth century was a systematic analysis of the ways in which professional people go mad. A prominent case, in German psychiatry, and one rich in implication for an understanding of early twentieth-century European culture, was that of the school-teacher and mass-murderer Ernst Wagner. On the night of 3 September 1913, Wagner cut the throats of his wife and children while they lay asleep in the family home in Degerloch, in the suburbs of Stuttgart, and then travelled by train and bicycle to the village of Mühlhausen-an-der-Enz, where he set fire to several buildings and shot down the inhabitants as they fled, killing eight and wounding a further twelve. Wagner had begun his career as an assistant teacher in the school at Mühlhausen, in 1901. Imagining, erroneously, that some of the villagers had been witness to a drunken act of bestiality, he developed over the next twelve years a systematic fantasy of persecution. The news had spread, he thought; everywhere he went, in Mühlhausen and beyond, people made fun of him, or commented obscenely on his sexual predilections. Wagner's fantasies developed into full-blown paranoia. The meticulously planned murders were the direct outcome of his persecutory delusion.

Wagner was articulate, well-read, and highly intelligent. Much of what is known about the terrible crime he committed derives from his three-volume autobiography. In the asylum, he wrote poems and plays. Robert Gaupp, professor of psychiatry at Tübingen, who more or less made a career out of Wagner, found the origins of his psychosis partly in the guilt induced by his sexuality, and partly in the absence of social recognition which is the lot of an assistant teacher at a village school. Wagner cannot not have been painfully aware that his unique abilities would never receive due acknowledgement in Mühlhausen-an-der-Enz. Robert Gaupp thought that teachers and governesses were particularly vulnerable to paranoia because their professions provided a milieu in which 'genuine mental superiority' gave rise to 'suppressed mental arrogance'. [33]

I find myself a long way from T. E. Hulme's career as an art-critic. My point, however, is that by 1900 expertise, although still highly valued as a form of symbolic capital, was no longer emancipatory; it no longer held out, as it had once done, the glittering prospect of a degree of social recognition not otherwise available to men and women from humble backgrounds. Dickens had meditated to brilliant effect on the last (and lethal) gasp of the delusions of grandeur once inscribed in professional training in *Our Mutual Friend* (1864-5). There, the monomaniacal schoolmaster Bradley Headstone, 'subdued to the performance of his routine of educational tricks, encircled by a gabbling crowd', breaks loose at night, as Ernst Wagner was to do, though not to the extent of mass-murder. [34] There is something of the slightly abashed contempt the novel expresses for Headstone in Wyndham Lewis's exoneration of Hulme from mere schoolmastering.

Such was the purchase bureaucratic rationalism had achieved on Western societies by 1900 that Max Weber was able to define 'charisma' as its antithesis. [35] To adapt Weber's terms, we might say that expertise, as commonly understood, had lost the charisma which, under particular social and political circumstances, in English society at any rate, it had once possessed. The task accordingly undertaken by the Edwardian intelligentsia, or at least by some members of it, was a renewal of expertise in the name not so much of 'efficiency' as of charisma. The *New Age*, the journal for which Hulme wrote, had been founded in disagreement with the policies put forward by those apostles of bureaucratic rationalism, Sidney and Beatrice Webb. However, although 'simple life' in tendency, under the editorship of Alfred Orage, the *New Age* did not by any means abandon the advocacy of what Lewis was to term 'technician-standards'. [36] Its dilemma was Bradley Headstone's, and Ernst Wagner's: how to develop 'technician-standards' which would illuminate rather than obscure a 'sensitive and original' mind. This became Modernism's dilemma, too. And it drove Hulme and Lewis, if not to pushing people into canals, as Headstone does, or setting light to villages, then at least to murderous impulse.

My final piece of evidence is Hulme's first contribution as the *New Age's* art-critic, an essay about 'Mr Epstein and His Critics' published on 25 December 1913. The essay makes it clear that Hulme meant to invest the intellectual capital accrued from his conversations with Worringer in equipping himself with the appropriate expertise. The charisma he brought to the role was an insider's knowledge of the imminent 'break-up' of the very foundations of 'all philosophy since the Renaissance' (*CW* 257). It was the 'business' of all honest men and women, he announced, with a sternness which would surely have won the Webbs' approval, to clean the world of the 'sloppy dregs' of humanism (258). And he proposed to get to work in the Augean stable of the magazine for which he himself wrote. For the main target of his vitriol was A. M. Ludovici, a member of the *New Age* staff, and no fan of Epstein's work. [37]

Ludovici had published a book about Nietzsche, which according to Hulme gave 'the impression of a little Cockney intellect which would have been more suitably employed indexing or in a lawyer's office, drawn by a curious kind of vanity into a region the realities of which must for ever remain incomprehensible to him' (*CW* 259). The book by Dickens in which this assault on Cockney intellect was shaped is not *Our Mutual Friend*, but *David Copperfield* (1849), where Uriah Heep, a young man of humble background, and a clerk in a lawyer's office, eventually gets, with the hearty approval of all concerned, what is coming to him. The thing to remember about Uriah is that he is nauseating, in David Copperfield's eyes, long before he has done anything wrong. Uriah is a slimy contamination, rather than a person. [38] The reason for the nausea he provokes becomes plain as soon as he identifies himself, which he does with some exuberance, as David's professional and sexual rival. Uriah's crime is mimesis. He seeks to obscure the essential differences between David and himself, and ultimately to *become* David, by mere slavish imitation. He is the first in a line of sickening Cockney intellects which culminates in the pimply young man in the draft of *The Waste Land*, his hair thick with grease and scurf, whom Eliot imagines either as a house agent's clerk or as a follower of the arts who hangs out in the Café Royal with the Futurist C. R. W. Nevinson. [39] The hesitation, effaced in the poem's published version, is symptomatic. Pimply young men were disgusting in large part because they aped the writer or artist of genuine talent. [40]

Contempt for Cockney intellects, for social mimesis, became a key weapon in Modernism's polemical armoury, and an argument for the reimposition of technician-standards. Thus Hulme expressed his amazement that Ludovici had been able to produce in the book about Nietzsche 'a shoddy imitation which may pass here in England, where there is no organised criticism by experts, but which in other countries, less happily democratic in these matters, would at once have been characterised as a piece of fudge' (*CW* 259). It is no surprise, then, that Ludovici should proceed to fail the art-critical 'test' Hulme sets him, by preferring a feeble cartoon by Augustus John to Epstein's *Carvings in Flenite*. The cartoon, Hulme fulminated, 'lacks precisely that quality of virility which Mr Ludovici finds in it, and is admired by precisely those "spinsterly", sloppy and romantic people whom, he imagines, dislike it' (261). What the advocacy of abstraction did for Hulme, and subsequently for Lewis, and indeed for Modernism in general, was to reunite charisma with expertise. One proof of the power it infused into Hulme's art-criticism lies in the generation of further forms of symbolic capital, including a self-conscious and self-assertive masculinity. Indeed, the antidote Hulme recommends to Ludovici and his like carries, in the pleasure it takes in the removal of sloppy dregs, a distant echo of Micawber's hugely gratifying expulsion of the loathsome Uriah Heep from *David Copperfield*. 'The most appropriate means of dealing with him would be a little personal violence' (260).

It was Hulme's campaign against social and aesthetic mimesis which Lewis resumed, on his return from the war, in 1919. 'Modern Art and its Philosophy' had included a call for the artist to take a 'more active part' in relation to the machinery by means of which and out of which the engineer had built the streets of London (*CW* 283). In *The Caliph's Design*, Lewis defined that more active part as the embedding of vorticist principles in architecture. He had not researched his subject in any depth, and he did not, in fact, have a great deal to say about, well, architecture as such. But his attempt to envisage contemporary art from the point of view of its usefulness to the architect provided plenty of scope for mordant reflection on its deficiencies. Unsurprisingly, the movements found to be most deficient of all were those which in one way or another threatened to eclipse the London vortex: Synthetic Cubism, in France, and Bloomsbury, in England.

The practice of collage – 'these assemblings of bits of newspaper, cloth, paint, buttons, tin, and other débris, stuck on a plank' – enabled Lewis to characterize the most recent work of Braque and Picasso as the dead-end of nineteenth-century naturalism: an ultimate passivity before that part of the world which happened to be in front of the painter's eyes at a particular moment in time. This immersion in the unfathomable entanglement of all phenomena of life, this susceptibility to the caprice of the organic, he cunningly associated with the 'English variety of art man' and his (or presumably her) pursuit of '"jolly" little objects like stuffed birds, apples, or plates, areas of decayed wall-paper': a tendency responsible, he added, for the 'distinguished amateurish gallantry and refinement' of Roger Fry's Omega workshops. 'Under a series of promptings from Picasso, then, painting in Paris has been engineered into a certain position, that appears to me to bear far too striking a family likeness, in its spirit, to the sensibility of the English amateur to give one much hope for it.'[41] This penetrating critique of contemporary art deliberately conflates the two main objects of Lewis's polemical aversion: mimesis, to which he opposed geometry; and amateurism, to which he opposed the technician-standards of the charismatic professional. Being against those things, which he regarded as *one* thing, was the basis of the books he wrote during the 1920s: both the social theory of *The Art of Being Ruled* (1926) and *Time and Western Man* (1927), and the satire of *The Childermass* (1928) and *The Apes of God* (1930). It *is* his Modernism: the will-to-abstraction incarnate.

And there is about it, in *The Caliph's Design*, just a whiff of paranoia. Like the paranoiac, as described in early-twentieth-century psychiatry, Lewis built himself, in the purity of the design he would substitute for the unfathomable entanglement of London, a refuge from appearance. 'I do not need to have a house built with significant forms, lines, masses, and details of ornament, and planted squarely before my eyes', he informed his readers, 'to know that such significance exists, or to have my belief in its reality stimulated. But *you* require that.' The freedom he thus claimed is one which depends on expertise. 'Theoretically, even', he went on, 'a creative painter or designer should be able to exist quite satisfactorily without paper, stone or paints, without lifting a finger to translate into forms and colours his specialised creative impulse.'[42] In so far as it cuts its exponent off from paper, stone, and paints, and from those of us who can envisage nothing without them, the urge to abstraction might be understood as a psychopathology of expertise. Such it was to become, to brilliant but also inhibiting effect, in Lewis's writing of the 1920s.

Notes

1   *Rude Assignment*, ed. Toby Foshay (Santa Barbara: Black Sparrow Press, 1984), p. 139.
2   'The Modernist Novel', in Michael Levenson, ed., *The Cambridge Companion to Modernism* (Cambridge: Cambridge University Press, 1999), pp. 70–99 (74–7).
3   *The Caliph's Design: Architects! Where is your Vortex?*, ed. Paul Edwards (Santa Barbara: Black Sparrow Press, 1986). In 'What Art Now?', an essay published in the *English Review* in April 1919, Lewis suggested that experiment in art involves 'a stepping aside from artistic production, almost, for the moment, into science'. In this case, he went on, the stepping aside had already taken place. 'So, because you had a revolution six years ago, you need not expect another next month. The revolution in painting of the

few years preceding the war has thoroughly succeeded': 'What Art Now?', in *Creature of Habit and Creatures of Change: Essays on Art, Literature and Society 1914–1956*, ed. Paul Edwards (Santa Barbara: Black Sparrow Press, 1989), p. 49. For Lewis's reflections on Blake and Rossetti as artist-writers, see 'Beginning' (1935), in *Creatures of Habit*, pp. 262–7.

4 And thus a precursor of the recent interest in Modernism's 'institutions': Lawrence Rainey, *Institutions of Modernism: Literary Elites and Public Culture* (New Haven: Yale University Press, 1999); Ian Willison, Warwick Gould, and Warren Chernaik, eds., *Modernist Writers and the Marketplace* (Basingstoke: Macmillan, 1996).

5 'A Commentary', *Criterion*, 2, 1924, p. 231. It may be significant that Peter Nicholls's justly influential 'literary guide' to the period includes no more than a single passing reference to this supposed forerunner of the twentieth-century mind: *Modernisms: A Literary Guide* (London: Macmillan, 1995), p. 179.

6 *Blasting & Bombardiering* (London: Calder and Boyars, 1967), p. 100.

7 In this respect, the enquiry I shall attempt here runs in parallel with recent investigations of the fantasies encoded in abstract painting, sculpture, and design. See, for example, Bryony Fer, *On Abstract Art* (New Haven: Yale University Press, 1997); and for a more general and rather more haphazard discussion, David Batchelor, *Chromophobia* (London: Reaktion Books, 2000). For a more distant parallel, but one which pays the same kind of attention to the circumstances in which and for which texts are produced, see Janet Stewart, *Fashioning Vienna: Adolf Loos's Cultural Criticism* (London: Routledge, 2000).

8 *A Genealogy of Modernism: A Study of English Literary Doctrine 1908–1922* (Cambridge: Cambridge University Press, 1984), chs. 3 and 6.

9 'The Philosophy of Intensive Manifolds', in *Collected Writings*, ed. Karen Csengeri (Oxford: Clarendon Press, 1994). Further references to Hulme's writing will be to this invaluable edition, and incorporated in the text.

10 It also features in the 'Notes on Language and Style' of 1907, for example, where it distinguishes the density of the poetic word, an image seen rather than a mere counter (*CW* 25), from prose; and in a 1909 review of William James's *A Pluralistic Universe*, where it is used to distinguish the 'complicated, intertwined, inextricable flux of reality' from the 'constructions of the logical intellect, having all the clearness and "thinness" of a geometrical diagram' (86).

11 This hostility to the imposition of pattern has given the essay a memorable afterlife in 'postmodern' aesthetic theory, in the writing of Robert Smithson: 'A Sedimentation of the Mind: Earth Projects' (1968), in *Collected Writings*, ed. Jack Flam (Berkeley: University of California Press, 1996), pp. 100–13 (102).

12 Notably, of course, the essay on 'Romanticism and Classicism', which can be dated to late 1911 or early 1912: *CW,* pp. 59–73.

13 *A Genealogy of Modernism*, p. 98.

14 *Ibid.*, pp. 80–1.

15 *Rude Assignment*, p. 115. The financial demands Lewis placed on his mother, who much to his embarrassment ran a laundry, are a constant theme in the early chapters of Paul O'Keeffe's *Some Sort of Genius: A Life of Wyndham Lewis* (London: Jonathan Cape, 2000). As late as September 1912, Mrs Lewis was still chiding her son for his lack of professionalism and his shortcomings 'from the business point of view': *Some Kind of Genius*, p. 117.

16 Alun R. Jones, *The Life and Opinions of T. E. Hulme* (London: Victor Gollancz, 1960), pp. 22–4.

38   *Rethinking Modernism*

17 Levenson, *Genealogy of Modernism*, p. 96.
18 O'Keeffe, *Some Kind of Genius*, p. 145.
19 *Abstraction and Empathy: a Contribution to the Psychology of Style*, trans. Michael Bullock (New York: International Universities Press, 1953), pp. 14–15.
20 O'Keeffe, *Some Kind of Genius*, p. 121.
21 *Letters*, two volumes, ed. Denys Sutton (London: Chatto & Windus, 1972), ii. 378.
22 O'Keeffe, *Some Kind of Genius*, pp. 147–8.
23 *Abstraction and Empathy*, pp. 15–17, 20–1.
24 An inclination no doubt exacerbated by the fact that my most recent publication is a book about 'paranoid Modernism', a literary and political habit of some consequence, I believe, for certain (mostly male, mostly English) writers of the period: *Paranoid Modernism: Literary Experiment, Psychosis, and the Professionalization of English Society* (Oxford: Oxford University Press, 2001).
25 *Mental Maladies: A Treatise on Insanity*, facsimile edition, with an introduction by Raymond de Saussure (New York: Hafner, 1965). I offer an extended account of the development of ideas of paranoia in *Paranoid Modernism*, ch. 1. On 'delusional disorder', see the psychiatrists' bible, the *Diagnostic and Statistical Manual of Mental Disorders*, Fourth Edition (Washington, DC: American Psychiatric Association, 1994), pp. 296–301.
26 *The Psychopathology of Everyday Life*, in *The Standard Edition of the Complete Psychological Works*, ed. James Strachey et al., 24 vols. (London: Hogarth Press, 1953–74), vi. 255. I choose Freud's description on account of its infallible lucidity. The phenomenon he observes was one familiar to turn-of-the-century psychiatry. See, for example, Richard von Krafft-Ebing, *Textbook of Insanity*, trans. Charles Gilbert Chaddock (Philadelphia: F.A. Davis, 1904), pp. 368–9, 382–3.
27 'Some Neurotic Mechanisms in Jealousy, Paranoia and Homosexuality', *SE*, xviii. 223–32 (226).
28 *Memoirs of My Nervous Illness*, ed. and trans. Ida Macalpine and Richard A. Hunter (London: William Dawson, 1955), p. 156. Freud's 'Psychoanalytic Notes on an Autobiographical Account of a Case of Paranoia (Dementia Paranoides)', of 1911, is in *SE*, xii. 1–82.
29 The 'modern town-dweller' for whose benefit the new abstract art will be produced has nothing at all to do, Lewis maintains, with the 'primitive' African who 'cannot allow his personality to venture forth or amplify itself, for it would dissove in vagueness of space'. The problem for the modern town-dweller is not space-shyness but entanglement. 'Life is really no more secure, or his egotism less acute, but the frontiers interpenetrate, individual demarcations are confused and interests dispersed.' The ego such conditions require will be an *abstract* ego: 'The New Egos', *Blast 1*, facsimile edition (Santa Barbara: Black Sparrow Press, 1992), p. 141.
30 For an informative exposition of the painting and its context, see Martin Cork, *David Bomberg* (New Haven: Yale University Press, 1987), pp. 48–52.
31 *Blasting & Bombardiering*, pp. 99–100.
32 *The Origins of Modern English Society 1780–1880* (London: Routledge and Kegan Paul, 1969), pp. 252–70; *The Rise of Professional Society: England since 1880* (London: Routledge, 1989).
33 'The Scientific Significance of the Case of Ernst Wagner' (1914), in S. R. Hirsch and M. Shepherd (eds), *Themes and Variations in European Psychiatry: An Anthology* (Charlottesville: University of Virginia Press, 1974), pp. 121–33 (130–1).

34 *Our Mutual Friend*, ed. Stephen Gill (Harmondsworth: Penguin Books, 1971), p. 609. It is in fact Headstone's bitter rival Eugene Wrayburn who identifies him as a 'monomaniac' (347), but Dickens gives us little reason to dispute the verdict.

35 'Charisma and Its Transformation', *Economy and Society: An Outline of Interpretative Sociology*, 2 volumes, ed. Guenther Roth and Claus Wittich (Berkeley: University of California Press, 1978), ii. 1111–57. 'In radical contrast to bureaucratic organization, charisma knows no formal and regulated appointment or dismissal, no career, advancement or salary, no supervisory or appeals body, no local or purely technical jurisdiction, and no permanent institutions in the manner of bureaucratic agencies, which are independent of the incumbents and their personal charisma. Charisma is self-determined and sets its own limits. Its bearer seizes the task for which he is destined and demands that others obey and follow him by virtue of his mission' (ii. 1112).

36 For a concise account of the *New Age* at the time of Hulme's association with it, see Jones, *T. E. Hulme*, pp. 25–9. 'Nominally Fabian,' as Norman and Jeanne Mackenzie put it, 'Orage was out of sympathy with the bureaucratic collectivism of Webb and closer to the Fabian mood of earlier days': *The First Fabians* (London: Weidenfeld and Nicolson, 1977), p. 344.

37 Ludovici had written about Epstein in the *New Age* of 18 December 1913. The dispute between Hulme and Ludovici rumbled on in the pages of the journal during the early months of 1914.

38 Hulme was to describe Nietzsche as a romantic passing his 'slimy fingers' over the 'classic point of view': *CW* 235.

39 *The Waste Land: A Facsimile and Transcript of the Original Drafts*, ed. Valerie Eliot (London: Faber and Faber, 1971), pp. 32–3.

40 In 'What Art Now?', in a passage strikingly similar in tone and intent to Eliot's, Lewis excoriated the '*café*-haunting microbe' liable to be mistaken for an artist. 'For, as he generally lets the hair at the back of his head grow long, and appears in many ways untidy and unusual, he is just the public's idea of an artist, and every small vulgarity that suggests itself to this shop-assistant allowed to stray is supposed by the unenlightened beholders to be the peculiar mentality that this occupation of picture painting engenders.' The proliferation of such impostors, Lewis argues, is a reason to start training an 'élite' audience for art: *Creatures of Habit*, p. 48.

41 *Caliph's Design*, pp. 124–5, 127.

42 *Ibid.*, p. 37.

3

'THE IMAGINATION':
A Twentieth-Century Itinerary

Lennart Nyberg

> 'it's in keeping with the best traditions
> For Travel Books to wander from the point'
> (W. H. Auden, *Letter to Lord Byron*)

In the autumn of 1955 the American poet Marianne Moore was contacted by the Ford Motor Company on rather peculiar business. Ford was developing a new series of cars and needed a suitable name for it, but the company had so far been unsuccessful, coming up with 'a list of three hundred-odd candidates' characterized, according to the Ford representative, by an 'embarrassing pedestrianism', and they had realized that they needed professional assistance. Consequently, Marianne Moore was now asked to lend them a hand. She was informed that she would, of course, be remunerated for her service, and to give her some idea of what they were looking for the Ford representative said that they wanted a colossal name and that 'another "Thunderbird" would be fine'. Marianne Moore responded a few days later that she was 'complimented to be recruited in this high matter' and that she, with the assistance of her brother, would see what she could do. After another week, she returned with a suggestion – The Ford Silver Sword – adding that the name was taken from a rare plant, only to be found in Tibet and Hawaii. Receiving a rather evasive answer from the company, only dealing with the contractual fee arrangement, Moore realized that she somehow must have failed to meet the expectations, and the rest of the year would be taken up with an exchange of design sketches of the car from Ford and lists of increasingly exotic suggestions from Moore. In January, her Ford correspondent told her that they still had not managed to arrive at a decision, but that the suggestions they had received from her rated 'among the most interesting of all'. The next time Moore heard from Ford was about a year after the correspondence had been initiated and she was then informed, with a note of disappointment, that the name they had eventually chosen was – 'Edsel'. This name was not among those suggested by Moore.[1]

Although Moore herself would later comment on this business as a 'very worthy pursuit' and something she enjoyed 'for all that it was abortive',[2] this episode in twentieth-century poetry has usually been seen at most as a charming anecdote, incongruously juxtaposing industry and one of its most successful products – the car – with the seemingly most unworldly and non-profitable of the arts, poetry. However, if we pause to take this episode seriously, it might be asked exactly what sort of professional capacity that Marianne Moore was asked to exercise for the Ford Company. The terminology used in the correspondence wavered. Ford needed a name of the car that, as noted in the first letter, would work through association and conjuration and it was pointed out that they needed the 'help of one who knows more about this sort of magic than we do', concluding that they hoped that they had managed to 'pique' Marianne Moore's 'fancy'. In her response, Moore said that she would try to bring 'ardor and imagination to bear on the quest'; but on later occasions she would also use the company's term – fancy – or even 'esprit', mostly with reference to the fact that she would not be able to come up with a suitable suggestion if she was to be remunerated in advance, stating that her 'fancy would be inhibited ... by acknowledgment in advance of performance' and 'that under contract esprit could not flower'. Towards the end of the correspondence the poetic faculty in question had been redefined as 'the art of precise word picking' in the Ford thank-you note, where it was said that 'We can scarcely begin to thank you for your interest and munificent help in our dilemma. The art of precise word picking is rarely joined with the mechanical genius of our automotive personnel.'

The art of precise word picking, esprit, fancy, imagination – when looked at closely these word choices would not seem arbitrary or exchangeable only for the reason of achieving variation. Rather, they can be identified as signposts for a concept in Western poetics, the concept of what makes a poet a poet. Fancy and imagination are, as is well known and surely was by Moore, the main operative and contrasting terms in Samuel Taylor Coleridge's largescale attempt at devising a theory of poetic creation, assigning 'fancy' to a lesser and more humdrum, associative aspect of the poetic act. Given the neoclassical orientation of Moore's aesthetics, appealing to such concepts as humility, concentration, and precision for its definition, it is not surprising that she would only hesitantly describe the poetic act as one of imagination, staying clear of the subjective and self-assertive connotations of the term in its Romantic formulation, and have few problems in accepting fancy and even the art of precise word picking as appropriate terms. Yet, the fact that the terminology wavered and that both parties seemed to have difficulty in putting a verbal finger on what sort of poetic capacity was required is telling.

It could be construed both as an expression of a certain type of twentieth-century tradition and as typical of its time.

At the time of the Ford correspondence, the apparent non-romanticism of Marianne Moore had a parallel in a budding poet across the Atlantic who had just published what would later turn out to be his breakthrough volume – *The Less Deceived* (1955). The poet in question, Philip Larkin, had already in 1943 described the imagination as an 'old-fashioned word'[3] and was now searching to define an aesthetic in which 'plain language, absence of posturings, sense of proportion, humour, abandonment of the dithyrambic ideal'[4] served as key elements. Although not entirely disavowing the possible existence of an unknown creative force which once might have gone under the name of the imagination, Larkin would usually talk about it in characteristic self-denigrating fashion, even when he started to mourn its frequent absence from the late 50s and onwards. When pressed to explain how he had come upon a particularly striking image in one of his poems he responded, surely with a note of exasperated mockery, 'Sheer genius'.[5] What he would talk about in more positive terms corresponded to the model of precise word-picking that we can recognize from Marianne Moore's practice: '… the putting down of good words for good things is the mainspring of my endeavours.'[6]

In the mid-fifties, Marianne Moore and Philip Larkin were commenting on and seeking to define the professional capacity of the poet in the wake of a second Romantic survival, if we think of the onslaught of modernist campaigning in the early twentieth century as directed not so much at Romanticism *per se* as at a *First* Romantic survival in the aestheticist, decadent, and sentimental poetry of the late nineteenth century. Moore and Larkin formulated their ideals of proportion and precision in the shadow of and perhaps to some extent against the examples of Delmore Schwartz in America and Dylan Thomas in Britain, Romantic copycats both in their vatic and dithyrambic evocations of the sublime and in their dramatically short-lived careers. In the early twentieth century, similarly, the ideals of objectivity and precision advocated by modernists like T. E. Hulme, Ezra Pound, and T. S. Eliot took shape against the work of aesthetes like Algernon Charles Swinburne and Ernest Dowson rather than that of the Romantics of a century earlier. With few exceptions – one of which was Eliot's constant animosity towards Shelley – the original Romantics seldom come in as representatives of the previous badness of poetry in modernist criticism, whereas Swinburne is frequently censured for bloodless aestheticism. As Raymond Williams pointed out as early as 1958, the modernist revolt was directed not so much at Romanticism proper as 'against something nearer and more oppressive: not Romantic theory itself but one of its specialized consequences, Aesthetic theory.'[7]

From examples like these it could be argued that the formulation of aesthetic principles is less to be seen as a question of essences than as a matter of self-defining gestures in relation to and against a previous generation, or a different set of aesthetic principles. Originality and newness, as well as avowed adherence to tradition and received usage, can be interpreted as relative rather than essential qualities. Nowhere, arguably, is this more evident than in the shadowlike itinerary of the word 'imagination' in twentieth-century poetry. It is often claimed that the word has disappeared from twentieth-century discourse on poetry, on account of its Romantic connotations of mysteriously subjective transformation of reality into unified vision. Few general surveys move beyond the nineteenth century when tracing the concept; but when they do it is to query its applicability, as when *The New Princeton Encyclopedia of Poetry and Poetics* claims that 'the notion of imagination as creating unity is generally opposed to the spirit of literary modernism and postmodernism.'[8] Yet, it would be patently absurd to try to narrate a history of twentieth-century poetry with the concept of the imagination silently erased when, for instance, two so prominent, and significantly dissimilar, poets of this history – William Carlos Williams and Wallace Stevens – based their whole conception of what poetry is and can do on the concept of the imagination.[9] Consequently, it has to be asked not so much whether the concept of the imagination has disappeared as how and why that disappearance has been effected and, insofar as it has not disappeared, what it has been used to mean.

If we return the focus to the early twentieth century and the first formulations of what would later become Anglo-American modernism, we need to examine the first two of what I would like to call the three myths of modernism and the imagination. These first two myths state that the imagination has disappeared from discourse on poetry on account of modernist erasure of it and that this erasure is the result of, according to the second myth, a technical and mechanical, even scientific, understanding of the creation of poetry as against the organic conceptions of Romantic theory. Looking at the second of these myths, it is certainly the case that whereas a Romantic poet like Keats could say that 'a poem should come, if it should come at all, as the leaves to a tree', modernists like Pound, Eliot, and Williams would be prone to seek analogies for poetic creation in technology or science rather than in nature. William Carlos Williams talked about a poem as a 'verbal machine',[10] implying that mechanical rather than metaphysical or organic ability would be called for in its making, and Pound often invoked the methods of science for defining the role of the artist. In his well-known 'A Few Don'ts by an Imagiste', he admonishes his readers to 'Consider the way of the scientists' and seeks an analogy in contemporary psychology in order to determine the aesthetic goal of Imagism.[11]

To what extent, however, does this choice of technical and scientific analogies involve essences as well as relations? That is, does it say more about modernist conceptions of poetic creation than that they wanted to achieve contrast to the vague and loose formulations of a previous generation of aesthetes? Does the choice of technical and scientific terminology in fact disguise a closer adherence to tradition than the modernists themselves would be prepared to acknowledge? Some recent criticism would indeed suggest that this is the case. Edward Larrissy, for example, argues that scientific terminology was one of the 'Modernist ruses' for dressing up or disguising ideas of Romantic provenance'[12] and George Bornstein states that the Anglo-American modernists 'began writing under the sway of debased, turn-of-the-century romanticism, freed themselves by an anti-romantic reaction, and then later reconciled themselves with their predecessors.'[13] In readings like these, the explicit aesthetic formulations are indeed seen as ways of relating oneself strategically to a previous generation rather than as essential conceptions of the act of imaginative creation.

In order to test the proposition that modernist erasure of the imagination is more a question of relations than essences we might look at one of the classic formulations of a modernist understanding of imaginative creation – Eliot's catalyst analogy in the fundamental essay 'Tradition and the Individual Talent':

> It is in this depersonalization that art may be said to approach the condition of science. I therefore invite you to consider, as a suggestive analogy, the action which takes place when a bit of finely filiated platinum is introduced into a chamber containing oxygen and sulphur dioxide ... When the two gases previously mentioned are mixed in the presence of a filament of platinum, they form sulphurous acid. This combination takes place only if the platinum is present; nevertheless the newly formed acid contains no trace of platinum, and the platinum itself is apparently unaffected: has remained inert, neutral, and unchanged. The mind of the poet is the shred of platinum. It may partly or exclusively operate upon the experience of the man himself; but, the more perfect the artist, the more completely separate in him will be the man who suffers and the mind which creates; the more perfectly will the mind digest and transmute the passions which are its material.[14]

This passage has been seen as a classic instance of modernist self-definition on account of its anti-Romantic tendency to approach art through the detached stance of science and to stress the impersonal, non-subjective nature of poetic creation. In trying to realise these aims, Eliot's choice of the experiment in question could be construed as arbitrary; in order to exemplify the function of a catalyst you do not *have* to pick the example of oxygen and sulphur dioxide. It is in fact an odd choice as the resulting product of the experiment would be rather unpleasant – an acid which, in contact with matter, would have corrosive and malodorous effects; to seek an analogy for poetry in this phenomenon would support the anti-Romantic strain and accordingly seem intentional. Yet, the choice of example has wider implications which not only make it appear non-arbitrary but which beyond, or below, the technical discourse Eliot employs betray a conception of poetic creation that has more *affinities* with Romanticism than is immediately apparent. When placed in a wider context, the analogy reveals an idea of poetic creation that is not inorganic or technical, but emphatically organic.

The wider context needed for pursuing this reading is Eliot's criticism in general and his recurring meditations on the nature of poetic creation in particular. The tropes which he constantly returns to in these reflections are those of alimentation and digestion on the one hand, and gestation on the other. We may note in the catalyst passage quoted above how the mind is perceived as digesting and transmuting its material, material which could be made up of the passions referred to in the passage as well as other experiences. In the later *The Use of Poetry and the Use of Criticism*, Eliot says that 'the mind of any poet would be magnetised in its own way, to select automatically, in his reading (from picture papers and cheap novels, indeed, as well as serious books, and least likely from works of an abstract nature, though even these are aliment for some poetic minds) the material – an image, a phrase, a word – which may be of use to him later.'[15] This material would then, in Eliot's conception, incubate within the poet, a period perceived by him as one of pain or pressure, until it would be ready for release or birth, an event associated with joy and relief. An example of this process is given further on in *The Use of Poetry and the Use of Criticism*:

> I know, for instance, that some forms of ill-health, debility or anemia, may (if other circumstances are favourable) produce an efflux of poetry in a way approaching the condition of automatic writing – though, in contrast to the claims sometimes made for the latter, the material has obviously been incubating within the poet, and cannot be suspected of being a present from a friendly or impertinent demon. What one writes in this way may succeed in standing the examination of a more normal state of mind; it gives one the impression, as I have just said, of having undergone a long incubation, though we do not know until the shell breaks what kind of egg we have been sitting on. To me it seems that at these moments, which are characterised by the sudden lifting of the burden of anxiety and fear which presses upon our daily life so steadily that we are unaware of it, what happens is something *negative*: that is to say, not 'inspiration' as we commonly think of it, but the breaking down of strong habitual barriers – which tend to re-form very quickly.[16]

If we take these formulations at face value they suggest that the basic analogy to

Eliot's conception of the poetic act is that of the organic process of the digestive system where the mind of the poet, as in the catalyst analogy, would indeed be detached except in the function of giving a signal for the process to start. The consistency in his considerations on this topic is further supported by the facts that sulphur, in small doses, was formerly used as a mild type of laxative and that eggs, when rotten, would give off a distinct smell of sulphide.

What is further apparent in Eliot's writing on poetry, as in *The Use of Poetry and the Use of Criticism* which was published in 1933, is that he is notably not averse to using the word imagination. It appears regularly in that work as it does in the criticism of a number of other modernists during the twenties and thirties, that of Marianne Moore and William Carlos Williams to name only two. This brings us back to the first myth of modernism and imagination mentioned earlier, that is, the notion that the word imagination has disappeared on account of modernist attitudes to it. Not only can it be argued, as I have just done, that the technological and scientific discourse employed by modernist poets was a temporary and strategic device for signalling newness and innovation, but that both the concept of the imagination in an essentially Romantic sense and the very term itself survive intact in the twentieth century. The sense that both concept and term have become untenable in the twentieth century is, I would like to argue, an effect less of consistently held attitudes among the modernists themselves than of a certain type of criticism, in many cases academic, that grew up around modernism in the twenties and thirties. This criticism picked certain elements from the repertoire of modernist pronouncements, usually originating in Eliot's early criticism, and formed the image of Anglo-American modernism as based on a non-romantic conception of self and art. It is also in this criticism, I submit, that the fundamental erasure of the word imagination itself takes place.

An interesting work in the transition from the attitudes evinced by poets themselves to a certain type of academic practice is the 1927 study *A Survey of Modernist Poetry* by Robert Graves and Laura Riding. This work is usually cited primarily for being one of the first pieces of criticism in which the term 'modernism' is used for certain types of literature produced in the early twentieth century. The explicit aim of the work is to explain the apparent obscurity of modernist poetry to what is described as the 'plain reader'; for this purpose, it mainly uses examples of E. E. Cummings's work to elucidate the obscurities of form and content in modernist verse. The choice of Cummings for this purpose would seem natural, as his poems could be argued to be the most apparently incomprehensible of its time and most alien to traditional expectations on poetry; but it is also historically interesting, as Cummings was the first Anglo-American poet, to my knowledge, to use the term 'modernist' for characterizing his own work.[17]

In the present context, Graves's and Riding's study is interesting primarily for its arguably Romantic sense of the nature of poetry and for its handling of the word and concept of the imagination. The imagination is here never used for determining the process of poetic creation, only for the work required by the reader in understanding the poetry produced. The poet, on the other hand, is conceived of as the impersonal and seemingly passive conduit for what is termed 'the poetic thought', which is 'as invisible and as inaudible as thought' and 'exists even before it is recorded on paper, before the poet is aware of anything more definite than that there is a poem to be written.'[18] What characterizes the modernist poet, in this argument, is the daring to handle the poetic thought as a 'sensitive substance' that should be allowed 'to crystallize by itself rather than poured into prepared moulds' (78) to find 'its own natural length in spite of the demands put upon poetry by critics, booksellers and the general reading public' (84). The ideal poem to result from this process is one in which 'naked ideas are found ... instead of ideas dressed up in rhetorical devices[.]' (121).

In its combination of idealism and organicism and in its conception of the poet as an instrument being played on by metaphysical or invisible forces, the argument betrays its profound Romantic legacy which is further codified in Graves's and Riding's statement, towards the end of the work, that 'True modernist poetry can appear equally at all stages of historical development from Wordsworth to Miss Moore. And it does appear when the poet forgets what is the correct literary conduct demanded of him in relation to contemporary institutions ...'(141). The key concepts linking Romantic and modernist are, in other words, non-conventionalism and individualism, circumstances that I will be returning to a little further on.

A Survey of Modernist Poetry was to be described as a 'very uneven book' in F. R. Leavis's *New Bearings in English Poetry* which appeared five years later, in 1932. The weakness, in Leavis's view, was that it had the temerity to discuss Cummings's poetry with 'equal gravity' as that of Gerard Manley Hopkins.[19] Leavis provided ample space for a discussion of Hopkins but, on the whole and as is well known, Leavis's cause was to champion Eliot's work and a certain version of Eliot's attitude to tradition and poetry. It was Eliot to whom the new bearings of the title were to be attributed: 'He has', Leavis claimed, 'made a new start, and established new bearings'(26). These new bearings were to be found in certain key concepts, partly picked up from Eliot's own writings on poetry, which were to be regurgitatad in New Criticism, 'impersonality', 'detachment', and 'control'. I see no reason to doubt Leavis's claim that this would have been a controversial and provocative cause to advocate at the time (218–19); but the fact remains that Leavis's study, as well as a number of others in the inter-war years, was instrumental in cementing a

version of modernism derived from Eliot that would become institutionalized, and arguably stifling, reading practice for several decades to come. This
was a version of modernism which served as a mirror image to the scholars
who produced it, favouring a kind of poetry that answered to academic practices of close scrutiny of textual cruxes and intertextual allusions and a version
of modernism in which Eliot, obviously, fitted more neatly than someone like
Cummings.[20]

In constructing this version of modernism, Leavis picked up the apparent
anti-romanticism of Eliot's stance and consequently had little use for a concept like the imagination, a word that is never mentioned in *New Bearings in
English Poetry*. In its place, Leavis talked about the productive mental faculties
of a poet in terms of 'consciousness' and 'awareness', arguing that these faculties should ideally be handled with 'impersonality', 'detachment', and 'control'. However, the erasure of the term 'imagination' in criticism could not
only be effected through actually leaving out the word, as in the two examples
just dealt with, but also by adapting it into a more controllable, and consequently non-Romantic, shape. This strategy is evident in I. A. Richards's
study *Coleridge on the Imagination* from 1934. It has been claimed that in
order for Coleridge to become acceptable for treatment by Richards in this
study, Richards first had to divest him of his metaphysics.[21] This is true in so
far as the 'imagination' dealt with in the study is a very controlled variety in
which sanity is the predominant characteristic, in obvious contrast to the
indulgence in poetic frenzy and madness in the Romantic construction.

The main interest of Richards's study, however, seems to me to be found
not so much in its status as a work of scholarship on Coleridge and Romanticism, nor as a polemic in academic and artistic power struggles, but as a statement of its particular historical moment, the early thirties. There were external factors at the time which made it imperative, in Richards's view, to redefine the imagination for modern purposes. This external world and its events
creep into Richards's argumentative web and direct his conclusions. When
considering Coleridge's theory of the imagination *qua* theory, Richards que-
ries the value of literary theory in general and answers that doubts concerning
theory are 'connected with the general disparagement of intellectual and theoretical effort, in literature as in life, which has been characteristic of our time.
They give us a convenient subsidiary field in which to examine the general
revolt against reason, which shows itself most flagrantly in mid-European
politics, but it is to be noticed, in varying forms, everywhere.'[22] Here, in
Hitler's Germany and elsewhere on the continent, Richards seems to be arguing, we see imagination in full freedom, and we see what it can lead to. This
placing of scholarship and literature squarely in the midst of political actuali-
ties raises the question of the responsibility of scholar and artist towards hu-

manity and civilization. Although Richards could probably only have been vaguely aware of this at the time, prominent modernist writers and ideas they propounded would have troubled trajectories in front of them, most notably in the indictment for treason of Ezra Pound during the second world war.

The relation between poet and society brings us to the final and third myth of modernism and imagination that will be examined here. This myth claims that modernist poets in their advocacy of impersonality and the fragmented versions of reality they produced in art would be diametrically opposed to the all-embracing subjectivity and unification of self and world that are essential to Romantic conceptions of the imagination. In order to investigate this nexus we need to backtrack to the early nineteenth century and take a closer look at both 'Romanticism' and 'imagination', words that I may have seemed to be using as more self-evident in definition than 'modernism', which of course they are not. Anyone trying to find common denominators for a period comprising authors like Percy Bysshe Shelley and Jane Austen, or a common set of aesthetic and ideological principles for poets like Coleridge and Byron, would necessarily run into trouble, the solution to which is usually generalized simplification. This is not least true when it comes to deriving a coherent sense of subjectivity and a single conception of the imagination from the Romantic era and its poets. If it is claimed that Romanticism established the individual self and its subjective vision as the prime epistemological arbiter and guide for thought and action, it can equally be claimed that Romanticism also disclosed how the self, when scrutinized, cannot be perceived as a self-contained entity but has to be understood as a fragmented and uncontrollable welter of past and present, child and madman, sense impressions and ideas. The self, although positioned as the source of vision in Romantic poetry, carries the seeds of disintegration that will come into full flowering in a modern, and modernist, sense of the absence of a firm centre in the individual self.[23]

A similar link between Romanticism and modernity can be found in the view of the relation between the self and the external world and the role of the imagination in bridging the gap between the two. Romantic definitions of the imagination involved, like the attempts at modernist self-definition dealt with earlier, both essences and relations. From the point of view of relations, Romantic theory attempted to distance itself from eighteenth-century association psychology, represented above all by David Hartley, according to which the imagination was a 'mechanistic operation linking existing data.'[24] This view of the imagination was emphatically empirical in character, and what the imagination could produce that would be new would necessarily be based on previous information, through memory. Taking off from the work of Immanuel Kant, the Romantics overturned this conception of the imagination and made it into the prime instrument for human perception and understanding and even making of the world. This conception can be seen in full swing in the perhaps most well-known and most cited instance of Romantic definition of the imagination, in Coleridge's *Biographia Literaria*:

> The IMAGINATION, then, I consider either as primary, or secondary. The primary IMAGINATION I hold to be the living power and prime agent of all human perception, and as a repetition in the finite mind of the eternal act of creation in the infinite I AM. The secondary I consider as an echo of the former, coexisting with the conscious will, yet still as identical with the primary in the *kind* of its agency, and differing only in *degree*, and in the *mode* of its operation. It dissolves, diffuses, dissipates, in order to recreate; or where this process is rendered impossible, yet still, at all events, it struggles to idealize and to unify. It is essentially *vital*, even as all objects (*as* objects) are essentially fixed and dead.
>
> FANCY, on the contrary, has no other counters to play with but fixities and definites. The fancy is indeed no other than a mode of memory emancipated from the order of time and space; and blended with, and modified by that empirical phenomenon of the will which we express by the word CHOICE. But equally with the ordinary memory it must receive all its materials ready from the law of association.[25]

As can be noted here, an eighteenth-century conception of the imagination as an association of memories is designated as the third and, I think one may venture to say, least valuable of the three types of imaginative operation. What is above all noticeable, however, is how the imagination is seen both as a unifying and a disintegrating force – the secondary imagination 'dissolves, diffuses, dissipates, in order to re-create' – and how the passage does not so much seem to comprise the external world as envisage the perceiving mind as being separated from a world which it 'struggles to idealize and unify'.

For all the assertive and all-encompassing traits found in Romantic pronouncements about the imagination, it could be argued that they reveal less of a positive sense of a unification of self and world than a negative, painful and acute awareness of a gap between them that had to be closed or healed.[26] Romantic poetry is no more expressive of subjective transformations of reality than of the oppressive presence of an external world, as in a poem like Wordsworth's 'The World Is Too Much With Us'. Looked at from this point of view, Romantic constructions of the imagination do not disclose confident assertion of self as much as a troubled awareness of the predicament of the autonomous individual having to relate to an outside world, a predicament, furthermore, that is clearly recognizable in modern and modernist constructions of the self.

No trope in modern poetry and discussions of it is more common, arguably, than that of the 'pressure of the world', that is, the sense in which the external world, with its confusing mixture of sense data, invades the mind of the individual and threatens to take over. Edmund Wilson, in a classic study of modernist poetry, *Axel's Castle* from 1931, argued that 'the modern poet … must create for himself a special personality, must maintain a state of mind, which shall shut out or remain indifferent to many aspects of the contemporary world';[27] and F. R. Leavis in the already cited *New Bearings in English Poetry* noted how 'the post-war world of power-house stacks and girder-ribs … presses so inescapably upon the intelligent and sensitive to-day … ' (203). Eliot, we may remember, referred to 'the burden of anxiety and fear which presses upon our daily lives so readily that we are unaware of it.' The question to be raised, however, is whether this sense of external pressure of the world is to be seen as primarily a modern predicament, or if it is, like the modern conception of the self as unstable and decentred, ultimately to be derived from versions of self and world constructed by the Romantics.

If we pursue the argument that a sense of a gap between self and world is to be noticed in both Romantic and modernist discourse, it could be said that there are two distinct ways of handling this sense, both of which involve the imagination. One way – a defensive one, it might be said – is to observe this gap but construe it as unbridgeable by art and the imagination, and reserve art and imagination for constructing a separate imaginative reality. This was the course taken by the poets of the First Romantic Survival at the end of the nineteenth century, expressed through the art-for-art's-sake doctrines of the time and also to be observed in William Butler Yeats's output from the period. In the twentieth century, this stance can also be seen to be taken up by Wallace Stevens, in whose work and comments on poetry the pressure of the world and the imagination are, it seems, in necessary and unbridgeable conflict. In Stevens's view, the pressure of the world could involve anything from noisy radio transmitters and the trivialities that issued from them to world affairs, making art and imagination means for escaping or pressing back against this pressure. In 'The Noble Rider and the Sound of Words' he claimed that 'The poetic process is psychologically an escapist process … My own remarks about resisting or evading the pressure of reality mean escapism, if analyzed.'[28]

The Romantics of the early nineteenth century and the modernists in general would, however, choose another course, an offensive one, in the attempt to find ways of fusing self and world through incorporating the artist and artistic activity in social affairs. This is where the question of the imagination takes on a more evident ideological colouring, as it pinpoints how the relation between poet and world will necessarily have to involve questions about the responsibility of the artist in society. Where Wallace Stevens would say that the poet has no 'sociological and political obligations',[29] someone like Coleridge would actively seek to harmonize the conflicts of his time through treatises on the constitution of church and state, activities which can be argued to be not separate from his work as an artist but extensions of it,[30] and activities to which there are obvious parallels in the work of dominant modernists like Pound and Eliot. It has been suggested that Yeats was the last poet to hold on to the Romantic belief that the 'power of poetry' could have effects in or change the external world,[31] but this is hardly true. Rather, as the poet Geoffrey Hill has suggested in a fascinating essay on Ezra Pound, modern poetry in general yearns for a sense of identity between saying and doing that would have the power of the word 'hereby' in a judicial sentence. "'Hereby'", he quotes speech-act theory, 'is an indication that the utterance *itself* is doing the job that it says is done.' But, Hill concludes, 'to Pound's embarrassment and ours [modern poetry] discovers itself to have no equivalent for "hereby".'[32]

If, then, Romantics and modernists can be said to evince distinct similarities in terms of the conception of self, of the relation of self and world, and of the role of the imagination in healing the gap between the two, it has to be asked, finally, what these similarities are founded on. This basic similarity, I would suggest, is to be found in the instituting of the poet as a professional in the early nineteenth century, a conception of the artist that is largely inherited in the twentieth century. In the Romantic era, more emphatically than previously, the poet perceives himself as an autonomous individual operating in a literary market with an, on the whole, unknown reading public. With this situation is also born the sense of alienation, so recognizable in the twentieth century, that would gradually transform itself into the sense of a pressure of an external world. The history of this professionalization of poetry, and its transformations in the twentieth century, is a long and complex narrative involving print technology and copyright negotiations that is gradually being put together in present-day scholarship[33] and to which I hope I shall be returning in the near future. Now, however, I would like to end by referring back to the correspondence between Marianne Moore and the Ford Motor Company with which I started and express a hope that I have managed to elucidate and give a background to the problems they had in identifying what the exact professional capacity of a poet really is.

Notes

1 The Moore–Ford correspondence was originally published in *The New Yorker*, April 13, 1957. I am quoting it from *A Marianne Moore Reader* (New York: Viking Press, 1961), pp. 215–24.
2 *Paris Review* interview, Winter 1961, quoted from George Plimpton (ed.), *Writers at*

Work: The Paris Review Interviews. Second Series (1963; Harmondsworth: Penguin, 1977), p. 85.

3 In a letter to J. B. Sutton, January 2, 1943. *Selected Letters of Philip Larkin 1940–1985*, edited by Anthony Thwaite (London: Faber and Faber, 1992), p. 53.

4 Letter to Robert Conquest, May 28, 1955. *Selected Letters*, p. 242.

5 'An Interview with *Paris Review*'. Philip Larkin, *Required Writing: Miscellaneous Pieces 1955–1982* (London: Faber and Faber, 1983), p. 74.

6 Letter to Kingsley Amis, January 11, 1947. *Selected Letters*, p. 133.

7 *Culture and Society 1780–1950* (1958; Harmondsworth: Penguin, 1963), p. 239. A year earlier, John Bayley had identified a 'romantic survival' in the work of Yeats, Auden and Dylan Thomas in *The Romantic Survival: A Study in Poetic Evolution* (London: Constable, 1957) but, typically, with Eliot posited as a counterforce: '…[Eliot] never admits or considers the claims of the imagination to possess a unifying power: indeed imagination, with all its romantic associations, is a term of which he is shy' (p. 55).

8 Alex Preminger and T. V. F. Brogan (eds), *The New Princeton Encyclopedia of Poetry and Poetics* (Princeton, N. J.: Princeton University Press, 1993), p. 573.

9 Albert Gelpi considers their differences and similarities in 'Stevens and Williams: The Epistemology of Modernism', Albert Gelpi (ed.), *Wallace Stevens: The Poetics of Modernism* (1985; Cambridge: Cambridge University Press, 1990), pp. 3–23, but also observes that 'By the early twentieth century the character and efficacy of the imagination were, at the very least, much in doubt' (p. 4).

10 'Author's Introduction', *The Wedge* (1944). In *The Collected Later Poems of William Carlos Williams* (1950; London: MacGibbon & Kee, 1965), p. 4.

11 *Poetry* I.6 (March 1913). Quoted from *Ezra Pound's Poetry and Prose: Contributions to Periodicals*. Vol. I (New York and London: Garland, 1991), p. 121.

12 *Reading Twentieth-Century Poetry: The Language of Gender and Objects* (Oxford: Blackwell, 1990), p. 53.

13 *Transformations of Romanticism in Yeats, Eliot, and Stevens* (Chicago: The University of Chicago Press, 1976), p. xii.

14 Quoted from the third enlarged edition of Eliot's *Selected Essays* (London: Faber and Faber, 1966), pp. 17–18.

15 *The Use of Poetry and the Use of Criticism: Studies in the Relation of Criticism to Poetry in England* (1933; London: Faber and Faber, 1948), p. 78.

16 *Ibid.*, p. 144.

17 In the December 1923 issue of *Vanity Fair* Cummings published 'Four Sonnets in the Modernist Manner'. It is to be noted, however, that T. E. Hulme in 'A Lecture on Modern Poetry' from 1908 or 1909 asked 'Starting then from this standpoint of extreme modernism, what are the principal features of verse at the present time?' *Further Speculations*, edited by Sam Hynes (Minneapolis: University of Minnesota Press, 1955), p. 73.

18 The text is quoted from the lightly revised version in Robert Graves, 'Modernist Poetry, with Laura Riding', in *The Common Asphodel: Collected Essays on Poetry 1922–1949* (London: Hamish Hamilton, 1949), p. 117. Further references are given in parentheses after the quotations.

19 *New Bearings in English Poetry: A Study of the Contemporary Situation* (1932; London: Chatto & Windus, 1961), p. 189n. Subsequent references will be given in parentheses after the quotations.

20 The role of academic criticism in determining and marketing a certain version of

modernism in the inter-war years has been the subject of numerous recent studies. See, for example, Stuart Laing, 'The Production of Literature', Alan Sinfield (ed.), *Society and Literature 1945–1970* (London: Methuen, 1983), pp. 122–171; Ian Willison, 'Introduction', in Ian Willison, Warwick Gould and Warren Chernaik (eds), *Modernist Writers and the Marketplace* (London: Macmillan, 1996); and Jeffrey M. Perl, 'Passing the Time: Modernism versus New Criticism', in Hugh Witemeyer (ed.), *The Future of Modernism* (Ann Arbor: The University of Michigan Press, 1997), pp. 33–47. The manifestation of the Eliot dominance in school and university teaching can be observed in several of the submissions in Michael Alexander and James McGonigal (eds), *Sons of Ezra: British Poets and Ezra Pound* (Amsterdam: Rodopi, 1995).

21   *The Princeton Handbook of Poetic Terms* (Princeton, N. J.: Princeton University Press, 1986), p. 102.
22   *Coleridge on the Imagination* (London: Kegan Paul, Trench, Trubner & Co, 1934), pp. 137–8.
23   For the reading of Romantic subjectivity suggested here, see Vincent Newey, 'Romantic Subjects: Shaping the Self from 1789 to 1989', in Philip W. Martin and Robin Jarvis (eds), *Reviewing Romanticism* (London: Macmillan, 1992), pp. 134–53.
24   Wolfgang Iser, 'The Imaginary', in Michael Kelly (ed.), *Encyclopedia of Aesthetics* (New York and Oxford: Oxford University Press, 1998), vol. 2, p. 469.
25   *Biographia Literaria*, Chapter 13, quoted from *The Norton Anthology of English Literature*. Sixth Edition. Volume 2 (New York: Norton, 1993), p. 387.
26   The ideological work of the notion of the imagination as a 'healing power' in Romantic discourse is interestingly studied in Forest Pyle, *The Ideology of Imagination: Subject and Society in the Discourse of Romanticism* (Stanford: Stanford University Press, 1995).
27   *Axel's Castle: A Study in the Imaginative Literature of 1870–1930* (1931; New York: Scribner, 1959), p. 39
28   *The Necessary Angel: Essays on Reality and the Imagination* (1960; London: Faber and Faber, 1984), p. 30.
29   *Ibid.*, p. 27.
30   This is an argument pursued by Forest Pyle in *The Ideology of the Imagination*: 'The power and difficulty of Coleridge's theory of the imagination is that it does not *presume* the unity of either subject or nation; it takes the divisions of both as the starting point of its ideological work. Coherence is not, in other words, a condition of the process but an imaginary outcome' (p. 57).
31   John Bayley, *The Romantic Survival*, p. 103.
32   'Our Word Is Our Bond', *The Lords of Limit: Essays on Literature and Ideas* (London: Andre Deutsch, 1984), pp. 153–4.
33   See, for example, Clifford Siskin, *The Work of Writing: Literature and Social Change in Britain, 1700–1830* (Baltimore and London: The Johns Hopkins University Press, 1998); Lee Erickson, *The Economy of Literary Form: English Literature and the Industrialization of Publishing, 1800–1850* (Baltimore: The Johns Hopkins University Press, 1996); and Thomas Strychacz, *Modernism, Mass Culture and Professionalism* (Cambridge: Cambridge University Press, 1993).

4

To Murder and Create: Ethics and Aesthetics in Levinas, Pound, and Eliot

Jewel Spears Brooker

> There will be time, there will be time
> To prepare a face to meet the faces that you
> meet;
> There will be time to murder and create . . .
> *T. S. Eliot, 'The Love Song of J. Alfred Prufrock'[1]*

These famous lines, like most by T. S. Eliot, can support any number of readings. They have a psychological dimension, a social dimension, a metaphysical dimension. The lines also have an ethical dimension, throwing into relief the encounter of the self with the other, and an aesthetic dimension, hinting that art may not be an innocent activity, that murder and creation, perhaps, are twins. Prufrock's intuition that meeting other faces may be momentous is consistent with the thinking of Lithuanian-born French philosopher Emmanuel Levinas. At the centre of his work is a claim that meeting others face-to-face can break open the closed circle of the self. To meet a face is to enter a zone of vulnerability; it requires dropping one's plastic social mask and piercing the mask of the other. Prufrock, of course, will never enter that zone, never speak to the ladies who come and go, talking of Michelangelo; he will never meet a human face in its nudity, never see the face behind and beyond the prepared face. Prufrock's hesitation is understandable, for if Levinas is to be believed, the shattering of the egoistic world and the creation of a responsible self can in prospect resemble murder and creation.[2] Prufrock fears this rupture, speculating that emerging into the social world would lead to disaster – when 'human voices wake us ... we drown.' So he endlessly wanders in the wilderness of the not-yet – 'there will be time, there will be time' –, endlessly defers entering the ethical world.

In exploring the interface between ethics and aesthetics, one could do worse than focus on the year 1948. In 1948, Levinas published 'Reality and its Shadow', an article arguing that ethics is prior to and more important than aesthetics. In 1948, Ezra Pound published the *Pisan Cantos*, which the Library of

Congress honoured with the Bollingen Prize for 'the highest achievement in American poetry' in that year, sparking intense public debate about ethics and aesthetics. And in 1948, at the Library of Congress, Eliot gave a talk entitled 'From Poe to Valéry', a talk tracing modernism's commitment to language and assessing the defensibility of that commitment in the age of Auschwitz. Eliot spoke with an authority rare in the arts, for in that very year, 1948, he had been awarded the Nobel Prize for Literature and the British Order of Merit. These three events, interconnected by various historical and thematic threads, provide a beginning point for reflection on the modern conflict between ethics and aesthetics, a conflict born of the Cartesian privileging of subjectivity and nurtured by Romantic poetry with its apotheosis of the poet and poetic imagination. I begin by looking at these events, and then in light of them, will comment on the commitment to the aesthetic in modernism, particularly in Eliot and Pound.

In 1948, in 'Reality and its Shadow', Levinas launched a critique of modern(ist) aesthetics. His quarrel was not with art itself, but with the claim in 'academic aesthetics' that art is separate from life and the artist responsible only to the work of art. Levinas does not use the word 'modernism', but the date of his paper and the terms in which he frames his argument clearly suggest that he was concerned with the human implications of the reigning orthodoxy regarding high art. Although he avoids naming names, he describes positions associated with such writers as Paul Valéry, James Joyce, T. S. Eliot, and Ezra Pound; in philosophy, the positions are those of Martin Heidegger. Levinas's argument has two parts. The first regards the ontology of art, its reality status. The second takes up the ethics of art, the issue of language and human responsibility. In regard to the first, he insists that, despite the claims often made for it, art is not reality, but its shadow. 'Art consists in substituting for an object its image.'[3] W. B. Yeats, in a rare moment of self-doubt, acknowledges as much in his great valedictory poem 'The Circus Animals' Desertion'.

> Players and painted stage took all my love,
> And not those things that they were emblems of.[4]

The idea that poetry is a kind of incarnation, suggested by Eliot in the wartime *Quartets*, is utterly rejected. On the contrary, says Levinas: 'Art is a disincarnation of reality by the image.' By its very nature, art converts the human into the non-human, spirit into matter. Poetry murders to create. Criticism, on the other hand, 'integrates the inhuman work of the artist back into the human world', bringing the reader back to the 'true homeland of the mind'.[5]

The reference to the 'true homeland of the mind' is a reminder that Levinas is responding in large part to Heidegger, by 1948 famous for his brilliant work in philosophy and infamous for his support of the racial and political ideas of the Third Reich.[6] Like many of his contemporaries, Heidegger felt a keen sense of spiritual dispossession, and in both his philosophical and political writings, he emphasized the need for a 'homeland'. He argued on numerous occasions that poetry can serve as the 'homeland of the mind'. Poetry, he claimed, is the establishment of being by means of the word and the poet is the shepherd of being, the priest who stands between the gods and the people in times of destitution.[7]

Heidegger's celebration of language is a celebration of language in itself, apart from any of its traditional uses. In an argument that echoed what *avant-garde* artists had been saying for decades, he insisted that language is self-grounding and self-reflexive: 'We do not wish to ground language in something else that is not language itself, nor do we wish to explain other things by means of language.'[8] Levinas, to come to the second major point in his essay, sees this uncritical praise for language as 'artistic idolatry', associating it with a collapse of concern for the Other/other. The worship of language, he claims, is related to the 'alleged death of God' which has left poets to find reality in their own productions, and to the related disregard for the human other which prepared the way for the slaughter of eight million innocent people. Levinas worries about the denigration of human responsibility in philosophic discourse and about the uncritical celebration of the language of the poet. The poet, Levinas maintains, 'speaks in enigmas, by allusions ... in equivocations.' The critic, on the other hand, 'speaks frankly, through concepts, which are like the muscles of the mind.' Poetry 'is an event of obscuring ... an invasion of shadow.' Levinas's attack on obscurity is not focused on the message that is obscured, but on the function of obscurity in sealing art off from life, its function in stopping dialectic and the movement of ideas.[9]

Levinas's thought is built on three foundations – Jewish theology, Russian literature, and the Holocaust – all of which foreground the ethical. As a child in a Lithuanian Jewish family, he absorbed the teachings of the Talmud. As a student in Russian schools, he immersed himself in Dostoyevsky, thus deepening his understanding of the relation between ethics and existence. As a European Jew coming to maturity in the 1930s, Levinas knew the horrors of the Final Solution. His family was killed by the Nazis, and he himself spent much of the war as a prisoner. These indelible memories shaped his post-war thinking in numerous ways, reinforcing his conviction that we are our brother's keeper and strengthening his belief that public intellectuals are responsible for the consequences of their ideas.[10]

Levinas entered philosophy proper by way of Heidegger's *Being and Time*, which he read in 1928, the year after it was published, and he studied with Heidegger's mentor, Edmund Husserl. In the 1948 article, Levinas was responding in part to the lectures on aesthetics that Heidegger gave in the 1930s, among them 'Hölderlin and the Essence of Poetry' (1936). Casting a cold eye on the separation of language from life, Levinas rejects the argument that poetry is a 'true homeland' and human 'dwelling place'. He maintains, conversely, that prose, not poetry, is the homeland and that interpretation is the dwelling place, the site of human-to-human engagement. He rejects aestheticism of any kind.

> Art for art's sake ... is false inasmuch as it situates art *above* reality and recognizes no master for it; and it is immoral inasmuch as it liberates the artist from his duties as a man and assures him of a pretentious and facile nobility.[11]

He concludes that in its narcissistic embrace of the self, its wilful rejection of the face-to-face, art for art's sake constitutes an evasion of moral responsibility.

In 1948, another work was published – Pound's *Pisan Cantos* – which highlighted in spectacular fashion the post-Romantic apotheosis of the poet and the modernist gap between aesthetics and ethics. The early Pound had been an aesthete, dedicated to art above all else. He was deeply disturbed by the loss of friends in the First World War and also by the cultural crisis epitomized by the War. He had come, in addition, to dislike London, and so, in 1920, in 'Hugh Selwyn Mauberley', he bade farewell to aestheticism and to England; henceforth his interest would be in big issues such as the relation between war and economics, and he would live in France and Italy. During the 1920s, his passion for art merged with his interest in economics, and his admiration for classicism and the Renaissance converged with his growing appreciation of Fascism. Impressed by Mussolini's economic reforms, he moved to Italy, where he continued to add to *The Cantos* and to write about culture and economics. Pound decided that usury was at the root of Western troubles and the Jews were the masterminds who were corrupting and destroying civilization. In 1938, with the Jews already under assault in Germany, Pound argued in the *New English Weekly* that two million Jews should be expelled from New York for 'harm done by Jewish finance to the English race in America.'[12] During the Second World War, he regularly voiced morally heinous and politically dangerous views on Radio Rome – for example, on April 27, 1943, he urged U.S. troops in North Africa to desert and said that President 'Roosevelt and a few hundred yidds' should be hanged.[13] In 1943, he was indicted for treason, and in 1945, arrested and brought to Washington. He was spared conviction and probable execution only because he was judged to be 'of unsound mind'.[14]

In 1948, when the *Pisan Cantos* appeared, Pound was the star patient in St. Elizabeth's, a Washington hospital for the criminally insane. These cantos, which had been written while he was in custody near Pisa, constitute the deeply moving, deeply conflicted memoir of a tormented survivor of a ruined civilization.

> As a lone ant from a broken ant-hill
> from the wreckage of Europe, *ego scriptor*. (C 76)[15]

As a modern Odysseus, now shipwrecked, imprisoned in a steel cage, he recalls moments of ecstasy and despair as he sailed the seas of human error. The poem begins as an elegy for Mussolini, a martyr 'twice crucified'.

> Thus Ben and la Clara *a Milano*
>   by the heels at Milano
> That maggots shd/ eat the dead bullock
> DIGONOS . . . the twice crucified. (C 74)

The poem includes his poisonous opinions about the Jews.

> the yidd is a stimulant, and the goyim are cattle
> in gt/ proportion and go to saleable slaughter
> with the maximum of docility. (C 74)

At the same time, the *Pisan Cantos* contain much beautiful poetry. In unforgettable language, Pound catalogues his lost companions: Possum – meaning Eliot, Jim – meaning Joyce, William – meaning Yeats, and others. More poignantly, he tries to hold on to beauty, and most poignantly of all, he examines his conscience.

> 'Master thyself, then others shall thee beare'
>   Pull down thy vanity
> Thou art a beaten dog beneath the hail,
> A swollen magpie in a fitful sun,
> Half black half white
> Nor knowst'ou wing from tail
> Pull down thy vanity
>   How mean thy hates
> Fostered in falsity,
>   Pull down thy vanity,
> Rathe to destroy, niggard in charity,
> Pull down thy vanity,
>   I say pull down. (C 81)

1948 was the year for the inauguration of the Bollingen Prize, funded by the Mellon family and intended as an annual prize for the best verse by an American. The jury was to consist of the Library of Congress Fellows in American Letters. In 1948, they were Conrad Aiken, W. H. Auden, Louise Bogan, Katherine Chapin, T. S. Eliot, Paul Green, Robert Lowell, Katherine Anne Porter, Karl Shapiro, Theodore Spencer, Allan Tate, Willard Thorp, and Robert Penn Warren. Aiken, Eliot, and Tate were longtime friends of Pound's, as were two important behind-the-scenes players, Archibald MacLeish and William Carlos Williams. In his capacity as Assistant Secretary of State and as Librarian of Congress from 1939–1945, MacLeish had been particularly well placed to serve as a buffer between Pound and the authorities. In 1943, MacLeish wrote to the Assistant Secretary of War that while the indictment of Pound was 'understandable', it was also regrettable because Pound was 'half-cracked and extremely foolish'. Concerned that the Allied military forces might execute Pound on the spot as they entered Italy, MacLeish maintained that he should be brought back to the United States for a proper civil trial.[16] Years earlier, in 1926, as an admirer of *The Waste Land* and of Pound's early poems, MacLeish had written the '*Ars Poetica*' of modernist aesthetics:

> A poem should be palpable and mute
> As a globed fruit,
> ...
> A poem should be equal to:
> Not true.
> For all the history of grief
> An empty doorway and a maple leaf.
> For love
> The leaning grasses and two lights above the sea–
> A poem should not mean
> But be.[17]

Anticipating a public uproar over the decision to award the Bollingen Prize to Pound, the jury prepared the following statement for release to newspapers:

> The Fellows are aware that objections may be made ... [But] To permit other considerations than that of poetic achievement to sway the decision would destroy the significance of the award and would in principle deny the validity of that objective perception of value on which civilized society must rest.[18]

This distinguished jury affirmed language over life, aesthetics over ethics, and objectivity over subjectivity. A decade later, with the help of MacLeish, Eliot, and others, Pound was released from St. Elizabeth's and immediately set sail for Italy. Arriving in Naples harbor, he gave the Fascist salute for reporters and announced 'All America is an insane asylum'.[19]

On November 19, 1948, at the Library of Congress, Eliot gave a lecture entitled 'From Poe to Valéry'. His speech is both a tribute to his old friend Paul Valéry, who died in 1945, and an evaluation of the tradition of poetry which culminated in Valéry's work. Pound is not mentioned, but he is the ghost in the room. He was, after all, just a stone's throw across the Anacostia River, confined in St. Elizabeth's on grounds with a view of the Jefferson Building in which Eliot was speaking. The day before Eliot's speech, the Fellows in American Letters had met to decide on the Bollingen award. Their meeting had been scheduled to coincide with Eliot's visit, and most if not all of the Fellows were in the audience for this speech. During the private deliberations on whether or not to honour the *Pisan Cantos* with this award, Eliot evidently had said very little, but in this public speech, de-personalized by its focus on Valéry, he explores the commitment to language and to art that had brought not only Pound but himself to the present moment. It is my view that his conclusions are a self-indictment and an indication that he has withdrawn from the tradition to which his earlier work had given so much prestige.

Eliot's speech consists of an analysis and a critique of the modernist tradition. He suggests that two notions originating in Baudelaire had reached their zenith in Valéry. The first regards the ontological status of poetry. Baudelaire had argued that 'A poem should have nothing in view but itself.'[20] This was accepted and extended by the modernists. In a clear allusion to MacLeish's 'A poem should not mean/But be', Eliot added that in more recent times Baudelaire's doctrine had been expressed as 'A poem does not say something – it *is* something.'[21] Eliot knew that his early essays and poetry were often given as 'Exhibit A' for this proposition, and he knew that his audience included younger poets who thought of themselves as his disciples as well as older poets who considered themselves his comrades. In this extraordinary situation, he turns away from these readings of his own early work and implicates himself, along with MacLeish and Pound, in the unspeakable sadness of current events.

The second notion stemming from Baudelaire is that 'the composition of a poem should be as conscious ... as possible, that the poet should observe himself in the act of composition.' In Valéry and other modernists, this culti-vation of self-consciousness led to the conclusion 'that the act of composition is more interesting than the poem which results from it.' Valéry 'continued to write poetry', it appears, 'simply because he was interested in the introspective observation of himself engaged in writing it.' Eliot quotes and by implication agrees with the assessment of Louis Bolle that, for Valéry, writing poetry dwindled to little more than an exercise in 'intellectual narcissism'.[22]

In critiquing this development, Eliot identifies three stages in experiencing poetry. In the first, the reader is interested primarily in the subject matter. In the second, he is interested both in the subject matter and the language in which it is expressed. In the third, he is interested primarily or exclusively in language and style. Although the third is the most sophisticated and the one associated with high modernism, it is not the one of which Eliot now approves.

> A complete unconsciousness or indifference to style at the beginning, or to the subject matter at the end, would … take us outside of poetry altogether: for a complete unconsciousness of anything but subject matter would mean … poetry had not yet appeared; a complete unconsciousness of anything but style would mean that poetry had vanished … poetry is only poetry so long as … the subject matter is valued for its own sake.[23]

Eliot concludes by suggesting that the '*art poétique* … which bore fruit in the work of Valéry has gone as far as it can go. I do not believe', he adds, that 'this aesthetic can be of any help to later poets.'[24] As for the future, he predicts that

> the extreme awareness of and concern for language which we find in Valéry … is something which must ultimately break down, owing to an increasing strain against which the human mind and nerves will rebel; just as … the indefinite elaboration of scientific … machinery … may reach a point at which there will be an irresistible revulsion of humanity and a readiness to accept the most primitive hardships rather than carry any longer the burden of modern civilization.[25]

In this speech, spoken to his peers and admirers, Eliot completes a process begun years before – a withdrawal of commitment to self-reflexivity in language. In my view, it was the war and particularly the Holocaust that underscored for him the folly of such a commitment. It was also, unavoidably, the ever-present example of Pound that made it important for Eliot to state this so clearly to this particular audience. Alluding to his own earlier belief, one shared and often repeated by Pound, that the artist's concern with language was actually a concern for civilization, Eliot concludes that civilization, so conceived, is a burden too heavy to carry.

Eliot once said that as a poet discussing other poets, he usually had in mind his own work and that of his friends. The shadow subject of 'From Poe to Valéry', I suggest, is 'From Baudelaire to Eliot and Pound'. The shadow issue is the relation of aesthetics to ethics, an issue of immense interest to both poets. Before turning to a further consideration of ethics and aesthetics in their work, I wish to return to Levinas and briefly explain the view of language and ethics in *Totality and Infinity*. His relevance to an understanding of modernism comes from the fact that his work was shaped in part by his complex response to his mentor Heidegger, a figure at the heart of the modernist understanding of language and also at the heart of modern crimes against humanity. Levinas's relevance here is also related to the fact that his work is deeply informed by an appreciation of modernist poetry, especially that of his friend Paul Valéry, and Valéry, as Eliot's Library of Congress talk makes clear, is emblematic of the modernist dilemma in aesthetics/ethics.

Levinas began his work in philosophy by grappling with Kant, Husserl, and Heidegger. The challenge in regard to ethics was to find some way of conceiving of human relationships that preserved genuine difference, that preserved the integrity of the other. With Kant, it is difficult to avoid turning the other into an object; with Husserl, difficult to avoid making her an aspect of my experience; with Heidegger, difficult to avoid subsuming her into Being. Another Jewish thinker, Martin Buber, had in the 1920s attempted to find a non-objectifying way to conceptualize the other. He developed a philosophy of dialogue based on a relationship of the self and the other, which he called the I and the Thou. Buber was reacting chiefly against the Existentialists, who emphasized solitariness, and the Kantians, who turned the other into an object. Levinas was far more radical, calling into question the entire Western tradition from Plato through Heidegger. He perceived that Kantian subjectivity was part of a major pattern in Western thought: a tendency to totalize, to absorb everything into a single system that obliterates difference. In Plato, the all-encompassing concept is the Idea; in Plotinus, the Soul; in Hegel, *Geist*; in Kant, the *Noumenon*; in Husserl, Consciousness; and in Heidegger, Being. As a corrective, Levinas suggests in *Totality and Infinity* that totality should be understood in relation to infinity. He associates totality with subjectivity or interiority, and infinity with objectivity or exteriority or alterity. When he says that the other or alterity is infinite, he means that the other cannot be totalized, cannot be grasped as an object or formulated as a concept; the other is always greater than my project to gain a total understanding or to incorporate her into my world. Levinas rejects any Hegelian move that would combine totality and infinity, any step that would collapse the self and the other into a synthesis. He rejects, for example, the notion that acknowledging the other involves sacrificing the self, for the very reason that both self and other have to be preserved in order for them to be in relation.

Levinas understands existence not in terms of substance or of subjectivity, but in terms of movement, in terms of breaking out of the self and living in relation. He argues that the world as I experience it is egocentric, a totality in which I experience others either as extensions of myself or as objects to manipulate. The question becomes, how can I break out into the ethical realm – that is, how can I ex-ist? His response is that one breaks into the realm of freedom by seeing the face of another. I see a face, an exterior to my self, and that face summons me out of my self. I can ignore that beckoning face, or I can welcome it with the Biblical words 'Here I am'. 'Here I am', in contrast to 'I understand', does not suggest that the other has been grasped or absorbed. It suggests, rather, an acceptance of the self and the other, and it allows the other to exist in her ineluctable strangeness and her irreducible alterity. The face of the other is always in a special sense the face of a stranger, and always greater than any concept I can have of her. It is important to note that the face is not identical with the other, but rather that it contains a trace of her passing, a pledge of the presence of the ungraspable, the unknowable – in short, of infinity. The question becomes: how can I welcome this face without making it an extension of myself, how can I have a relation with the other that leaves its otherness intact?[26]

The face can be welcomed and the walls of the self tumbled, Levinas claims, through language. It is speaking that enables one to respond to the face of the other, and thus, it is language that makes possible the movement from the egocentric to the ethical realm. Language is an essential part of the movement between totality and infinity. When a face appears before me, it is language that enables me to say 'Here I am'. With this saying, I put part of my self into words and offer it as a gift to the other, without demanding reciprocity. With this saying, I accept responsibility in the ethical realm. What is said is not as important as the saying, for the saying always exceeds any possible said. Language is my response to epiphany, and thus it enables me to glimpse the trace of infinity, the trace of the ultimate Other.[27]

The ethics articulated by Levinas in *Totality and Infinity* can now be folded into his resistance to academic aesthetics, with which I began. His understanding of the function of language in breaking through the shell of the self and establishing existence provides a powerful alternative to the Heideggerian understanding of language and being; it is also a forceful refutation of modernist claims about art and moral responsibility. His analysis of the philosophic tradition of totalizing is helpful in understanding political developments in twentieth-century Europe, among them the totalitarian regimes in Italy and Germany. And of course, the totalizing tendencies are everywhere evident in the Holocaust. In European history, the face of the other has often been the face of the Jew, the stranger who could not be assimilated. As a European Jew in the age of Auschwitz, Levinas was acutely aware of what it meant to be the other, and this gave him a special perspective in the construction of his ethics.

Levinas's distinction between totality and infinity can be profitably compared to Eliot's contrast between 'Tradition and the Individual Talent'. Eliot extends his title binary to include classic vs. romantic, past vs. present, intellect vs. feeling, objectivity vs. subjectivity, the mind of Europe vs. the individual mind, and much more. And then he deconstructs it. His thesis, suggested in his title by the use of the coordinating conjunction 'and', is that these categories are not opposites but complements; he argues that the binaries are related and can be understood only in terms of each other. Tradition is defined not as something that is past, specifically not as a canon, but as a continuously evolving complex constantly being re-shaped by the present and by the individual talent, by the new work of art. Much like Levinas, he is trying to resist both totalizing and fragmentation, both turning the tradition into an aspect of his own mind and turning it into an object. But it is important to acknowledge that Eliot is trying to have it both ways. He resists the totalizing elements in tradition, but at the same time, he defines tradition as an 'ideal order of monuments' and he privileges the 'Mind of Europe' as 'more important' than the individual mind. But then again, he also argues that it is only in an individual mind that the Mind of Europe can exist, only in the present moment that the past can exist.[28] Although he is less than consistent, he is at least self-critical, returning to the issue in his social and religious criticism, in *Four Quartets*, and in his postwar comedies.

I have suggested that self-criticism is implied by the older Eliot's critique of modernism in 'From Poe to Valéry'. The two characteristics he associated with Valéry are, first, a fastidious concern with language for its own sake, and second, extreme self-consciousness in which the poet's attention is displaced from the real world to the writing process. A version of these qualities, I would argue, can be seen in Eliot's own work from 'Prufrock' to *Four Quartets*. The concern with language is explicit from the start. Prufrock's anxious 'Shall I say' is parallel with his desperate 'Do I dare?' His weary 'it is impossible to say just what I mean' leaves him forever stranded on half-deserted 'streets that follow like a tedious argument/Of insidious intent' on the way to an 'overwhelming question' interrupted by an ellipsis. As for self-consciousness, it is clear that Prufrock is paralysed by self-reflection. He imagines himself ascending a stair and then, as he changes his mind, descending, and as he descends, he sees his own head as an object moving down with a 'bald spot in the middle of [his] hair'; and then he observes others observing his bald spot – 'They will say: "How his hair is growing thin!"' He imagines, further, observing his own head carried on a platter. The interplay of self-consciousness and language makes it impossible for him to break through his solipsistic shell.[29] The references to language (speaking, saying, asking questions, dropping questions on plates) in 'The Love Song of J. Alfred Prufrock' show, however, that even though Prufrock is so obsessed with language that the poem becomes to some extent self-reflexive, Eliot could not be said to be concerned with language for its own sake. Prufrock is obsessed with language because it does not work, because of its epistemological and existential and social insufficiency. The fact that Eliot constantly recurs in his poetry to the failure of language means that he had to some extent an instrumental view of language – language was supposed to do something – existentially, epistemologically, socially.

The insufficiency of language continues to be a major topic in Eliot's work. In his middle period, he writes of Sweeney's struggle with language – 'I've gotta use words when I talk to you'.[30] And in *Four Quartets*, the poet narrator devotes section five of each poem to the endless struggle with language and meaning.

> Words strain
> Crack and sometimes break, under the burden,
> Under the tension, slip, slide, perish,
> Decay with imprecision, will not stay in place,
> Will not stay still.[31]

The Eliot of *Four Quartets* remains self-referential, but in a different mode, now deeply self-critical, even self-effacing.

Eliot's allegiance to the aesthetic waxed and waned in tandem with personal crises which called into question the sufficiency of art. One such crisis, I would suggest, was vocational. In 1915-1916, he abandoned philosophy as a career and decided to be a man of letters. Ezra Pound was at this time trying to 'save' Eliot for art and partially through Pound's influence, Eliot intensified his allegiance to the aesthetic. This commitment peaks in the polished quatrains of 1917–1920 in which the other is objectified, caricatured, and treated primarily as material for art. Among these are the most ethically disturbing of Eliot's poems, the ones which most expose his prejudices – for example, 'Mr. Eliot's Sunday Morning Service', 'Sweeney Among the Nightingales', 'Burbank with a Baedeker: Bleistein with a Cigar'. It is in these poems too that Eliot's language is most self-reflexive. 'Polyphiloprogenitive', for example, refers first and foremost to itself as a word.

Another crisis re-aligning Eliot's relation to the aesthetic can be seen in the circumstances surrounding the writing of *The Waste Land*, including the failure of his marriage, the collapse of his health, and economic stress. It could be argued that Eliot's tendency to totalize, to bind all fragments together through art, reaches its zenith in his use of the mythical method in *The Waste Land*. One way that he copes with fragments is by using a myth older than recorded history and theoretically common to all people, an all-inclusive Ur-myth from which all fragments can be seen as fall-outs. It could be argued, moreover, that his use of language is self-reflexive. With its trademark dislocation of syntax and use of foreign phrases, the poem does force the language to point to itself, making it self-reflexive. In spite of the myth, however, the poem refuses to be grasped; in spite of the self-reflexivity of its language, it refuses to refer primarily to language. It ends with a cascade of fragments that further undercuts the commitment to totalizing visions and indeed to language itself. 'These fragments I have shored against my ruins' is followed by its negation in the reference to Kyd's *Spanish Tragedy*. In *Reading* The Waste Land, Joseph Bentley and I argue that this conclusion undermines grand solutions, undermines the grounding myth, undermines the idea that art enables one to salvage the ruins of life. In our reading, the poem ends on the margin, the shore, between art and life, between damnation and salvation.[32] To use the language of this essay, it ends on the margin between totality and infinity.

Two other crises must at least be mentioned – one ending with Eliot's baptism in 1927 and the other associated with World War II. In regard to his conversion, the retreat from aestheticism was immediate and unambiguous. In the 1928 preface to *The Sacred Wood*, Eliot backs away from the repeated proposition in his early essays that art has no master but art.[33] In the great Dante essay of 1929 and in the Harvard lectures of 1932, he rejects the idea that art can be a substitute for religion.[34] In the first poems written after his conversion, he presents the stylistic equivalent of a new commitment to content, most noticeably in the austere and simple dramatic monologues, 'Journey of the Magi' and 'Song for Simeon', and in the philosophical meditation 'Animula'.

Eliot's retreat from aestheticism continued throughout the 1930s, with his *Criterion* editorials and cultural criticism showing increasing concern for the social and religious dimensions of art.[35] Like Pound, he was much exercised by the war, but unlike Pound, he supported the Allies. In a strange way, the war was energizing for Eliot and many others. He took his war duties seriously, and in a draft of 'The Three Voices of Poetry' referred to the wartime *Quartets* as 'patriotic poems'.[36] Most of his prose of the 1940s, when not patriotic, is also focused on issues raised by the war. Jeffrey Perl suggests that the main subject in Eliot's prose in the 1940s is 'germanism of the sensibility', and argues that the war and the Holocaust changed the poet more than his conversion to Christianity did.[37] On the evidence of the wartime *Quartets* alone, it seems clear that Eliot has moved quite close to the position articulated in 1948 by Levinas. In 'East Coker', the poet includes a sample of beautifully polished poetry, and then remarks:

> That was a way of putting it – not very satisfactory:
> A periphrastic study in a worn-out poetical fashion,
> Leaving one still with the intolerable wrestle
> With words and meanings. The poetry does not matter.[38]

One can see in the formal beauty of the *Quartets* a continuation of the interest in history, in order, in form, in art, but this is carefully balanced by an emphasis on place and time and the individual talent. Art as a totalizing concept is transformed, with the whole and the part seen, as in the later Yeats, as part of a dance. The artist, similarly, is demoted. He is seen as a workman, a bricoleur.

> Trying to learn to use words, and every attempt
> Is a wholly new start, and a different kind of failure ...[39]

The most important moral characteristic of the artist in the *Quartets* is humility, humility before language, before history, before the other.

Turning to Pound: Of the great modern poets, he remained the most consistently committed to a totalizing aesthetic. He referred to *The Cantos* not only as an epic, 'the tale of the tribe', but as a 'poem containing history'.[40] He conceived of his poem(s) as a twentieth-century *Odyssey*, with himself as both Homer and Odysseus. He also claimed that it was a modern version of the *Divine Comedy*, with himself as the Dante (both poet and pilgrim) who visits the world of the dead to gain the secrets of past, present, and future, and then passes through the purgatory of human error.[41]

Any attempt to make sense of aesthetics and ethics in Pound must address an issue that has sharply divided critics for years: whether or not he was 'of sound mind' and thus responsible for his actions. In 1945, his defenders (including MacLeish, Fitts, and Laughlin) argued that the insanity plea was the only way for him to avoid execution.[42] On the other side, there is ample evidence that Pound was mentally ill. According to Wendy Flory,

> Beginning in 1935, Pound's mental condition deteriorated precipitously. From
> then on, characteristics of his behavior and his writings exactly fit the diagnostic
> criteria for ... Delusional Disorder.[43]

Flory argues that Pound suffered both from delusions of grandeur (i. e., he was possessed by a single keystone idea) and delusions of persecution. Pound's 'insight' was his belief that the economics of Social Credit could prevent war and depression, and he did his best to convince not only ordinary people but world leaders, including Mussolini and Roosevelt. His belief in the superior intelligence of the artist fed his confidence about this 'great insight', and the repertoire of European anti-Semitism provided him with a ready-made villain. Pound's radio broadcasts and his letters are the best evidence for Flory's position. It is shocking to realize that these incoherent and bitter broadcasts were penned by a major poet. His private letters are just as startling. The recently published letters he and Dorothy exchanged between his arrest and her arrival in Washington reveal that as soon as he was arrested, he dashed off a cable to President Truman: 'BEG YOU CABLE ME MINIMUM TERMS JUST PEACE JAPAN'. Pound continues: 'LET ME NEGOTIATE VIA JAPANESE EMBASSY ... FENELLOSA'S EXECUTOR AND TRANSLATOR OF CONFUCIUS CAN WHAT VIOLENCE CANNOT. CHINA ALSO WILL OBEY VOICE OF CONFUCIUS'.[44] This is a serious offer. He thought he could negotiate the end of the war in the Pacific because he was an artist, superior to bureaucrats and politicians. To say that he was suffering from delusions is to put it mildly. He was also manic, alternating between gloom and excitement. The complication, as was noted in the swirl of journalism surrounding the Bollingen Award, is that the acknowledgment that Pound was of unsound mind means that the best American poetry in 1948 was written by a madman.

Pound's earliest commitments were aesthetic, but in retrospect, they can easily be seen as part of his developing politics. In 1913, he published in *The Egoist* an essay which explains his view of the relation of aesthetics and ethics. In 'The Serious Artist', he argues that the function of the artist is to provide raw data for the study of ethics. The arts, he claims, are a science, like biology, and, just as the biologist provides data on the physical person, so the artist provides data on the spiritual. The ruling principle in ethics, he says, should be achieving the 'greatest good for the greatest number'. The formula, of course, is Bentham's. This is straight utilitarianism. The good of the whole takes precedence over the good of any part; morally speaking, one is required to determine 'what percentage of maximum happiness [man] can have without causing too great a percentage of unhappiness to those about him.' This is, again, Bentham's relentlessly totalizing, hedonistic calculus.[45]

When Pound says that art is a 'scientific report' on the 'inner nature of man', he does not mean man in the abstract, but man as represented by himself or another artist.

> The serious artist is scientific in that he presents the image of his desire, of his hate, of his indifference as precisely that, as precisely the image of his own desire, hate or indifference. The more precise his record the more lasting and unassailable his work of art.[46]

The criterion for distinguishing good art from bad is the same as that distinguishing good science from bad – accuracy. 'Bad art is inaccurate; [it] falsifies.' The bad artist is immoral because he is dishonest, equivalent to a physician who lies about his data. The serious artist, on the other hand, is accurate; he is moral because he tells the truth. Pound concludes that 'good art', by which he means the 'most precise' art, is 'wholly a thing of virtue', 'however "immoral" [its content].'[47] By this standard, *Cantos* 14 and 15 are not only good, but virtuous, for they seem to constitute an accurate image of Pound's hatred for Londoners, capitalists, the middle class.

The poet as conceived in this early essay has three main characteristics. The first is sensuous: he is in touch with the world around him and with his own feelings. The second is intellectual: he knows more than other people, in part because of his living contact with tradition. The third is moral: he is accurate, he tells the truth. *The Cantos* begin with the initiation of the poet, a ritualistic descent to the underworld, a descent through layers of culture in which the poet gives blood and thus a voice to ghosts on every level, all the way back to pre-history, and then comes back like Lazarus to tell us the truth about ourselves. As he puts it in *The Cantos*, he is interested in correcting 'error'. This is behind Pound's famous didacticism, his urge to scold people for being wrong.

Pound's position in this essay is rendered more powerful and more dangerous because it is combined with Baudelaire's contempt for the middle class. By 1913, Pound's assumptions that other people are emotionally, intellectually, and morally inferior to the artist are plainly displayed in his poems. In 'The Garden', for example, he presents three classes – a male narrator as representative of the intellectual aristocracy, an exquisitely bored female as specimen of the middle class, and filthy, sturdy children as emblematic of the very poor. The poem is written from the point of view of the analytical male, who observes in the silken-clad lady 'the end of breeding'. His complex class-drenched image touches on both the purpose and the effect of breeding (both animal and human/social). This anemic and sterile lady of the middle class is surrounded, ironically, by children, 'a rabble/Of the filthy, sturdy, unkillable infants of the very poor'.[48] Alluding to the *Beatitudes*, Pound concedes that the alarmingly fertile, mindlessly breeding masses will inherit the earth. Their sturdy issue will survive the effete woman, and in what may be an unintended irony, the filthy rabble will also survive the connoisseur of beauty and truth. They will survive, not because of their intellectual or moral qualities, nor even their human qualities; they will survive because among the very poor, there is no end (in both senses) of breeding and, like rabbits or roaches, they are unkillable. Pound's garden of death suggests 'the end of breeding' in another sense too, for his image recalls a better garden, lost now, a paradise in which the Lord commanded all creatures to 'Be fruitful and multiply'. Pound will continue until the end to associate the middle class with stupidity, with error, with suburban prejudice, and only occasionally will he include in his poetry the self-criticism that makes Eliot's early poems so moving. Whatever one might think of the ethics represented in Pound's early work, one should not doubt the sincerity of his commitment to the artist as representative of an intellectual aristocracy. His generosity to other artists, most famously Eliot and Joyce, is well-known.

In 1920, Pound published *Hugh Selwyn Mauberley*, a major poem that in retrospect can be seen as a watershed, both for him and for modern poetry. It is his farewell to London, and his acknowledgment that an artist has limits; he cannot 'wring' lilies from acorns.

> For three years, out of key with his time,
> He strove to resuscitate the dead art
> Of poetry; to maintain 'the sublime'

In the old sense. Wrong from the start –

...

Bent resolutely on wringing lilies from the acorn;
Capaneus; trout for factitious bait;

...

His true Penelope was Flaubert ...[49]

Pound blames the situation of the modern artist on the 'tawdry cheapness' of late capitalist culture, in which the large and powerful middle class prefers the classics in paraphrase to sculpture in rhyme. He takes leave of aestheticism, ditching the idea that a poem is a beautiful object, a well-wrought urn; at the same time, he reiterates his conviction that the artist embodies moral and intellectual *areté* and the middle class embodies not only stupidity but immorality. His commitment to art is more militant than ever and more convincing. It is in this watershed poem that Pound brings together the mix that will dominate his future poems – economics, war, usury, art, and contempt for the middle class and the Jews.

Pound's obsession with the superiority of the artist permeates everything to come and can be seen by focusing on almost any of his prose pieces, almost any of the infamous broadcasts, almost any of *The Cantos*. 'Murder by Capital', published in the *Criterion* in the middle of the great Depression (1933) is typical. 'The unemployment problem', he insists, 'is not ... the unemployment of nine million ... etc.; it is and has been the ... unemployment of Gaudier-Brzeska, T. S. Eliot, Wyndham Lewis, E. P. the present writer, and of twenty or thirty musicians.' He argues that the situation can only be corrected by an enlightened statesman with 'values', saying that Mussolini is the first to appear since the Renaissance.[50] As the decade wore on and events accelerated toward the second world war in a single generation, Pound's health deteriorated and his voice – 'Ezra Pound Speaking' – grew bolder and more shrill. He was now on the road to Pisa.

One of the recurring puzzles about this endlessly complicated poet is the meaning of the obstinate silence into which he retreated after his return to Italy. He said almost nothing, and the few things he did say were as self-deprecating as his earlier words had been self-aggrandizing. In regard to *The Cantos*, he told Daniel Cory, 'I botched it', saying that his way was 'not the way to make a work of art'.[51] He now insisted that his epic made no sense, that it was simply double talk.[52] One of the young poets who travelled to Italy to pay court to Pound was Allen Ginsberg. To Ginsberg's praise of *The Cantos*, Pound said, 'Any good spoiled by my intention. Worst mistake was the stupid suburban prejudice of anti-Semitism.'[53] This sounds like a recantation, especially since it was said to a Jewish poet in the presence of witnesses. But in fact, although Ginsberg seemed to consider it an apology for Pound's sins against the Jews, and although many critics accept it as such, Pound clearly says that his worst mistake was adopting a 'suburban', i.e. middle-class, prejudice. His regret is that it spoiled the poem. There is not the slightest hint that he had Auschwitz or Buchenwald in mind, or that it mattered to Ginsberg, who was thrilled to have received the master's blessing. While it is difficult to know why Pound retreated into silence, one can surmise that it had to do with depression and illness, but also that he may have come to reassess his commitment to art in the light of his painful experiences over many decades. He may have decided that silence was the only appropriate response for one who realized too late that he could not re-make the world with words. In the *Pisan Cantos*, Pound presents himself as the mind of Europe. His claim lends retrospective poignancy to Valéry's early essay describing the contemporary crisis as a collapse of the mind of Europe. Europe has cracked up, lost its mind, had a nervous breakdown.[54]

To conclude: It is my view that Levinas's mid-century critique of Heideggerian notions of language and of academic aesthetics is illuminating in regard to the complicated failures in community that culminated in the middle decades of the twentieth century. The close connection between totalizing theories of history and ethical blindness is strikingly illustrated by Heidegger's collaboration with Hitler, a collaboration he not only accepted but sought and never repudiated. As one of Germany's leading intellectuals, Heidegger supported the Third Reich with his prestige; as a leader in Freiburg University, 'he energetically implemented the antisemitic "cleansing laws" against his colleagues and students.'[55] Levinas's analysis of totality and infinity is particularly helpful here, because unlike most poststructuralists, he does not de-authorize the other and thus facilitates rather than blocks enquiry into responsibility. Responsibility, in fact, is a cornerstone of Levinas's philosophy. One of his favourite quotations was the statement by the old holy man in *The Brothers Karamazov*: 'We are all responsible for everyone else, but I am more responsible than all the others.'[56]

The link between Pound's totalizing tendencies and his early convictions about art can be seen in the 1910s in his essays on Vorticism and on the serious artist. He often associated his aesthetics with totalitarianism, and he thought of his accomplishments in terms of synthesis. For example, in *Guide to Kulchur*, he writes:

> If I am introducing anybody to Kulchur, let 'em take the two phases, the nineteen tens, Gaudier, Wyndham L. and I as we were in *Blast*, and the next phase, the 1920s. The sorting out, the *rappel à l'ordre*, and thirdly, the new synthesis, the totalitarian.[57]

Synthesis, as Levinas has argued, involves the overcoming of difference and the move to a higher unity. What is often called Pound's commitment to

history was actually a commitment to synthesis and to his own 'grand concept', a concept that is a textbook example of what Levinas refers to as totality.
Pound never had the influence that Heidegger had, in part because he had no
official position, in part because he was recognizably suffering from delusions. This circumstance mitigates somewhat his responsibility for those incoherent and possibly traitorous radio broadcasts.

The early Eliot was far more self-critical and far more aware of the dan-
gers of totalizing, but he too longed for unity and experimented with ways
of overcoming the fragmentation of modern life. As he grew older, he
seemed even more aware of 'our first world', and he made 'wholeness' and
'universality' key words in his critical lexicon. The impulse to totalize is part
of the mentality of the age and can be associated with some of its greatest
thinkers and artists. Some of these artists, admittedly, were not particularly
conscious of the political and ethical dimensions of their work. Levinas saw
the modern tendency to totalize as in part a compensation for the alleged
death of God and the consequent failure of community in modern intellectual and political life. I agree with him and would add, as others have said,
that modernism in the arts was born of the same spiritual crisis; I would
also argue that one of the hallmarks of modernist style in classics like *The
Cantos*, *The Waste Land*, and *Ulysses* – their formal experimentation – derives from the need to overcome fragmentation and difference in a situation
in which the centre had not held. The strenuous metaphysics of these
thinkers and artists is inseparable from their sense of crisis. In a time of
spiritual vacuum, or to use Heidegger's term in his essay on Hölderlin, in a
time of destitution, the artist tends to become a shepherd of being, tends to
help us re-collect our fragments and re-construct our world.

It can be argued that Eliot and Pound came in old age to see the inhuman-
ity of their association of language with civilization. Certainly Eliot's late
comedies can be seen as a recantation. In *The Cocktail Party*, Edward defines
hell, not as Sartre defined it in *No Exit* – 'Hell is other people' – but as the
polar opposite of that. 'Hell is oneself.'[58] The 'other' is my salvation. To inter-
ject Levinas, that can be interpreted as meaning that it is only in an encounter
with the face of the other that one can even imagine, to say nothing of experience, self-transcendence. In an unpublished letter to the Librarian of Congress explaining his vote in favor of giving Pound the Bollingen award, Eliot
says that he and all members of the committee are dismayed by Pound's politics and his anti-Semitism, but they still consider the *Pisan Cantos* to be the
best volume published in 1948. Eliot says that although he himself deplores
Pound's attacks on England and on religion, he does not feel it would be best
in the present circumstances to point out in public just how antithetical
Pound's views are to his own. [59]

In regard to Pound: one longs to be generous, for although he did great harm, not least to himself, he was without doubt a great poet and without doubt a shattered human being. It is possible to read his magnificent chant, 'Pull down thy vanity', as a self-accusation and an expression of remorse. But it is possible to read the second part of it as self-vindication.

> But to have done instead of not doing
>   This is not vanity
> To have, with decency, knocked
> That a Blunt should open
>   To have gathered from the air a live tradition
> or from a fine old eye the unconquered flame
> That is not vanity,
>   Here error is all in the not done,
> all in the diffidence that faltered . . (C 81)

Whether from the hand of a patriot, as his defenders claim, or from the hand of a traitor, these lines are beautiful and possibly true. In them, Pound reminds the reader that at least he did make a choice. This defence, associated with the Existentialists, has been problematized by postmodernists; Levinas, for one, considers it as another example of defining the world in terms of one's own subjectivity. Be that as it may; Pound sides with those who associate choice with authenticity, even if the choice turns out to be wrong. He admits in the end that he chose error, but he takes heart in knowing that at least he chose, that he was not guilty of the diffidence that faltered. From his point of view, in choosing, he has saved himself from the non-existence of many of his contemporaries. Pound could say of himself what Eliot said of Baudelaire, that he was at least man enough to be damned, that he was worthy of a 'damnation denied to the politicians and the newspapers editors of Paris' or London or Washington, D.C.[60]

Note: I wish to express my gratitude to Cyrena N. Pondrom, who read this essay and made helpful suggestions.

Notes

1   T. S. Eliot, *The Complete Poems and Plays* (London: Faber and Faber, 1969), p. 14.
2   Emmanuel Levinas, *Totality and Infinity: An Essay on Exteriority* (1961), trans. Alphonso Lingis (Pittsburgh: Duquesne UP, 1969). See section IIIB.

3 Emmanuel Levinas, *Collected Philosophical Papers*, trans. Alphonso Lingis (Pittsburg: Duquesne UP, 1987), p. 3.
4 W. B. Yeats, *Collected Poems* (New York: Macmillan, 1956), p. 335.
5 Levinas, *Collected Philosophical Papers*, p. 5.
6 Heidegger's deep and enduring identification with the Nazis was based on his often-stated conviction that his philosophy was the spiritual counterpart of Hitler's leadership. For an account of Heidegger's collaboration with Hitler, see Thomas Sheehan, 'Reading a Life: Heidegger and Hard Times', in *The Cambridge Companion to Heidegger*, ed. Charles Gufgûon (Cambridge: Cambridge University Press, 1993). For a brief overview of the documents, see Hugo Ott, *Martin Heidegger: A Political Life*, trans. Allan Blundan (New York: Basic Books, 1993), pp. 1–9.
7 For Heidegger's view of the poet, see 'What Are Poets For', *Poetry, Language, Thought*, trans. Albert Hofstadter (New York: Harper & Row, 1975), pp. 91–142; and 'Hölderlin and the Essence of Poetry' (1936), trans. Douglas Scott, in *The Critical Tradition*, ed. David H. Richter (Boston: Bedford Books, 1998), pp. 560–70.
8 Heidegger, *Poetry, Language, Thought*, p. 191.
9 Levinas, *Collected Philosophical Papers*, p. 13.
10 Levinas's penetrating work on language, *Otherwise than Being*, was dedicated to the memory of the millions of Jews slaughtered by the 'National Socialists'. The title of this book suggests his quarrel with Heidegger, and the dedication suggests that all members of the party, including Heidegger, are implicated in the Holocaust.
11 Levinas, *Collected Philosophical Papers*, p. 2.
12 Quoted in Humphrey Carpenter, *A Serious Character: The Life of Ezra Pound* (Boston: Houghton Mifflin, 1988), p. 552.
13 Ezra Pound, *'Ezra Pound Speaking'. Radio Speeches of World War II*, ed. Leonard W. Doob (Westport, Conn.: Greenwood Press, 1978), p. 289.
14 Carpenter, p. 751.
15 Ezra Pound, *The Cantos* (New York: New Directions, 1950), p. 478. In subsequent references, the canto number will be indicated parenthetically in the text.
16 Carpenter, p. 626.
17 Archibald MacLeish, *Collected Poems 1917–1952* (Boston: Houghton Mifflin, 1962), pp. 50–51.
18 Quoted in Carpenter, *A Serious Character*, p. 792.
19 C. David Heymann, *Ezra Pound: The Last Rower: A Political Profile* (New York: Viking, 1976), p. 257.
20 Quoted by Eliot in *To Criticize the Critic* (London: Faber and Faber, 1965), p. 40.
21 *Ibid.*, p. 37.
22 *Ibid.*, p. 41.
23 *Ibid.*, pp. 38–9.
24 *Ibid.*, p. 41.
25 *Ibid.*, p. 42.
26 Levinas, *Totality and Infinity*, pp. 194–204.
27 Levinas, *Totality and Infinity*, pp. 204–12. For Levinas's views on the language of poetry, see 'The Servant and Her Master' in *The Levinas Reader*, ed. Séan Hand (Oxford: Blackwell, 1989), pp. 151–9.
28 T. S. Eliot, 'Tradition and the Individual Talent', *Selected Essays*, third enlarged edition (London: Faber and Faber, 1966), pp. 13–22.
29 Eliot, *Complete Poems and Plays*, pp. 13–17.

30 *Ibid.*, p. 125.
31 *Ibid.*, p. 175.
32 Jewel Spears Brooker and Joseph Bentley, *Reading* The Waste Land: *Modernism and the Limits of Interpretation* (Amherst: University of Massachusetts Press, 1990), pp. 200–7.
33 T. S. Eliot, *The Sacred Wood,* 2nd ed. (London: Faber and Faber, 1928), pp. viii-ix.
34 See especially T. S. Eliot, 'The Modern Mind', *The Use of Poetry and the Use of Criticism* (London: Faber and Faber, 1933), pp. 121–42.
35 T. S. Eliot, 'Last Words', *Criterion* XVIII (January 1939), 269–75.
36 Quoted by Peter Ackroyd, *T. S. Eliot: A Life* (New York: Simon and Schuster, 1984), p. 264.
37 Jeffrey Perl, *Skepticism and Modern Enmity* (Baltimore: Johns Hopkins University Press, 1989), pp. 118–19.
38 Eliot, *Complete Poems and Plays*, p. 179.
39 *Ibid.*, p. 182.
40 Ezra Pound, *Guide to Kulchur* (1938) (New York: New Directions, 1970), p. 194; interview with Donald Hall in *Paris Review* (1962), in *Ezra Pound: A Critical Anthology*, ed. J. P. Sullivan (Baltimore: Penguin, 1970), pp. 278–9.
41 Pound, Interview with Donald Hall, p. 279.
42 E. Fuller Torrey, *The Roots of Treason: Ezra Pound and the Secret of St. Elizabeth's* (New York: McGraw-Hill, 1984), p. 182.
43 Wendy Flory, 'Pound and antisemitism', in *Cambridge Companion to Ezra Pound* (Cambridge: Cambridge University Press, 1993), p. 287.
44 Ezra and Dorothy Pound, *Letters in Captivity: 1945–1946*, ed. Omar Pound and Robert Spoo (New York: Oxford University Press, 1999), p. 51.
45 Ezra Pound, *Literary Essays* (London: Faber and Faber, 1960), p. 41.
46 *Ibid.*, p. 46.
47 *Ibid.*, p. 44.
48 Ezra Pound, *Selected Poems*, ed. T. S. Eliot (London: Faber and Faber, [1948] 1968), p. 92.
49 *Ibid.*, p. 173.
50 Pound, 'Murder by Capital', 589.
51 Noel Stock, *The Life of Ezra Pound* (New York: Avon Books, 1974), p. 590.
52 Carpenter, *A Serious Character*, p. 898.
53 Heymann, *Ezra Pound*, p. 297.
54 Paul Valéry, 'Letters from France: The Spiritual Crisis', *Athenaeum* (11 April 1919), 182–4.
55 Flory, p. 299; Sheehan, pp. 86–7.
56 Fyodor Dostoyevsky, *The Brothers Karamazov*, trans. Constance Garnett (New York: Norton, 1970), II.6.
57 Ezra Pound, *Guide to Kulchur* (New York: New Directions, 1970), p. 95.
58 Jean-Paul Sartre, *No Exit*, trans. Stuart Gilbert (New York: Vintage, 1989), p. 45; Eliot, *Complete Poems and Plays*, p. 397.
59 Unpublished letter from T. S. Eliot to Leonie Adams, Library of Congress, 5 July 1949.
60 Eliot, *Selected Essays*, p. 429.

5

Modernism and the Georgians

Marianne Thormählen

According to most handbooks and surveys dealing with English poetry of the early twentieth century, an adversarial relationship prevailed in that period. The enemies were on the one hand a group of writers referred to as 'modernists' and on the other a set of producers of 'largely unexceptionable but also unexceptional verse' [1] commonly known as 'Georgians'. There is no doubt that 'modernism' gained the upper hand in terms of critical prestige: having secured control of the media in the course of the 1930s, its advocates had a couple of decades in which to entrench the picture of Georgian poetry as conventional in subject matter and technique and nostalgic, not to say sentimental, in tone. That picture has been questioned from the 1960s onwards; [2] but as late as 1996 an American study of modern poetry dismissed Wilfred Owen's juvenile verse as 'mostly mannered and late romantic – or Georgian, as the current group of poets were called in England'.[3] Clearly there is still work to be done for people to whom the word 'Georgian' does not signify a mere derivative versifier.

This essay challenges the dismissive attitude referred to above, not primarily in order to defend the Georgians but to erase an artificial frontline in the drawing of which Academe has played a prominent role. Using Georgian poetry as reference material, it criticizes the idea that the poets known as 'modernists' were a breed apart who represented a uniquely innovative and vigorous element in early-twentieth-century poetry.

The word 'modernism' is notoriously difficult to define; indeed, that difficulty is the *raison d'être* of the research project of which this book is the outcome. The concept 'Georgian poetry' is not, however, straightforward either. Some use it as a blanket term for any verse written in the second and third decades of the 20th century that does not in their view belong within the hallowed halls of 'modernism'; for others it denotes the work published in Edward Marsh's five anthologies called *Georgian Poetry*, published between 1912 and 1922. In the present context, it will be employed with reference to poets included in these anthologies: for instance Gordon Bottomley, Rupert Brooke, Walter de la Mare, Edmund Blunden, and W. H. Davies. In addition, it is extended to some other poets who were closely associated with the Georgians, for example Laurence Binyon and Edward Thomas. The term 'traditionalist' would have been an inappropriate designation for these writers; there was never a 'modernist' who was not also in a very real sense a traditionalist. As early as 1920, Edwin Muir had seen the necessity of situating the modern – 'modernism', as he actually called it – in an overall context which incorporates the past as uncompromisingly as T. S. Eliot's roughly contemporary 'Tradition and the Individual Talent': 'If modernism be a vital thing it must needs have roots in the past and be an essential expression of humanity, to be traced, therefore, in the history of humanity: in short, it can only be a tradition.' [4]

Before the First World War there was plenty of bickering between different coteries in which men like Ezra Pound, Richard Aldington, Rupert Brooke, and Lascelles Abercrombie played prominent roles. There was little real rancour in their squabbles, though, and every now and then they all squeezed in together to listen to readings in Harold Monro's 'Poetry Bookshop' – Harold Monro, a Georgian poet and a critic with catholic tastes, who published both Marsh's *Georgian Poetry* anthologies and Pound's 1914 collection *Des Imagistes*.[5] In fact, Pound was asked to contribute 'The Goodly Fere' to the first volume of *Georgian Poetry*. He refused because he was just bringing out that poem himself, and added that it was not a good idea anyway as 'The Goodly Fere' did not 'illustrate any *modern* tendency' – which says something about the view he took of Marsh's initiative.[6] As has often been pointed out, the inclusion of D. H. Lawrence and Robert Graves in the first *Georgian Poetry* volumes is an indicator of Marsh's range and readiness to promote emerging talent of a high order.

Not until after the War did the Georgian enterprise come under sustained attack from quarters associated with 'modernism'; but that onslaught was only part of a pattern of general critical disapproval. Indeed, some of the first-wave Georgians were openly sceptic about Marsh's selections for volumes IV and V. [7] Even in the mid-1920s, however, writers still extended urbane recognition to the merits displayed by colleagues whose ideals and practices were not obviously similar. Muir suggested that this patent – and, as he conceded, imperfectly justified – courtesy had something to do with a shared wish that what they did all have in common, the moment in history, would come to be seen as being of peculiar importance:

> Nothing is more amazing in our time ... than the amiability of literary men towards one another. Dozens of intelligent critics have not scrupled to call Mr. de la Mare a great writer; Mr. Chesterton has accorded the same title to Mr. Squire, and Mr. Strachey, of all people, has bracketed Shakespeare and Mr. Eliot together, evidently as poets of the same quality. Politeness cannot account for such happenings; it would be perfectly satisfied with the acknowledgement that Mr. de la Mare and Mr. Eliot are writers of indubitable and acknowledged talent. The thing

which makes our praise of contemporaries involuntarily too high is the genuine desire that they should be great, the necessity to see significance in our era, whether it is precisely where we are discovering it or not. [8]

Muir, writing in the mid-1920s, clearly felt that de la Mare was as representative of his time as Eliot. A decade earlier, the absence of anything that might be called a rift between 'modernists' and 'Georgians' before the War is illustrated by an intriguing work published in 1914, the *Collected Poems* of Ford Madox Ford (then still Ford Madox Hueffer). Towards the end of a preface which urges poets to register their own times in terms of their own time, and to avoid sentimentality, affectation, and verbosity, Ford listed some contemporary poets in whose work he took a special interest: W. B. Yeats, Walter de la Mare, F. S. Flint, D. H. Lawrence, Thomas Hardy, and Ezra Pound. While Ford recognized the individual characteristics of and dissimilarities between these writers, he did not assign them to different 'schools'.

Ford is usually thought of as belonging to the 'modernist' 'side'. Six years later, a poet and man of letters commonly associated with the Georgians demonstrated a similar lack of awareness of a gulf between experimentalists and traditionalists in early-twentieth-century verse. Harold Monro's book *Some Contemporary Poets (1920)* consists of a review of the situation just after the War; a 'glance backward' in which Yeats features as one of yesterday's masters along with, for instance, Hardy, Bridges, and Kipling (who were all still alive and writing); and a long section entitled 'Poets and Poetasters of our time'. Monro claimed that the forming of groups and coteries is natural among poets, and that affiliation with a group may be a helpful move for a young talent. He also pointed out that a group tends to uphold some shared ideal, a 'secret unknown to those outside its circle'. That 'secret' must, according to Monro, be connected with the choice of subject, the method of treatment, the idiosyncracy of rhythm, or style.[9] The description sounds familiar: it would fit both the Georgians and the Imagists.

Monro proceeded to group the poets he included along lines that a present-day 'modernism' scholar recognizes. For instance, he put in Pound with Ford, Flint, Aldington, and H. D. However, he never suggested that there was a radical distinction between them and the two groups he placed on either side – groups containing such names as A. E. Housman, John Masefield, de la Mare, and Davies on the one hand, and Abercrombie and Bottomley on the other. When Monro discussed Pound, he dwelt on the American's bookishness, his interest in the pre-Renaissance literature of Latin Europe and Chinese poetry, and his irascible temperament. Monro predicted that the recognition of Pound's 'genius [would] be gradual and tardy', because it was not readily apparent on the surface and because Pound, in Monro's opinion, kept getting in his own way in his communication with readers.[10] But nobody who read *Some Contemporary Poets* in 1920 could have been led to believe, on the basis of Monro's appraisal, that Ezra Pound stood for something radically new that was peculiarly responsive to the spirit of his age. It is interesting that a paragraph in Monro's introductory chapter talks about a 'new movement' in poetry which gathered direction and force between 1910 and 1915 and goes on to exemplify this movement, and the publications it generated, in the following terms: 'Besides *Georgian Poetry* there was *Oxford Poetry*, and *Cambridge Poetry*. There were the "Imagist" anthologies; later there was the annual anthology, *Wheels*.'[11] To a present-day student of the poetry of the early twentieth century, such insouciant juxtapositions – and within the framework of one 'movement', too – seem breathtaking.

The Imagists have often been set up as inimical or antithetical to the Georgians, and both groups have served as metonymic representations of 'modernism' and 'literary conservatism' respectively; but there was never much of a basis for such an antithesis. As Edwin Muir pointed out in the late 1930s, the theory of Imagism 'was merely a selected part of the theory of all good poetic writing'.[12] The Georgians shared the Imagist loathing of stale post-Victorianism. There were differences between the two groups, of course, and some harsh words were said on both sides even in the 1910s; but neither group's adherents would have consigned the other's to a place on the other side of an abyss, or experienced any desire to see them at the bottom of one. In any case, they had enemies in common: both Georgians and Imagists had to contend with hostile reviewers whose allegiance was with such late-Victorian and Edwardian poets as Stephen Phillips and William Watson.[13]

It was during the 1920s and 1930s that a sense of polarization made itself felt. There were several reasons for this. Some were political in a rather narrow sense of the word: a poet's stance (or lack of one) on the Right-Centre-Left scale came to affect his or her position in the contemporary literary debate; and as so often happens, where ideological zeal went in, alertness to diversity and complexity went out. Besides, the neo-Georgian quarter was increasingly often and loudly represented by the poet J. C. Squire, who though a generous man, like Pound, was also like him in not being averse to a fight.[14] Another factor was the development of English Literature as an academic discipline. Many of the earliest books on 'modern poetry' had been written by men (for men they usually were) of letters, some of them poets. As the above quotation from Muir's *Transition* shows, these men had the practitioner's respect for a colleague's craft even when the manifestations of that craft diverged from his own preferences. The academic critics were less inhibited, though, and among them the valorizers of 'modernism' gradually came to prevail. The example of F. R. Leavis alone should be a sufficient illustration of the readiness with which those who were reviewers rather than doers added contempt to rejection.

Even so, it would be incorrect to suppose that Academe has always argued that there was a division between 'modernists' and 'conservatives' and declared the former more worthwhile. For instance, one notable trend in academic criticism of twentieth-century poetry is the idea that 'modernism' is essentially an American phenomenon whose foreign influence on poetry in Britain has been damaging to the domestic product.[15] Another view one sometimes hears is that tides or cycles operate in this sphere: an experimental phase is sure to be followed by a more traditional one and vice versa.[16] In addition, Paul de Man has argued that '[t]he appeal of modernity haunts all literature', suggesting – as Rainer Emig has pointed out – that 'modernism is not so much the feature of one historic era as a recurring element within literature itself'.[17] All these dissimilar perspectives militate against the idea that the elusive phenomenon known as 'modernism' is of greater specific importance to a student of English poetry in the twentieth century than any other factor. And still – for one book on an early-twentieth-century poet who is not associated with 'modernism', academic publishers bring out dozens on someone who is. The assumption is, of course, that the 'modernists' were better poets and hence more worth investigating; but that assumption remains rooted in another: the contention that the subject belongs to a new, revolutionary, and at least in some sense victorious tendency in literature.

There are different ways of probing the tenability of this dual assumption. The one adopted here consists in reviewing qualities usually associated with 'modernism', trying to establish whether those qualities are in fact exclusive to, or in any case peculiarly characteristic of, those writers who are commonly known as 'modernists'. It is not a particularly sophisticated procedure, and it cannot yield any definite conclusions; but it has the merit of concreteness in that it supplies tangible examples for everyone to assess according to their own views and conceptions. Besides, the instances referred to were not gleaned from obscure sources: it would have been easy to locate 'modernistic' passages in long-forgotten Georgian works and drag them in through the back door to prove a point; but all the evidence presented below is familiar material. What I am suggesting is that there are 'modernist' dimensions in it which have not usually been perceived as such, or perceived at all. That circumstance explains why I have chosen to talk about 'Georgians' rather than, for instance, 'anti-modernists' (David Lodge's term) [18] or even 'non-modernists'. There are difficulties with the term 'Georgians', certainly; but at least it does not postulate a programmatic divide.

The relation between the 'modernist' work of art and history is an intensely problematic one, and this is not the right place to go into it. However, it is usually held that the 'modernist' is 'of' his or her age and that his/her art responds to it, though that response is often troubled, even antagonistic. Stephen Spender built a system of categorization on the principle of recognition and condemned the Georgian poets as the classic examples of 'non-recognizers': they failed to recognize and engage with 'the modern situation', and they believed that 'modern life can be got away from in [a poetic] dream'.[19] Spender's prime example of this attitude is Walter de la Mare, whom he accuses of dealing in a kind of 'impersonal, mediumistic dreaming of the past'.

It is natural for an analysis of this allegation to proceed from de la Mare's best-known poem, 'The Listeners'. It was an immediate success when the collection named after it appeared in 1912; Pound and Ford were among those who recognized it as an important work.[20]

> 'Is there anybody there?' said the Traveller,
> Knocking on the moonlit door;
> And his horse in the silence champed the grasses
> Of the forest's ferny floor:
> And a bird flew up out of the turret,
> Above the Traveller's head:
> And he smote upon the door again a second time;
> 'Is there anybody there?' he said.
> But no one descended to the Traveller;
> No head from the leaf-fringed sill
> Leaned over and looked into his grey eyes,
> Where he stood perplexed and still.
> But only a host of phantom listeners
> That dwelt in the lone house then
> Stood listening in the quiet of the moonlight
> To that voice from the world of men:
> Stood thronging the faint moonbeams on the dark stair,
> That goes down to the empty hall,
> Hearkening in an air stirred and shaken
> By the lonely Traveller's call.
> And he felt in his heart their strangeness,
> Their stillness answering his cry,
> While his horse moved, cropping the dark turf,
> 'Neath the starred and leafy sky;
> For he suddenly smote on the door, even
> Louder, and lifted his head:—

'Tell them I came, and no one answered,
    That I kept my word,' he said.
Never the least stir made the listeners,
    Though every word he spake
Fell echoing through the shadowiness of the still house
    From the one man left awake:
Ay, they heard his foot upon the stirrup,
    And the sound of iron on stone,
And how the silence surged softly backward,
    When the plunging hoofs were gone.

The element of dream is certainly potent in 'The Listeners'; but it is not a case of idyllic reverie. The Traveller, 'the one man left awake', intrudes on a world with which he cannot communicate; those who people it cannot speak or act, only listen. They hear the crude, blunt real-world sounds he makes – the beating on the door, the noise of his horse's hoofs. The Traveller senses the presence of the listeners, but his original message is not for phantoms. All he can pass on to them is another message: that of a mission undertaken, a promise honoured, but with an abortive outcome. The 'lone house' with the 'empty hall' is clearly a large building, and equally clearly not inhabited by people of flesh and blood.

    'The Listeners' is a very suggestive poem and there are many interpretations of it, [21] incidentally a circumstance which counteracts the notion of facile escapism and serves as a reminder that there was a good deal of 'defamiliarization' in Georgian poetry. To me it conveys a scenario which would become even more common a few years after de la Mare wrote it, but was common enough during the heyday of the British Empire: someone – perhaps a young man of good family, gone out into the world to civilize it – has died out there, and before he did he asked another man, perhaps a comrade, to go and see his people for him when he got back to England. Many missions of that kind were solicited and undertaken by British people at that time. But whatever the Traveller's original message contained, there was nobody at home to give it to: the ancestral home itself was abandoned by all except the ghosts of the past. 'The Listeners' presents a place where a story ended. Houses live and die, as the greatest 'modernist' wrote. This house does not live. The last word of the poem is 'gone', and it also serves to define the fate of that small piece of old civilization that a country house encompasses.

    Read this way, 'The Listeners' may certainly be said to recognize something happening in its time. In fact, one might call it prophetic: the wars and the progress of modern civilization in the first half of the twentieth century would divest many stately homes of any other inhabitants than phantoms, disturbed by occasional visitors who come and go without making any lasting impact.

Many of the Georgians chronicled and explored the cataclysmic events of their time in poems where the use of traditional forms and the adoption of muted tones enhance rather than detract from the recognition that nothing will be the same again, that the world has changed utterly. Edmund Blunden's 'The Sunlit Vale' is sometimes quoted as an example of how '[t]he guns in France had ripped off the green surface of the world'.[22] I think the same writer's poem 'Forefathers', an anthology favourite like de la Mare's 'Listeners', also recognizes the magnitude of societal and historical transformations. It starts by looking back to the lives of the speaker's ancestors, but the perspective is neither mimetic nor nostalgic; it might be recapitulated as follows: 'I know these men lived here and more or less what they were up to, but I don't feel any continuity between those lives and mine'. The concluding stanza emphasizes the rupture in a peculiar way:

> Like the bee that now is blown
>   honey-heavy on my hand,
> from his toppling tansy-throne
>   in the green tempestuous land –
> I'm in clover now, nor know
> who made honey long ago.

For a moment the sensuousness of the bee simile may seduce the reader away from recognizing the radical import of the poem. The almost flippant colloquialism 'I'm in clover' also superficially detracts from its seriousness. Actually, though, the last stanza reinforces the sense of deracination that the whole poem conveys: the speaker shares the animal's ignorance of anything but a present conceived in purely material terms. The lives of the forefathers are also sketched with reference to secular pursuits, but they are overlaid with a sense of dignity which the speaker's present lacks. The same features are found in such 'modernist' classics as *Hugh Selwyn Mauberley* and *The Waste Land*.

One distinction between 'modernists' and Georgians to which few exceptions can be found is the contention that poets like Eliot and Pound belong in an urban, even metropolitan, setting, whereas the Georgians are chiefly located in the countryside. It is true that the latter were far more given to writing about rural flora and fauna than the leading 'modernists', though we should remember that much Imagist poetry also drew its materials from the natural sphere. But the notion that Georgian verse combines Nature as material for poetry with a naively eulogizing attitude is unfounded. The work of Edward Thomas alone is a powerful counter-argument. In the eight lines of 'Cock-

Crow', for instance, a natural phenomenon cuts through and redirects an intellectual's troubled mental processes; evokes a heroic-heraldic image which can only arise in the mind of a student of history; and sends farm labourers about their work:

> Out of the wood of thoughts that grows by night
> to be cut down by the sharp axe of light, –
> out of the night, two cocks together crow,
> cleaving the darkness with a silver blow:
> and bright before my eyes twin trumpeters stand,
> heralds of splendour, one at either hand,
> each facing each as in a coat of arms:
> the milkers lace their boots up at the farms.

Anyone who even approaches the word 'realism' today does so with misgivings, not to say trepidation; but connoisseurs of Georgian verse have often commented on these poets' realism, and their reasons are apparent. In the very limited sense of alertness to unpleasant aspects of earthly existence, realism may certainly be said to prevail in many well-known poems by Georgians. For instance, W. H. Davies' frequently anthologized poem 'The Truth' suggests that a robin sings with particular sweetness and intensity because the killing of his parents will leave him with more to eat.[23] The same Davies, so often thought of as embarrassingly naive, wrote about wife-battering in harrowing terms and class-consciousness in subtle ones. Even his often-reprinted poem 'Sweet Stay-at-home' is in no way a celebration of contented life in one quiet place. On the contrary, most of it constitutes an evocative catalogue of the excitements of world travel written by an unusually seasoned traveller, and it ends on a downright patronizing note:

> Sweet Well-content, sweet Love-one-place,
> Sweet, simple maid, bless thy dear face;
> For thou hast made more homely stuff
> Nurture thy gentle self enough;
> I love thee for a heart that's kind –
> Not for the knowledge in thy mind.

While the dichotomy between urban 'modernists' and rural Georgians does stand up, other aspects of subject-matter are less clear-cut when it comes to distinguishing between them. For instance, neither the 'modernists' nor the Georgians explored passionate love between men and women to any great extent, a circumstance which contemporary critics and anthologizers deplored in them all.[24] In view of the fact that an interest in sexuality has often been said to be a typically 'modernist' characteristic, it is noteworthy that D. H. Lawrence's erotic poems were so roundly condemned by Ezra Pound. Reviewing Lawrence's *Love Poems and Others* in 1913, a year after Lawrence's début as a Georgian, Pound called them 'middling-sensual ... slush, disgusting or very nearly so', and supplied a merciless one-line parody, 'I touched her and she shivered like a dead snake'. (But typically, Pound softened the blow by adding: '... when Mr. Lawrence ceases to discuss his own disagreeable sensations, when he writes low-life narrative ... there is no English poet under forty who can get within shot of him'.[25])

A couple of months earlier, Pound had commented on the innovations of the machine age as material for poetry: 'Whatever may be said against automobiles and aeroplanes and the modernist way of speaking of them, and however much one may argue that this new sort of work is mannered, and that its style will pass, still it is indisputable that the vitality of the time exists in such work.'[26] The sentence is noteworthy for more reasons than one: it acknowledges that there is a 'modernist' way of dealing with the objects of the modern age, and Pound (writing in 1913) recognizes that it may turn out to be a passing fashion.

It is interesting to compare Pound's statement with a discussion on modern poetry by a fellow American, Edward Davison, published 15 years later, in 1928. Davison's analysis distinguishes between convention, which should be challenged, and tradition, which is another thing altogether – a view in which Eliot and Pound would have concurred. On subject-matter, Davison says: 'It need not be denied that an automobile, or any other machine, is potentially as worthy and likely a subject for poetry, especially today, as the reddest of roses that ever faded in a moonlit garden. But is a good poem about a machine necessarily better than a good poem about a rose?'[27] One 'modernist' who would not have given an affirmative answer to that question was T. S. Eliot, who was exploring the symbolic properties of the rose for the new departure that would become *Ash-Wednesday* at the time when Davison wrote his book.

William Empson called death 'the trigger of the literary man's biggest gun', and literary men and women kept pulling it throughout the 1910s and 1920s, especially of course after 1914 when the taste of death was everywhere. It made no difference whether they were 'modernists' or Georgians. An example might be mentioned: In a 1919 collection edited by W. Kean Seymour, *A Miscellany of Poetry*, the war is a strong presence, but there is no trace of chauvinism. F. V. Branford's 'Over the Dead' extends compassion to the enemy fallen; in 'Bacchanal (November, 1918)' the arch-Georgian W. W. Gibson recoils from the victory celebrations, sensing an element of ancient madness there; and G. K. Chesterton hurls his bitter accusations against England's rulers in 'Elegy in a Country Churchyard'. Seymour's collection is largely non-experimental, though he included four poems by Edith Sitwell. But it is easy to hear other laments for the war through the ones printed by Seymour, laments that were written though not yet published at about the same time: 'These fought in any case, / and some believing, / pro domo, in any case ...' 'So many, / I had not thought death had undone so many'. These days it should no longer be necessary to clear Rupert Brooke of facile chauvinism; he could not help being made into a war-glorifying icon after his death of septicaemia. Nor should people have to be reminded that the greatest of the war poets, Wilfred Owen, was proud to be regarded as a peer by the Georgians,[28] or that some of the harshest anti-war verse was written by the Georgians Edmund Blunden and Siegfried Sassoon. But it may serve some purpose to point out that when it comes to the horrors of war, there are no essential distinctions with regard to tone and stance between 'modernist' poets and others.

Nor does the 'Georgian' label entail a greater measure of evolutionary optimism than the 'modernist' one. For instance, the apocalyptic dimension in *The Waste Land* has a notable counterpart in Gordon Bottomley's *The End of the World*. Later, in the 1930s, Edwin Muir picked it up for his poem 'The Horses' and made it the stuff of a great modern poem.

When Michael Roberts compiled *The Faber Book of Modern Verse* in the mid-1930s, he excluded such poets as de la Mare, Blunden, and Muir because they had not produced a 'notable development of poetic technique'.[29] If the issue of subject-matter is inconclusive when it comes to establishing a clear distinction between 'modernists' and Georgians, at least in a manner which will unquestionably leave the honours with the former, what about technique?

The received wisdom runs along the following lines: The 'modernists' experimented with form, language, and structure to give innovative expression to the experience of the modern world. They abandoned conventional idioms and restrictive metres and measures, turning towards colloquial language, speech rhythm, and free verse. If their experiments entailed a loss of clarity and coherence, it was because they could not express what they thought and perceived in any other way: chaos and fragmentariness made sequential argument impossible. In any event, the modern poet should present, not discourse. The aim was not to engender an echo in every human breast but to jolt, producing shock rather than recognition.

In response to this, it would be possible to say that the Georgians experimented as much with free verse as Eliot and Pound did, and that it reached a high-water mark in D. H. Lawrence's poems published in Marsh's *Georgian Poetry*. Besides, one could point to Pound's hatred of slushiness and his advocacy of Gautier's severe stanza as a disciplinary measure. It would also be true to say that common speech was used to great effect by poets who were not 'modernists', and a good many things besides. But it would be useless to try to deny that an experimental streak was more in evidence among the writers usually called 'modernists' than among the Georgians. What is less immediately obvious to me is that it is this that makes the 'modernists' better poets, supposing we agree that they are.

Michael Roberts claimed that the truly modern poets achieved an extension of significance by exploring the possibilities of language.[30] That, of course, is what good poets have always done, in different ways. But it seems reasonable to maintain that such extension by exploration was a particularly wide-ranging and deliberate undertaking for Eliot and Pound in Europe, and for Wallace Stevens in America. The best example, for me, is the poem which an incredulous Ezra Pound greeted in the words, 'He has actually trained himself *and* modernized himself *on his own*': [31] 'The Love Song of J. Alfred Prufrock'. Less than a third of the length of *The Waste Land*, which Pound was later to call 'the justification of ... our modern movement, since 1900', [32] 'Prufrock' encompasses a wide range of registers without once losing its distinctive note of individual existential *Angst*. Its prosody is also superb. Not everybody realizes how greatly 'Prufrock' relies on rhyme: over 100 of its 131 lines belong in some sort of rhyme scheme. The element of rhyme is fused with an interplay of metrical and stress patterns, speech rhythm, and repetition. The outcome is a prosody which makes the superficially irregular lines of Eliot's poem more memorable, in my view, than those of any early-twentieth-century poem of more than epigrammatic length set to a perfectly regular metre. There is nothing quite like it anywhere else, even in Eliot.

However, I would not wish to suggest that experimentation must be visibly radical and extensive to have an impact. The only 'modernist' poem I am sure I could recite entire if woken up in the middle of the night is T. E. Hulme's 'Above the Dock', which develops its masterly image with the aid of rhyme and another unobtrusive but effective prosodic device. The last two lines were lengthened one foot at a time, leaving the concluding line a perfect alexandrine:

> Above the quiet dock in midnight,
> tangled in the tall mast's corded height,
> hangs the moon. What seemed so far away
> is but a child's balloon, forgotten after play.

The 'modernists' were not alone in avoiding composition 'in sequence of a metronome', to quote Pound.[33] Harold Monro went on record as saying that '[u]nsuccessful experiment is far more interesting than successful imitation'.[34] Many of the best-known early-twentieth-century poems by others than 'modernists' contain challenges to established patterns of various kinds. One example must suffice: a line from Laurence Binyon's 'For the Fallen', written in the early days of the First World War and still the most frequently quoted tribute to the British dead in the twentieth century's wars. Binyon wrote: 'They shall grow not old, as we that are left grow old'. It would of course have been perfectly possible to say 'They shall not grow old, as we that are left grow old'; but by shoving in the negation between the two components of the verb phrase Binyon achieved several effects at once. He forced the reader of the line to stress three consecutive monosyllabic words, and he avoided a simple re-production of 'grow old' at the end of the line – repeating with a difference, as the 'modernists' were fond of doing. As a result, what could have been a mere truism becomes an expression of dislocation and wrongness. It compels the reader to move slowly past the familiar verb phrase 'grow old' – slowly enough to gain some sense of what it means both to die young and to go on living without those for whom the sun did not set to rise again. Binyon was a con-scious artist, as Pound would have been the first to confirm. He knew what he was doing when he made an unforgettable line out of what would have been an unexceptional one by means of having two consecutive monosyllabic words change places.

Binyon's 'For the Fallen' is dignified, but not mawkish. A good deal of Georgian verse is sombre, but the charges of sentimentality and humourless heavy-footedness that have sometimes been levelled against its leading repre-sentatives are erroneous. Twentieth-century academic criticism has tended to valorize irony and pessimism, of which there is plenty in 'modernist' writers; [35] but the attitudes of their contemporaries and predecessors were hardly Pan-glossian either. There is little sanguinity in Hardy and Housman, for instance, and an ironic, not to say satirical, streak is palpable in some of Rupert Brooke's best poems. It is a pretty bleak period; and the works that do strike a hopeful note usually do so against grave undertones – for example a resolu-tion to endure as there is no alternative, or a half-despairing trust in an unseen power. Both among 'modernists' and Georgians, this lack of optimism is bound up with what one might call a crisis of the ego: there is a fundamental lack of harmony between the speaking subject and his/her context. I think it would be fair to say that 'modernist' writers problematized the self more profoundly and persistently than their contemporaries; but the difficulty of finding an identity in a larger existential framework is a ubiquitous concern.

If I am right in thinking that the academics are to a large extent responsible for the low esteem in which the Georgian poets of the early twentieth century are still held, it is time we faced some challenging questions. Have we valor-ized the 'modernists' because they provided us with more material to work on – because, to put it crudely, they were more difficult than the others and so needed us as explicators? How good is 'modernist' poetry in relation to that which is not usually regarded as 'modernist'? How 'modernist' is the best work by people known as 'modernists'? Have we academics seized on and made exaggerated use of what we have seen as polarizing trends, but what were really little more than expressions of the need naturally felt by writers working out their own position to lash out against others whom they saw as working along somewhat different lines? Why is it that for one member of the literate public who can quote two consecutive lines by Pound, a dozen are able to quote two lines by W. H. Davies? The issue of mass culture and popularity is at the heart of the 'modernism'/'postmodernism' debate; should we not ask ourselves whether our discipline has raised obstacles in the way of the large-scale recognition of fine and accessible writers? How far is the notion of 'modernist' subversiveness and outrage an academic construct, fashioned to impart a heroic and revolutionary dimension to our own labours?

It should of course be pointed out that several academic critics have questioned the dominance of 'modernism' in the Anglo-American academy in the last few decades.[36] In the 1950s and 1960s, Frank Kermode and C. K. Stead challenged the idea of the Image as the predominant mode of presentation, arguing that the poet who has something to say must be able and willing to use discourse to say it. More recently similar points have been raised by Richard Hoffpauir,[37] who has maintained that the 'modernist' emphasis on presentation short-changed the intellect – an intriguing point in view of the fact that the 'modernists' have so often been referred to as super-intellectuals, sometimes in contrast to the 'postmodern' preoccupation with the body. [38]

One issue which is partly contingent on these questions is that of the relationship between what Eliot called 'the music of poetry' and reader response. Robert Lynd's introduction to Methuen's *An Anthology of Modern Verse*, first published in 1921, contains a statement that seems uncannily prescient to me. Lynd, himself a poet, said: 'The chief danger of the modern poet is not indifference to form, but indifference to phrase.' [39] Even in his day, there was discussion as to whether the image was the essential thing to put across, rather than the words that conveyed it. But as the 'modernists' knew, poetry is made with words and if the words do not stick the poet has failed. They used various expressions to describe the essence of that phenomenon which Lynd was afraid twentieth-century poets would lose sight of – 'cadence' and 'musical phrase' are two of them; Eliot's 'auditory imagination' belongs in this context, too. Like their Georgian contemporaries, they created poetry which owes its impact to the phrase rather than, or as well as, to metre or rhyme. The lesson was not lost on the best poets in the generations who followed them.

Something happened in the early twentieth century that altered the writing of poetry, and 'modernism' is as good a name for it as any other. Revolutions and evolution, in science and technology as well as in the lives of nations, brought new modes of perception, new ways of grappling with the great existential issues, and new modes of exploring them in art.[40] But these transformations were felt and recorded by many besides those who are commonly referred to as 'modernists'. In England, for instance, Hardy represented 'the ache of modernism' for many writers in the early twentieth century; in December 1934 Pound wrote from Rapallo, 'Nobody has taught me anything about writing since Thomas Hardy died. More's the pity.'[41] By giving the 'modernists' the status of foreign bodies and postulating a domestic line from Hardy through the Georgians to Larkin, Hughes, and R. S. Thomas, academics are not only denying either side a part in the real action; they are obscuring the universality of that action *and* the degree to which each participant proceeded according to his/her individual impulses.

Generalizing and classifying are natural pursuits for the academic, and there is no harm in that. The damage is done when labelling becomes an excuse for contemptuous dismissal, especially if that labelling and the consequent dismissal are contaminated by the particularly regrettable form of ignorance that is known as prejudice. English Literature as an academic discipline can ill afford to be seen to invoke such notions as a reason for failing to engage with poetry which wins thousands of new readers in generations born half a century after it was written.[42] If Eliot was a better poet than Walter de la Mare – and I believe he was –, it was not because he was a 'modernist' and de la Mare was a 'Georgian'. In any case, being 'of' one's age is no longer a central issue when that age has passed from living memory: the sound of plunging hoofs in the night is hardly more remote from us today than the noises emitted by the 'horns and motors' of the 1920s. Similarly, the challenges to convention that were audacious in the 1910s are barely perceived, let alone be felt to be in any way striking, today. The twentieth-century poetry that continues to be read and analysed in the twenty-first will owe its survival to other qualities – qualities whose existence is independent of the 'modernist' label.

Notes

1 Peter Childs, *The Twentieth Century in Poetry: A Critical Survey* (London and New York: Routledge, 1999), p. 7.
2 See, above all, C. K. Stead, *The New Poetic: Yeats to Eliot* (first published in 1964 by Hutchinson, subsequently reprinted by Penguin); Robert H. Ross, *The Georgian Revolt: Rise and Fall of a Poetic Ideal 1910-1922* (London: Faber and Faber, 1967); and Myron Simon, *The Georgian Poetic* (Berkeley/Los Angeles/London: University

of California Press, 1975). A more recent, and spirited, attack on anti-Georgian prejudice is delivered by Martin Stephen in *The Price of Pity: Poetry, History and Myth in the Great War* (London: Leo Cooper, 1996), pp. 25–41.

3 William Pratt, *Singing the Chaos: Madness and Wisdom in Modern Poetry* (Columbia and London: University of Missouri Press, 1996), p. 110.

4 Edwin Muir, *We Moderns: Enigmas and Guesses* (New York: Alfred A. Knopf, 1920), p. 138. For a contemporaneous voice from Academe whose utterance is germane to Muir's and Eliot's views (and Pound's, too, for that matter), see John Livingston Lowes's *Convention and Revolt in Poetry* (first published in 1919; I quote from the 1938 reissue from Constable & Co., London): 'The great constructive element in both life and art is the dealings of genius with the continuity of tradition. And poetry becomes original by breaking with tradition at its peril. Cut the connection with the great reservoir of past achievement, and the stream runs shallow, and the substance of poetry becomes tenuous and thin.' (Page 81 in the 1938 edition.)

5 See Ross, *The Georgian Revolt*, p. 94.

6 *Ibid.*, p. 122.

7 *Ibid.*, pp. 226–8. Hailing the fifth – and, as it turned out, last – volume of *Georgian Poetry*, Edmund Gosse suavely praised the quality of the writing but commented on its uniformity in less than enthusiastic terms and repeatedly expressed his regret that 'the three most energetic of the Georgian set – Mr. Masefield, Mr. Ralph Hodgson, and Mr. Siegfried Sassoon' – were missing from the book (*More Books on the Table*, 3rd rev. ed. of 1925, pp. 230 and 235).

8 Edwin Muir, *Transition: Essays on Contemporary Literature* (London: The Hogarth Press, 1926), p. 10.

9 *Some Contemporary Poets (1920)* (London: Leonard Parsons, 1920), p. 16.

10 *Ibid.*, pp. 87–93.

11 *Ibid.*, p. 25.

12 *The Present Age from 1914*, Vol. V in *Introductions to English Literature*, ed. by Bonamy Dobrée (London: The Cresset Press, 1939), p. 51.

13 It is important to distinguish between these critics and those that were connected with the Georgians. In the Introduction to Kevin J. H. Dettmar (ed.), *Rereading the New: A Backward Glance at Modernism* (Ann Arbor: The University of Michigan Press, 1992), the label 'Georgian' is affixed to anyone who was hostile to the 'Modernists' (see pp. 3–8).

14 See Ross, *The Georgian Revolt*, pp. 206–210, and Simon, *The Georgian Poetic*, pp. 87–90. Cf. also pp. 186 and 200–1n15 below.

15 See, for instance, Philip Hobsbaum, *Tradition and Experiment in English Poetry* (London: Macmillan, 1979), pp. 289–307, and Peter Faulkner, *Modernism* (London: Methuen, 1977), pp. 70–71 (among other things, Faulkner summarizes A. Alvarez's views on the subject).

16 See Harry Levin's famous lecture/essay 'What Was Modernism?', pp. 281-3 in the version printed in his *Refractions: Essays in Comparative Literature* (London/Oxford/New York: Oxford University Press, 1966), and David Lodge, *Modernism, antimodernism and postmodernism*, Inaugural lecture at the University of Birmingham, 2 December 1976; published by the University of Birmingham in 1977, pp. 5–9.

17 *Modernism in Poetry: Motivations, Structures and Limits* (London and New York: Longman, 1995), p. 5; see also p. 239. Muir expressed a similar idea in 1920: 'Is there a "modern spirit" not dependent upon time and place, and in all ages mod-

ern? If there is – and there is – the possession of it in some measure will alone entitle us to the name of moderns ...' (*We Moderns*, p. 139).

18 See Lodge's *Modernism* lecture, pp. 4ff.

19 *The Struggle of the Modern*, Part Three (London: Hamish Hamilton, 1963); I have used the 1965 Methuen paperback, where the relevant discussion is on pp. 159ff.

20 See Pound's review – which admittedly praises de la Mare with some rather deafening damns – of *Peacock Pie* in *New Freewoman* I.6 (1 September 1913), 113, reprinted in *Ezra Pound's Poetry and Prose: Contributions to Periodicals* in ten volumes, ed. by Lea Baechler, A. Walton Litz, and James Longenbach (New York and London: Garland, 1991), Vol. I, p. 152. For Hueffer/Ford, see the Preface to his *Collected Poems* (London: Max Goschen, 1914), p. 26.

21 See, for instance, Monro, *Some Contemporary Poets*, pp. 63-4, and R. L. Mégroz, *Walter de la Mare: A Biographical and Critical Study* (London: Hodder and Stoughton, 1924), pp. 119–20. There is a judicious section on de la Mare in David Perkins, *A History of Modern Poetry: From the 1890s to the High Modernist Mode* (Cambridge/Mass. and London: The Belknap Press of the Harvard University Press, 1976), pp. 180–91 (this is the first volume of two of Perkins' *History*).

22 G. S. Fraser, *The Modern Writer and His World* (first published in 1953; I have used the 1970 Pelican Books reprint), p. 255.

23 There is plenty of Nature in Georgian poetry; but it is strikingly often Nature at its most cruel. It is symptomatic that a poem along these lines by E. N. Da C. Andrade is called 'A Song for Edmund Blunden: The Boy and the Birds'; J. C. Squire included it in his *Second Selections from Modern Poets* (London: Secker, 1927; first published in 1924), pp. 12–13.

24 See, for example, Robert Lynd's introduction to A. Methuen's *An Anthology of Modern Verse* (London: Methuen, first published in 1921; I have used the 22nd edition of 1927), pp. xxviii–xxix, and the preface to the exceedingly traditional *Poems of To-Day: First and Second Series* (London: The English Association, 1924), p. viii.

25 *Poetry* II.4 (July 1913), 149–51; reprinted in *Ezra Pound's Poetry and Prose*, Vol. I, p. 148.

26 Review of P. J. Jouve, *Présences*, in *Poetry* I.5 (Feb. 1913), 165–6, reprinted in *Ezra Pound's Poetry and Prose*, Vol. I, p. 117.

27 Edward Davison, *Some Modern Poets and Other Critical Essays* (New York and London: Harper, 1928), p. 16. Davison makes a number of interesting comments, for instance 'I have usually found that those who insist loudest that the modern poet should take care to reflect the particular life and thought of his own generation are the same people who object most noisily to dead poets (Tennyson, for instance) who were at pains to do the same thing for their own age' (p. 18), and the opinion according to which the only 'recent poet whose revolutionary theories appear to have a basis tenable in terms of reasoned literary criticism is Mr. T. S. Eliot' (p. 19; Davison adds, however, that even Eliot needed I. A. Richards as an apologist before people could make sense of him).

28 See, for instance, Anthony Thwaite, *Twentieth-Century English Poetry: An Introduction* (London: Heinemann, 1978), p. 5.

29 Michael Roberts (ed.), *The Faber Book of Modern Verse* (London: Faber and Faber, first published in 1936; I have used the seventh impression of 1943), p. 1. It should be pointed out, however, that Roberts did not set technique and subject-matter apart: 'In a good poet a change [or] development of technique always springs from a change or development of subject-matter' (p. 7).

30 *Ibid.*, p. 3.
31 *The Selected Letters of Ezra Pound 1907–1914*, ed. by D. D. Paige (London: Faber and Faber, 1971; originally published in 1950), p. 40.
32 *Ibid.*, p. 175n. The qualification 'since 1900' is a noteworthy detail.
33 'A Retrospect', first published in *Pavannes and Divisions* (1918); quoted from *Literary Essays of Ezra Pound*, ed. T. S. Eliot (London: Faber and Faber, 1960 (1954)), p. 3.
34 *Some Contemporary Poets*, p. 110.
35 William Pratt's *Singing the Chaos* suggests that the early twentieth century should be called 'The Age of Irony'; see the opening chapter.
36 See, for instance, pp. 75ff. in Astradur Eysteinsson's *The Concept of Modernism* (Ithaca and London: Cornell University Press, 1990).
37 *The Art of Restraint: English Poetry from Hardy to Larkin* (Newark: University of Delaware Press and London and Toronto: Associated University Presses, 1991).
38 Cf. Levin, 'What Was Modernism?', p. 292.
39 Page xxvi in Lynd's introduction to the Methuen anthology.
40 For a profound and yet accessible analysis of these processes in science and philosophy as well as art, see Thomas Vargish and Delo E. Mook, *Inside Modernism: Relativity Theory, Cubism, Narrative* (New Haven and London: Yale University Press, 1999).
41 *The Selected Letters of Ezra Pound*, p. 264.
42 Seán Street makes this point, drawing on Timothy Rogers' *Rupert Brooke: A Reappraisal and Selection* (London: Routledge and Kegan Paul, 1971) and Peter Miller's *The Rugby Centenary Brooke* (The Rupert Brooke Association, 1987), in a pamphlet from the Dymock Poets Archive & Study Centre, *Rupert Brooke – The Unimpeded Self* (1996).

6

Tribal Drums and the Dull Tom-Tom: Thoughts on Modernism and the Savage in Conrad and Eliot

Claude Rawson

In a famous speech in Jean Genet's *Les Nègres* (*The Blacks*, 1959), the protagonist Archibald urges blacks to 'negrify' themselves, to realize an authentic identity by allowing themselves to become all the things the white man says they are. These range all the way from obscene dances to cannibalism. The speech is quoted in Norman Mailer's review of the play, which goes on to say, in an escalation of Archibald's meaning, that a reversion to tribal barbarism, including the cannibal urges supposedly buried in the human psyche, is the only way Western civilization can return to its own instinctual roots.[1] Mailer comments, in the original version:

> [W]here do nightmares go when they are gone? Who is to say the gates of heaven are not manned by cannibals mumbling: Lumumba! ... it is possible that Africa is closer to the root of whatever life is left than any other land on earth.[2]

This, down to the jargon of nightmares, reads like a reductive parody of what is sometimes taken as a 'theme' of *Heart of Darkness* (even the naming of Lumumba may be Mailer's little joke, identifying Conrad's location).

Mailer's version, if not Genet's, is an incremental variation on one of the classic formulas of Western primitivism, that 'primitive' peoples are closer to their passional life than 'we' are. The addition of cannibalism, not normally included in the formula, adds a frisson, grinningly designed to elicit outrage in the bourgeois soul. It contributes nothing to the original idea but its own detail, and seems innocent of the notion, held by many anthropologists, that cannibalism is normally a matter of tightly restricted ritual rather than instinctual gratification. Archibald's speech makes a different point from Mailer's idea of it. He is recommending not primarily an instinctual release, but something which is if anything the opposite of this, a willed and deliberate political, as well as psychological, adoption of traits imputed to his race by a conquering oppressor. Both writers share a concern, not necessarily inherent in conventional primitivism, with a form of self-authentication to which the word 'existentialist' tends sooner or later to become attached. Mailer is fond of the word 'existential', which sug-

gests that it may be idle to look for its meaning, though part of its justification
in the present context seems to reside in the Sartrean origins of, or association
with, the doctrine which is articulated by Genet's protagonist and which Mailer
thinks he is expressing or extending.[3]

The idea that pariah groups (thieves, homosexuals, 'inferior races') tend
naturally, or need, or ought, to assume the characteristics foisted on them by
their oppressors is one which Genet and Sartre seem to have fed one another
through a series of interrelated texts, which include Sartre's *Réflexions sur la
question juive* (1946) and Genet's *Journal du voleur* (*Thief's Journal*, 1949),
dedicated to Sartre and Simone de Beauvoir, and which culminate in but do
not end with Sartre's voluminous study of Genet himself, *Saint Genet, comédien et martyr* (1952).[4] The idea may have contributed to the ideologizing of
'negritude', though its fullest expressions, like those of classic primitivism,
tend to come from white writers. Its interest in the present context is that it is
also, even in its guises of flaunted artifice (Genet's *Blacks*) or attitudinizing
obfuscation (Mailer), the expression of a modernist conception of 'authenticity', of self-realization through extreme experiences.

The aspiration to 'authenticity' has a variety of antecedents: cults of self-
realization and 'total possibility' which flourished in the extremer fantasies of
the sentimental movement in Europe (the nostalgia, in the words of the
Monthly Magazine in the 1790s, for an – allegedly recently abandoned – ideal
of 'experiencing endless varieties of warmth', or the earlier boast by Werther
that there was no single force in his soul 'that remained untried'),[5] and which
achieved their *jusqu'auboutiste* flowering in the absolute permissiveness of Sa-
deian immoralism. But it is ultimately different from all these, or from the
claims made for inquisitorial soul-baring, or the confessional rituals of revolutionary cultures, from 1789 to the present, which are in some respects the
secular counterpart of religious Inquisitions. Nor does it necessarily involve
the hideous sincerities of sectarian worship, which early Christian writers
identified in heretical sects, and Swift and Burke among Dissenters, or the
orgiastic activities of more secular revivalisms, although orgiastic states are
included in Archibald's scenario and play their part in *Heart of Darkness*.

The state described by Archibald is not so much an expressive as a self-
realizing one. As Archibald conceives it, it is the protean expression of disparate roles or selves combining into a distinctive identity that had no prior
existence. There is no suggestion in Archibald's speech, as there is in Mailer's
understanding of it, of a return to an innermost self. Indeed Sartre had written, in 'Orphée noir' (1948), his introduction to Léopold Senghor's founding
text of the negritude movement, *Anthologie de la nouvelle poésie nègre et mal-
gache*, that self-recognition or self-realization ('prise de conscience') in op-
pressed groups is the exact opposite of such a return, 'exactement le contraire

d'une redescente en soi.'[6] A related paradox is that of a radical 'truthfulness' deriving, as in Archibald's speech, from a willed fabrication, the product of ideological pretension and a flaunted declarative artifice (like the donning of blackface masks in Genet's plays). The gesture is often rebellious and alienated, an assertion of the 'me' as other, and the more authentically 'me' when most fully and wilfully affirmed and bedecked as 'other'. It is no accident that Rimbaud's 'Je est un autre' reappears as the title of a key section of Sartre's study of Genet.[7]

In the evolution of this story, the specific 'other' whom one authenticates oneself as being is, for certain Western minds, their most visible opposite, the Negro. Rimbaud also famously said: 'Je suis une bête, un nègre', a declaration which reverberates across the long history of modernist alienations and which issues ultimately in the pirouetting fatuities of Mailer's 'existential' hero, the White Negro. The idea of white negroes is itself an old one, going back at least as far as the seventeenth century. It typically referred to degraded whites, the Irish in English eyes, the poor of Chamfort or Dostoyevsky, and the amalgam of Irish-and-poor which settled into a stereotype of British imaginations, the helot conceived as simultaneously alien savage and domestic mob.[8] There is a postmodern, in some ways campy, overturning of this, in which the pariah state is flaunted as honorific, and becomes an untormented variant of Sartre's transmutation of despised subgroups into what the dominant group chooses to call 'them'. The most genial example is Roddy Doyle's version of Mailer's White Negro in *The Commitments*, whose characters revel in the idea that the Irish are the 'Niggers of Europe'.[9]

Theirs is a cheerful extravert version. Rimbaud's original formula, variously replayed by Sartre, Genet, and Mailer, is one in which the transmutation seems or claims to have been fully internalized. The great fictional type, nearly contemporaneous with the later Rimbaud who became an African ivory trader, is Conrad's Kurtz, who combines in varying degrees of self-awareness and self-deception a similar blend of imperious and aggressive contempt for the natives, and a self-implicating sense of kinship. The canting imperial do-gooder, who knows he wants to 'Exterminate all the brutes' only in the lucidity of a fevered delirium, eventually achieves self-realization and self-knowledge through a reversion to tribalism and the practice of 'unspeakable rites' (118).[10] As in Genet, this is something more than the stereotype of the tribesman as closer to instinctual truth than his 'civilized' counterpart or oppressor. It includes the fact that in looking into the heart of darkness, and seeing 'The horror! The horror!', Kurtz is described as achieving a 'supreme moment of complete knowledge', one which confronts not only the brutishness of primitive barbarism (alongside the seductive vitality of tribal drums) and his secret sharing of this, but the fact of his own falsity and self-deception (149). It is no accident that, in Trilling's *Sincerity and Authenticity*, the discussion of *Heart of Darkness* as 'the paradigmatic literary expression of the modern concern with authenticity' comes immediately after an exposition of existentialist doctrines of authenticity, chiefly in Sartre and Sarraute.[11]

Trilling's concept of 'authenticity' is not exclusively, or even mainly, concerned with primitivist themes. But it seems arguable that the specifically modernist interest in the primitive is defined by having some such concept at its core, and that this separates it from its Romantic or pre-Romantic antecedents. If this is so, the concept must be distinguished, as in Trilling, from any idea of 'sincerity', though Conrad's Marlow sometimes uses the latter term in his groping efforts to describe a quality in Kurtz which Trilling associates with 'authenticity'. The fact is paradoxical because, as in Genet or Mailer, the process of self-authentication, if that is what it is, is pervaded with artifice, falsehood, and self-deception. In so far as Kurtz's authenticity has to do with 'extreme' experiences, with a total self-abandonment to every possible impulse or mode of being, of the sort that Rimbaud projected in the *lettres du voyant* and Genet's Archibald and Mailer's review of the *Blacks* expressed on a more politicized plane, it is also part of a Romantic inheritance that Modernism, for all its efforts, never shook off.

In his own furtive and secretive way, the white man gone native achieves what Genet's Archibald exhorts Africans to take on, because of what white men describe them as being. The gaudy expressionism with which Archibald wants his blacks to adopt 'unspeakable rites' reads like an aggressively playful fantasy of what Kurtz did covertly and for real. That Kurtz is a white man is less of a difference than it seems. Such fantasies of primitive reversion, even when they transcend the formulaic simplicities of European primitivism, are as surely the products of an imperial conscience as the shepherds of pastoral were the inventions of cities and courts. If Kurtz is white, so is Archibald's author, who seems himself to have seen the situation with an insolent lucidity, demanding in particular that his Blacks should be played with suggestions of the black-and-white-minstrel show. The play is subtitled 'clownerie', and Genet was much concerned with the *maquillage*, or makeup, of the actors, requiring that his white characters be played by black actors with white masks, but with their black skins, and kinky hair, clearly showing.[12] And it is Mailer the white writer who, in his review of Genet's *Blacks*, wondered whether a return to cannibalism might yet be the salvation of the Western psyche, and who, in doing so, brought the issue back full circle, to a reductive and unreconstructed old-style primitivism. Genet offers a witty signposting of such ironies when he tells us that his play is written by a white, for whites, but that even if it were played before a black audience, one white man would have to attend every performance, preferably in the centre of the front row.

The play will be directed at him ('on jouera pour lui'). If no white agreed to this, white masks would be distributed to the audience, and if no black agreed, then a dummy must be used.[13]

The black playwright Lorraine Hansberry, commenting on all this, remarks that 'there is certainly nothing fresh in the spectacle of white people insisting on telling all sorts of colored peoples how they should behave to satisfy them.' She described Mailer's White Negro as a 'manufactured ... absurdity' he 'locked himself' into, initiating a prolonged 'life-eating sense of fatigue' in black readers. But her argument goes beyond Mailer to perceive in Genet himself the kind of falsifying appropriation which the play purports to neutralize by its flaunted theatricality.[14] Genet may or may not have been a step ahead of her in his awareness of this point too.

There are no flamboyant theatricals in Conrad. But the whiteness of Kurtz, busily operating in the heart of darkness, is a bravura antithesis to which Conrad seems to have attached an importance almost as insistent as that of Genet's version. It is harped on by a relentless parade of schematisms of light and darkness, of bringing light to dark places, of twinned adoring women, one a black enchantress from the bush, the other a white lady whose delicate pallors (fair hair, pale visage, pure brow, ashy halo) are set off by her dark eyes and mourning clothes, 'all in black, with a pale head, floating towards me in the dusk'(156–7). She reminds Marlow of her black counterpart:

> a tragic and familiar Shade, resembling in this gesture another one, tragic also, and bedecked with powerless charms, stretching bare brown arms over the glitter of the infernal stream, the stream of darkness.(160–1)

So Marlow lies to the white Intended about Kurtz's last words. To have done otherwise 'would have been too dark – too dark altogether'. 'The sunlight', as Marlow reports earlier, 'can be made to lie, too' (154).

The schematism of the light and dark imagery of *Heart of Darkness* is as relentless in its way as Genet's, with its own insistent evocations of the moral black-and-white-minstrel show. Repeatedly, the call of the wild comes over as a blackface act: 'you could see ... the white of their eyeballs glistening' as they 'shouted' and 'sang', with 'faces like grotesque masks' (61); 'hands clapping ... feet stamping ... bodies swaying ... eyes rolling ... they howled and leaped, and spun, and made horrid faces' (96). There is an inside-out or antithetical version, represented by the savage fireman, who 'ought to have been clapping his hands and stamping his feet', but who has been 'instructed' in the white man's machinery and becomes guardian of the deity in the boiler. This inversion of roles highlights rather than dims the showbiz artifice: 'He was an improved specimen; he could fire up a vertical boiler ... to look at him was as edifying as seeing a dog in a parody of breeches and a feather hat, walking on his hind legs' (97–8). The vaudeville of the 'improved specimen', whose acquisition of expertise is a small achievement of empire, is balanced by that of the frightened helmsman, whose 'eyes rolled', and whose loss of nerve cost him his life (110–13). The sense of theatrical fatuity is comparable to Genet's, though Conrad's version operates on a plane of tentative questioning or earnest introspective casuistry rather than stagey artifice. In lacking the element of play, though in its own way it is not unplayful, it might be said to differ from Genet's drama as modernism differs from postmodernism, and from Mailer's review as both differ from an old-fashioned sentimental primitivism in he-man clothes.

The self-questioning intimacy with which Marlow observes Kurtz's progress, and the sensitive narrative with which Conrad registers both, should not be allowed to obscure the formulaic schematism. Kurtz is not only the white man gone native, he is also the 'nigger in all of us' in an insistently literalized sense. 'All Europe contributed to the making of Kurtz' (117).[15] In this too he resembles the Rimbaud of *Une Saison en Enfer*, who is 'une bête, un nègre', entering the kingdom of the sons of Ham ('j'entre au vrai royaume des enfants de Cham'), who is at the same time the representative of 'all Europe'. 'Pas une famille d'Europe que je ne connaisse.'[16] That Rimbaud ended up, like Kurtz (and ahead of him), as a merchant in Africa, with something of Kurtz's outlook and trading instincts, is an irony not to be overlooked.

Somewhat as in the real-life case of Rimbaud, Kurtz's adoption of a pariah role is an expression of exalted alienation which becomes internalized as self-contempt. The fiction perhaps probes further, making the self-contempt itself part of the terrible lucidity with which Conrad invests Kurtz's 'victory' in looking 'the horror' in the eye: 'It was an affirmation, a moral victory paid for by innumerable defeats, by abominable terrors, by abominable satisfactions' (151). The 'affirmation' is not noble, but a recognition or constatation, neutral and unglorious, of the ignoble:

> Droll thing life is ... The most you can hope from it is some knowledge of yourself
> – that comes too late – a crop of unextinguishable regrets. I have wrestled with
> death. It is the most unexciting contest you can imagine. It takes place in an
> impalpable grayness, with nothing underfoot, with nothing around, without
> spectators, without clamour, without glory, without the great desire of victory,
> without the great fear of defeat, in a sickly atmosphere of tepid scepticism, with-
> out much belief in your own right, and still less in that of your adversary. ... I was
> within a hair's-breadth of the last opportunity for pronouncement, and I found
> with humiliation that probably I would have nothing to say. This is the reason
> why I affirm that Kurtz was a remarkable man. ... He had summed up – he had
> judged. 'The horror!' (150–1)

Trilling describes Kurtz as 'a man whose foul and bloody deeds make him what the terms of the story permit us to call a devil', noting also, however, that the decent and honest Marlow 'accords Kurtz an admiration and loyalty which amount to homage, and not, it would seem, in spite of his deeds but because of them'.[17] But Marlow refuses, or fails, to emulate Kurtz, or perhaps counts his refusal as a failure. He tells us that his experience falls short of Kurtz's, and also that it is Kurtz's 'extremity' that he has 'lived through'(151), though he also speaks of 'my own extremity', and of having, in some sense, 'remained to dream the nightmare out to the end' (150). Kurtz's cry

> was the expression of some sort of belief; it had candour, it had conviction, it had a vibrating note of revolt in its whisper, it had the appalling face of a glimpsed truth – the strange commingling of desire and hate. And it is not my own extremity I remember best – a vision of grayness without form filled with physical pain, and a careless contempt for the evanescence of all things – even of this pain itself. No! It is his extremity that I seemed to have lived through. True, he had made that last stride, he had stepped over the edge, while I had been permitted to draw back my hesitating foot. And perhaps in this is the whole difference; perhaps all the wisdom, and all truth, and all sincerity, are just compressed into that inappreciable moment of time in which we step over the threshold of the invisible. (151)

Stripped of its wordy Marlovian glosses, the moral (or mental) landscape of *Heart of Darkness*, 'impalpable grayness, ... with nothing around', is a secularized 'misère de l'homme sans Dieu' which recalls the bleak solitudes of Camus's Absurd. Such landscapes have been seen as describing a peculiarly modern experience of alienation, and it is an arresting fact that, in his examination of that concept, Lionel Trilling should see Diderot's *Neveu de Rameau* rather than Pascal's *Pensées* as the chief precursor text of a modern concept most fully embodied and developed in the Kurtz of *Heart of Darkness*:

> For Pascal, ... man's existence in society is but the manifestation of his cosmic alienation, whereas for Diderot the silence of the infinite spaces is not frightening; it is not even heard. For Diderot society is all in all, the root and ground of alienation. It is social man who is alienated man.[18]

If this analysis is correct, it bears awkwardly on those Conradian heroes who find their crisis in solitude, away from a policed civilization and the solace of civilized crowds. Their defining predicaments are precipitated not by alienation from or within society, but by the (usually physical and circumstantial) withdrawal of society's support system from them. The result may be disintegration, as in those prototypes of Kurtz in the 'Outpost of Progress', Kayerts and Carlier; or in white men gone native, like Willems in *An Outcast of the Islands*; or in the more fastidious case of Martin Decoud in *Nostromo*. Or it may be a 'victory', never an unironic concept in Conrad, as the novel of that name makes clear. The victory, in Kurtz's case, is bought at a heavy price, 'paid for by innumerable defeats, by abominable terrors, by abominable satisfactions', a victory which is achieved at precisely the point of 'disintegration', when, adrift from society, 'alone in the wilderness'(145), Kurtz is placed in those 'infinite spaces' whose silence Trilling says is 'not frightening ... not even heard' in the post-Pascalian experience.

If the full bleakness of this, in Marlow's account, stands out starkly from his verbose glosses, these glosses are themselves of cardinal importance. Though in one sense so much the voice of the bewildered, bluff Englishman, they contain what enables Trilling to see in *Heart of Darkness* a 'paradigmatic' or exemplary text in the full development of the modern concept of 'authenticity', that idea of self-realization through a descent into self and a confrontation of the horror within which is very different from, and in some ways the antithesis of, the more benign concept of 'sincerity'.

Marlow's language has many premonitory features of the vocabulary of 'authenticity', though the word itself was not yet fully available in the senses explored by Trilling (still unrecognized in the *OED*). If it had been, the bluff Marlow would not be the one to use it, typically falling back on an old-fashioned impressionistic and approximate language of wisdom, truth, sincerity. *Heart of Darkness* is full of 'inauthentic' sincerities. Marlow 'had not the slightest doubt' that the Manager 'was sincere' in his concern for Kurtz, but as a 'man who would wish to preserve appearances' (106). Kurtz's altruistic enthusiasms to improve the lot of the natives are, notwithstanding the underlying rage to exterminate, also 'sincere', with the kind of curdled passion we similarly encounter in the hideous sincerities of Swift's Dissenting sects. But Marlow has no single term for the lucidity of self-realization, the experience of clear-eyed discovery, which are the marks of Kurtz's 'victory', and has to use the approximations of an older vocabulary. He speaks of Kurtz's 'final burst of sincerity' (145), 'the appalling face of a glimpsed truth' (151). And Marlow himself, both as Kurtz's proxy, and by virtue of his following Kurtz to the edge of the abyss, feels sure, on his return to the 'sepulchral city', that its citizens 'could not possibly know the things I knew' (152).

This 'knowledge' comes, not discursively, but in an experience of fierce and disturbing revelation. At times, its language is that of an epiphany of the depths, of experience at its 'extremity', of 'that inappreciable moment of time' (151) which claims a downbeat kinship with Eliot's 'still point of the turning world', even as Marlow's reaction, the drawing back of his hesitating foot, is the language of Eliot's

backward half-look
Over the shoulder, towards the primitive terror,

though Eliot's confrontations of the heart of darkness do not often take this sombre and sonorous form.[19]

Marlow's language about Kurtz's 'extreme' experience even has some of the connotations of 'revolt' which, from Sade to Genet, belong to the strong traditional line which continues, for all the coy demurring, to link Romanticism and Modernism. The 'vibrating note of revolt in its whisper' (151) shows that Conrad is not free of the inflated rhetorical gesturing that goes with the territory, but the 'whisper' (a Conrad word, occurring, as noun or verb, some twenty-two times in *Heart of Darkness*) may be a *frisson nouveau*, as though the horror was experienced in understated form, like the surreal 'whisper music' of the woman's hair in the *Waste Land*, full of sexual menace and the downfall of civilizations. 'Whisper' is an Eliot word, and much possessed by death in his writings. When Phlebas lay dead, 'A current under sea/ Picked his bones in whispers.'[20] Its two dozen or so appearances in the poems and plays are nearly always sinister, but the two *Waste Land* occurrences have exceptional resonance. Perhaps, especially in that poem, the word was appropriated from *Heart of Darkness*, where there is a lot of whispering, including the low-grade conspiratorial whispering of the manager and his cronies (91) and the 'hurried whispers' of the quarrelling 'pilgrims'(106). But whispers are also part of the aura of Kurtz, to whom the wilderness 'had whispered ... things about himself which he did not know ... and the whisper had proved irresistibly fascinating' (131). The quotation from *Heart of Darkness* Eliot planned to use as an epigraph to *The Waste Land* was that in which Kurtz 'cried in a whisper ... a cry that was no more than a breath – "The horror! The horror!"'(149) The story is well known. Pound urged him to remove it and, though Eliot pleaded that it was 'much the most appropriate I can find, and somewhat elucidative', he replaced it with the passage from the *Satyricon* about the Sibyl.[21] *Heart of Darkness* subsequently provided the related epigraph for 'The Hollow Men', 'Mistah Kurtz – he dead'(150).

But whispers already had a potent life in Eliot's poems, in 'Rhapsody on a Windy Night', for example, or 'Gerontion'. In 'Whispers of Immortality', the word seems to announce itself as a replacement for Wordsworth's 'Intimations'. The whispers hint at the skull beneath the skin, at breastless creatures with a lipless grin, with a nascent modern surrealism grafted onto the Jacobean spookiness:

> Daffodil bulbs instead of balls
> Stared from the sockets of the eyes![22]

We should also note, in this language of whispers and hints, not only that this is a language of bleak negation rather than of Wordsworthian joy, but also that 'whispers' are, more or less literally or by definition, low-key. They may be to sound what hints, or intimations, are to meaning, but in any event these bleak whispers are a language of Prufrockian understatement, whereas Wordsworth's intimations, or hints, are in reality grandly affirmative.

That the language of epiphany, of intense clear-eyed recognition, takes this downbeat or rhetorically lowered form, is one of the things which bring Conrad and Eliot together. In both, as Marlow puts it, the epiphany is 'without glory', not an epiphany of high points but of soured discovery, a view of the naked lunch. For all the distinctions Marlow makes between Kurtz's 'last stride' and drawing back his own 'hesitating foot', it is remarkable how much Marlow has internalized everything undergone by Kurtz: 'It was his extremity that I seem to have lived through' (151). Since all we can ever know of Kurtz's psyche is what Marlow tells us, there is in these late pages of *Heart of Darkness* a constant interpenetration of the states of mind of the two men. The run-up to the 'last stride' had for both men the demoralized ordinariness of that 'sickly atmosphere of tepid scepticism', that 'grayness without form filled with physical pain', which Marlow reports of his own close encounters with the Eternal Footman, 'the most unexciting contest you can imagine' (150–1). On this reading, Kurtz's 'expression of some sort of belief' comes precisely at the 'last stride', reaching beyond the 'sickly scepticism'. This 'belief', a kind of Straussian secret, connects with many explorations of the idea of the saving lie in *Heart of Darkness*. 'It had candour, it had conviction', but it does not seem to have had much content (151).

The 'belief' that animates self-deceiving colonial enterprises, enabling the bringing of light, and even electric light, to dark places, or which leaves the Intended's faith in Kurtz undisturbed, seems also to penetrate Kurtz's confrontation with the horror, and with the recognition that the mission to bring light is the acceptable, perhaps the necessary, gloss to a reality whose underlying and unacknowledged desire is to 'exterminate all the brutes'. If that 'belief' is inseparable from Kurtz's 'affirmation' and 'moral victory', it may be that for all its 'candour' and 'conviction', it is itself intrinsically a falsehood, that its 'authenticity' entails the recognition of this, and rests, like that of Genet's *Blacks*, on artifice, though without the garish spectacle.

At the same time, Marlow's refusal to follow Kurtz over the brink, on which he exercised much introspective humility, not to say abasement, is also one of the tale's moments of truth. For one thing, Marlow's sober and thoughtful 'restraint', which Kurtz lacks (131), is what gives authority to his admiration for Kurtz. This restraint is treated more respectfully by Conrad than by Marlow himself. Perhaps, as we now say, the book valorizes it. It is consonant in its own way with a vocabulary of whispers, which, we should remember, is Conrad's word before it becomes Marlow's. It is not without connection to the hesitations and shrinkings of J. Alfred Prufrock in the well-furnished drawing-rooms which are his version of the nightmare of existence, even though Marlow's canvas is the vastness of the Dark Continent, and Marlow has a sober maturity, an ability to be humbled and awed, and a simple forthrightness, which seem a long way from the mincing distresses of Eliot's ageing dandy.

A hint, or whisper, of the detached Prufrockian register even gets into Marlow's mode of speech. 'Some sort of belief', at all events, is a gruff sailor's version of the flip concessiveness that we find in Eliot's own acknowledgments of our link to the heart of darkness, as in the closing paragraph of *The Use of Poetry and the Use of Criticism*: 'Poetry begins, I dare say, with a savage beating a drum in a jungle'.[23] It is not hard to imagine Marlow speaking the same words, with his own intonation and his own version of the oracular perplexity. The common element of respectful puzzlement at facts of awe-inspiring or soul-shaking portent is matched by a shared refusal to use words that might be thought grand enough to express them properly. The Marlow who meets the call of the wild by embracing the primitive, not with a self-authenticating howl but with respectful hesitancy, who hears tribal drums, salutes their appeal and simultaneously domesticates them to chapel bells, and who ultimately draws back his 'hesitating foot' from the abyss Kurtz stepped into, is replayed on a different plane by the great poet of the early twentieth century on whose work *Heart of Darkness* exercised some of its most compelling influence. The words of the *Use of Poetry*:

> Poetry begins, I dare say, with a savage beating a drum in a jungle, and it retains
> that essential of percussion and rhythm,

are a version of the Marlovian holding back, mutated to a dandy detachment or non-committal sagaciousness. It concedes the call of the drumbeat, half-neutralizes it by 'I dare say', and orchestrates the half-hearted flirtation further with 'hyperbolically one might say that the poet is *older* than other human beings'. The idea of poetry as the oldest, the primal, utterance, is domesticated to the dimensions of a little old man, as it might be 'gerontion', and again hedged in by 'hyperbolically one might say', before petering out with 'but I do not want to be tempted to ending on this sort of flourish'.

It is interesting that a decade or so before the *Use of Poetry*, Eliot published a short article entitled, by him or by his editor, 'The Beating of a Drum'.[24] Reviewing a book on the fool in Elizabethan drama, Eliot found it disappointing for not getting beyond the concept of the 'comic servant' to the primitive or shamanistic nature of the Fool in *Lear*, the witches in *Macbeth*, and Caliban. Eliot's tribute to savagery and primitive extremism is delivered with a parade of pedagogic precision, including at least two perhapses: 'The comic element, or the antecedent of the comic, is perhaps present, together with the tragic, in all savage or primitive art; but comedy and tragedy are late, and perhaps impermanent intellectual abstractions ...

Such abstractions, after developing through several generations of civilization, require to be replaced or renewed'. At the end of the review, affirming
that 'drama was originally ritual' and bound up with sacred dancing, Eliot
contests another scholar's view that 'the origin of the sacred dance' lay in a
desire to imitate the 'supernatural powers'. Eliot thinks primitive behaviour
might have been instinctual and pre-rational:

> It is equally possible to assert that primitive man acted in a certain way and
> then found a reason for it. An unoccupied person, finding a drum, may be
> seized with a desire to beat it; but unless he is an imbecile he will be unable to
> continue beating it, and thereby satisfying a need (rather than a 'desire'),
> without finding a reason for so doing. The reason may be the long continued
> drought. The next generation or the next civilization will find a more plausi-
> ble reason for beating a drum. Shakespeare and Racine – or rather the devel-
> opments which led up to them – each found his own reason. The reasons may
> be divided into tragedy and comedy. We still have similar reasons, but we
> have lost the drum.

Despite the gestures of scholarly caution, the two perhapses, a declaration
that he holds no one else responsible for his views, and that 'it is equally
possible to assert', this is both more categorical and less assured than 'Poetry
begins, I dare say, with a savage beating a drum in a jungle'. It has a lecturing
insistence which the remark from the actual lecture in *The Use of Poetry* wholly lacks, as though the earlier Eliot had not, at least in critical prose, developed the courage of his hesitancies. 'We have lost the drum' is very declarative. It sounds on first impact like a lament for the loss of instinctual rhythms,
those rhythms to which Marlow was so responsive in the bush, and which
Eliot partly experienced through Marlow. The phrasing sounds exactly like
the 'sort of flourish' he did not want to end on in the later statement. The
whole closing passage of the review is bizarrely emphatic. The instinctual and
non-rational impulse is said to be the operative and initiating one, but Eliot
re-imagines the savage in a condition of distinctly 'modern' boredom, like any
idle gramophone user in an apartment, with a dash of primitive decor ('the
long continued drought') added, offhand, for local colour.

It is such a person, hardly an archetypal bush savage, who would have had
to be an imbecile to continue beating the drum without a reason. And we,
like him, need the 'reasons', but only because we need to continue the drum-
ming. The display of dogmatic assertion betrays a conflicted sense of how to
accommodate himself to the idea of the primitive roots of poetry. The affirmation of primitive origins is undercut by a wilful refusal to imagine them in
other than drawing-room terms. It is also deflated by the exasperated nega-
tions, pointing to the imbecility of the savage state left to itself. One senses
that Eliot would like to admit he cannot take the idea seriously, while taking

it seriously. The necessary nostalgia, and the fastidious distancing, which come together in the faintly weary concessiveness of *The Use of Poetry*, have not yet found their proper discursive tone.

It is, however, through the speakers of the poems, of 'Portrait of a Lady' and 'Rhapsody on a Windy Night', that Eliot found, at a much earlier date, his voice for dealing with 'drums', and displacing them from the tribal bush to the celestial ennui of apartments:

> Among the windings of the violins
> And the ariettes
> Of cracked cornets
> Inside my brain a dull tom-tom begins
> Absurdly hammering a prelude of its own.[25]

The dull monotony of this *thé-dansant* ragtime is a ghostly residue, decorously reprocessed, of what Marlow remembers of 'the beat of the drum, regular and muffed like the beating of a heart', when Kurtz was being carried on a stretcher (155). Earlier, we read that

> Mr. Kurtz's adorers were keeping their uneasy vigil. The monotonous beating of a
> big drum filled the air with muffed shocks and a lingering vibration, (140)

and before long Marlow is confounding the beat of the drum with 'the beating of my heart' (142). The common analogy between primitive rhythms and those of the systole and diastole works far differently from the dull thudding in the brain of Eliot's speaker.[26] They beat a sonorous lament for an ailing 'adored' tribal demi-god, a passionate soul which 'for the moment had had its fill of all the emotions' (135), of vast sexual and homicidal gratifications, and whose 'savage and superb, wild-eyed and magnificent' (135-6) black lover we are shown confronting the wilderness in her grief. Kurtz himself, when Marlow sees him shortly after, is under

> the heavy, mute spell of the wilderness – that seemed to draw him to its pitiless
> breast by the awakening of forgotten and brutal instincts, by the memory of grat-
> ified and monstrous passions. This alone, I was convinced, had driven him out to
> the edge of the forest, to the bush, towards the gleam of fires, the throb of drums,
> the drone of weird incantations; this alone had beguiled his unlawful soul beyond
> the bounds of permitted aspirations. (144)

Eliot's 'dull tom-tom' is also erotic, though his speaker barely rises to the 'permitted aspirations', let alone beyond them. And it offers its own shadowy version of the correspondence between the rhythms of the wilderness and those of his own body, except that this is experienced 'inside my brain' rather than on his pulses, in an unusually literal sense of what Lawrence called 'sex in the head' or 'sex in the mind.'[27] Eliot took a lot of trouble to get the tom-toms right, changing the adjective from 'droll' [?] to 'strong' to 'rude' to 'dull', evidently poised between connotations of savage vigour (never an unqualified Eliot note, but endlessly flirted with) and urbane distance (the first and last impulse).[28]

The main evocation, initially, is of a cocktail-party version of African rhythms, ragtime, where the

> negro (teeth and smile)
> Has a dance that's quite worth while
> That's the stuff!
> (Here's your gin
> Now begin!)

Even the primitive Bolovians, in Eliot's most unbuttoned verses, the long-standing series about King Bolo, 'wore bowler hats'.[29] In 'Portrait of a Lady', among the ragtime of cracked cornets, the mental tom-tom is vaguely suggestive of Chopin, 'hammering a prelude of its own.' The tribal drum is variously assimilated to a tinkling piano and its 'capricious monotone'. By the end of Section II, this has become a 'street-piano, mechanical and tired', beating out 'some worn-out common song', 'Recalling things that other people have desired'. It is a classic Eliot scenario: tribal rhythms disturbing self-possession, and both the rhythms and the self-possession a subdued or muted parody of feelings self-consciously understood not to have been experienced, ghostly emanations of unexercised passions. The number of removes from a primary experience suggested by 'Recalling things that other people have desired' calls for a subtle arithmetic, but the mood survives into 'Burnt Norton''s account of the roses that 'had the look of flowers that are looked at.'[30]

In the tom-tom's other incarnation, in 'Rhapsody on a Windy Night'(1911–1915),

> Every street lamp that I pass
> Beats like a fatalistic drum,

the retreat is not to the etiolated harmonies of 'the latest Pole' transmitting 'the Preludes' but to the surreal and scary grin of an Elizabethan mad scene:

> And through the spaces of the dark
> Midnight shakes the memory
> As a madman shakes a dead geranium.[31]

Southam offers sources and analogues, from Heywood's *Woman Killed with Kindness*, from Oscar Wilde, and of course Laforgue's geraniums (actually very unlike). But the real force is that of the surreal icons in the *Waste Land*, which follow the image of the woman drawing her long black hair out tight, an image of haunted sexuality, of challenge and menace, instantly followed by 'bats with baby faces in the violet light' (l. 379). It is such things, for Eliot's speakers, which constitute 'The horror! The horror!', not the Kurtzian abyss, but a stagey repertoire of ghoulish frissons from the stock of 'decadent' or pre-surrealist special effects. It is from this prefabricated parlour spookiness that they draw back their hesitating foot, with limp flourishes of dandy deflection. Their tom-toms both mimic, and shrink from, a scaled-down version of passionate rhythms, far removed from the wild vitality of jungle drums which arouse in Marlow the notion of their perhaps not being altogether inhuman; or the frenzied tam-tams of Céline's *Voyage au bout de la nuit*, one of whose characters would exterminate all the brutes if he were not so tired, because their noise keeps him awake, like the peccant humanity which gave the gods insomnia in the Mesopotamian flood myth.[32]

It is a truism that Eliot and his speakers get their primitivism at second hand, from reading Frazer, from vaudeville, from ragtime and gramophone records. It is this attenuated apprehension itself which, in its own lower key, is either a derivative or an analogue of Marlow's. This is not because Marlow himself passed through the same intermediaries, but because he provided, on another plane, a model for keeping the jungle at bay. It is Kurtz, not Marlow, who fascinated Eliot, but it is Marlow who is in another sense closer to Eliot, because Kurtz fascinated Marlow too, and perhaps for the same reason, which has, after all, partly to do with tribal drums. If Kurtz succumbed to the call of the drums, and Marlow held back, Marlow's drums are nevertheless those which drew Kurtz too. There is nothing attenuated or tentative about these drums. It is Marlow who is tentative towards them. In Eliot, all this has become internalized. The drums themselves have become tentative. In the poems, they are simulacra, sometimes merely 'mental' or imagined, of the speakers' irresolute yearnings. In *The Use of Poetry*, the words 'I dare say' give them a thin and ultimately speculative identity, and they have a remoteness in time which removes any suggestion of instinctual immediacy. If *Heart of Darkness* is a modernist book, as we all assume and as Conrad did not know, then 'some sort of belief' may suggest that perhaps the genuinely modernist gesture is not the self-implicating invocation of tribal drums, Marlow's or Kurtz's or Eliot's, which taps into traditional primitivisms, but the fastidious caution which links it to Eliot's 'I dare say'.

Notes

1 Jean Genet, *Les Nègres* (Paris: Décines, 1963), p. 76; *The Blacks*, trans. Bernard Frechtman (London: Faber and Faber, 1960), p. 52; Norman Mailer's review, *Village Voice*, 11 May 1961, 11–14, which discusses Archibald's speech, and 18 May, 11–15 (reprinted in a modified form in Mailer's *The Presidential Papers*, Harmondsworth: Penguin, 1968, pp. 216–29; briefly discussed, in relation to *Heart of Darkness*, in Claude Rawson, *Gulliver and the Gentle Reader: Studies in Swift and Our Time*, London: Routledge & Kegan Paul, 1973, p. 146). There is a subsequent exchange between Lorraine Hansberry and Mailer, *Village Voice*, 1 June, 10–18 and 8 June, 11–12.

2 *Village Voice*, 11 May 1961, 14.

3 In the *Blacks* controversy, the ubiquitous word turns up in Mailer's answer to Hansberry, *Village Voice*, 8 June 1961, 12.

4 For some notes on the interrelationships, see Philip Thody, *Jean Genet: A Study of his Novels and Plays* (London: Hamish Hamilton, 1968), pp. 151–4.

5 *Monthly Magazine and British Register*, II (1796), 707; Goethe, *The Sorrows of Young Werther* (1774), trans. William Rose (London: Scholartis Press, 1929), p. 6.

6 Jean-Paul Sartre, 'Orphée noir', *Situations, III* (Paris: Gallimard 1949), p. 235.

7 Arthur Rimbaud, letters to Georges Izambard, 13 May 1871, and Paul Demeny, 15 May 1871, in *Lettres du voyant*, ed. Daniel Leuwers (Paris: ellipses, 1998), pp. 89, 92; Rimbaud, *Oeuvres complètes*, ed. Antoine Adam (Paris: Gallimard/Pléiade, 1972), pp. 249, 250; Sartre, *Saint Genet: comédien et martyr* (1952; Paris: Gallimard, 1969), pp. 159–71.

8 Rimbaud, *Une Saison en enfer* (1873), in *Oeuvres complètes*, p. 97; for early uses of 'white negro' see Claude Rawson, *God, Gulliver, and Genocide: Barbarism and the European Imagination 1492–1945* (Oxford: Oxford University Press, 2001), pp. 219, 306, 359n.99, 378 nn.125–6.

9 Roddy Doyle, *The Commitments* (1987), in *The Barrytown Trilogy* (Harmondsworth: Penguin, 1995), p. 13.

10 Joseph Conrad, *Heart of Darkness* (1899), in *Youth, Heart of Darkness, The End of the Tether*, Collected Edition (London: Dent, 1956). All page references are to this edition, and appear in brackets in the text.

11 Lionel Trilling, *Sincerity and Authenticity* (Cambridge/Mass.: Harvard University Press, 1972), p. 106. 'Authenticity' as a key concept in existentialist thought is tangential to the concerns of the present discussion, but for a useful summary treatment see John Macquarrie, *Existentialism* (Penguin: Harmondsworth, 1973), pp. 161–72.

12 *Les Nègres*, pp. [5] ('Pour jouer les *Nègres*', not translated in *The Blacks*), 16; *The Blacks*, p. 8.

13 *Les Nègres*, note by J.G., p. 13; *The Blacks*, p. 4.

14 Lorraine Hansberry, 'Genet, Mailer, and The New Paternalism', *Village Voice*, 1 June 1961, 14, 10.

15 Conrad says he 'took great care to give Kurtz a cosmopolitan origin', letter to Kazimierz Waliszewski, 16 December 1903, in *Collected Letters of Joseph Conrad, Volume 3: 1903–1907*, ed. Frederick R. Karl and Laurence Davies, p. 94, cited in *Heart of Darkness and other Tales*, ed. Cedric Watts (Oxford: Oxford University Press/World's Classics, 1998), p. 273n207.

16 Rimbaud, *Une Saison en enfer*, in *Oeuvres complètes*, pp. 97, 94.

17 Trilling, *Sincerity and Authenticity*, p. 106.

18 *Ibid*, p. 30.

19 T.S. Eliot, 'still point', 'Coriolan, I' (1931), and 'Burnt Norton', II and IV (1935); 'backward half-look', 'Dry Salvages', II (1941), in *Collected Poems and Plays* (London: Faber and Faber, 1982), pp. 128, 173, 175, 187, hereafter *CPP*.

20 *Waste Land*, ll. 378, 316, *CPP*, pp. 73, 71.

21 See *The Waste Land: A Facsimile and Transcript*, ed. Valerie Eliot (London: Faber and Faber, 1971), pp. 3, 125n; for a brief account, see B. C. Southam, A *Guide to the Selected Poems of T.S. Eliot*, 6th edn. (San Diego: Harcourt Brace, 1994), pp. 134–5. The Sibyl may herself have an unstated connection to *Heart of Darkness*, if, as, Cedric Watts's note suggests, the knitters of black wool, 'guarding the door of Darkness' in the sepulchral city, are an evocation of her (*Heart of Darkness and Other Tales*, World's Classics, Oxford 1990), pp. 147, 266n145.

22 *CPP*, p. 52.

23 T. S. Eliot, *The Use of Poetry and the Use of Criticism* (1933; London: Faber and Faber, 1964), p. 155.

24 T. S. Eliot, 'The Beating of a Drum', *The Nation and Athenaeum*, 6 October 1923, 11–12.

25 Eliot, 'Portrait of a Lady' (1910–1915), *CPP*, p. 19.

26 Compare the speech on 'rhythm' in Saul Bellow, *Henderson the Rain King* (1959; Harmondsworth: Penguin, 1966), p. 307 (also p. 69).

27 D. H. Lawrence, *Fantasia of the Unconscious* (1923; Harmondsworth: Penguin, 1971), p. 125; 'Leave Sex Alone' (1929), *Complete Poems*, ed. Vivian de Sola Pinto and Warren Roberts (New York: Viking Press,1971), p. 471.

28 T. S. Eliot, *Inventions of the March Hare: Poems 1909–1917*, ed. Christopher Ricks, (London: Faber and Faber, 1996), pp. 328, l. 33, 332n33. See Robert Crawford, *The Savage and the City in the Work of T. S. Eliot* (Oxford: Clarendon Press, 1990), p. 77, who deciphered the third attempt ('rude') as 'male'.

29 *Inventions of the March Hare*, pp. 70, 321; see Crawford, *The Savage and the City*, p. 83.

30 *CPP*, pp. 19–20, 172.

31 *CPP*, pp. 24, 18.

32 Louis-Ferdinand Céline, *Voyage au bout de la nuit* (1932; Paris: Livre de Poche, 1952), p. 167; *Journey to the End of the Night*, trans. Ralph Manheim (New York: New Directions, 1983), p. 142; for the Mesopotamian Flood myth, see *Atra–Hasis: The Babylonian Story of the Flood*, II.viii.35, ed. W. G. Lambert and A. R. Millard (Oxford: Clarendon Press, 1969), pp. 67, 109, 117, and introduction, pp. 12–13; Alexander Heidel, *The Gilgamesh Epic and Old Testament Parallels* (Chicago: University of Chicago Press, 1963), pp. 225–6.

7

Modernism and the Classical Tradition: The Examples of Pound and H. D.

Lars-Håkan Svensson

John Ashbery's 'Syringa', one of the most acclaimed and most frequently quoted poems of his 1977 collection *Houseboat Days*, draws on the Orpheus myth for an exploration of a classic elegiac motif: pain as the precondition of art, art as the alleviation of loss. In the first six lines Ashbery provides a characteristically deflated version of the myth up to Orpheus' grief for Eurydice. At this point, in contravention of traditional accounts of the story, Apollo, the god of song, appears to the distraught singer and gives him the following advice:

> Then Apollo quietly told him: 'Leave it all on earth.
> Your lute, what point? Why pick at a dull pavan few care to
> Follow, except a few birds of dusty feather,
> Not vivid performances of the past.'

Ashbery exegetes have not failed to note that Apollo's intervention recalls similar scenes in classical poetry. John Shoptaw, for example, refers us to Callimachus, *Aitia* I, and to Virgil, *Eclogue* VI.[1] An equally apposite parallel would be Propertius III.3. In Propertius, Apollo commands the poet to specialize in subjective love poetry rather than shoulder the drab and demanding task of composing an official epic. In illustration of his point, he couches his advice in symbolical language itself expressive of the stylistic ideal he prescribes, thus repeating a procedure found in Callimachus and, less explicitly, in Virgil.[2] Interestingly, Ashbery's Apollo has recourse to a similar technique. Though, surprisingly and utterly un-Apollo-like, he urges Orpheus *not* to write, the metaphors he employs in bolstering his argument ('dull pavan', 'birds of dusty feather') look back to corresponding tropes in Propertius (and Callimachus) just as the casual, dryly ironic tone of his quiet man-to-man talk recalls, while intensifying, the deprecatory tone employed by the Apollo of the Latin poem.

The notion that Propertius III.3 colours Apollo's speech in 'Syringa' should, however, be supplemented with a reference to a more recent intertext. In section II of 'Homage to Sextus Propertius' Ezra Pound renders the relevant passage in Propertius III.3 as follows:

> And Phoebus looking upon me from the Castalian tree,
> Said then 'You idiot! What are you doing with that water:
> Who has ordered a book about heroes?
>   You need, Propertius, not think
> About acquiring that sort of a reputation.
>   Soft fields must be worn by small wheels
>
> ...
>
> No keel will sink with your genius
>   Let another oar churn the water,
> Another wheel, the arena; mid-crowd is as bad as mid-sea.'³

Several of the features observed in 'Syringa' recur in these lines as they do in Propertius' original, but my point is not that 'Syringa' imitates Pound's adaptation of Propertius in specific detail (nor of course that Pound is, in a general sense, a precursor of Ashbery).⁴ Rather, it is the combination of the generic features observed in Callimachus, Propertius, and Pound and the modernist diction and manner Pound developed in 'Homage to Sextus Propertius' that makes Pound's poem a powerful presence in 'Syringa'.

The subtle conflictual relationship of Ashbery's and Pound's poems –Ashbery's Apollo advises *against* writing while Pound's (and Propertius') Apollo argues *for* writing (though of a particular kind) – directs our attention to some issues pertinent to a discussion of modernist poetry's relation to classical poetry. The most obvious question concerns what may be referred to as 'the politics of appropriation': what authors and what works do modernists align themselves with (or reject) and for what purpose? In this context it is essential to remember that poets and their works are always already interpreted. Recent criticism (to be adumbrated shortly) has taught us that the modernists' perceptions of their classical models are influenced not only by the meanings ascribed to the poets by classical philologists but by the translations, imitations, and assessments found in the works of previous writers. It is, in other words, such constructions which are mediated (or modified or rejected) by the modernist imitators or translators.

Closely related to this question is the vexed issue of poetic diction, always an important and tricky factor in translations or adaptations of classical poetry. The campaign for the modernization of poetic diction associated with modernism has been extremely successful. Though 'conventional' translations – translations relying on metre, standard syntax, homogeneous vocabulary, and perhaps even rhyme – are by no means an extinct category, it is now absolutely normal for a translator of Sappho or Callimachus to discard metre altogether, use fragmentized syntax, simplify the vocabulary so as to exclude any references that might be obscure to a modern reader, and imitate the forms of modern poetry; in other words, to employ techniques associated with Pound's procedures as a translator and imitator. In fact, Pound's and other modernists' influence has been so pervasive that we sometimes forget that they were far from consistent in their own theory and practice. Thus, in both his 'major personae' – poetic appropriations so free as to be virtually new poems – and in the works he labelled 'translations', Pound makes frequent use of archaisms, dialectal expressions, convoluted syntax, and so forth in order to signal the foreignness of the appropriated text, though his reasons for doing so may not be the same in his personae as in his translations.[5]

It should come as no surprise after what I have said so far that Pound will serve as my main example here of modernism's use of the classics. Though the classics make some sort of appearance in the work of nearly all the great modernists, Pound's engagement with the classics is outstanding, paralleled only by that of H. D. and, perhaps, T. S. Eliot, at least if we stick to poets currently deemed to be of the first order. In this short survey I will, for practical reasons, limit my discussion to a fairly small group of poets – Ezra Pound, H. D., and their circle – and to a fairly short but significant period in the history of modernism and the respective careers of Pound and H. D.: from 1908 when Pound arrived in London to the early 1920s when he left England for France (December 1920) and H. D. published her fourth volume – *Heliodora* (1924) – and her first *Collected Poems* (1925). In other words, I shall be concerned with only *one* modernism and only with an early but formative phase of Pound's and H. D.'s involvement with the classics. Though it would be tempting to move on into the *Cantos* and H. D.'s later work, I believe that the period I have restricted myself to will yield interesting conclusions. Both poets had achieved important results by the early 1920s and were entering new phases of their careers. During the period in question, both Pound and H.D can be seen to tackle similar issues regarding the translation, imitation, and appropriation of the classics and to attain artistic results which are vital to a discussion of the points I raised.

Given the modest scope of this essay, other limitations will be necessary as well. While I hope to be able to demonstrate how Pound's and H. D.'s treatment of classical material evolved into its first characteristic phase, it is clear that this cannot be done in full detail. I aim to examine a number of poems which, in my view, constitute important phases in their respective careers and which also indicate that modernism's treatment of classical material is not uniform. In particular, I want to suggest that even if they choose diverging directions after the creation of Imagism in 1912, their engagement with the classics up to the early 1920s constitutes two different ways of responding to 'Alexandrianism' as a poetic ideal and practice (a practice also noticeable in the 'Syringa' passage discussed earlier). 'Alexandrianism' as understood here refers both to a literary mode and to the influence exerted by an important site of cultural transmission. In the latter sense, 'Alexandrianism' has opened up interesting critical vistas in the last few years, particularly as regards the work of H. D.

*

As I have already suggested, our understanding of the transition from late-Victorian romanticism to the flowering of high modernism has been undergoing important changes in recent years. As far as poetry is concerned, there is now a strong tendency to downplay the difference between the Imagists and their contemporaries and immediate predecessors and to stress the ties between the modernists and the late Victorians. The use made of the classics provides interesting insights into the changes – and continuities – that characterize the period in question. To appreciate these, it is necessary first of all to recognize that what is sometimes somewhat vaguely referred to as 'the classical tradition' is not a monolith but the partial remains of a vast body of literature created over a period of at least 1,000 years. Some of its most prized achievements, such as Virgil's *Aeneid*, were uppermost in the minds of many of the poets under survey since they had studied them at school and knew large portions of them more or less by heart. Thus, Pound's constant references to the *Aeneid*, a work he thoroughly disliked, cannot be understood other than as the effect of reluctant close familiarity with its high points.[6] Other poets, most spectacularly Sappho, were in the process of being re-appraised at about the same time as the precepts of Imagism and Vorticism were formulated, and the recovery of Sappho's works is inscribed in the works of Pound and H. D. The circumstances under which this recovery was presented throw interesting light on the role played by the classics in public life. Before 1906 only two complete poems by Sappho were known. As a result of the excavations performed at Oxyrhyncus in Egypt some ten new substantial fragments were discovered, an event deemed so important that on 14 May, 1914, *The Times* printed one of these fragments in Greek with a prose translation and commentary by J. E. Edmonds, the future editor of the three volumes of Greek lyric, *Lyra Graeca*, included in the Loeb Classical Library. (Incidentally, only two years later, *The Times* would carry other news with a special and disturbing resonance for classically educated readers: in the 1916 reports on the battle of

Gallipoli the place-names were given now in Turkish, now in Greek, so as to suggest that the war of Troy was being fought once more.[7])

Despite the promulgation of certain standard authors by the educational system in both Britain and America, the prominence or popularity of others is likely to reflect the preferences of specific groups or individual strong readers. Thus, reference to or use of a particular classic poet is a way of demonstrating one's allegiances and position in the literary field,[8] and the difference between late-Victorian romanticism, the aesthetes of the 1890s, and the various groupings of the early twentieth century can be perceived in the classics they promoted, translated, and imitated. On the whole, it would seem that from the time of Matthew Arnold's hellenism there was a preference for Greek over Roman literature.[9] Thus, since for the Victorians the classical world provided models for discussing contemporary issues, their examples were mainly Greek—Athenian democracy versus Spartan oligarchy; the erotic Plato of the *Symposium* versus the authoritarian Plato of the *Republic* and the *Laws*. The stern Aeschylus and the sage Sophocles were contrasted with the effeminate and unruly Euripides. Theocritus, the author of bucolic *Idylls*, was looked upon as a paragon of landscape poetry while his portraits of shepherds, despite their largely heterosexual bias, were held in high esteem in homosexual circles. Swinburne and Rossetti translated Greek poetry, setting a standard which seemed valid well into the days of Imagism; Rossetti's versions of Sappho were looked upon as unsurpassable by H. D. who never attempted to render an entire Sappho poem into English.[10]

If, generally speaking, the late Victorians prized Greece more highly than Rome and preferred Greek to Roman writers, an interesting tendency can be noted as regards Roman literature. Walter Pater famously wrote about the literature of the late Roman empire in *Marius the Epicurean*, especially singling out authors such as Apuleius and the anonymous author of the *Pervigilium Veneris* and emphasizing the connection between late Latinity and Provençal poetry. Late Latinity was also a favourite period with the French symbolists and decadents. Des Esseintes, the hero of Huysmans' *Against the Grain (A Rebours)*, is an avid reader of Apuleius, and the speaker of Mallarmé's prose poem 'Plainte d'Automne' consoles himself after the loss of a beloved sister by reading 'the works of one of the last poets of the Roman decadence'. Although the English writers of the 1880s and 1890s picked up some of these ideas, which to some extent parallel Pater's preferences, it is nevertheless difficult to claim that the aesthetes fully imported the ideas of their French counterparts in this respect. Ernest Dowson, for example, sticks to the Augustan classics in his identifiable Latin titles and epigraphs, his best-known poem deriving its title, of course, from Horace ('Non sum qualis eram bonae sub regno Cynarae').[11]

Though individual emphases may vary, at times considerably, some writers, with whom everyone can be expected to be familiar, seem to be endowed with a variety of identities. A case in point is Virgil, long considered to be an exemplar both in view of his progression from frivolous pastoral through didactic georgic to serious epic, the so-called *rota Vergiliana*, and in view of the moral and political values embodied in the *Aeneid*. Not unexpectedly, Virgil has elicited widely different responses from the poets of the period under survey, the modernists among them. To Wallace Stevens, who makes a number of passing references to him, he was a type of major man.[12] Thomas Hardy treats him with great respect, modelling some of his war poems on passages from the *Aeneid*.[13] Willa Cather, raised and educated in the mid-West, refers on a number of occasions in her novels to saddened heroes who console themselves for life's inequities by reading Virgil at the end of their day's work.[14] As I have already mentioned, Virgil's *gravitas* did not appeal to Ezra Pound, whose dismissal of him generously includes other epic poets writing in his spirit such as Spenser, Camoens, Tasso, and Milton.[15] Eliot, on the other hand, highlighted the encounter between Aeneas and Dido in *The Waste Land*, setting off the squalor and inanity of the modern world against the heroic passions of antiquity, and later came to view the *Aeneid* as the most central poem of the Western tradition. Nor is this all. As Theodore Ziolkowski has reminded us, there were a number of other Virgils, constructed so as to allow various categories of readers to view him as both proto-Fascist and anti-Fascist; there was a German millenialist Virgil, a Virgil with a Southern accent, and an *Aeneas Americanus*.[16] This battle of the Virgils has not lost impetus. In the 1960s, Robert Graves attacked Eliot's attempts at sanctifying Virgil, alluding to the view, prevalent at the time of the First World War, of Virgil as the apologist of Romano-British imperialism, a view which he had repudiated even as a young man.[17] In this connection, it might be added that the 1960s were also a period when classical philologists, especially American ones, perhaps under the impact of the Vietnam war, began to question the notion that the *Aeneid* lends unqualified support to Roman imperialism; this view has caught on, and many Latinists today see the *Aeneid* as a tortured poetic document about the intrinsic conflicts of imperialist designs.[18]

*

As attested by one of his earliest attempts in verse, a poem written towards the end of the summer term of 1898 when he was 13 and enrolled at the Cheltenham Military Academy, Ezra Pound was a student, if not initially an avid one, of both Latin and Greek from an early age onwards.[19] During the next eight years which he spent at various institutions of learning, chiefly the University of Pennsylvania and Hamilton College in the New York State, he seems to have concentrated on Latin, acquiring sufficient competence to read this language with ease throughout his life. Though the authors he selected appear to have been the usual ones, Pound later claimed that his study of Martial and Catullus (on whom he concentrated in the year 1905–6) had made him specially aware of the need for 'clarity and hardness' in verse.[20] It is noteworthy, however, that Pound read widely in various other languages, including English, and later claimed that he had done so because he had decided at the age of fifteen that he wanted to be a poet and to learn more about the craft of poetry than anyone else.[21] This hunger for arcane knowledge also led him to take an interest in Neo-Latin poetry and even to consider the possibility of writing a thesis on Neo-Latin poets.[22] In fact, some of his earliest articles and translations, dating from 1906 to 1908, and inspired to some extent by his trips to Europe in those years, highlight the Neo-Latin work of sixteenth-century luminaries such as Castiglione, Bembo, and Angeriano.[23] All of these are of course better known for what they wrote in the vernacular, but this is an aspect of their careers that Pound appears to have paid little or no attention to. In matters of diction and style, he was still very much under the influence of Browning, Pater, and other writers of the Victorian era, as is apparent not only from his translations of the Neo-Latin poets just mentioned but from his original work in English as well. Nevertheless, it is interesting to note that Pound's life-long habit of mediating classical literature through neo-Latin translations presumably dates from this early exposure to neo-Latin poetry.

Though Pound's earliest volumes contain a number of references to classical texts ('Famam Librosque', 'Threnos', and 'Greek Epigram'), the engagement with the source texts often merely reflects the influence of the late-Victorian romantics and the aesthetes of the 1890s. A more tangible involvement with classical texts can be detected in the *Canzoni* of 1911, but the choice of texts and the way in which they have been appropriated are not original. Titles such as 'Speech for Psyche in the Golden Book of Apuleius' and 'Blandula, tenula, vagula' ('Dear little fleeting pleasing soul') really tell us little more than that Pound may have found both Apuleius and the Emperor Hadrian's poems in Pater. It is perhaps a little more noteworthy that the collection has an epigraph from Propertius and that it contains a translation of a poem by Propertius, 'Prayer for his Lady's Life'; the diction of the poem is conventional and old-fashioned, however, and the choice of Propertius cannot in itself have surprised contemporary readers since even a poet of the 90s such as Dowson was a keen admirer of the Roman poet. Pound's next volume, *Ripostes* (1912), marks a change: not only does this collection contain 'The Complete Works of T. E. Hulme' and some of Pound's earliest Imagist poems ('Δώρια' among them), it also offers a free adaptation of one of Catullus' epigrams, 'Phasellus Ille' ('The yacht which you see'), used by Pound to clarify his position in the contemporary literary debate. This is perhaps the first example of how Pound uses a classical poem to make a contemporary point (though he had of course used Italian and Provençal poems earlier for similar purposes). Interestingly, at the same time as Pound modernizes his diction in the Imagist poems, he does not hesitate to use archaizing features in a poem written in Sapphics ('Apparuit').

The same characteristic mixture of features originating from a variety of sources continues in the poems Pound wrote during the next few years and collected in *Lustra* (1913–15). On the whole, their titles reflect the Imagist or satirical bent of the poems. Some of them are in Greek and Latin but do not convey the aesthetizing impression found in earlier volumes. Thus, there are no poems called 'In tempore senectutis' (recalling the manner of 90s poets such as Dowson and Johnson) but only sharp, concise titles such as 'Coitus' or titles consisting of a quotation which engages in intertextual play with the poem, such as 'Dum Capitolium Scandet' (from Horace). The new aesthetic underlying this book is announced in the epigraph which tellingly repeats the opening line of Catullus' volume: 'Cui dono lepidum novum libellum', in which the two key-words 'lepidus' ('pretty') and the diminutive 'libellus' ('little book') strike the chord: elegance, concision. Though the volume contains a number of satirical and epigrammatic poems castigating contemporary mores in the manner of Catullus, it is worth remembering that Pound wrote in the famous 1913 issue of *Poetry* magazine that his search for hard, dry, imagistic concision was guided by the examples of Sappho, Villon, and Catullus – and of course by that of T. E. Hulme. Though we should in all probability add the epigrams of the *Greek Anthology* as another important influence, there exists apparently a curious affinity between Pound's imagistic poems and his satirical epigrams. Catullus has strictly speaking no images of the visual kind that Pound, Hulme, and H. D. perfected in some of their poems, yet his brand of concision involves features that were of interest to Pound. This is how *The Oxford Companion to Classical Literature* characterises 'Alexandrianism':

> a development of new, miniature genres ... a regard for form ... the cult of erudition; and the emergence of a subjective and personal way of writing.[24]

Alexandrianism's Roman imitators, the neoterics,[25] are said to have honoured the following ideals:

> perfection in miniature, and experimenting with new metres, different kinds of language, new words (often Greek), new themes (romantic, exotic, some bizarre) and a mannered style.[26]

While the two definitions comprise features that are found in most author-

itative discussions of Alexandrianism and neoteric poetry, they do not suffi-
ciently stress the shift in emphasis that characterizes the work of the Romans, who 'use [Callimachus'] language ... to develop a conception of ...
poetry ... far richer and more insidious than Callimachus' overt conception
of his'.[27] They also leave out an important dimension which, despite the
scantiness of the extant material, is in full evidence in Alexandrianism's
leading poet, Callimachus, and his Roman successors: a wry sense of humour, ranging from subtle metafictive irony to biting epigrammatic sarcasm.[28] In view of Pound's interest in *logopoeia*, 'the dance of the intellect
among words',[29] it seems important to point out that both Alexandrians
and Romans have a number of stylistic code-words at their disposal and
that they are fond of metapoetic imagery of the kind discussed in connection with the Ashbery poem.

Several similar features are discernible in Pound's verse from this period
onwards, in contrast to what is typical of his earlier work. At the same time his
actual appropriations of specific poems are informed by new techniques, indicative of a more far-reaching and self-willed manner of imitation. Two of
the most interesting cases are 'Coitus' and 'The Spring'. The first of these is, as
the title suggests, a drastic reworking of motifs only hinted at in the source,
Pervigilium Veneris, a late Latin poem praised by Pater, whereas 'The Spring' is
a an early precursor of the freedom which will later come to fruition in the
'Homage'.

'The Spring' is based on a fragment of a poem by the 6th-century Greek
poet Ibycus, whose first line recurs in Pound's Greek epigraph. As critics have
pointed out, the original contrasts the fragility and beauty of spring with the
passion constantly raging inside the speaker's breast.[30] Pound's version down-
plays this conflict, defamiliarizing certain features – 'Cydonian spring',
'maelids', and 'water-girls' are hardly intelligible expressions in ordinary English – while simultaneously suggesting that all the details mentioned are
symptoms of one and the same phenomenon: the omnipotence of love. The
contrast comes in the very last two lines which have no counterpart at all in
the original: 'She, who moved here amid the cyclamen, / Moves only now a
clinging tenuous ghost', and the powerfully shaken or devoured heart of the
original is 'bewildered' in Pound's version. In the process, the poem has assumed an elegiac tone not found in the original, and the language is strikingly
modern by comparison with that of earlier poems.

Certain of the linguistic devices found in 'The Spring' may suggest the
neoteric or Alexandrian manner. Other poems play linguistic games of a similarly modern kind. The humorous three-word poem 'Papyrus' plays with a
Sapphic fragment, translating its syllables in a self-willed, perverted way,
while another poem, bearing a Greek title ('Ἰμέρρω' – Aeolic dialect for

'ἱμείρω', 'I yearn') is an improvisation, inspired, it would seem, in equal measure by a poem by Sappho and some phrases in Richard Aldington's translation of it.[31] The 'Homage to Quintus Septimius Florentis Christianus' is a sequence based on epigrams from the *Greek Anthology*; in several of these, Pound deviates from the models, suppressing some statements and conflating others while making his diction much more contemporary, adding sarcasm in a number of cases, sometimes of a misogynistic kind. Textually, some of these versions thus differ considerably from the Greek originals.

Although there is not enough space here to discuss these textual changes in detail or to relate them to other Poundian poems which exemplify similar tendencies, it is clear that terms such as 'translation', 'adaptation', or even 'imitation' are inadequate as characterizations of Pound's involvement with his models. Nor do they fully describe the nature of Pound's next major work, 'Homage to Sextus Propertius'. In this, Pound appropriates the work of a minor Roman classic, creating a new whole out of a selection of his poems – or sometimes even sections of individual poems; in the process, some features of the originals are highlighted, others are left out. While the format of the sequence – 12 sections – appears to hint at the twelve books of Virgil's *Aeneid*, its elegiac ethos, celebrating love and art while being pervaded by feelings of transience and futility, is an indictment of the epic mode, represented in the poem by Virgil.

The poem's derivative yet independent character is indicated by its title. In a letter to Thomas Hardy written from St Raphael on 31 March 1921, Pound explains that the poem's title is

> a term of aesthetic *attitude* borrowed from a French musician, Debussy – who uses 'Homage [*sic*] à Rameau' for a title to a piece of music recalling Rameau's manner. My 'Homage' is not an English word at all.[32]

Pound's statement that 'My "Homage" is not an English word' means that the English word does not carry the connotations that Debussy's 'Hommage' does.[33] (Pound had previously used the word in 'Homage to Quintus Septimius Florentis Christianus' and in an uncollected poem published in *The Times*, Jan. 20, 1914, entitled 'Homage to Wilfrid Scawen Blunt'.) In French music and literature the genre of the *hommage* and the *tombeau* is a well-established one, some of the most famous examples being Mallarmé's *tombeau* sonnets commemorating Baudelaire, Verlaine, and Poe ('Tel qu'en Lui-même enfin l'éternité le change'); in fact, the section in Mallarmé's *Poésies* containing these poems is subtitled 'hommages et tombeaux'. As *The New Grove Dictionary of Music and Musicians* explains, the idea is to commemorate a deceased musician, preferably by appropriating the very forms that the predecessor so honoured had excelled in.[34]

What these French associations might have suggested to the poem's early

readers is that Pound approaches Propertius with the sophisticated artistic
and linguistic sensibility of one familiar with French symbolist poetry. In a
letter written in 1922 Pound claims that 'after his first "book" S.P. ceased to be
the dupe of magniloquence and began to touch words somewhat as [Jules]
Laforgue did'.[35] What Pound has in mind here is *logopoeia*, 'the dance of the
intellect among words', realized in the poem in a variety of ways: as knowing-
ly inverted clichés, a predilection for polysyllabic or pompous words (usually
of Latin origin), 'translationese', and a general propensity for energetic over-
statement. When the historical Propertius expresses admiration, real or
feigned, for Virgil's *Aeneid*, he is content with a single distich:

> cedite Romani scriptores, cedite Grai;
> nescio quid maius nascitur Iliade.

> ('Yield ye, bards of Rome, yield ye, singers of Greece! Something
> greater than the Iliad now springs to birth')

In Pound's 'Homage' this is amplified into self-conscious bombasm which
uses both archaisms and repetition to drive home its point:

> Make way, ye Roman authors,
>   clear the street, O ye Greeks,
> For a much larger Iliad is in the course of construction
> (and to Imperial order)
> Clear the streets, O ye Greeks!

As other passages make clear, the 'Homage' is also a linguistic joke, the fruit of
Pound's imaginative use of Lewis-Short's *Latin-English Dictionary* or simply
reflecting his delight at the superficial similarity between Latin and English
words. Thus, the Latin word *minae*, 'threats', yields a reference to 'Welsh
mines'; and the lines

> quippe coronatos alienum ad limen amantes
> nocturnaeque canes ebria signa fugae,

> ('For thou shalt sing of garlanded lovers watching before an-
> other's threshold, and the tokens of drunken flight through the
> dark')

become

> Obviously crowned lovers at unknown doors,
> Night dogs, the marks of a drunken scurry,

simply because *canes*, 'you will sing', is superficially identical with *canes*, 'dogs'. However amusing details such as these may be to those familiar with the Latin original, they also form part of a tendency which readers who have no Latin can grasp. The 'Homage', as it stands, is an English-language poem which has a meaning available without the Latin originals though it is reinforced by familiarity with them and with the Propertius corpus *in toto*.

The basis of this meaning is Pound's famous contention that the

> 'Homage' presents certain emotions as vital to me in 1917, faced with the infinite and ineffable imbecility of the British empire as they were to Propertius some centuries earlier, when faced with the infinite and ineffable imbecility of the Roman Empire.[36]

To set forth his discontent Pound appropriates certain carefully selected poems in the Propertius corpus while drawing on others for colour or tone. The resulting selection highlights what I have referred to as the Alexandrian aspect of Propertius, especially prominent in Bks 2 and 3 from which all the poems selected and reworked by Pound are taken. The result is a sequence which gives pride of place to metapoetic statements, to poems identifying and describing the subjective elegist's melancholy predicament: on the one hand, he has to fend off suggestions from high places that he compete with epic poets for the position as 'Phoebus' chief of police'; on the other hand, his only readers are 'ladies of indeterminate character' who honour him at their banquets 'with yesterday's wreaths'. As as result of this dichotomy, Pound's 'Homage' spans a variety of emotions, ranging from vatic exuberance to moments of sadness and sordid futility, and an equally wide stylistic variety, as is made clear in the very first lines where the solemn and musical invocation of the 'Shades of Callimachus, Coan ghosts of Philetas' soon leads on to a sarcastic denunciation of epic poets: 'Out-weariers of Apollo will, as we know, continue their Martian generalities'.

The effect of these shifts is to create a new type of poem, which I would claim is a modernist invention. It resembles the dramatic monologue in that it intrudes 'the personal utterances of ancient poets ... into a modern consciousness';[37] it adopts certain attitudes peculiar to the decadent and aesthetic poets of the 90s; it draws on and rearranges a selection of texts derived from an ancient predecessor so as to form a new entity; [38] it is dialogical in a Bakhtinian sense since it mimics a variety of voices and stylistic tropes;[39] it is intertextual since it draws on Propertius and in particular on the Alexandrian or neoteric manner as practised by him. The Alexandrianism of the 'Homage' is noticeable not only in the stylistic features discussed but in the speaker's pervasive sadness and his occasional bitter elitism, induced by the competing claims of art-for-art's sake and the reigning values. When he lashes out against the populace ('For the nobleness of the populace brooks nothing below its own altitude') he does not deviate from the Alexandrian manner *per se* – after all, Callimachus had expressed violent dislike of everything popular[40] – but he does give Propertius' attitude a new complexion.

*

The Alexandrianism displayed in Pound's early poetry can be interestingly contrasted with that encountered in the early work of H. D. Pound's Alexandrianism is largely a textual and stylistic one, filtered through the Roman poets whom he admired and imitated. His interest in Alexandria in a more general, cultural sense was less in evidence – in fact, in his letters and critical writings he often treats Alexandria with contempt, considering it second-rate in relation to Athens.[41] H. D., on the other hand, as Eileen Gregory has suggested in her recent book, appears to have seen Alexandria as the cultural centre through which the civilization of classical Greece was refracted to the modern world and, in addition, as emblematic of specific cultural values and attitudes which she promoted in her own original work and in her critical writings.[42] However, her perception of the multicultural Egyptian metropolis and its role as a centre of cultural transmission is less a philological or textual affair – though it contains that element too – than a general sense of complicity with writers and tendencies that she looks upon as 'Alexandrian'. In some important ways, her view of Alexandria reflects the late-nineteenth-century fascination with Alexandria as the mythical capital of decadence. However, while some Victorians and some modernists – usually male ones – were troubled by the equation of Alexandria with effeminacy, H. D. and other early women modernists saw the sexual ambiguity often associated with Alexandria as a strength, interpreting the city's alleged decadence as, among other things, an open-mindedness about erotic behaviour, including homoeroticism. In this respect, H. D.'s view of Alexandria is consonant with that of Constantine Cavafy (who, incidentally, was introduced to English readers at an early stage through E. M. Forster's articles for the *Athenaeum* from 1919 onwards and *Pharos and Pharillon*, his 1923 book about Alexandria).[43]

Although H. D. scholars have detected a number of parallels between her poems and passages in the works of writers usually typifying Alexandria such as Callimachus and Theocritus, the poet whom she herself seems to have regarded as the embodiment of Alexandrianism is Meleager, the 1st-century B.C. epigrammatist and anthologist. Curiously, though Meleager was a native of Gadara in Syria, H. D. bestows the honorific title 'Meleager of Alexandria' on him, two of Meleager's crucial distinctions in H. D.'s eyes being that he included women poets in his anthology and that he was reputed to be bisexual (and certainly used a bisexual persona in his poetry).[44] Meleager appears also to have been associated, in H. D.'s mind, with her own ongoing project of collecting, exploring, and re-writing works by cherished predecessors. As the site of a famous library where heterogeneous works were collected, Alexandria becomes a powerful symbol of H. D.'s own early work (largely pursued in the British Library and museums throughout Europe). As is well known, H.D.'s early poems are in a sense an anthology of fragments culled (and reworked in different ways) from Meleager and other Greek poets (some of whom figured prominently in Meleager's anthology, such as Anyte and Nossis). There can be no doubt that H. D. read these poems in the original Greek versions, though she also had recourse to modern translations and bilingual editions;[45] her chief source as regards epigrams, at least during the early stages of her career, appears to have been Mackail's *Select Epigrams from the Greek Anthology* (1890), from which she picked the epigrams, by Meleager and other epigrammatists, which provided the impetus for several of her earliest poems, in particular the ones put forward as models of Imagism by Pound.[46]

H. D.'s appropriations of her classical models follow different patterns. In 'Orchard', one of the poems pronounced Imagist by Pound during the legendary visit to the tea shop near the British Museum in August 1912, the basic notion of an offering to Priapus is derived from an epigram (Zonas, *AP* VI.22); but there are only a few verbal parallels at the end.[47] The other poem that served as Imagism's midwife, 'Hermes of the Ways', appears to be based on a poem by Anyte (*AP* VI.314); nearly all the words found in the Greek epigram have counterparts in H. D.'s poem which, however, expands the scene described by Anyte into a little drama, centring on the speaker's fateful (and fearful) encounter with Hermes.[48] As Gregory observes, H. D.'s engagement with the epigrams of the anthology can be divided into two sharply defined groups (both in terms of chronology and her way of appropriating the Greek text): the first, belonging to 1913–14, is 'lyric'; the second is 'almost entirely amatory' and 'narrative'.[49] An example of the latter, more elaborate type is found in 'Lais', which uses a short epigram by Plato as its starting-point (*AP* VI.1). The four lines of the model are expanded into a poem nearly fifteen times as long; in the process, the bare details of the terse original are rehearsed, transformed, and reformulated, until, at the very end of the poem, a fairly faithful rendition of the epigram states the theme on which the poem is an elaboration. An even more complex example of intertextual play along these lines is found in 'Heliodora', an amalgam of at least two epigrams by Meleager (*AP* V.144 and V.147) which are quoted, alluded to, and finally transformed into a narrative about two lovers writing verse. In the case of both these epigrams, H. D. can be shown to have used the Greek text rather than Mackail's English translation.

It is obvious even from such a short survey as this that H. D.'s way of exploiting the Greek text during both the periods sketched above differs in vital respects from Pound's. While Pound's use of epigrams or elegies results in new poems that often stand in a line-to-line relationship with their models, H. D. frequently singles out and adapts individual words and concepts in the Greek original to entirely new ends. The thematic concerns of the original are partly suppressed, partly transformed in order to establish new imaginative structures of H. D.'s own devising. Many of the poems display a marked thematic (and topographical) resemblance to one another. Usually set in a bare landscape near the sea, they enact scenes of pursuit and waiting. Contrary to the epigrams upon which they draw, they rarely depict the scenes or predicaments they present in concrete visual and narrative detail, although many of the components employed are specific enough. While Pound resorts to the classics in order to lash out against contemporary aberrations of taste and morality, H. D. uses her Greek models to represent concerns of a more personal and intimate character. Sometimes the situations suggested depict clashes between male and female sensibility; sometimes – and increasingly after her first two collections – the emotional attachments explored are of a bisexual or lesbian character.

Consonant with this thematic orientation is H. D.'s choice of source texts. Meleager and the Alexandrians apart, H. D. in her elective affinities largely adheres to late-Victorian taste though in her own work she favours a modern diction. In drama, for example, unlike Pound and Eliot, who advocate Aeschylus,[50] her favourite is Euripides, considered too effeminate and erratic by Pound and Eliot (but admired by the preceding generations) and also prone to sweeping lyricisms and an almost operatic effusiveness which may seem difficult to harmonize with the hard, dry classicism advocated by Pound and his circle. Euripides is famous for making the choruses of his plays to some extent independent of the action and transforming them into semi-separate lyrical entities. At a more general level, he is known for his 'feminine' sensibility, discernible for example in his portrait of Medea, and his disbelief in war as a means of resolving conflicts.

An important portion of H. D.'s early work – a portion probably composed at about the same time as her short lyrics – consists of what she herself refers to as translations from Euripides. Translations they are in a general sense, since they provide English versions of choruses from *Iphigeneia in Aulis* and *Hippolytus*. At the same time the similarity between the free forms which H. D. has invented for her versions of these choruses and the form of her own original poems is striking. The complex grammatical and metrical patterns of the original have been simplified at the same time as repetitive syntactical patterns similar to the ones found in her original poems are established. This view of the lyrical – one is almost tempted to say 'Imagist' – qualities of the Greek chorus is something H. D. shares with Pound, who in a short piece called 'The Tradition' suggests that the works of Euripides or 'almost any notable Greek chorus' might serve to illustrate the effects of *vers libre*.[51] In her renditions of Euripides, H. D. leaves out the high-flown rhetoric of the original, concentrating instead on simplicity, clarity, and concretion to an extent that makes it doubtful, *pace* Eliot, if the word 'translation' is the most adequate description of the end result.

Indeed, H. D.'s freedom in transforming the classical materials that she engages with is often so striking that the question may well be raised whether the resultant poems should in fact be looked upon as 'imitations' or 'appropriations' or as new poems bearing little or only superficial resemblance to the originals that supposedly inspired them. Is 'Eurydice', spoken by Eurydice herself, a imitation of Ovid's version of the myth in *Metamorphoses* X.1-63 or is it a free revision of it, so free in fact that it should be seen as a latter-day counterpart to Ovid's own revisions of standard interpretations of mythical matter in some of the letters making up his *Heroides*? Is 'Adonis' a mosaic drawn on hints and themes derived from a variety of sources such as Bion's *Lament for Adonis*, Theocritus, *Idylls* 15 and 30, and Sappho LP 140a and 168? The issue is brought to a head in the case of H. D.'s appropriations of Sappho. Some readers seem to feel that H. D. merely alludes 'to Sappho in epigraphs to a handful of poems'[52] while others consider Sappho to be H. D.'s chief elective affinity, arguing that Sappho's influence is a pervasive one extending far beyond title references ('Fragment Forty-three') to the standard numbering of Sappho's preserved fragments. On the one hand, the reader might be left with the curious impression that although H. D. in her prose writings reveals a profound interest in Sappho, almost amounting to an identification, her own poetry contains no interesting intertextual exchanges. What is true is that H.D. never translated any of Sappho's poems; nor, on the face of it, does she seem to have taken an active interest in the new fragments published during the heyday of Imagism. The standard explanation of her failure to translate Sappho is that she valued Rossetti's and Swinburne's versions too highly to wish to enter the competition herself. (Pound appears to have taken a similar view.) As regards the allegation that Sappho did not provide materials for her poetry, we now know better. As Diana Collecott shows in a recent study, Sappho's poetry informs H. D.'s work to a very large extent, though in ways which only close familiarity with both writers – and with perceptions of Sappho current in H. D.'s time – permits us to see.[53] From an appendix setting forth similarities between H. D.'s and Sappho's works it appears that during the period relevant to this survey H. D. makes consistent use of Sappho in her work, picking up individual lines, phrases, and words, charging them with poetic and erotic meaning, inserting them into new contexts and making them serve new purposes. In this exchange, H. D. also draws on the work of her Victorian predecessors, inscribing her vision of Sappho and Sapphism in a poetic context widely different from that of Pound.

I have argued that terms such as translation, adaptation, and even imitation are inadequate as descriptions of the intricate transformations of classical poems that characterize the first phase of one of the most highly publicized modernisms of the early twentieth century. Irrespective of whether the term I have proposed here, 'appropriation', is more suitable, it seems to me that Pound and H. D. used the classics to create forms that are unique to modernism. In his path-breaking study *The Light in Troy*, Thomas M. Greene identifies a type of imitation which he refers to as 'heuristic imitation' and considers the most intricate kind.[54] The characteristic feature of such an imitation is that it transcends its model, transforming it into a text fully integrated with the historical conditions of the imitator's own era; the poem thus takes us on a new dimension, expressing new tensions, giving new experiences a form at once recognizable and innovative. A case in point is Sir Thomas Wyatt's version of a Petrarchan sonnet, 'Who so list to hount', whose idealized vision of courtly love is modified by the erotic and political constraints of Henry VIII's reign. Pound's 'Homage to Sextus Propertius' and some of H. D.'s poems seem to me to be modern equivalents – in fact more than that: their play with the textuality of classical models, their application of the political and erotic valencies of the originals to their own situation, and their reconstruction of established poetic genres all combine to create new forms and expressions unique to modernism. The fleeting recurrence of one of these modes in an Ashbery poem is just one manifestation of their success.

Notes

1 John Shoptaw, *On the Outside Looking Out: John Ashbery's Poetry* (Cambridge/Mass. and London: Harvard University Press, 1994), p. 368 n. 29.
2 For a discussion of these and other relevant passages, see G. O. Hutchinson, *Hellenistic Poetry* (Oxford: Clarendon Press, 1988), pp. 77–84 and 277–96.3.
3 'Homage to Sextus Propertius', II, in *Personae: The Shorter Poems of Ezra Pound*, a revised edition prepared by Lea Baechler and A. Walton Litz (New York: New Directions, 1990), pp. 207–8.

4 Ashbery is rightly mentioned only in passing in surveys such as Christopher Beach, *ABC of Influence: Ezra Pound and the Remaking of American Poetic Tradition* (Berkeley, Los Angeles, and Oxford: University of California Press, 1992), and Marjorie Perloff, *Poetic License: Essays on Modernist and Postmodernist Lyric* (Evanston: Northwestern University Press, 1990).

5 For a discussion of Pound and poetic diction, see Emerson R. Marks, *Taming the Chaos: English Poetic Diction Theory Since the Renaissance* (Detroit: Wayne State University Press, 1998), pp. 265–87. For a survey of Pound's techniques as a translator, see Lawrence Venuti, *The Translator's Invisibility: A History of Translation* (London and New York: Routledge, 1995), *passim*.

6 For Pound's views on Virgil, see, for example, the following statement: 'Virgil is a second-rater, a Tennysonianized version of Homer' (*The Letters of Ezra Pound 1907–1941*, ed. D.D. Paige, London: Faber and Faber, 1951, p. 316). For a discussion of Virgil and the *Cantos*, see Peter Davidson, *Ezra Pound and Roman Poetry: A Preliminary Survey* (Amsterdam–Atlanta: Rodopi, 1995), pp. 130–40.

7 Eileen Gregory, *H. D. and Hellenism: Classic Lines* (Cambridge: Cambridge University Press, 1997), p. 260, n.17. It should perhaps be added that the *Times* was only one of several important dailies.

8 Sometimes such allegiances could carry connotations with wider significance. Thus 'Hellenism' was at times a codeword for homosexuality.

9 This is a point demonstrated, for example, by Richard Jenkyns, *The Victorians and Ancient Greece* (Oxford: Basil Blackwell, 1980).

10 For Ezra Pound's admiration of Rossetti as a translator, see Venuti, *The Translator's Invisibility*, p. 192.

11 Some of Dowson's allusions and affinities with Roman poets are pointed out by Mark Longaker in his edition of Dowson's poems (*The Poems of Ernest Dowson*, Philadelphia: University of Pennsylvania Press, 1962).

12 For Stevens' treatment of Virgil, see Eleanor Cook, *Poetry, Word-Play, and Word-War in Wallace Stevens* (Princeton: Princeton University Press, 1988).

13 See Tom Paulin, *Thomas Hardy: The Poetry of Perception* (London: Macmillan 1986 (1975)), pp. 49–50.

14 For a discussion of Cather's use of the classics, see Hermione Lee, *Willa Cather: A Life Saved Up* (London: Virago, 1989), and Erik Ingvar Thurin, *The Humanization of Willa Cather: Classicism in an American Classic* (Lund: Lund University Press, 1990 [Lund Studies in English 81]).

15 'Milton ... is the worst possible food for a growing poet, save possibly Francis Thompson and Tasso', *Literary Essays of Ezra Pound*, ed. T. S. Eliot (London: Faber and Faber, 1954), p. 217.

16 Theodore Ziolkowski, *Virgil and the Moderns* (Princeton: Princeton University Press, 1993).

17 'The Cult of Virgil', *The Virginia Quarterly Review* 38 (1962), 13–47.

18 For an authoritative account of Virgil along these lines, see Michael C. J. Putnam, *The Poetry of the Aeneid* (Ithaca and London: Cornell University Press, 1988 (1965)).

19 The poem contains the line 'No more Latin, no more Greek' (Noel Stock, *The Life of Ezra Pound*, London: Routledge & Kegan Paul, 1970, p. 10).

20 *Ibid.*, p. 21.

21 *Ibid.*, p. 12.

22 *Ibid.*, p. 23.

23 See, in particular, 'Raphaelite Latin' (*Books News Monthly*, Sept 1906), 'To the Rapha-

elite Latinists' (*Book News Monthly*, Jan. 1908) and 'M. Antonius Flaminius and John Keats' (*Book News Monthly*, Feb. 1908), all now conveniently reprinted in *Ezra Pound's Poetry and Prose: Contributions to Periodicals*, edited by Lea Baechler, A. Walton Litz, and James Longenbach (New York: Garland, 1991), vol. I.

24 *The Oxford Companion to Classical Literature*, ed. M.C. Howatson (Oxford: Oxford University Press, 1989), *s.v.* 'Alexandrianism'.

25 The term was originally coined by Cicero who disparagingly referred to the poets in question as *hoi neoteroi* ('the young ones') and *novi poetae*. Given the resources of Latin, the phrases come very close to 'modernists'.

26 *Oxford Companion to Classical Literature, s.v.* 'neoterics'.

27 Hutchinson, *Hellenistic Poetry*, p. 283.

28 For a discussion of these aspects of Callimachus' work and its repercussions in Roman poetry, see Hutchinson, *Hellenistic Poetry*, chs. 2 and 6.

29 See further below.

30 For an analysis of the poem, see C. M. Bowra, *Greek Lyric Poetry: From Alcman to Simonides* (Oxford: Clarendon Press, 1961), pp. 260–63.

31 As pointed out by Hugh Kenner, *The Pound Era* (Berkeley and Los Angeles: University of California Press, 1971), pp. 61–2.

32 The correspondence between Hardy and Pound was first discussed by Patricia Hutchins, 'Ezra Pound and Thomas Hardy', *The Southern Review* 4.1 (1968), 90–104. See also Donald Davie, *Ezra Pound* (New York: The Viking Press, 1975), pp. 46ff.

33 Michael North, in his otherwise very illuminating essay on 'Old Possum and Breer Rabbit: Pound's and Eliot's Racial Masquerade' (in *The Dialect of Modernism: Race, Language, and Twentieth-Century Literature*, New York: Oxford University Press, 1998), mistakenly explains Pound's comment that 'homage' is not an English word at all as due to his 'tenuous linguistic position, even in the years of his greatest success' (p. 79).

34 *The New Grove Dictionary of Music and Musicians*, ed. Stanley Sadie (London: Macmillan, 1980), *s.v.* 'tombeau'.

35 *Letters*, p. 246.

36 *Letters*, p. 310.

37 Robert Langbaum, *The Poetry of Experience: The Dramatic Monologue in Modern Literary Tradition* (Harmondsworth: Penguin, 1974 (1957)), p. 89.

38 Pound's engagement with the Propertian text was first discussed in detail by J. P. Sullivan, *Ezra Pound and Sextus Propertius: A Study in Creative Translation* (London: Faber and Faber, 1965). For a recent discussion of the structure of the 'Homage', see Davidson, *Ezra Pound and Roman Poetry*, pp. 83–115.

39 For a discussion of the 'Homage' from a Bakhtinian perspective, see Stan Smith, 'The Poetry of a Democratic Aristocracy: *Homage to Sextus Propertius*', in *The Origins of Modernism: Eliot, Pound, Yeats, and the Rhetoric of Renewal* (New York: Harvester Wheatsheaf, 1984), pp. 59–74.

40 The most famous instance is 'I loathe all common things' (*Epigram* 28 (II), l. 4) but it should be added that the statement is made in a context of erotic rivalry; the speaker's lover has been found out to be unfaithful.

41 'You advertise "New Hellenism". It's all right if you mean humanism, Pico's *De Dignitate*, the *Odyssey*, the Moscophoros. Not so good if you mean Alexandria, and worse if you mean the Munich-sham-Greek "Hellas" with a good swabian brogue' (Letter to Margaret C. Anderson, January [?] 1917), *Letters*, p. 61.

42 See n. 7.

43 'The vision that informed his conversation, a disbelief in racial purity and high valu-

ing of 'bastardy' in civilization, fitted perfectly with Forster's own mood of the time' (P. N. Furbank, *E. M. Forster: A Life*, New York: Harcourt Brace Jovanovich, 1978, vol. II, p. 33).

44 H. D.'s phrase occurs in *Paint It Today*, ed. Cassandra Laity (New York: New York University Press, 1992), p. 70. For a general discussion of H. D. and Meleager, see Rachel Blau Duplessis, *H. D.: The Career of That Struggle* (Brighton: The Harvester Press, 1986), pp. 20–23, and Gregory, *H. D. and Hellenism*, pp. 50–1.

45 Like (and perhaps to an even higher degree than) Pound, H. D. consistently looks back to translations made by the previous generations, Swinburne, Rossetti, and others.

46 Incidentally, Mackail's anthology was important not only to H. D. and Pound. Wallace Stevens made a thorough study of it in his youth (Joan Richardson, *Wallace Stevens: The Early Years, 1879–1923*, New York: William Morrow, 1986, p. 269) and returned to it in 'Effects of Analogy' (*Collected Poetry and Prose*, ed. Frank Kermode and Joan Richardson, The Library of America, 1997, p. 712).

47 The similarity between Zonas's poem and 'Orchard' was pointed out by Joan Retallack, 'H. D., H. D.', *Parnassus* 12.2–13.1 (1985), 70–71.

48 The parallels between Anyte's and H. D.'s poems were first pointed out by Thomas Burnett Swann, *The Classical World of H.D.* (Lincoln: University of Nebraska Press, 1962), p. 85n. Robert Babcock, 'Verses, Translations, and Reflections from "The Anthology": H. D., Ezra Pound, and the Greek Anthology', *Sagetrieb* 14 (Spring–Fall 1995), 205–6, draws attention to an anonymous epigram (*AP*, x.12), which bears the title 'Hermes of the Ways' in Mackail's edition. The title (which translates the phrase 'Hermeîen einódion' found in line 8 of the original) has no doubt been lifted from the Greek, but almost none of the significant details of the poem are echoed in H. D.'s poem.

49 Gregory, *H. D. and Hellenism*, p. 168.

50 Cf., for example, Eliot's comments on Gilbert Murray's and H. D.'s translations of Euripides: 'The choruses from Euripides by H. D. are, allowing for errors and even occasional omissions of difficult passages, much nearer to both Greek and English than Mr. Murray's. But H. D. and the other poets of the 'Poets' Translation Series' have so far done no more than pick up some of the more romantic crumbs of Greek literature; none of them has yet shown himself competent to attack the *Agamemnon*'; 'Euripides and Professor Murray', *The Sacred Wood: Essays on Poetry and Criticism* (London: Methuen, 1960), p. 77. Eliot seems to have attempted to translate *Agamemnon* during the crucial period when he and Pound were exchanging views on the manuscript of what was to become *The Waste Land* (*The Letters of T. S. Eliot. Volume I: 1898–1922*, ed. Valerie Eliot, New York: Harcourt Brace Jovanovich, 1988, pp. 499, 504, 505, and 508). See also Ezra Pound, *Guide to Kulchur* (New York: New Directions, 1970), pp. 92–3.

51 'The Tradition' was first printed in *Poetry* III.3 (Dec. 1913) and later reprinted in *Literary Essays*, pp. 91–3. The quotation is found on p. 93.

52 Peter Jay and Caroline Lewis (eds), *Sappho through English Poetry* (London: Anvil Press, 1996), p. 24.

53 *H. D. & Sapphic Modernism 1910–1950* (Cambridge: Cambridge University Press, 1999).

54 *The Light in Troy: Imitation and Discovery in Renaissance Poetry* (New Haven and London: Yale University Press, 1982).

8

D. H. Lawrence and the Meaning of Modernism

Michael Bell

'Modernism', like many literary-historical terms, should always carry a health warning for elementary misuses of which the most common is reification. As has been especially evident with 'romanticism' in recent decades, the designations of literary movements are to a large extent retrospective creations. Countless articles on romantic topics have begun by making this point, often in a tone of scandal at its then assumed illegitimacy. But such terms, even if coined by the original artists or their contemporaries, will always be retrospective in so far as later usage endorses them. However they arise, they are now for us essentially heuristic devices indicating a way of grouping a set of phenomena *as* a set, and they should neither be identified with the phenomena, nor reified into a substitute for them. Recognizing this in principle is part of academic apprenticeship although, as with many elementary protocols, it requires constant vigilance to observe it in practice. We are all open to linguistic seduction.

The more serious problem perhaps for 'modernism' is its ambiguous status as descriptive or honorific. Just as 'Enlightenment' may present eighteenth-century texts in a new light, so modernism encourages not only the presumption of a common project, but a habit of regarding the authors in question as part of an elite club. The iconoclasm of its progenitors lives on and to be 'outside modernism' is to be presumptively second league.[1] For this reason, perhaps, revisionary views have often sought to demonstrate the modernist qualifications of apparent outsiders or of neglected writers, particularly women.[2]

The term 'modernist' has come to define some generic features of artistic preoccupation and expression in the early part of the twentieth century. This usage could be changed as with the now widely established use of 'early modern' to refer to developments from the fifteenth to the eighteenth centuries. Yet 'romanticism', for all the fuss, has survived and its recurrent questioning may perhaps be seen rather as a beneficial thought-experiment than as a literal project. It is a constant prophylactic against reification. One might emphasize the same point in relation to 'modernism' since its value lies largely in its uncertain boundaries and multiple epicentres, as is reflected in the plural title of Peter Nicholls' excellent survey of *Modernisms*.[3] The authors thought of as modernist had not only very varied, but mutually opposed, conceptions and practices.

In this respect, the fact that D. H. Lawrence is not usually placed in any of the modernist groupings makes him especially revealing as a test case, and his marginal status is worth unpacking into several aspects. Half in and half out of the circle, he usefully resists a self-fulfilling relation between texts and definitions. More importantly, the widespread sense that he is not merely marginal, but beyond the pale, is clearly evaluative as well as definitional. But if the canonical British and American modernists, such as Eliot, Joyce, Pound and Wyndham Lewis, were largely dismissive of him, this is where his true interest lies in relation to modernism.[4] He was not just accidentally outside it as doing something else, he was actively outside it as a significant opposition concerned with the same issues and questions. In short, Tony Pinkney is right to claim Lawrence as a 'meta-modernist' although, as I will go on to indicate, his reading partly misses Lawrence's internal rationale.[5] Pinkney argues that Lawrence developed an alternative, anti-classical, female, Northern 'Gothic' modernism invested in the architectural symbolism of *The Rainbow* which was then undermined, unconsciously, by the more familiar modernism of *Women in Love*. This claim depends on a working conception of 'modernism' and indicates its double value. For if Lawrence critiques modernism, he is also revealed in its light.

The modernists' rejection of Lawrence is a function of their perception, and this is particularly important because critical practice in the Anglophone academy has descended very largely from their principles and examples. Lawrence has probably had some underground impact on the practice of reading but, apart from his often-quoted injunction 'Never trust the artist. Trust the tale', he is not commonly regarded as one of the exemplary figures for defining the activity of criticism, or for our sense of what literature is.[6] As he became aware at an early stage, you would have to read differently to read him.[7] Notoriously, his work often seems, to the unsympathetic or uninitiated reader, precisely lacking in all the disciplined impersonality that the techniques of modernism sought to achieve. For although he meditated closely on questions of representation, he did not wear his technique on his sleeve and saw such self-consciousness as a symptomatic modern vice. A besetting danger of modernist technique was the reifying assumption that it had an instrumental value: that it could produce, as well as embody, the essential qualities and recognitions achieved in the work. It is revealing that two modern critics who made a heavy professional investment in such modernist-derived notions of technique as efficacy, Mark Schorer and Wayne Booth, both stumbled badly over Lawrence.[8] But if the characteristic mindset of modernism was often imperceptive in relation to Lawrence, it therefore provides a useful template against which to see how his language and narrative forms gradually evolved to suit the changing demands of his understanding of modernity. It becomes evident that he achieved modernist ends by his own, apparently contrary, means.

What follows is a brief account of the process by which Lawrence worked out his own form of modernism, and why it was resistant to the overt technical mastery that he associated with the imposition of will. The crucial instance here, of course, is Flaubert who was the acknowledged master of the major Anglophone modernists. The Flaubertian tradition effectively defines the modernism to which Lawrence was significantly opposed. [9] If Flaubert produced great art out of his quarrel with romanticism, Lawrence's struggle was internal to romanticism itself.

Lawrence was, in a sense, a modernist *malgré-lui*. Modernism happened to him rather than being actively sought. As Ford Madox Ford noted, the young Lawrence was deeply imbued with romantic and nineteenth-century literature and thought. [10] He had relived its major intellectual struggles, especially its negotiation between science and religion, as an urgent personal quest. [11] His 'modernism' arose gradually by its own internal logic from the matrix of modernity as he conceived it, and the process can be traced in his writing. To be more precise, *Women in Love* is perhaps his only truly modernist work, which might initially suggest a marginal relevance of the term in his case, except that *Women in Love* is also the centre of his novelistic *oeuvre*, and the fulcrum on which it turns. In the context of his other novels, *Women in Love* is the culmination of a combined development in historical vision, psychological insight, and literary technique.

After *Women in Love*, the novel form effectively dissolved under the contradictory pressures to which Lawrence subjected it. His novels of the twenties are mixtures of autobiography, travelogue, essayistic reflection, and Nietzschean thought experiment, in which he rode out his oppositional relation to the culture as a whole. He acknowledged, and thematized, the lack of assumed readerly consensus on which the novel ultimately depends. Rather than being modernist, his later fiction anticipates some of the mixed genres of the late twentieth century. Yet Lawrence never lost faith in the function of the novel and it was precisely in the nineteen-twenties that he produced his classic affirmative statements of the value of the form. [12] In praising the novel for its unique capacity to assess experience, he encompassed the form trans-historically and perhaps with primary reference to its nineteenth-century embodiments. He explicitly excluded the modernism of Joyce and Proust. [13] If Lawrence retained to the end his commitment to the novel conceived in traditional, pre-Joycean terms, then this lends a special significance to the transformations it underwent in his hands. He discovered, and raised to consciousness, the deeper logic of the form in his day precisely because he was not otherwise committed to changing it.

From the retrospect of *Women in Love* his earlier novels reveal themselves as stages in shedding the nineteenth century models of modernity by which he had been formed. In his first novel, *The White Peacock* (1911), although he drew consciously on George Eliot for his structure of the two couples, Lawrence had already left her predominantly ethical interest behind for a more naturalistic understanding of emotional states.[14] It communicates an immense sensitivity to natural and emotional conditions while refraining, at least overtly, from large claims to significance. In effect, the major Lawrencean themes are there, but with an uncertainty as to their true significance and mutual relations. The novel is Edwardian in its sensibility. Edwardian poetry, as enshrined in the famous anthologies to which Lawrence contributed, was conceived of as modern in its day; yet it has since come to seem innocently unaware of modernity because it was almost immediately overrun by, in a double sense, the 'men of 1914': the modernist generation and the impact of the Great War.[15] The novel depicts the emotional timidity of its narrating character, Cyril Beardsall, and the degeneration of his friend, George Saxton, with a mixture of diagnostic observation and over-riding Hardyesque emotional fatalism, much of which finds its rationale in a misogyny not entirely attributable to the male characters. The white peacock of the title, though a minor thread in the narrative, stands near its emotional centre. Above all, there is, along with the sensitivity to the natural environment, a sense of entrapment in both the natural and social worlds. It may be that the recurrent preoccupation of the narrator with the violence of nature is itself a projection of an emotional frustration which pervades the book. Although still only symptomatic rather than dramatically expressive, this indicates a potential growing point. Like much of Hardy's fiction, the novel partly acquiesces in the emotional impasse it dramatizes, but the first-person narrative brings this acquiescence closer to being acknowledged as the locus of the problem.

The uncertainty of *The White Peacock* is partly located in the weakness of its male characters, and some reviewers of Lawrence's earliest publications assumed their author to be female.[16] The question of gender is of obvious thematic significance for Lawrence, but for his relation to modernism its importance is not just thematic or ideological: it lies most crucially in the gender of the writing itself. Several of his novels involved collaboration with a woman, and *The Trespasser* (1912) is his version of a novel by his school-teacher friend, Helen Corke. Her subsequently published version makes clear that the failure of the central relationship between the younger woman, Helena, and her married music teacher, Siegmund, arises from Helena's lesbian nature.[17] Lawrence made it a study in damaging emotional idealism. This is still partly laid at the door of the heroine's inability to respond with physical passion, but it is also the condition of her music teacher and lover, Siegmund. Although the narrative, once again, acquiesces in male pathos, it suggests, in Siegmund's eventual suicide, the self-destructive turn of his emotional frustration. More importantly, the music theme develops a Wagnerian parallel which incipiently generalizes the action into an internal critique of romantic love. By recognizing this massive historical formation, Lawrence gained a more impersonal insight into his own struggle to overcome his personal tendency to emotional idealization, and the associated danger of being emotionally dominated by a woman. Once again, the novel hovers on a knife-edge between expressing and diagnosing its emotional fatalism but has begun to question romantic love at a more impersonal, mythic, level.

In his next novel, *Sons and Lovers* (1913), he effectively 'shed' his own 'sicknesses' although the text suggests an almost Pyrrhic cost personally and artistically.[18] If he managed to 'kill' the mother-figure, Mrs Morel, some such violence was required and he was not able to present her in quite the impersonal spirit he showed in his play *The Daughter-in-Law* (1912). In the play, the now married son is still dominated by the mother, and the necessary struggle, and consequent reconciliation, come from the daughter-in-law, Minnie. In the novel, by contrast, the potential daughters-in-law are not allowed to challenge the mother and the principal contender, Miriam Leivers, is partly blamed for Paul Morel's inability to free himself emotionally for another woman. A certain narrative predisposition in this regard may reflect the fact that in the last reworkings of the book, Lawrence was consulting the responses of Frieda rather than Jessie Chambers, the 'original' of Miriam. Nonetheless, the strength of the novel is precisely that Lawrence, as so often, is fighting the situation, achieving his insights, from the inside. The pervasive tendency to emotional identification with Paul impairs the novel's impersonality yet is a condition of its achievement. At the same time, there are episodes such as the pregnant Mrs Morel's recovery in the garden after being driven out by her husband, or Paul's love-making with Clara Dawes in a field, which anticipate the mature Lawrence.[19] Here he renders with complete artistic objectivity emotional experiences which take on an impersonal dimension for the characters themselves. These episodes, while integral to the narrative at the level of the action, are also isolated premonitions of the mature 'metaphysic' of impersonal feeling that Lawrence was to soon to develop.[20] At the same time, the temptation to emotional despair in the novel indicates the crucible from which Lawrence's intuition of the impersonal arose. He was no less aware than T. S. Eliot of the crises in which one might wish to 'escape' personal emotion.[21]

That his metaphysic, and its means of representation, were developing in a partly groping fashion is strikingly exemplified in the way his next novels came into being. In 1913, he began with some ambition the work that was to become *The Lost Girl* (1920). Since he was separated from the manuscript by the war, and rewrote it radically for later publication, we cannot know how he might have completed it at the time. But it is evident that it took some of its impulse from a desire to critique the mode of realism associated with Arnold Bennett, as well as the emotional resignation that seemed to be integral to that mode. In the published version the heroine, Alvina Houghton, leaves the Midlands, recognizably the world of the potteries, for a peasant existence in the Abruzzi with Ciccio, an Italian she has met through a Red Indian show performed in the town. Likewise, the novel itself transcends the realism of Bennett and anticipates Lawrence's later interest, partly literal and partly through psychological fables, in alternative or 'primitive' cultures. Meanwhile, Lawrence interrupted work on this novel, in March 1913, for a 'pot-boiler' which gradually developed into his principal novelistic project: the work variously called 'The Sisters' and 'The Wedding Ring' before becoming the two novels *The Rainbow* (1915) and *Women in Love* (1920). These major works, with their increasingly modernist core, seem almost to have waylaid him, as did the 'nightmare' of the Great War.

The initial desire to tell the story of his modern heroine, Ella (later Ursula Brangwen), led Lawrence to see a need to sketch her background. After several rewritings, this eventually developed into a full-scale novel, *The Rainbow*, which narrates three generations of the Brangwen family through the nineteenth century. If Lawrence had spent his career to date slowly fighting his way through the major formations of nineteenth-century culture without a sense of where it was leading, this novel enabled him to recapitulate that experience consciously from the standpoint of modernity. In effect, this was an implicit reflection on the modernist theme of tradition as it affected him. Indeed, although we read the novel in a conventional historical present moving into an unknown future, the retrospective impulse from which it arose lends it a metaphysical significance beyond the moment-by-moment narrative. Lawrence had by now read contemporary anthropological works and had come to resolve the classic nineteenth-century conflict of religion and science by seeing them not as a choice of beliefs but as incommensurable world-views and psychological formations meeting in the form of myth. His novel, therefore, took on a temporal purview way beyond its apparent historical range over three generations. Starting with an indeterminate historical location in 'Marsh' Farm, and placing the whole action within the model, structurally as well as rhetorically, of Genesis, he runs together two opposed myths of origin, the biblical and the 'Darwinian,' to form the internal dynamic of the family's generational evolution. If the Bible gives a myth of the fall and loss of Eden, evolution suggests progress. Lawrence transmutes these into two fundamental psychic motives: on the one hand a need to stay rooted in a spot, and within a communal tradition, and on the other a need to develop into separate individuality. This is the mythic centre of the novel: not the nostalgia for an illusory pre-modern existence which some readers have seen in it. Thomas Mann's description of his own modern version of the Genesis narrative, *Joseph and His Brothers*, applies equally to *The Rainbow*: it tells of 'the birth of the ego out of the mythical collective.'[22] Perhaps accepting a contemporary belief that ontogeny rehearses phyllogeny, Lawrence sees the longer evolutionary past, as well as the more immediate family past, as active in the individual characters. His three generations, therefore, rehearse those massive phases of human cultural development proposed by various nineteenth-century and modern thinkers: the mythic, the religious, and the scientific world-views.

Lawrence, then, presented individual character as part of a much larger evolutionary process, and his last reworking of *The Rainbow* was affected by his rereading of Hardy, as reflected in the 'Study of Thomas Hardy'. If Hardy, like Schopenhauer, saw the human individual as caught in a vast inhuman process, the Schopenhaurian Will, Lawrence performed the same reversal as Nietzsche in assimilating that impersonal process into the self. Nietzsche's early turn on Schopenhauer in *The Birth of Tragedy* was, if not foundational, then premonitory, of the modernist generation. In a formula, Schopenhauer's privileging of the aesthetic stands to nineteenth-century aestheticism and symbolism as Nietzsche stands to modernism. Both Nietzsche and the modernists continued to privilege the aesthetic but not in a separatist spirit: it became the model for life rather than an escape from it. Lawrence was less concerned than Joyce and Yeats with the Nietzschean metaphysics of art, but he shared their interest in the psychological problematics of human wholeness as manifest in the realms of love and power. The aesthetic, and a related conception of myth, were crucial categories in *The Birth of Tradgedy* because Nietzsche's process of the Apollonian gradually suppressing the Dionysian was otherwise on a course of decadence. By contrast, Lawrence's dual and still active mythopoeia in *The Rainbow* is open-ended if not optimistic.

Lawrence's narrative over-voice in *The Rainbow* recreates the world as seen through this nineteenth-century metaphysic. It is written from the standpoint of the internalized Will. Its obscurity and strangeness are of the essence, and the novel is more truly Wagnerian than *The Trespasser*. If it is not completely successful, it is remarkable in what it achieves. The idealist and rationalist world-views, to which it is most opposed, have to be dramatically and diagnostically encompassed in this rhetoric without being merely traduced. The Cathedral episode particularly exemplifies how Lawrence uses this over-voice and its mythopoeic compression of time scales to represent the condition of an individual. Lawrence catches in the idealistic, significantly named, Will, of the second Brangwen generation, a nineteenth-century, Ruskin-influenced psy-

chological formation. Will's mixture of sexual, aesthetic, and religious subli-
mation is period-specific and yet, in so far as crucial scenes are set in an actual
medieval cathedral, we can also understand this period formation as itself a
later working out of a more ancient, long-term idealizing shift from mythic
holism to religious dualism. Tony Pinkney has argued that Lawrence creates in
the Ruskinism of *The Rainbow* an alternative, Northern, gothic modernism.[23]
Although he is right to see Lawrence jostling canonical modernism with an
opposed conception, I believe the whole Gothic ambience is itself placed as
part of the process by which we arrive at the fully modern predicament of
Women in Love. Where Pinkney sees the modernism of *Women in Love* closing
in on Lawrence, I believe Lawrence shows the modernist spirit closing in on
the culture. Will's internal struggle is indeed on the brink of modernity yet
swerving from it for an atavistic return.

Lawrence's creation of a viewpoint beyond that of the characters has implications for his authorial relation to them. *The Rainbow* is the first major work
written out of his new relation to Frieda. Life with Frieda was hardly peaceful,
and the novel embodies the outcome of their struggles with each other. Will
Brangwen rehearses something of Lawrence's own early idealism, and our
awareness of its inauthenticity is partly focused by his wife's angry, Frieda-like
reaction to his aesthetic, religiose, sexually-sublimating ecstasy. Lawrence was
highly conscious of the seismic shift occurring during the rewritings, and
when he spoke of the novel as being 'the work of both of us' he was far from
intending authorial collaboration.[24] He was referring to something more fundamental: the shift within his own consciousness which had enabled the writing. Once again, this places Lawrence in a critical relation to other modernists. As Lisa Appignanesi has pointed out, several male authors of this generation espoused a creative merging of the genders.[25] Leopold Bloom is valued
for being a womanly man. Yet Joyce's own writing, like Pound's, or Lewis's,
has been found by many readers to be highly masculinist. Although Lawrence's insecurities led to notorious moments of reactive misogyny, homo-
phobia and male assertion, these are in large part the epi-phenomenal outcome of his internal braving of this realm. They are symptoms of how much
he accepted the female in himself. Once again, he illuminates a modernist
theme from an opposite angle.

I have suggested that, following pre-eminently in the wake of Nietzsche,
Lawrence achieved the multi-layered continuity of psychic life in *The Rainbow* through his encompassing conception of myth. Even science, without
ceasing to be science, is caught in its mythic aspect as an order of human
significance. The point may be expanded to encompass Lawrence's relation to
the novel form itself: *The Rainbow* is not just a novel containing myth, it is a
novel mythopoeically conceived. Over and above its central use of a Biblical

structure and rhetoric, the social-historical narrative itself takes on the quality of myth as a culturally-specific world-form. For the novel adopts the model of a generational saga as the appropriate embodiment of its evolving subject and in doing so it implicitly acknowledges its own historical specificity; that it is no longer simply the 'natural' form to use. Where Joyce might have overtly parodied the earlier form, Lawrence rather invests it with a significance at once richer and more relative. Once again, it is unlikely that he consciously excogitated the formal question in quite this way. It is rather that the internal logic of the material led him to find the appropriate form, and he uses the world-view of nineteenth-century historical narrative as if with an implicit recognition of its historical relativity. *The Rainbow* is a literary, as well as an historical, farewell to the nineteenth century.

In view of this, it is not surprising that *Women in Love* develops a fully modernist form to deal with the contemporary generation, yet even this proved to be a gradual process of discovery internal to the composition. The earlier version of the novel that Lawrence sought to publish in 1916 remains significantly closer to a conventionally sequential narrative. The substance of the story is essentially the same in the published version of 1920, albeit with much local modifying and sharpening, and with a less bitter impact overall. But the later version makes a crucial change in presentation. The 1916 version has a series of numbered chapters, some of which incorporate several episodes that occur as separate chapters in the final text. It therefore invites being read as a continuous, progressive narrative, whereas the final version is a series of iconically titled episodes which function less as a sequential progress than as a series of depth explorations. The major characters have all already absorbed their significant life experiences. In their various ways they have reached, or reach in the book, a point of crisis. What unfolds, therefore, is more a matter of discovering the inner logic of what they now are; a shift that also manifests itself as a dissolving of the rhetoric of love into the exercise of power. The many acts of violence in the novel prove for the most part to be not liberational so much as 'Gladiatorial'.[26]

In so far as the difference between these two novels was to be increased by the impact on Lawrence of the Great War, Thomas Mann's *The Magic Mountain* provides an illuminating parallel to *Women in Love*. Conceived before the war as a comedic counterpart to *Death in Venice* (1912), *The Magic Mountain* eventually incorporated the war into its compendious critique of modern culture. Just as significantly for the present theme, Mann consciously understood his narrative as spatialized: it 'seeks to abrogate time itself by the technical device that attempts to give complete presentness at any given moment to the entire world of ideas that it comprises. It tries, in other words, to establish a magical *nunc stans*...'[27] The comment could apply to *Ulysses* and *Four Quartets*. Although Lawrence made no such explicit comment on this aspect of his form, and his informing spirit was different, the dominant symbolic structure changes from the historical and evolutionary implications of *The Rainbow* to a spatial, geographic mapping. Myth may be thought of in the abstract as timeless or trans-historical but the mythopoeic imagination is more varied. The mythic order of *The Rainbow* is dynamic, evolutionary and full of promise, whereas the cultural and psychic geography of *Women in Love*'s 'barren tragedy' (*Women in Love*, 476), its psychic map from Nordic to African, represents a fixed order within which most of the characters have little room for manoeuvre. Joseph Frank's cardinal observation that modernist literature typically found spatial form is strikingly exemplified, and even thematized, in the shift from *The Rainbow* to *Women in Love*.[28] If spatialized form as myth enables what Nietzsche called the superhistorical standpoint, that itself is open to varying use.[29] Whereas *Ulysses* has something of the transcendence of Nietzsche's account, *Women in Love* has a sense of entrapment. But the common element lies in their invoking of trans-historical values against which history itself is to be judged. Both works are packed with history but refuse to be bound by it.

It should also be noted that for all the abundance of mythic allusion in *Women in Love*, its symbolic structure of Nordic to African suggests anthropological awareness rather than mythic identification, a difference which reflects the shift from mythic participation to modern knowledge. Heidegger saw the rise of anthropology, and its underlying logic of relativism, as a quintessentially modern turn.[30] As myth becomes an object of knowledge, becomes aware of itself as myth, it ceases to be participatory and becomes instead part of the modern predicament rather than a solution of it, or an alternative resource. When assessing more generally the modernists' use of myth as literary structure, therefore, it is necessary to discriminate degrees of self-consciousness and inwardness with respect to myth. Lawrence constantly sought to recover the active power of mythopoeic sensibility within modernity. That is why his mythopoeia does not typically require allusion to pre-existing mythic figures or motifs: it is essentially a mode of being. The function of overtly mythic allusion may be to focus this rather than create it. Whatever else it may also be, therefore, Lawrence's mythopoeia is always in the first instance a character's creation of the world, or what Heidegger might call a specific mode of being-in-the-world. *Women in Love* enforces the relativity of worlds, a theme given its classic modernist expression in the perspectivism of *Ulysses* created under the sign of myth. But whereas this has the aspect in Joyce of a general cultural recognition, in Lawrence the characters' worlds are specifically functions of their own beings. The unwittingly 'murderous' Gerald is eventually destroyed by a murderous world of his own creation. In this regard, Lawrence differs from those other modernists who use myth essentially externally as a self-consciously structuring device, and often over the heads of the characters, as in *The Waste Land*. Eliot's reference to the 'mythic method' in relation to *Ulysses*, and perhaps to his own poem, suggests the difference: Lawrence, with his participatory holism, would not think of myth as a *method*; it is the inescapable mode of being for mythopoeic creatures.[31]

What has been said so far may suggest how Lawrence conceived the inter-related themes of identity and impersonality which were a major preoccupation of modernist writers. It was while working on the early version of *The Rainbow* and *Women in Love* that he explained to Edward Garnett his need to discard the 'old stable ego' of nineteenth-century characterization.[32] In so far as his narrative was concerned with the creation of the individual, it had to have a purview beyond that of the ego itself. He also believed, as he later put it in *Lady Chatterley's Lover* (1928), that 'it is the way our sympathies flow and recoil that chiefly determines our lives.'[32] To honour this in narrative representation likewise required a way of registering movements of feeling below the level of immediate consciousness, or elusive of external causality. This is different from Woolf's 'halo of consciousness' which at least suggests an arena of awareness.[34] Lawrence's ambition to catch experience at this level entailed the creatively risky paradox of putting the subconscious into words. His way of doing so had his characteristic mixture of boldness, brilliance, sophistication, and naivety. Like other modernists, he largely elided the distinction between narrative voice and the consciousness of the character but with an opposite effect to Flaubertian/Joycean irony. The character's consciousness is ambiguously absorbed into a larger emotional process while the process nonetheless exists only inside the character. *The Rainbow* risks an over-voice of insistent, straining, circling, repetitious, heavily rhythmic prose expressing the moments of, often obscure, intensity and crisis which are its principal concern.

Lawrence's later remarks, in a review of Verga, on the 'emotional mind' indicate something of what he is after:

> ...when we are thinking emotionally or passionately, thinking and feeling at the same time, we do not think rationally ... the mind makes curious swoops and circles. It touches the point of pain or interest, then sweeps away again in a cycle, coils round and approaches again ... there is a curious spiral rhythm, and the mind approaches again and again the point of concern, repeats itself, goes back, destroys the time-sequence entirely, so that time ceases to exist, as the mind stoops to the quarry, then leaves it without striking, soars, hovers, turns, swoops, stops again, still does not strike, yet is nearer, nearer, reels away again, wheels off into the air, even forgets, quite forgets, yet again turns, bends, circles slowly, swoops and stoops again, until at last there is the closing-in, and the clutch of a decision or a resolve.[35]

Typically, even as Lawrence describes the process of emotional thought he is drawn into a stylistic enactment of its circling indirections, and it is evident how closely his creative endeavour is invested in the life of the character. His characters typically provide the imaginary arena for his own process of emotional discovery. These remarks also explain the elasticity and compression of time in *The Rainbow*.

Whether or not Lawrence, in his fiction, succeeds in expressing processes taking place on the fringes of consciousness as this passage implies, much hinges on recognizing that the animating spirit of his narrative is a dramatic enactment as opposed to the authorial rhetoric it has frequently been taken to be. As with Will Brangwen in the Cathedral, the narrative prose would at times be pseudo-mystical rant if it were coming simply from the author rather than from the inner life of a character for whom this rhetoric is symptomatic. It enacts perverse, confused, inauthentic feeling which is at the same time neither insincere for the character nor overtly ironized by the narrative. In *Women in Love* the language is typically different in that the characters tend to be highly articulate and self-conscious to the extent of conducting much of the novel's heuristic process in their own conversations. But in being more articulate they are even less in touch with themselves, and the impersonal process of the novel tends to be a plumbing of the self rather than a progression. And reflecting their self-alienation, the subconscious states of the characters are typically registered for us as they are unwittingly projected on to their world. Most strikingly, the novel's many water scenes gradually give way to the frozen environment of the Tyrol which proves to be Gerald's self-created destination.

Two related aspects emerge from the risky 'subjectivity' of Lawrence's narrative methods. By the time he was working on *The Rainbow*, he had developed his own 'metaphysic' of impersonal feeling. The early Brangwens had less individually developed egos and their emotions more readily took on, in moments of crisis and intensity, a felt connection to something beyond themselves. This was not just a response to something external, but a quality of their own feeling. Lydia looks at Tom after the birth of their first child with an 'impersonal' look, 'female to male'; a look which gives him a 'great scalding peace.'[36] If in such scenes Lawrence is able to communicate convincingly the impersonal dimension of the characters' feeling, then the corollary is his own artistic impersonality in representing it. This points to the most crucial, and critical, aspect of his relation to modernism.

Artistic impersonality was a central theme of the canonical modernists: most notably in Joyce's thematizing of it in *A Portrait* and *Ulysses*, and Eliot's 'impersonal theory' of poetry in 'Tradition and the Individual Talent'.[37] Despite their mutual differences, the modernists shared a settled hostility to sentimentality which was central to their literary and cultural programme. For them, it was a major modern scourge for which literature was at once the symptom and the antidote. Sentimentalism was a personal, social, and artistic vice which they associated with their immediate nineteenth-century inheritance and with the whole romantic tradition. In the grip of this justified hostility, however, they tended to distrust the whole realm of feeling, as in Eliot's remark on wishing to 'escape' the feelings. Lawrence shared this general critique of sentiment. In his essay 'The Crown', which is a discursive companion to *Women in Love* as 'Study of Thomas Hardy' is to *The Rainbow*, he says: 'Sentimentality is the garment of our vice. It covers viciousness as inevitably as greenness covers a bog.'[38] But his way of conceiving the question was opposite to that of the other modernists. He worked critically from inside the romantic heritage and its reworkings in Victorian fiction. For him, feeling was fundamental and of the essence. There is no alternative standpoint outside of feeling, a pure and disinterested idea, from which to contain or judge it. In some sense feeling has to be trusted, and in the face of all the internal and external seductions to falsity of feeling, the important capacity is to find its truth.

Identifiable moments of emotional truth may be rare, and only obliquely known. Tom's 'scalding peace' after the birth is a characteristic Lawrencean oxymoron. If this experience feels like an obliteration of the self, that is exactly what it is, momentarily. In some sense, true feeling, in so far as it takes on an impersonal dimension, has of necessity a noumenal elusiveness. It cannot be known directly by the conscious ego. Meanwhile what the personal consciousness experiences is almost inevitably falsified. Without this capacity to transcend, in feeling, the viewpoint of the personal ego, '...emotion turns into sentiment, and sentimentalism takes the place of feeling. The ego has no feeling, it has only sentiments. And the myriad egos sway in tides of sentimentalism.'[39] The collectivity of modern sentiment here, which Lawrence's generation experienced powerfully in the war years, is a grotesque, chiasmic counterpart to the impersonality of what Thomas Mann called the 'mythical collective' preceding the birth of the ego. It is not surprising, therefore, that *The Rainbow* and *Women in Love* are made up almost entirely of false feeling as characters struggle, or not, to overcome its temptations. In *The Rainbow*, the over-voice of the narrative tends to carry the noumenal, or unarticulated, dimension of the characters' life of feeling. In *Women in Love*, by contrast, the characters' own articulacy typically brings them, and the reader, face to face with the problem of experiencing true feeling in consciousness. Birkin hates his own articulacy, his 'telling way of putting things' (*Women in Love*, 189), because he sees its capacity for falsification and avoidance. This is why he is used seriously by Lawrence as the thematic mouthpiece, and heuristic growing point, of the novel while being constantly exposed to ridicule, largely from a female viewpoint. Likewise, his initial attempt to propose to Ursula has a farcical unreality even as he hangs on to the idea of marriage as an expression of the impersonal conjunction he seeks to form with her. In *The Rainbow* marriage genuinely expressed a supra-personal union for which modern personality, as indicated in the opening conversation of the Brangwen sisters, has lost not just the capacity but the conception. The very 'word' love has become unusable for Birkin, and his image of star 'equilibrium' (*Women in Love*, 148–52) is an abstract attempt to express an equivalent emotional conjunction beyond the ego, a felt givenness rather than a personal commitment, something for which there is no working model in the contemporary culture.

For Lawrence, then, impersonality was first and foremost an emotional quality, and one difficult to achieve for the modern individual, whether artist or not. At least since Schiller's essay *On Naïve and Sentimental Poetry* (1795), European thinkers had defined their own problematic modernity by invoking the impersonal, pre-sentimental quality of an earlier culture often seen to be instantiated in ancient Greek poetry. Lawrence is part of this larger discussion, as was Joyce in his invocation of Homer in *Ulysses*. Both resisted the judgement that it was impossible for the modern self to escape this damaging form of self-consciousness. Joyce expressed this using the artistic standpoint, and the example of his impersonalizing techniques, to create inferentially the value of Leopold Bloom's transcendence of ego. He creates a Homeric lens through which to represent Bloom and to define his significance. Lawrence works in reverse. By pursuing the falsities of feeling in the individual characters, and invoking the impersonal processes of feeling in which they are caught, he effectively creates the artistic standpoint of impersonality, as it were, from the inside. For the artist, too, is on test emotionally. As Lawrence remarked *a propos* Giovanni Verga, an artist who has the capacity for such impersonality will not require a special technique, and the imposition of it will only damage the representation with the wrong kind of self-consciousness. [40] If on the other hand the artist lacks the emotional capacity, imposed technique will only expose the condition. From this point of view, the self-conscious investment in technique that is a hallmark of modernism takes on a symptomatic value. Lawrence was unfair to Joyce and Proust whose massive achievements were won through the very processes of artistic self-consciousness in a way that he did not conceive. Yet his capacity as a literary critic lies largely in his incisive emotional judgement, and his response to his modernist contemporaries, while not the last word, and formed before their careers were complete, is still relevant to an overall assessment of them.

In conclusion, the very division of *The Rainbow* and *Women in Love* into two separate novels sits on the cusp of Lawrence's marginal relation, whether parallel or oppositional, to modernism. Written from the retrospect of modernity, *The Rainbow* presents a Tolstoyan sense of the self in history in an internalized version of the Tolstoyan novel. By placing the narrative under the epic sign of the rainbow, Lawrence approaches a modernist method of invoking the archaic past in relation to the present, yet this mythopoeic conception serves a dynamic psychological process of internal evolution. Only in *Women in Love* does a fully modernist, spatialized narrative emerge expressing the felt impasse of the culture. These metaphysical dimensions of Lawrence's fiction have often been overlooked as readers have responded to the narrative foreground of personal relations, social history, or sexual politics. These latter aspects are important, of course, but their meaning is crucially governed by the epochal formations that link them to modernism. His work loses part of its point without its oppositional objects and, by the same token, high modernism represents sophisticated and challenging versions of what he opposed. It is necessary to an assessment of him just as he is part of the meaning of modernism. As creative writers, he and Joyce did not need each other, but we need both to read either.

Notes

1 For a view of writers outside the modernist grouping see *Outside Modernism*, ed. Lynne Hapgood and Nancy L. Paxton (London: Macmillan, 2000). The volume questions not the category of modernism but its tendency to limit understanding of the period. See also Maria DiBattista and Lucy McDiarmid (eds), *High and Low Moderns: Literature and Culture, 1889–1939* (New York and Oxford: Oxford University Press, 1996).

2 For an examination of gender within modernism see *The Gender of Modernism* ed. Bonnie Kime Scott (Bloomington: Indiana University Press, 1990). For a female counter-tradition see Suzanne Clark, *Sentimental Modernism: Women Writers and the Revolution of the Word* (Bloomington: Indiana University Press, 1995). [See also pp. 260f. below on women and modernism. *Ed.*]

3 Peter Nicholls, *Modernisms: A Literary Guide* (London: Macmillan, 1995).

4 T. S. Eliot's best known criticism of Lawrence was in *After Strange Gods* (London: Faber, 1934); for Joyce's view that Lawrence wrote 'very badly' see Richard Ellmann, *James Joyce* (New York and London: Oxford University Press, 1959), p. 628; a critique of Lawrence's primitivism appears in Wyndham Lewis's *Paleface: the Philosophy of the 'Melting Pot'* (London: Chatto and Windus, 1929). Of the major modernists, only Pound acknowledged Lawrence's ability although he privately disliked him and was bored by his writing: *The Letters of Ezra Pound* ed. D. D. Paige (New York: Harcourt, Brace and World, 1950), pp. 17, 34, 301.

5 Tony Pinkney, *D. H. Lawrence* (London: Harvester, 1990), p. 168.

6 *Studies in Classic American Literature* (London: Heinemann, 1924), p. 2.

7 Letter to Edward Garnett, 5 June 1914. *The Letters of D. H. Lawrence* vol. 2, ed. George Zytaruk and James T. Boulton (Cambridge: Cambridge University Press, 1981), p. 182.

8 Mark Schorer missed the narrative control of *Sons and Lovers* in 'Technique as Discovery', *Hudson Review* 1, i (Spring, 1948), although he developed an appreciation of the novel, and Lawrence generally, by the early 1950s. Wayne Booth acknowledged his earlier impercipience concerning Lawrence but without gaining a significant insight into its causes. See *The Company We Keep: An Ethics of Fiction* (Berkeley: University of California Press, 1988), p. 286.

9 'Review of *Cavalleria Rusticana* by Giovanni Verga', *Phoenix: The Posthumous Papers of D. H. Lawrence* ed. Edward D. Macdonald (London: Heinemann, 1936), pp. 240–50 (247–8).

10 See John Worthen, *D. H. Lawrence: The Early Years 1885–1912* (Cambridge: Cambridge University Press, 1991), pp. 121–2.

11 See especially Lawrence's correspondence on religious belief with the Rev. Robert Reid in Worthen, *op. cit.*, pp. 174–83, and *The Letters of D. H. Lawrence* vol. 1, ed. James T. Boulton (Cambridge: Cambridge University Press, 1979).

12 See 'Morality and the Novel', 'Why the Novel Matters' and 'The Novel and the Feelings' in *Study of Thomas Hardy and Other Essays*, ed. Bruce Steele (Cambridge: Cambridge University Press, 1985).

13 See 'The Future of the Novel' ['Surgery for the Novel – or a Bomb'] in *Study of Thomas Hardy*, pp. 151–5.

14 See E. T. [Jessie Chambers Wood], *A Personal Record* (London: Cape, 1935), p. 103.

15 Lawrence had poems in the *Georgian Poetry* anthologies 1911–12, 1913–15, 1918–19, 1920–22.

16 See *D. H. Lawrence: the Critical Heritage* ed. R. P. Draper (London: Routledge, 1970), p. 3.

17 *Neutral Ground: A Chronicle* (London: Arthur Barker, 1933).

18 *Letters of D. H. Lawrence*, vol 2, p. 90.

19 *Sons and Lovers* ed. Helen Baron and Carl Baron (Cambridge: Cambridge University Press, 1992), pp. 33–5, 397–8.

20 Lawrence took the term 'metaphysic' from Lascelles Abercrombie's *Thomas Hardy* (London: Secker 1912). See Bruce Steele's comments in *Study of Thomas Hardy*, pp.xxvii–xxix.

21 See 'Tradition and the Individual Talent', *Selected Essays*, third enlarged edition (London: Faber and Faber, 1966), pp. 13–22 (21).

22 Thomas Mann, '*Josef und seine Brüder*, Ein Vortrag', *Gesammelte Werke* (Frankfurt: Fischer, 1960) vol. 11, p. 665.

23 Pinkney, *D. H. Lawrence*, pp. 54–99.

24 See, for example, *Letters of D. H. Lawrence* vol. 2, pp. 164, 181, 218.

25 *Femininity and the Creative Imagination* (London: Vision Press, 1973).

26 Although the chapter with this title is Birkin's attempt to resist such an outcome. *Women in Love* ed. John Worthen (Cambridge: Cambridge University Press), pp. 266–76.

27 'The Making of the Magic Mountain' in *The Magic Mountain* trans. Helen T. Lowe-Porter (New York: Knopf, 1927), pp. 717–27 (723).

28 'Spatial Form in Modern Literature' in *The Widening Gyre: Crisis and Mastery in Modern Literature* (New Brunswick, NJ: Rutgers University Press, 1963), pp. 3–62.

29 'On the Uses and Disadvantages of History for Life' in *Untimely Meditations* trans. R. J. Hollingdale (Cambridge: Cambridge University Press, 1983).

30 Martin Heidegger, *The Question Concerning Technology and Other Essays*, ed. and trans. William Lovitt (New York, Harper and Row, 1977), p. 130.
31 *Dial*, 75 (1923), 483.
32 *Letters of D. H. Lawrence*, vol. 1, p. 183.
33 *Lady Chatterley's Lover* ed. Michael Squires (Cambridge: Cambridge University Press, 1993), p. 101.
34 'Modern Fiction' in *The Common Reader* (London, 1925), pp. 145–53 (148–9).
35 *Phoenix*, pp. 249–50.
36 *The Rainbow*, ed. Mark Kinkead-Weekes (Cambridge: Cambridge University Press, 1989), p. 77.
37 *Selected Essays*, pp. 17–18.
38 'The Crown' in *Reflections on the Death of a Porcupine and Other Essays*, ed. Michael Herbert (Cambridge: Cambridge University Press, 1988), pp. 253–306 (285).
39 'The Crown', p. 280.
40 *Phoenix*, p. 248.

9
Joyce and the Making of Modernism: The Question of Technique

Derek Attridge

I want to take you back to the year 1922 – perhaps the year that was to change the course of literature more decisively than any other in the entire twentieth century[1] – and to the publication of the complete version of a novel that had appeared in part over the immediately preceding years, a novel written on a vast scale and remarkable both for its minute reconstruction of the mundane realities of day-to-day life in an earlier period and for its depiction of the most intimate psychological currents, especially those that swirl around the vortex of sexual desire – offering, in this respect at least, one of the fullest portraits of a marriage ever to have been written. The author of the novel I have in mind was not, as you might think, an Irishman in exile in Paris but a woman who lived most of her life, and set her fiction, in Norway: Sigrid Undset, whose three-volume novel *Kristin Lavransdatter* was published between 1920 and 1922. The historical world which she recreated was as far from early twentieth-century Dublin as one could imagine: it was that of fourteenth-century Norway, seen primarily through the eyes of a girl, and then woman, of strong passions and equally strong moral sentiments. Although this work gained international esteem between the wars – Undset received the Nobel Prize in 1928 – and remains both highly regarded and immensely popular in the Scandivanian countries, it has had nothing like the world-wide success of another work which my first sentence could equally well have been describing.

Why these very different fates for *Ulysses* and for *Kristin Lavransdatter*, appearing in full as they did in the same year (the year, incidentally, that both authors turned forty)? The simplest explanation is just that one is a better work than the other, but any such judgement of quality presupposes a cultural foundation, and it is that basis for judgement in which I am interested. Readers who do not know Undset's novel will have to take my word for it that it is not in any *obvious* way a markedly inferior aesthetic production – it is huge in scale (its three volumes total well over a thousand pages in the Penguin translation), meticulously detailed, strongly yet intricately plotted, and, as many readers have testified, powerfully moving in its depiction of human characters and their relations. In its recreation of the quotidian realities of fourteenth-century existence in the farms and towns of Norway and in its handling of the political and religious events of that century it absorbs and transmutes an entire library of medieval texts.[2] Perhaps its most remarkable feature is its capacity to produce the illusion of complete familiarity with the milieu it describes, so that the sense of historical distance we experience as readers is never *within* the novel, but rather between the novel's assumption of intimate acquaintance with the texture of medieval daily life and our extra-novelistic awareness that this world is in fact quite other than our own. Undset achieves this in part by throwing historical caution to the winds when imagining psychological states, which are immediately recognizable to a contemporary reader, so that we have no difficulty in identifying with the mind through which the fourteenth-century world in all its foreignness is perceived. Although *Ulysses* or, to take another work which makes for a fruitful comparison, Dorothy Richardson's *Pilgrimage* (six volumes of which had been published by 1922) invites a similar experience of intimacy with the lived consciousness of a period before that in which they were first read, the gap in those novels is a matter of decades, not centuries; and now that another eighty years have passed we barely notice it as we read.

Clearly, one reason for the relative obscurity of *Kristin Lavransdatter* on the global scene is that it was written in Norwegian, though the example of Ibsen a couple of decades earlier shows that this need not have been an insuperable barrier to wider attention. Perhaps Undset was simply unlucky in her original translator in the 1920s; instead of William Archer, whose versions of Ibsen made a strong impact on at least one aspiring author in Dublin in the 1890s, she had *Charles* Archer, whose fondness for *methinks*'s and *'twas*'s turned her carefully-judged prose into neo-Victorian pseudo-medieval embroidery. (The translation also excised some passages – here we find ourselves thinking of Joyce again – deemed to be too sexually explicit for the 1920s readership.) It was actually only very recently that an adequate English version of the whole three-volume text become available: Tiina Nunnally's new translation, the first volume of which appeared in 1997, the second in 1999, and the third in 2000. Although my total lack of Norwegian means that I cannot judge its fidelity to the original, I can say that from the point of view of the English reader it is superbly rendered, and this new version deserves to win for it many more admirers.

(If Joyce read *Kristin Lavransdatter* – and I have seen it claimed that he knew Undset's work[3] – he would not have needed Archer's translation, since he had taught himself Norwegian in order to read Ibsen in the original, and, in the years 1926–27, when Undset's fame was approaching its zenith, he sought out, as part of his labours on 'Work in Progress', a series of Norwegian teachers in Paris to help him refresh his acquaintance with the language.[4])

I think we can safely say, however, that even in a good translation *Kristin*

Lavransdatter would never have achieved the cultural centrality of *Ulysses*, and the reasons clearly go beyond matters of geography, original language, and translation. They include the gender of the author, the waning allure of medieval subjects by the 1920s, and the conservative ideology underpinning the novel. (In a trajectory the reverse of Joyce's, Undset underwent conversion to Catholicism two years after the publication of the final volume of *Kristin Lavransdatter*, an event which early readers of the novel would not have found surprising.[5]) Another possible factor, and this is the issue on which I want to focus, is Undset's *technique* (a rather unsatisfactory term which I shall attempt to sharpen in due course). We non-readers of Norwegian are told that Undset developed a style that is eminently readable yet tinged with a flavour of Old Norse, since she eschewed modern vocabulary that was not derived from Old Norse and utilized features of Old Norse syntax.[6] Nunnally's English equivalent is straightforward, workmanlike prose, unmistakably modern but with very few explicit markers of the twentieth century, which is in keeping with one critic's description of Undset's use of Norwegian:

> Perhaps the first thing that impresses us in *Kristin Lavransdatter* is the apparent *effortlessness* of the artistic performance, the seeming lack of any conscious narrative devices or tricks, the complete absence of *style* in the narrow literary sense of the word.[7]

It is hard to imagine a description that would be less appropriate for *Ulysses*.

Joyce, however, or rather the cultural reception and construction of Joyce, is my main topic in this essay. The question I want to pose is this: did Joyce's technique in *Ulysses* play a central role in achieving for that work the status it now enjoys as the modernist novel *par excellence*? (I do not think there is any doubt that in all parts of the globe the most frequent answer to the question, 'Name a modernist novel', would be, for those who understood the adjective, Joyce's *Ulysses*.) Conversely, does our (admittedly vexed) understanding of modernism as a distinct and distinctive literary movement emerge to a significant degree from the technical aspects of *Ulysses*? It is a scarcely thinkable proposition, but if Joyce had continued to use the 'scrupulously mean' style of *Dubliners* to elaborate at enormous length a day in the lives of three Dublin characters, would his novel have suffered something like the fate of *Kristin Lavransdatter*?[8] Or is it conceivable that the connotations of the term 'modernism' would have turned out rather differently, its scope perhaps broad enough to have included Undset's work?

Unanswerable questions, of course, and I am raising them only as a means of speculating about the role played by technique in our current conception, or conceptions, of modernism, and the influence which Joyce's work, and *Ulysses* in particular, have had upon that role. But I cannot go any further without attempting to clarify this vague word 'technique'. Of course, any writer uses technical devices, and Undset is no exception. What we mean by modernist technique, presumably, is the use of formal features that, instead of being entirely in the service of communicative effectiveness, draw attention to themselves in some way. We become conscious of, and perhaps are at first puzzled by, for example, the relation of one word or sentence to the next, the absence of the usual markers identifying a speaker or a consciousness, or the intrusion of other languages or nonverbal signs. One reflex of this is the notorious modernist 'difficulty' – which does not mean difficulty in the sense of a complex mathematical theorem or abstruse philosophical argument, but difficulty experienced when the relatively passive mode of reading that almost all texts allow has to give way to a more active engagement in the interpretative process. What is more, and I suspect this is of peculiar importance in thinking about modernism, this foregrounding of technique often means that we have to be prepared to accept that reading is always a matter of making sense only of *some portion* of the linguistic (or musical or visual) material we are engaging with, and not the whole of it. Putting this another way, modernist technique, in what I would argue is its most characteristic mode, destroys the illusion that every significant element in the text we are reading feeds into a continuous meaning that, however rich and complex, is single and whole, and that any failures of comprehension are either minor or merely temporary, to be made good fairly quickly as one reads on. The random, the contingent, the inorganic, the inexplicable, the radically ambiguous: in the full-blooded modernist work these are not dismissable but demand to be acknowledged and dealt with.

There are two rather easy responses to this phenomenon: one is that the modernist work is deliberately chaotic, avoiding the orderliness and coherence traditionally expected of art; the other is that it is a complex whole of such elaborate interconnectedness that the meaning of individual items remains inaccessible until an intellectual apprehension of the whole scheme is achieved (usually with the help of some kind of external critical apparatus). And when the work's historical context is seen as a period of rapid change and loss of certainty, these two responses give rise to two easy ways of relating it to the world: in the first case, it is taken to be reflecting the chaos of the time in its disorder; in the second case, it is taken to be containing or controlling the chaos of the time in its order. All four of these views were forcefully articulated in early responses to *Ulysses*.

Of course, formal technique cannot be separated from the other aspects of a text by a simple division. When, in an otherwise straightforwardly presented tale, an ape speaks or a man turns into an insect, we could describe this moment either as a (formal) transgression of conventional narrative codes or as a (thematic) departure from normal subject-matter. The insertion of snatches of popular song in a poem of high intellectual pretensions is an infringement of formal organic unity but also an unexpected choice of content. However, it is perfectly clear that, whereas the major impact of *A Portrait of the Artist as a Young Man* arose from what was regarded as its 'realism' or 'naturalism', *Ulysses* was immediately perceived to be radically unconventional in technique. Even before the publication of the whole work, Clive Bell was writing in the *New Republic*:

> Mr. Joyce does deliberately go to work to break up the traditional sentence, throwing overboard sequence, syntax, and, indeed, most of those conventions which men habitually employ for the exchange of precise ideas.[9]

The early reviews contain many reactions to Joyce's technical innovations: here are four from 1922:

> There are whole chapters of it without any punctuation or other guide to what the writer is really getting at. Two-thirds of it is incoherent...[10]

> His style is in the new fashionable kinematographic vein, very jerky and elliptical...[11]

> Every trick that a keen-witted man could conceivably play with the English language, and some that were inconceivable until Mr. Joyce arrived, is played somewhere in this book.[12]

> All the conventions of organised prose which have grown with our race and out of our racial consciousness which have been reverently handed on by the masters with such improvements as they have been able to make, have been cast aside as so much dross.[13]

The frequent references to 'boredom' and 'dullness' in many of the early reviews (sometimes by reviewers who are otherwise very positive – Edmund Wilson, for instance, refers to the book's 'appalling longueurs'[14]) are primarily responses to Joyce's technical innovations (as well as the sheer length at which he indulges in some of them).[15] Readers are bored because they cannot understand what they are reading, and they cannot understand what they are reading because the text does not follow the normal conventions of narrative prose. The result is that it seems 'formless'. (This does not prevent many reviewers from fulminating against the book's depravity and salaciousness.[16])

Now the history of literary form provides many examples of technical innovations that are at first puzzling and hard to deal with, but which soon become new conventions that readers process without turning a hair. Defoe's real-seeming fictions or Whitman's free-flowing verse did not cause problems for very long. One of Joyce's most significant and influential technical innovations, the use of present-tense syntactic fragments to create the illusion of spontaneous thought, quickly becomes as easy to read and enjoy as the normal sentences of past-tense narrative reporting. Although the following passage has few precedents in literary history, it poses no lasting challenge to the reader schooled in Victorian novelistic practices:

> Another slice of bread and butter: three, four: right. She did not like her plate full. Right. He turned from the tray, lifted the kettle off the hob and set it sideways on the fire. It sat there, dull and squat, its spout stuck out. Cup of tea soon. Good. Mouth dry.[17]

Technique of this kind is deployed in the service of greater naturalism, more delicate responsiveness to the internal world of thoughts and feelings, and in that sense functions as an extension of, rather than a break with, the tradition of the nineteenth-century novel. This is what Wilson, for example, admired and enjoyed in 1922:

> Mr. Joyce manages to give the effect of unedited human minds, drifting aimlessly along from one triviality to another, confused and diverted by memory, by sensation, and by inhibition. It is, in short, perhaps the most faithful X-ray ever taken of the ordinary human consciousness.[18]

Much of the achievement of Woolf, Lawrence, and Richardson can be understood in similar, if not equally extreme, terms. The interior monologue of *Ulysses*, then, stands as a highly successful instance of this refinement of the tradition of psychological realism, not that far removed from the supposedly styleless style of Sigrid Undset. This is not modernist technique in the fullest sense of the word.

But there are other kinds of technique in *Ulysses* that posed a great challenge to its first readers, and demanded a mode of interpretation very different from that required by Undset and, indeed, most other novelists of the period or of earlier periods. We can turn to Wilson again for an early and influential articulation; this is from his chapter on Joyce in *Axel's Castle*, published in 1931:

> What is the value of all the references to flowers in the Lotus-Eaters chapter, for example? They do not create in the Dublin streets an atmosphere of lotus-eating – we are merely puzzled, if we have not been told to look for them, as to why Joyce has chosen to have Bloom think and see certain things, of which the final explanation is that they are pretexts for mentioning flowers.[19]

There is thus a certain *excess* of technique in Joyce – and it is an excess of technique not designed to thwart meaning, but to multiply meanings. It works as a joke, of course – revealing unsuspected congruities in the apparent arbitrarinesses of language in the same manner as the pun[20] – but at the same time it highlights the operations of language and narrative which normally function so smoothly as to be unnoticeable. The references to flowers in the 'Lotus-Eaters' chapter are an *addition* to everything else that is going on in the chapter in terms of event, thought, and feeling; and the scandal is not just that they have no organic relation to the events and thoughts being narrated in the chapter, but that they even appear at times to *determine* the events and thoughts being narrated, to provide, as Wilson astutely observes, pretexts for the use of flower-related words.

We find something similar happening in many of the episodes, notably in passages where the style is otherwise geared to naturalistic representation. To take one example out of hundreds: in 'Sirens', the terms Miss Douce chooses to express her annoyance with the boots – 'If he doesn't conduct himself I'll wring his ear for him a yard long' – are there not because, or not only because, they are naturalistically appropriate, but because the reader can relate 'conduct' and 'wring' (differently spelled) and 'ear' to the chapter's theme of music. In order to do so, however, he or she has to stop treating the text as the evocation of a scene and treat it as a series of words selected by an author – or rather, *possibly* selected by an author, since one of the crucial properties of this type of device is that it rapidly becomes a machine that continues to operate for its readers irrespective of any authorial intention. The opposition between the willed and the fortuitous breaks down; not only is it impossible to say where an effect of this kind is deliberate and where it is a chance product of the language, it no longer matters to our enjoyment of the work.[21] The same is true of all the eyes (often blind ones) in the 'Cyclops' episode, the various kinds of windiness in 'Aeolus', the words suggestive of food and eating in 'Lestrygonians', and so on. And this particular technical device is only a minor version of the ascendancy of style over content that characterizes all the later chapters of the book, with the partial exception of 'Penelope'.[22]

To many readers, this use of technique represented what was worst about Joyce's technical innovations; Wilson's objection is mild in comparison to the well-known complaints made by D. H. Lawrence ('too terribly would be and done-on-purpose, utterly without spontaneity or real life') or Wyndham Lewis ('What stimulates him is *ways of doing things*, and technical processes, and not *things to be done*') or, somewhat later but very influentially, F. R. Leavis ('There is no organic principle determining, informing, and controlling into a vital whole, the elaborate analogical structure, the extraordinary variety of technical devices').[23] More recently, as I have argued in the final chapter of *Joyce Effects*, Leo Bersani's critique of *Ulysses* owes not a little to the discomfort produced in a certain kind of reader by the work's foregrounding of technique ('a text to be deciphered but not read', he calls it, objecting that the 'technical machinery ... obscures our view of what is happening').[24] Had Joyce not had powerful early defenders in a number of countries – Pound, Eliot, and Valéry Larbaud at the start, and soon Gilbert, Wilson, Hermann Broch, Harry Levin, and perhaps I should add Morris Ernst and Judge Woolsey – technique might have proved his downfall, and the story of modernism in literature would have been very different.

Those early supporters of *Ulysses* cannot be said to have stressed its most innovative technical features, however, and this was no doubt the wisest course for them to have followed. They tended to ignore or make excuses for Joyce's verbal extravagances (we have seen that Wilson was quite open about his un-happiness – which may in fact have helped rather than hindered his effort to win readers for the book), or to lay emphasis on the systematic coherence of the whole. By emphasizing the vividness of psychological detail and the concrete-ness of the setting it was possible to turn the book into a super-realist novel; by stressing the structural ingenuity of the book as a rewriting of the *Odyssey* one could reassure readers that it was not the chaotic mess it seemed at first. Follow-ing the early critics who first laid down these paths, Joyce scholars of the fifties – primarily American – helped to establish *Ulysses* as a coherent, humane fictional masterpiece, whose techniques are fully in the service of a consistent view of the world (though there was some disagreement about the exact nature of that view). They also lodged it in the centre of what was becoming a clearly-defined period of literary history: modernism.[25]

Without the rapid success of *Ulysses* made possible by its early proselytizers, it is doubtful whether Joyce would have written *Finnegans Wake*, and if, under those conditions, he had, it would simply have clinched his reputation as the writer of extravagantly unreadable works of technical interest only (for many readers, of course, it did). *Ulysses* would have been consigned to the side-alley of interesting experimentation. (In 1948 Leavis was still able to assert that *Ulysses* was a dead end, and many potential readers of the novel in Britain and its colonies nodded wisely in agreement.[26]) Modernism would still have made its mark as a rejection of traditional expectations of continuous sense-making – if anything, Pound, Stein, and Eliot showed even less respect than Joyce for such demands – but it might not have seemed such a triumph of technique, such an explosive increase in the possibilities inherent in language and in literary con-ventions, such a showing-up of the one-dimensionality of traditional forms.

But what is the place of *Ulysses*, and of its excess of technique, now, as we reassess modernism from the threshold of a new millennium? Accounts of modernism that treat is as the response to an increasingly complex, chaotic, and meaningless world – whether that response is taken to be an imitation of exter-nal chaos or an attempt to reduce it to order – have come to seem naïve, based as they are on an excessively simple model of literature's relation to historical change. The experience of a loss of sense in the world, of increasing complexity, of information overload, is one that many generations throughout history have experienced; and the violence with which the modernists provoked and chal-lenged existing habits of thought, moral norms, and conventions of representa-tion suggests a willingness to increase, rather than control or merely reflect, the changes afoot in the culture at large. Critical responses to *Ulysses* in the past twenty years, influenced by what became labelled as 'theory', have ceased, by and large, to be embarrassed by Joyce's technical feats; his comic revelation of the workings of language, narrative, and the many other ways in which we try to make sense of ourselves and of the world has come to seem central to his achievement, and to at least one brand of modernism. Though many readers still balk at the arbitrariness of the flowers in 'Lotus-Eaters' or the parodic styles of 'Oxen of the Sun', it has become much easier to take pleasure in these verbal games, and to find them working as an ensemble in a project that goes beyond, while it never cancels, the convincing representation of the realm of consciousness and its objects. Many of the literary practices that we rather inadequately label 'post-modernist' have accustomed us to operations of contingency and chance in our texts, and although the realist narrative thrives as much as it has ever done, we have come to understand that convincing representation can quite happily go hand-in-hand with exposure of the means of representation.[27] *Ulysses*, therefore, becomes even more central to our account of the literary revolution of this period. It sums up the double drive of modernism as described by T. J. Clark in *Farewell to an Idea* (Clark is talking about painting, but the relevance to literature is clear):

> Modernism had two great wishes. It wanted its audience to be led toward a recognition of the social reality of the sign (away from the comforts of narrative and illusionism, was the claim); but equally it dreamed of turning the sign back to a bedrock of World/Nature/Sensation/Subjectivity.[28]

I will end with a postscript in the form of a personal reflection, which will bring me back to Sigrid Undset's novel. I enjoy and admire *both Ulysses and Kristin Lavransdatter*, and I would like to think that, rather than reflecting a hopeless inconsistency in my literary taste, this dual allegiance indicates that the two works have important features in common. Although Undset's novel is often, and not inaccurately, represented as a signal example of anti-modernism, which does anything but attempt an exposure of the means of representation or draw the reader's attention to the writer's choices, it seems to me to participate in other ways in modernism's expansion of the possibilities of literary form. It shares with *Ulysses*, and with the work of many other modernists, an immense confidence in the power of literary language to accomplish tasks not hitherto attempted, and part of the pleasure of reading it is experiencing the effects of that confidence *in the writing itself*, the pleasure of self-imposed challenges triumphantly met. The challenges Undset sets herself are, of course, very different from Joyce's, and do not involve overt technical flourishes, but I would argue that they do involve an element of display, of conjuring with words. (Hence the signal importance of a convincing translation.) My familiarity with *Ulysses*, and my relishing of its unapologetic technical devices, do not constitute a bar to my enjoyment of *Kristin Lavransdatter*; on the contrary, I believe that my pleasurable engagement with Undset's great novel is actually enhanced by my Joycean predilection for linguistic prestidigitation.

Notes

1 An entire book has been devoted to the literary production of this year, Michael North's *Reading 1922: A Return to the Scene of the Modern* (New York: Oxford University Press, 1999), and it has frequently been cited as a watershed year; see, for example, Harry Levin, 'What Was Modernism?', in *Varieties of Literary Experience: Eighteen Essays in World Literature*, ed. Stanley Burnshaw (New York: New York University Press, 1962), p. 317, and Stanley Sultan, *Eliot, Joyce and Company* (New York: Oxford University Press, 1987), p. 129.

2 For a brief discussion, see Sherrill Harbison, Introduction to *The Cross*, volume 3 of *Kristin Lavransdatter* (Harmondsworth: Penguin, 2000), pp. vii–xviii.

3 B. J. Tysdahl, *Joyce and Ibsen: A Study in Literary Influence* (Oslo: Norwegian Universities Press, 1968), p. 126.

4 *Ibid.*, p. 127.

5 In 'Unfashionable *Kristin Lavransdatter*', Otto Reinert acknowledges the novel's conservative, religious temper, and defends it as a great work 'that comes late in a long line of works great in the same way' (*Scandinavian Studies* 71.i [Spring 1999], 67–80; quotation on p. 69). This is to underestimate the degree to which the novel is of its time, however.

6 Sherrill Harbison, Introduction to *Sigrid Lavransdatter*, vol. 3, *The Cross*, p. xx.

7 Alrik Gustafson, *Six Scandinavian Novelists* (Minneapolis: University of Minnesota Press, 1966), p. 315.

8 John Wyse Jackson and Bernard McGinley, in their introduction to their annotated edition of *Dubliners* (London: Sinclair–Stevenson, 1993), offer this intriguing tidbit: 'Robert McAlmon reported that Joyce wondered in the mid–1920s whether it might not have been better to have developed his writing in the "*Dubliners*" style "rather than going into words too entirely"' (p. xiv).

9 'Plus de Jazz,' *New Republic* xxviii (21 September 1921), 95; quoted in Robert H. Deming, *James Joyce: The Critical Heritage*, vol. 1 (London: Routledge, 1970), p. 183.

10 'The Scandal of *Ulysses*', *Sporting Times*, No. 34 (1 April 1922), 4; quoted in Deming, vol. 1, p. 192.

11 'A New *Ulysses*', *Evening News*, 8 April 1922, 4; quoted in Deming, vol. 1, p. 194.

12 John Middleton Murry, Review, *Nation & Athenaeum*, 22 April 1922, xxxi, 124–5; quoted in Deming, vol. 1, p. 196.

13 Holbrook Jackson, Review, *To–Day*, June 1922, ix, 47–9; quoted in Deming, vol. 1, p. 199. The quoted sentence is not exactly a model of 'organised prose'!

14 Review, *New Republic*, xxxi, No. 396 (5 July 1922); quoted in Deming, vol. 1, p. 230.

15 A few examples from 1922: '*Ulysses* is not alone sordidly pornographic, but it is intensely dull' (Review, *Sporting Times*, No. 34 [1 April 1922], 4; quoted in Deming, vol. 1, p. 194); 'There are the deadliest of Dead Seas in this ocean of prose. You get becalmed by them – bored, drowsed, bewildered' (Holbrook Jackson, review, *To–Day*, June 1922, ix, 47–9; quoted in Deming, vol. 1, p. 199); 'A more serious objection to the novel is its pervading difficult dulness' (Arnold Bennett, Review, *Outlook*, [29 April 1922], 337–9; quoted in Deming, vol. 1, p. 220); 'It requires real endurance to finish *Ulysses*' (Joseph Collins, review, *New York Times Book Review* [28 May 1922], 6, 17; quoted in Deming, vol. 1, p. 223).

16 One reviewer tries, unconvincingly, to marry these incompatibles: 'Our first impression is that of sheer disgust, our second of irritability because we never know whether a character is speaking or merely thinking, our third of boredom at the continual harping on obscenities (nothing cloys a reader's appetite so quickly as dirt)...' (S. P. B. Mais, 'An Irish Revel: And Some Flappers,' *Daily Express* [25 March 1922], n.p.; quoted in Deming, vol. 1, p. 191).

17 *Ulysses*, The Corrected Text, ed. Hans Walter Gabler with Wolfhard Steppe and Claus Melchior (London: The Bodley Head, 1986), 4.11–14.

18 *Op. cit.*, p. 228.

19 *Axel's Castle: A Study in the Imaginative Literature of 1870–1930* (Glasgow: Collins–Fontana, 1961), p. 172. Wilson cites the interpolations of 'Cyclops' and the parodies of 'Oxen of the Sun' as further examples.

20 See my discussion of the pun and the portmanteau in chapter 7 of *Peculiar Language: Literature as Difference from the Renaissance to James Joyce* (Ithaca: Cornell University Press and London: Methuen, 1988).

21 I have commented on this phenomenon in the reading of *Finnegans Wake*, where it is exploited much more fully, in *Peculiar Language*, pp. 206–7, and *Joyce Effects: On Language, Theory, and History* (Cambridge: Cambridge University Press, 2000), p. 121.

22 There are signs of this technique as early as *Dubliners*: in their edition Jackson and McGinley provide notes to 'The Dead' that point out the suggestions of death in apparently innocent terms and phrases such as 'three mortal hours', 'toddling' (c.f. German *Tod*), 'perished alive' (meaning 'very cold'), and 'the subject ... was buried.' See notes 159k, 159m, 159n, and 179h.

23 D. H. Lawrence, *Selected Literary Criticism*, ed. Anthony Beal (London: Heinemann, 1967), p. 149; Wyndham Lewis, *Time and Western Man*, ed. Paul Edwards (Santa Rosa: Black Sparrow Press, 1993), p. 107; F. R. Leavis, *The Great Tradition* (New York: Doubleday, 1954), p. 36.

24 Leo Bersani, *The Culture of Redemption* (Cambridge/Mass.: Harvard University Press, 1990), p. 156.

25 Literary modernism's relation to the other arts was, and remains, problematic, and I do not propose to tackle this large question here; let me just say that analogies to the development I am tracing are clearest in painting and least clear in architecture.

26 *The Great Tradition*, p. 36.

27 To take one example of many, Kate Atkinson's highly popular novel *Behind the Scenes at the Museum*, which gives a vivid, comic portrayal of a girl's formative years in the city of York, includes between the chapters lengthy footnotes which elaborate on her parents' and grandparents' lives (London: Doubleday, 1995).

28 T. J. Clark, *Farewell to an Idea: Episodes from a History of Modernism* (New Haven: Yale University Press, 1999). The last sentence in fact ends '...which the to and fro of capitalism had all but destroyed', introducing a historical explanation which raises many more questions than can be dealt with here.

10

'Modernism', Poetry, and Ireland

Edna Longley

For me 'modernism' is not so much elusive as pervasive: a powerful system well able to suppress both its contradict*ions* and its contradict*ors*. Forty years ago the late Karl Shapiro wrote of T. S. Eliot: 'Eliot resembles one of those mighty castles in Bavaria which are remarkably visible, famed for their unsightliness, and too expensive to tear down. Life goes on at the bottom; but *it* is always up there.'[1] Shapiro, significantly, was the sole voter against Ezra Pound's being awarded the Bollingen Prize in 1948. To change tack and image: the profile of 'modernism' recalls the magazine *Antichrist* in *Keep the Aspidistra Flying* which 'gave the impression of being edited by an ardent Nonconformist who had transferred his allegiance from God to Marx, and in doing so had got mixed up with a gang of *vers libre* poets'. Although Orwell's image targets the ideological confusions of the literary 1930s, it might also fit the way in which 'modernism' can present itself as radical, behave as conservative, and recognize poetry only when poetry suits its agenda.

That is, when poetry suits the agenda of the literary academy. The 'modernism' I mean is not, for instance, Marshall Berman's sense of an exhilarating artistic quest to 'make oneself somehow at home in the maelstrom',[2] but the narrower Anglo-American academic tradition whose hegemony enraged Shapiro. Astradur Eysteinsson in *The Concept of Modernism* (1990), a fine exposé of contradiction and inconsistency, stresses that '"modernism" is not a concept that emanates directly from literary texts; it is a construct created by the critical enquiry into a certain kind of texts'. Yet Peter Nicholls in *Modernisms: A Literary Guide* (1995) and the contributors to Michael Levenson's *Cambridge Companion to Modernism* (1998) are typical when they use the term to denote a protean literary actor at work in the early twentieth century. Eysteinsson also stresses the neglect of literary history in modernist 'critical enquiry', despite 'the extent to which every discussion of an author or a literary work is an act of literary history'.[3] The 1998 anthology *Modernism: An Anthology of Sources and Documents* illustrates the point. On the one hand, the editors accept that 'modernism' is a post-dated term which 'masks conflict, upheaval and any number of contradictory positions'; on the other, they refuse an 'evolutionary model of literary history'. Hence their 'modernism' 'does not follow from "Romanticism" or "Symbolism", nor does it precede "Post-modernism" as a literary category'.[4] Yet to talk of sources and documents is to imply history. And the anthology's final section is headed: 'The 1930s: Modernist regroupings'. But this piece of historicism is both an appropriation and a fudge since it overrides, *inter alia*, the fact that the 1930s were not quite as *vers libre* as Orwell thought. Here literary history eludes a 'modernist' synchronicity which tries to engross it.

Nonetheless modernism (inverted commas understood from here on) is currently invading the literary 1930s in an attempt to join forces with late twentieth-century 'postmodernism' and thus span the century. Two examples are Keith Williams' and Steven Matthews' *Rewriting the Thirties: Modernism and After* (1997) and the teleologically titled *W. H. Auden: Towards a Postmodern Poetics* (2000) by Rainer Emig. Emig desires to show that Auden was first devoted to 'the modernisms of Yeats and Eliot', then 'their critic and parodist', finally 'their successor'. This genealogical as well as teleological project is revealingly anxious to detach Auden from 'an anti-modernism that often amounts to a relapse into pre-modernist patterns of thought and artistic expression' and to situate his poetry in a postmodernism which is not 'a false antithesis to modernism, but ... its critical continuation'.[5] In another quarter, Michael Schmidt's *Harvill Book of Twentieth-Century Poetry in English* (1999) pronounces a global *fait accompli*: 'An anthology that takes Modernist bearings is an anthology that believes it is possible to find coherence within so large a body of work, from so many corners of the world.'[6] Coherence and modernism seem strange bedfellows. I would suggest that clearer perspectives might be achieved by considering (what I prefer to call) 'the modern movement' in a more dialectical as well as historical spirit that makes room for critical enquiry into other kinds of text. Here structural questions – as regards poetry, the dialectic between free verse and a reanimation of traditional forms – are centrally at issue. More pan-generic and thematic markers (such as reflexiveness or transcultural references or engagement with modernity or with the city) can be found in a wide range of writings. When critics notice this, however, they tend to claim another text for proto-modernism rather than complicate their map.

In considering some ways in which modernism has impinged on poetry, Ireland, and both together, I will outline how my thinking on modernism and modern poetry has developed, and review critical debates about modernism and Ireland. Then I will illustrate some points about modernism, Ireland and poetry with reference to Louis MacNeice and to the contemporary Northern Irish poets, Ciaran Carson and Paul Muldoon. Finally, I will revisit Yeats and Pound at the supposed moment of modernism around 1920.

A few years ago I gave a paper on 'Yeats and American Modernism' at a conference on Anglo-American poetic relations.[7] Its main argument was that overviews with modernism in their title invoke Yeats selectively, inaccurately, and opportunistically. Modernist studies are obsessed with lists – a function of their hegemonic drive. Thus Yeats is often cited to boost some characteristic that more properly belongs to Pound or Eliot. He is read through Pound and Eliot (see below). His index-entries are thinner than those for Pound and Eliot. At the same time, the team clearly needs this strong player. My point was, or is, not that his role in such compendiums shows Yeats to be less modernist, but that it betrays modernism as being less modernist. His simultaneous inclusion and exclusion protects modernism's heavy founding investment in the poetics of Pound and Eliot. John Harwood has called for 'a revised history of modernism which would dispel the illusion of Pound's centrality [and] would call into question almost everything that is ... taken for granted in orthodox studies of the period'.[8] In my paper I discussed the aesthetic dialectics between Yeats and Eliot, Yeats and Pound, stressing that they *were* dialectics: the latter a profound twenty-five-year mutually-defining argument with a poet 'whose art', Yeats concluded, 'is the opposite of mine, whose criticism commends what I most condemn'.[9] This argument or antinomy staked out the twentieth-century poetic field as regards the English language, and it culminated in Yeats's Introduction to his *Oxford Book of Modern Verse*. Here Yeats's central objection to the form of the *Cantos* is that it constitutes 'flux eternal and therefore without movement'.[10] I suggested that Yeats, in contrast with Pound (I will return to this difference), takes a dynamic view of form, history, and their inter-relations. That is, his poetry crosses history as process with form as sequence. I also argued that Yeats's strong presence in American and British poetry at that time, and his own sense of his juniors – sharpened by working on an anthology which brought the 1930s up against the 1890s – again signifies something more dialectical than 'regrouping'. Yeats's Introduction to the *Oxford Book* claims Auden and Co. as defectors from *vers libre* (Auden would seem to agree).[11] And Yeats elsewhere disparages the Pound *protégés* paraded in his *Active Anthology* (1933) as 'shell-shocked Whitmans'.[12] Here national differences surface in the battle to propagate formal genes among the young.

While Ireland, America, and Scotland have often showed solidarity on the common point of literary independence from England, that does not preclude rivalries or cultural and aesthetic differences between, as within, these countries. The youthful Yeats, for instance, was competitively aware of American and Scottish role-models for advancing a literary culture. However, categories like 'international modernism' or 'Anglo-American modernism' efface Ireland, Scotland, and Wales. Indeed, T. S. Eliot wrote patronizing reviews of two important 'regional' British Isles critical works, Gregory Smith's *Scottish*

Literature and Yeats's *The Cutting of an Agate*, at precisely the moment in 1919 when he was incubating 'Tradition and the Individual Talent'. Moreover, this *locus classicus* of the Anglo-American 'we' shows undeclared debts to Yeats's 'Poetry and Tradition' (1907, reprinted in *The Cutting of an Agate*). Thus perhaps we should conceive the 'inter-national' thrust of the modern move- ment as active rather than passive: once more, a dialectic rather than the over- arching canopy implied by 'cosmopolitan'.

Ireland has fought back during the past decade, especially by repatriating James Joyce from the modernist imperium and its more rarified theoretical domains. Elizabeth Butler Cullingford can even refer to 'the bad old days, when Joyce was an apolitical Modernist'.[13] Yet some repatriations of Joyce, such as Emer Nolan's pioneering *James Joyce and Nationalism* (1995), argu- ably represent him as too national*ist* rather than national*. I prefer the more open-ended approach of Joseph Kelly's ironically titled *Our Joyce* (1998), which examines the shifting relation between Joyce's work (in progress, too) and various interpretive communities from the implied Dublin reader of *Dubliners* to the multinational Joyce industry. Kelly's conclusion regarding Pound's and Eliot's 'Joyce' is that 'Pound de-Irished Joyce's reputation, and, in the process stripped his early fiction of its political force.'[14] A contextual point here is that the realism, not symbolism, of *Dubliners* was radical. As we have seen, Yeats was less amenable to what K. K. Ruthven terms Pound's 'attempts at controlling the discursive reproduction of literary texts pro- duced by his contemporaries' (which he sees as a major factor in 'the institu- tionalisation of Anglo-American modernism inside literary studies').[15] This resistance may be one reason why Joyce figures more centrally than Yeats in later canons. Thus as regards academic modernism, lack of attention to Irish cultural and political specifics had complementary results: a de-Irishized Joyce and a shadowy Yeats (whose Irish contexts history had also made less and less accessible). Some of this, it must be said, reflects the late development, internal rifts, and weak voice of Ireland's own literary academy.

Yet, as with Nolan's book, I want to enter a *caveat* against turning a salutary correction into a new orthodoxy. Current attention to Joyce's Irish contexts is bound up with two academic tendencies. The first is the continuing reaction against New Critical readings: a reaction which fails to see that (nationalist) politics was not their only lacuna regarding Ireland. Nor can Cullingford's 'bad old days' be redeemed by simple reversal, by proclaiming a wholly Irish, wholly political 'Joyce'. The second tendency is the liaison between postcolo- nial theory and the politics of Irish studies. Derek Attridge and Marjorie Howe, who stress that the postcolonial paradigm should not override other approaches, are probably right to conclude (in their introduction to *Semicolo-*

nial Joyce, 2000) that 'the difficulties presented by the Irish case ... make the crossroads between [postcolonial studies] and Joyce's works ... a rich ground for further investigation'.[16] Not every critic, however, is so scrupulous about 'difficulties' or 'investigation'. Again, Howard J. Booth and Nigel Rigby, the editors of *Modernism and Empire* (2000), are probably right to contend that 'colonialism needs to be considered in accounts of modernist writing' even as they rebuke Fredric Jameson's 'crudely oversimplified' account of 'Ireland's relation to modernism and empire'.[17] Nonetheless, since the empire or colonialism in question is invariably British, the prominence of Britain's extra-European domains tends to distance Ireland from intra-European contexts for modernism.

As regards Yeats and Joyce, for instance, should 'metropolis' be opposed to province or region rather than to 'colony'? Apart from the fact that historians term Ireland a 'metropolitan colony', mobility, publishing media, and getting away from restrictive folks back home remain crucial factors in the 'hybridity' – a word which may simply be replacing 'cosmopolitanism' – of the Anglophone modern movement. In *Modernism and Empire*, Elleke Boehmer misreads Yeats's relation to Tagore as denoting an anti-colonial modernism: 'Yeats understood the compulsion to retrieve or reinvent images of the homeland untouched by the colonial presence ... In Yeats's Introduction to *Gitanjali* the unsettling of the Western writer's superiority over another culture is sharpened and complicated by the writer's own culturally subordinate position relative to the metropolis.'[18] Yeats writes: 'A whole people, a whole civilisation, immeasurably strange to us, seems to have been taken up into this imagination; and yet we are not moved because of its strangeness, but because we have met our own image, as though we had walked in Rossetti's Willow Wood'.[19] Here Yeats does not show a particularly radical side either of the Romantic literary imagination or of his own eastern-mystical disposition. Nor is his first-person plural clearly Irish. Roy Foster comments: 'Yeats's affinity with Tagore was rooted in mysticism and religion, rather than in a shared sense of colonial oppression; and many Irish people benefited from Imperial spoils (and Raj careers)'.[20] Indeed, from another postcolonial angle, the passage would be condemned as Celto-Orientalism.

The problem with some criticism that links postcolonialism, modernism, and Ireland is that it perceives 'Ireland' as both internally homogeneous and as distinct from an equally homogeneous 'Britain'. In *Modernism and Empire*, for instance, C. L. Innes writes that Joyce and Yeats 'but Joyce more insistently so, assert ownership of a "double" language or idiom, one which asserts mastery over standard literary English, and another which asserts the distinctiveness of Irish English, and so implicitly excludes a constructed British reader such as Haines from its community'.[21] This recognizes the significance of audience and language but in too binary a fashion. The English (not British) Haines in *Ulysses* is a Revival groupie: a Joycean joke against Yeats and Douglas Hyde which highlights intra-Irish literary quarrels. Again, there is no such thing as 'standard literary English' or standard Irish-English. Innes constructs herself as a postcolonial English reader who atones for Haines's sins by accepting her allegedly 'marginalised status' as a non-Irish reader. *Ulysses*, full of anti-Irish as well as anti-English and anti-imperial satire, hardly calls a homogeneous reading-community into existence. The point is that Irish (like American) writers of the period were potentially self-conscious about language and audience in ways that sometimes (but not always) led to radical revisions of literary structure. Helen Carr's essay in *Modernism and Empire*, discussing 'Pound and the Celts', makes the uncontroversial case that Yeats and the Irish Revival influenced Pound and Imagism. But Carr pushes her argument too far when she maintains that the Revival offered modernists 'an alternative cultural tradition from which to critique the values of the present power structures and Western modernity'.[22] This implies that Irish culture (and cultural nationalism) is a single, non-Western formation. It also disregards the wider role of Celticism in English-language poetry.

The most remarkable convergence of postcolonial and modernist readings – a shotgun marriage which exposes basic incompatibilities – is Máire ní Fhlathúin's essay 'The anti-colonial modernism of Patrick Pearse'. Here Pearse's 'bi-culturalism' (English father, Irish mother) is seen as unusual rather than commonplace, and as enabling Pearse to occupy 'a position in the multiplicity of cultures and traditions which characterised both the modernist mode of thought and twentieth-century Ireland'.[23] This proposition tries to capitalize on the prestige of modernism by turning Pearse, with his mono-cultural Gaelic ideology, into Joyce. The metamorphosis renders both Pearse and modernism unrecognizable. Conversely, in other readings, Joyce mutates into Pearse. Modernism, hitherto regarded (not only in Joyce studies) as unhelpful to Irish nationalism, is being recruited *via* postcolonial theory for a more supportive role.

Attridge and Howe argue that 'postcolonial studies offers ways of articulating nationalism, both imperialist and anti-imperialist, and modernism as interdependent rather than opposed phenomena'.[24] But no twentieth-century European culture is restricted to nationalism nor its literature to modernism. *Modernism and Empire*, more scattergun than *Semicolonial Joyce*, elasticates modernism to the point of redundancy. Yet so do other recent books, with modernism in their title, which seek to diversify the field while retaining its market-niche. Here again Yeats, rather than modernism, proves elusive. Thus in *Institutions of Modernism: Literary Elites and Public Culture* (1998) Lawrence Rainey mentions how Yeats published works in both Dun Emer/ Cuala

166 *Rethinking Modernism*

Press and Macmillan editions: a practice Rainey sees as influencing Yeats's 'young admirer Ezra Pound' and 'the emerging English avant-garde'.[25] It may well have done so, but Yeats himself had been influenced by William Morris, and dual publication helped him to maintain his credibility as an Irish cultural nationalist. Michael North in *Reading 1922* (1999) broadens the textual and historical field, yet such revisionism can make the modernist list even more pointless: '[D. H.] Lawrence and Yeats defy the common requirement that modernist works are organised paratactically rather than hypotactically'. North continues with one of those escape-clauses whereby academic modernism maintains its hegemony: 'modernism ceaselessly creates forms and in so doing confounds critical desires for formal consistency'.[26]

Of course Joyce and Yeats have foundational roles in Irish literary studies which lie outside the brief of academics who put Ireland in their index but not America. Yet if that literary dialectic is also foundational for 'Anglo-American modernism', if it turns on form and epistemology as does the modernist paradigm itself, if form is of the poetic essence, perhaps 'Ireland' might be given a more complex place – somewhere between absence and nationalism – in the proceedings.

*

What this critic desires is less 'formal consistency' than more consistent recognition that literary forms are historical and dialectical, and continue to be so. Yeats's or Lawrence's poetry does not just 'happen' to defy a 'paratactical' norm (and who, exactly, 'requires' this?). Earlier twentieth-century literary history is still working its way through the practice and theory of contemporary poetry. This – if we were to apply rather than merely quote Eliot's most fruitful insight into 'tradition' – should modify our picture of the past. Yet if modernism does not care, or cares only selectively, about contemporary poetry, why should contemporary poetry care about modernism? After all, other modern poetry is discussed in other ways in the academy. Yet this is less the case than formerly. And the academy, especially in the United States, controls more and more of poetry's surviving audience. The English poet James Fenton said after returning from America: 'if I now write a very plain lyric, it's actually in protest against people writing in a very muzzy, neither-here-nor-there, anti-metrical, very cautious, take-it-or-leave-it style, that seems to have been forced on them by the Academy'.[27] Further, academic modernism now promotes its own theorized version of poetry.

In fact, the piece of academic inbreeding now offered as 'language poetry' or 'the new poetics' reproduces older tendencies. One is that such university-based groups proclaim their marginalization by a metropolitan establishment portrayed as monolithic and powerful. Thus Marjorie Perloff (who has attacked Fenton's position) deplores the fact that poetry reviewing has not absorbed 'the scholarly reception and theorisation of [contemporary] poetry'. She also responds to Glyn Maxwell's remark that no-one is interested in language poetry, by saying it 'is belied by so many *articles, books and symposia* not only in the US' [my italics].[28] Perloff's rhetoric is neo-Poundian: the (American modernist) professional putting down the (English) amateur. Similarly, Andrew Crozier, introducing the neo-modernist anthology *A Various Art* (1987), castigates 'current constructions of British poetry' for licensing work that is 'either provincial or parasitically metropolitan'.[29] By 'provincial' he may partly mean 'Irish'. Nor is Ireland itself immune. An anthology of critical essays called *Modernism and Ireland: The Poetry of the 1930s* (1995), allied to some contemporary 'experimental' Irish poetry, heralded a continuing surge in academic writing about a rather frail group of so-called 'modernists', principally Brian Coffey, Denis Devlin, and Thomas MacGreevy. Contradictions surface when the editors (Patricia Coughlan and Alex Davis) term Yeats 'undeniably an Irish modernist' while excluding him from influence on these modernist poets. Yeats, who appears on both sides of the modernist, as of the colonial, equation, is most typically a modernist in America but not in Ireland. Coughlan and Davis avoid the issue of value when they broach the 'somewhat vexed question of [the poets'] reception both by later generations of poets and by the Anglo-Irish critical establishment over the last twenty years'. But they take comfort from the fact that 'these poets ... have functioned as models for successive groups of later literary dissidents from the dominant forms of Irish poetry'.[30] What might be dissident, what dominant, in contemporary Irish poetry or its criticism is by no means clearcut.

I would conclude that in Ireland, as in England, modernism can serve as the sign whereby academically touted poets represent themselves as in touch with an 'international' – i.e., American – dynamic that sets them beyond the uncomprehending provincialism of their own country. It also seems to function similarly within America itself. Perloff, in her internal campaign, has to insist that American language poetry interests the British, French, Chinese, Japanese, Australians, and so on. So modernism also signifies a transcendental global orbit possibly traceable to Pound's successive deracinations.[31]

Up to a point I prefer Robert Crawford's Scottish perspective on 'Modernism as Provincialism'. Crawford stresses the national dimensions of *The Waste Land* and *Ulysses*, plausibly links Pound with Hugh MacDiarmid, and says: 'Drawing so strongly on both anthropology and dialect, and aiming to outflank the Anglocentricity of established Englishness through a combination of the demotic and the multicultural, Modernism was an essentially provincial phenomenon'.[32] However, MacDiarmid's best poems may be his least modernist, and we should not forget that the modern movement also criticizes all our provincialities. Perhaps it was simultaneously provincial and anti-provincial. Yet twentieth-century Scottish poetry has been more productively experimental than has Irish or English poetry, as in the work of Edwin Morgan and Ian Hamilton Finlay. These poets too have invoked modernism to elude certain tropes and categories of 'Scottish literature', including those urged by MacDiarmid. But perhaps their modernism qualifies more as avant-gardeism. Its main roots are in the revived liaison between poetry and the visual arts represented by concrete poetry in the early 1960s. In both cases this has stimulated a rich range of work, deeply in touch with Scotland itself, and alert to the American poets who revised Pound and Williams rather than to the modernist academy.

My current awareness of Scottish poetry derives from another recent undertaking: editing an anthology of twentieth-century British and Irish poetry. Of course, my own taste may have preconditioned any patterns that I see as emerging from this experience – such as the fact that Yeats's traces seem more marked than Eliot's. Nonetheless, some points may be worth recording. First, both 'tradition' and traditional forms have been intricately woven and unwoven across the century. Second, interaction across the Atlantic (and Channel) has not been confined to the modernist circuits. Third, at certain points American modernist poetry makes a particular impact – in the 1950s, for instance, the influence of Pound and Williams as filtered more vitally through Robert Creeley and Robert Duncan. Here the Black Mountain evidently came as a relief from Ben Bulben. But the same period also shows a continuing influence from modernism in its guise as New Criticism: the seventeenth--century lyric still going strong as model of 'complexity'. Yet New Criticism as a poetic and critical enterprise inspired by Yeats and Eliot (or by a confused belief in their similarity) itself differs crucially from any neo-Poundian formation.

Not that poets and poems align themselves neatly. Thom Gunn, whom the term 'Anglo-American poet' actually fits, and which he accepts as doing so, speaks for the stimulus of creative dialectics. 'We should all be fertilising each other', he says. Gunn's early sonnets 'Lerici' and 'From the Highest Camp' are influenced by Donne and the Auden sonnet. Later, syllabics became his bridge between stanzaic form and the freer verse he would write under the stimulus of Williams, Creeley, Ginsberg and Duncan. Yet Gunn's most recent collection *Boss Cupid* cannot be categorized as subscribing either to 'open' or 'closed' form. (He speaks of himself as moving between 'spontaneity and finish'.) And in 1989 he recalled how the *Collected Poems* of Yeats, who had been out of print during the war, appeared in 1950 and 'we all bought copies. It was extraordinary because we'd always understood that Eliot was the king of the world, that Eliot was *the* modern poet. There was no possible rival, and suddenly here was somebody as good or better, it seemed to us, someone with a lot more vigour, a bigger range, and more exciting. And we discovered him for ourselves, which was a wonderful thing to be able to do with a major poet, because every other major poet by that time has been presented to you as part of a curriculum.'[33] However, two letters in a recent *London Review of Books* (20 July 2000) indicate that Gunn's fans insist more than he does on a particular, modernist, value attaching to his American dimension. An English reviewer who under-emphasized it was accused of 'tweedy bearings', 'trivialisation', and 'willed blindness'.

*

My own long-term interest in Louis MacNeice may have Irish-tweedy bearings, but I would cite him, too, as a category-disturber whom orthodox categories fail to fit. These categories include modernism along with 'thirties poetry' and 'Irish poetry'. Indeed, one of MacNeice's own critical themes is the procrustean critic who forces poets or poems into pre-fabricated moulds. Another recent undertaking with a bearing on the present context has been my re-reading of MacNeice's criticism in the context of modernism, i.e., the reception of Eliot and Pound in 1930s Britain and Ireland. This has reinforced my long-standing belief that MacNeice was uniquely well placed to weigh the formal models of Yeats and Eliot. And he did so in relation to the raised European historical consciousness which he shared with his English contemporaries. MacNeice's other credentials include: a knowledge of avant-garde painting and its theory (in which he had been tutored at Marlborough by Anthony Blunt); an absorption of philosophical relativism given further meaning by personal displacements; an ability to re-imagine the modern/modernist city and specifically (in *Autumn Journal*) Eliot's London; an interest in literary criticism which led him to synthesize the views of I. A. Richards and the Marxist poet-critic Christopher Caudwell; his creative dialogue with Auden about aesthetics and politics.[34]

MacNeice responded to Pound's *Cantos* much as Yeats did – a point suggestive of Irish continuities. In 1935, before Yeats had published the *Oxford Book*, MacNeice wrote: 'What Mr Grigson has called "the cultural reference rock-jumping style", even if feasible in a poem of the length of *The Waste Land* ... is bound to lose its virility in a work as vast as the Cantos [whose faults] should remind us of certain practical, if pedantic, truths. Quantity must always affect quality ... Mr Pound does not know where to stop. He is a born strummer.'[35] MacNeice came to see Yeats, in contrast, as having prompted himself and Auden to 'put shape on' the world.[36] Shape (also Samuel Beckett's term for form) need not imply 'closure' in the totalitarian sense the word has somehow acquired: ironically so, if its opposite is Poundian strumming. In *The Poetics of Fascism* Paul Morrison argues with reference to the *Cantos*: 'It may be ... that today power operates all the more insidiously for its refusal of centres and that "a structure lacking any centre" [Derrida] is best characterised not as "unthinkable" but as strategically resisting thought, as a modality of power that would not be known as such'.[37] For MacNeice, 'Yeats's formalising activity began when he *thought* about the world'.[38]

At the beginning of the 1960s MacNeice re-entered the modernist fray as critic and poet. His Clark lectures *Varieties of Parable* offer 'parable' as a wide-ranging, and inherently poetic, literary structure that informs works as seemingly diverse as *The Faerie Queene, The Waste Land*, and *Waiting for Godot*. Arguing implicitly *for* shape, MacNeice maintains that language *functions* in Beckett, that the silences 'are there to throw the words into relief'.[39] MacNeice's own 'parable-poems' at this period are reflexively occupied with how the mind or poem organizes the world. They admit greater relativism than do Yeats's structures, while also continuing the Yeatsian trajectory whereby the poetic unity denoted by 'symbolism' was progressively disturbed by history. The relation between symbol, syntax, and stanza becomes a performative, dialectical rhetoric. Where poetry is concerned, symbolism still seems more of a watershed than what was later construed as modernism. MacNeice's poems 'Variation on Heraclitus' and 'Reflections' relate to one another in a Yeatsian counterpoint. 'Variation' uses an emblematic 'room' to suggest how perceptual relativism might open up life, poetry, and reading:

> Even the walls are flowing, even the ceiling,
> Nor only in terms of physics; the pictures
> Bob on each picture rail like floats on a line
> While the books on the shelves keep reeling
> Their titles out into space ...
>
> No, whatever you say,
> Reappearance presumes disappearance, it may not be nice
> Or proper or easily analysed not to be static
> But none of your slide snide rules can catch what is sliding so fast
> And, all you advisers on this by the time it is that,
> I just do not want your advice
> Nor need you be troubled to pin me down in my room
> Since the room and I will escape for I tell you flat:
> One cannot live in the same room twice.[40]

'Reflections' uses the 'room' to suggest, conversely, how relativism might close down life, poetry, and reading. The poem ends with the speaker's image 'pinned down' in an alternative, unreadable reality:

My actual room stands sandwiched between confections
Of night and lights and glass and in both directions
I can see beyond and through the reflections the street lamps
At home outdoors where my indoors rooms lie stranded,
Where a taxi perhaps will drive in through the bookcase
Whose books are not for reading and past the fire
Which gives no warmth and pull up by my desk
At which I cannot write since I am not lefthanded.[41]

Of course, neither poem, not only in their own dialectical relationship, closes down the movements of consciousness that they enact. The scenarios of positive and negative dislocation in time/space logically continue *ad infinitum*. And their dialectic does more than what 'language poems' are said to do when they disrupt the syntagmatic chain. It may be more 'disruptive' to follow MacNeice's angled syntax into space or into the cognitive nihilism of his hall of mirrors. These poems also fulfil a supposed modernist aspiration: MacNeice makes a modern room in a modern city signify in the same manner as George Herbert's emblems. Yet, rather than abandoning syntax or rhyme, he maximizes their resources. Thus the line 'And all you advisers on this by the time it is that' exploits syntax – and poetry – as sequence. Again, he uses a favourite device, internal rhyme, to dramatize flux: 'But none of your slide snide rules can catch what is sliding so fast'. And in 'Reflections', asyndeton and syntactical refrain (parison) help to produce 'aporia' in an experiential rather than a purely theoretical sense. Not all literary experiment is uncontrolled.

Paul Muldoon and Ciaran Carson are sometimes called 'postmodernist' poets. Certainly they grew up in a late twentieth-century ethos influenced by collisions and collusions between high art and popular culture – though that has happened before. Their poetry also takes a deconstructive approach to language (though that is not all it does) and abounds in intertextual quotation as does their prose. Carson produced three prose works during the 1990s, *Last Night's Fun*, *The Star Factory*, and *Fishing for Amber*, which proceed by association and digression. So does the specimen of Muldoon's criticism called *To Ireland, I* which has more courage of its author's formal convictions than does criticism by most 'modernist' poets. At one point Muldoon pursues a 'digression within a digression within a digression'.[42] Nonetheless, 'free, ungrounded play' (Nicholls's definition of postmodernism)[43] ultimately fits neither aesthetic. Indeed, the more digressive both poets become the more obsessively they join things up.

Both *The Star Factory* and *To Ireland, I* employ an alphabetical scheme. Muldoon's most recent collection *Hay* (1999) is intricately rhymed, and he transfers rhyme-schemes from one collection to another.

Carson's 'Last Orders' (1989) and Muldoon's 'Sushi' (1987) are loosely related to the MacNeice poems in that each presents a speaker located or dislocated in urban space, having a night on the town. These speakers also try to make sense of their environment in a way that reflects on poem-making. In Carson's 'Last Orders' questions of 'appearance' are a matter of life and death. This is the first stanza:

> Squeeze the buzzer on the steel mesh gate like a trigger, but
> It's someone else who has you in their sights. Click. It opens,
>   like electronic
> Russian roulette, since you never know for sure who's who, or what
> You're walking into. I, for instance, could be anybody. Though I'm told
> Taig's written on my face. See me, would *I* trust appearances? [44]

The scenario of getting into a security-fenced Belfast pub, and how best to behave once inside, adds a political dimension to the parable of perception, of self and world. Carson exploits the colloquial Belfast exclamation 'See me' to underline the conundrum of identity construed from within and/or without. Here again, relativized readings are a more than theoretical matter. And syntax is again prime mover in dramatizing the conundrum. Yet Carson corrugates and extends, rather than abandons, the line.

'Sushi' is a formally more introverted poem, indeed that introversion is part of its theme:

> 'Why do we waste so much time in arguing?'
> We were sitting at the sushi-bar
> drinking Kirin beer
> and watching the Master chef
> fastidiously shave
> salmon, tuna and yellowtail
> while a slightly more volatile
> apprentice
> fanned the rice
> every grain of which was magnetized
> in one direction – east.
> Then came translucent strips
> of octopus,
> squid and conger,

pickled ginger
and pale-green horseradish ...
'It's as if you've some kind of death-wish.
You won't even talk ...' ...

I saw, when the steam
cleared, how this apprentice
had scrimshandered a rose's
exquisite petals
not from some precious metal
or wood or stone
('I might as well be eating alone.')
but the tail-end of a carrot:
how when he submitted his work to the Master –
Is it not the height of arrogance
to propose that God's no more arcane
than the smack of oregano,
orgone,
the inner organs
of beasts and fowls, the mines of Arigna,
the poems of Louis Aragon? –
It might have been alabaster
or jade
the Master so gravely weighed
from hand to hand
with the look of a man unlikely to confound
Duns Scotus, say, with Scotus Eriugena. [45]

The first and last lines rhyme (as do the intermediate irregular couplets) and
their rhyme-sounds also reverberate with the italicized aria on *rgn* towards the
end of the poem. The unspoken rhyme-word, it seems, may be 'origin' since
the difference between the like-named philosophers turns on whether God is
located in Nature or is too 'arcane' for human reason and art. Some of this
may appear postmodern enough. 'Sushi' nods to T. S. Eliot as regards the
need for explanatory notes, and perhaps the situation of (presumably) a
woman's attempt to talk being ignored by a male speaker. Nonetheless, in
reflecting on how we pattern the world, the poem depends on its own patterns, however these patterns might be open to question.

The italicized rhyme words shape, rather than disperse into free association,
another parable-poem concerned with personal and modern instabilities. These
instabilities include the problematic status of art: does it violate Nature as the

sushi-scenario, 'scrimshandered' and the imagery of innards and mines might suggest? Is it all about craft and 'mastery'? Or does such masculine aestheticism deny life, flux and emotion? Perhaps the Master's final balancing-act with the carrot-rose leaves the poem itself as evenly weighed in its artistic 'thisness' – a relevant Duns Scotus concept. The notion that he is 'unlikely to confound' (not 'confuse') one philosopher with another suggests that neither the poem nor poetry is in the business of absolute conclusions – not only where spirit and matter are concerned. Both, however, are in the business of 'pattern-making' (to use MacNeice's favourite term for 'formalising activity'). To read 'Sushi' as a poem about poetry, or a poem relevant to modernism and to reading poetry, is not entirely arbitrary but fits its textual position in Muldoon's *Meeting the British* (1987). There 'Sushi' prefaces '7, Middagh Street': a sequence that adopts the voices of MacNeice, Auden, Salvador Dalí, and others to explore form and history with reference to Europe in 1940, Ireland in the 1980s. In both contexts of a work also saturated with Yeats, Muldoon possibly warns against confounding one poet with another. And while 'the tail-end of a carrot' may satirize Yeats's architectonic rhetoric of working with metal, wood, and stone, 'Sushi' clearly offers itself as more than a carrot and perhaps as a variation on how the Yeatsian gyres pattern history.

My point is that we may not need modernism or postmodernism to talk about these 'Irish' poems – although these Irish poems may talk about modernism and postmodernism. Nor do MacNeice, Muldoon, and Carson resort to free verse when they dramatize the existential or cognitive problematics of modernity. It might be argued, indeed, that a poetry still in touch with traditional forms (and in touch with Yeats) has retained more complex means of phrasing such questions. The formal dialectic between Yeats and Joyce has something to do with different (Protestant and Catholic) religious or post-religious epistemologies, as well as with their own historical position in Ireland. Similar theological influences condition contemporary Northern Ireland along with Irish/ British political faultlines and language-questions. Complex tensions between authority and relativism thus criss-cross the cultural field. Some of this may explain why Carson and Muldoon subject Yeatsian form (itself earlier revised in the poetry of MacNeice, Derek Mahon, and Michael Longley)[46] to Joycean linguistic deconstruction. So if there has been a multiplication of creative 'play' by Yeats's 'more volatile apprentices', it is hardly 'ungrounded'. Yet perhaps all these dialectics have been poetically fertile because neither Yeats nor Joyce 'confounds' the other. In contrast, some postcolonial criticism uses a modernist-nationalist 'Joyce' to displace a traditionalist-colonialist 'Yeats'.

*

Hugh Selwyn Mauberley, 'Nineteen Hundred and Nineteen', and *The Waste Land* share a reflexive narrative of the poet trying to find his creative bearings amidst postwar circumstances that seem to invalidate European art, thought and civilization. It may be symptomatic, however, that Pound's title is a personal name that brings the artist-hero upfront, however mock-heroic or mocked he may be (critics are revealingly divided as to the degree of irony in *Mauberley*); that Eliot's title is spatial and symbolic; that Yeats's is temporal and historical. If Eliot's and Yeats's titles imply (differently angled) judgments of Christendom, Yeats places the Christian era historically as well as critically.

The Pound voice does appear to blame history, together with English literary culture, for not respecting the artist and his own labours to 'resuscitate the dead art / Of poetry'. Whether or not you agree with K. K. Ruthven's opinion that Pound's 'farewell to London' turns literary history into 'a myth whose function is to align readers of the poem with its own point of view',[47] the poem's perspective is dominated by literary priorities which portend the next Poundian phase. Yeats's irony, in contrast, neither detaches the artist from the age nor sees him as mistaken (Pound's 'Wrong from the start') as opposed to inadequate or self-deceived ('crack-pated'). Both poets return to the 1890s, their common aesthetic point of origin, in a effort to comprehend what has gone 'wrong'. They conflate various art-forms in nineties style, and wistfully evoke nineties reverie: Pound's 'inward gaze', Yeats's 'secret meditation'. Both poets also depend on structures which present stark contrasts between the present and various pasts: Yeats's 'We who seven years ago/ Talked of honour and of truth', Pound's 'What god, man, or hero/ Shall I place a tin wreath upon!' Pound and Yeats come close in these sequences. Yet Yeats seems to initiate a deeper formal engagement with the crisis that his poem perceives. A collective 'we' – which incorporates shattered Irish and British political optimism as well as artistic disillusionment – is his most common pronoun, and conveys an imagination more implicated in events than Pound's 'I/he'. Yet all Yeats's pronouns serve a 'polyvocality' of dramatic variation. Tones of irony, lament, anger, self-reproach, and numbed horror figure, to quote Marshall Berman, somebody 'trying to survive and create in the maelstrom's midst',[48] somebody who reconstitutes 'formalising activity' even as he mourns its disruption:

When Loie Fuller's Chinese dancers enwound
A shining web, a floating ribbon of cloth,
It seemed that a dragon of air
Had fallen among dancers, had whirled them round
Or hurried them off on its own furious path;

So the Platonic Year
Whirls out new right and wrong,
Whirls in the old instead;
All men are dancers and their tread
Goes to the barbarous clangour of a gong.[49]

Yeats's recall of a nineties dance-ensemble mutually involves a performative artwork and the historical 'dragon of air'. This condenses and defines the poem's larger trajectory: its dialectic of images, the way in which symbolism has been forced to engage with history, or the poem as sequence with history as process. The intense patterning makes every variation matter. For instance, the final section – which intermingles the nineties motifs of Salome and apocalypse – hides its stanzaic structure (three six-lined stanzas rhymed ABCA-BC) and occasionally omits the verb 'to be'. That purposeful aporia, in the first and seventh lines, helps to power the rhetorical sweep from actual 'Violence upon the roads' to apocalyptic symbolism, while further ellipsis makes 'Their purpose in the labyrinth of the wind' all the more sinister:

Violence upon the roads: violence of horses;
Some few have handsome riders, are garlanded
On delicate sensitive ear or tossing mane,
But wearied running round and round in their courses
All break and vanish, and evil gathers head:
Herodias' daughters have returned again,
A sudden blast of dusty wind and after
Thunder of feet, tumult of images,
Their purpose in the labyrinth of the wind ...
...
But now wind drops, dust settles; thereupon
There lurches past, his great eyes without thought
Under the shadow of stupid straw-pale locks,
That insolent fiend Robert Artisson
To whom the love-lorn Lady Kyteler brought
Bronzed peacock feathers, red combs of her cocks.[50]

If Yeats's images appear heterogeneous – and here he did learn a thing or two from Pound – heterogeneity *per se* (in contrast with *The Waste Land*) is never upfront: his images are primarily actors, like the finally opposed Lady Kyteler and Robert Artisson, in a dialectical and dramatic counterpoint. This does not imply that everything is under control or resolved. The finale is left open to what history – and poetry – might do next.

I will end by citing two readings of 'Nineteen Hundred and Nineteen': the first in terms of modernism and Eliot; the second, in terms of postmodernism and Pound. On the one hand, Rainer Emig sees Yeats's sequence as pre-modernist: he refers to its 'deterministic and mythical outlook' and says 'the text is not content with factual historic events. They have to be put into a universal frame'.[51] On the other hand, Hillis Miller reads the poem as post-modernist: Yeats has now been postmodernized quite a bit as that gyre gradually reaches every text, still required for curricular credibility, that used to fit the New Critical bill. But Miller's reading is wonderfully extreme. He argues that 'Yeats ... speaks as no one, from nowhere, at no time, to no identifiable listeners; that [the poem] can by no effort be shown to have an organic unity; and that there is no identifiable central, literal thing of which all else is figure. The poem, in short, is a labyrinth of the wind.'[52] Readings against the grain can be refreshing, and Yeats's dialectic with Pound, as with 'modernity', absorbed more than his poetic surfaces admit. Miller, however, reduces the great-rooted blossomer to an unrecognisable scatter of twigs. He also turns Ireland into 'nowhere'. *If* it is the case that the literary-critical 'concept of modernism' has significant roots in early twentieth-century inter-national dialectics about poetry, perhaps modernism should pay wider attention to those dialectics and their continuing history. This might, of course, bring about its own dissolution into 'a labyrinth of the wind'.

Notes

1 Karl Shapiro, 'T. S. Eliot: The Death of Literary Judgment', in Shapiro's *In Defense of Ignorance* (New York: Random House, 1952; Vintage edn, 1965), pp. 35–60 (35).
2 Marshall Berman, *All That Is Solid Melts into Air: The Experience of Modernity* (New York: Simon and Schuster, 1982; Penguin edn, 1988), p. 345.
3 Astradur Eysteinsson, *The Concept of Modernism* (Ithaca and London: Cornell University Press, 1990), pp. 100, 50.
4 Vassiliki Kolocotroni, Jane Goldman, and Olga Taxidou (eds), *Modernism: An Anthology of Sources and Documents* (Edinburgh: Edinburgh University Press, 1998), p. xvii.
5 Rainer Emig, *W. H. Auden: Towards a Postmodern Poetics* (London: Macmillan, 2000), p. 4.
6 Michael Schmidt (ed.), *The Harvill Book of Twentieth-Century Poetry in English* (London: Harvill, 1999), p. xxxviii.
7 Edna Longley, '"Why should men's heads ache?" Yeats and American Modernism' will appear in the conference proceedings edited by Mark Ford and Steve Clark.
8 See John Harwood, 'The Hollow Man', review of Humphrey Carpenter, *A Serious Character: The Life of Ezra Pound* and James Longenbach, *Stone Cottage*, in *Yeats Annual* 8 (London: Macmillan, 1991), p. 256.

9   W. B. Yeats, *A Vision* (London: Macmillan, 1962 edn), p. 3.

10   W. B. Yeats (ed.), *The Oxford Book of Modern Verse 1892–1935* (Oxford: Clarendon Press, 1936), p. xxiv.

11   'The poet who writes "free" verse is like Robinson Crusoe on his desert island: he must do all his cooking, laundry and darning for himself. In a few exceptional cases this manly independence produces something original and impressive, but more often the result is squalor – dirty sheets on the unmade bed and empty bottles on the unswept floor.' W. H. Auden, *The Dyer's Hand and Other Essays* (London: Faber and Faber, 1963), p. 22.

12   See Brigit Patmore, 'Some Memories of W. B. Yeats', in E. H. Mikhail (ed.), *W. B. Yeats: Interviews and Recollections* (London: Macmillan, 1977), vol. II, pp. 355–63 (361).

13   Elizabeth Butler Cullingford, 'Phoenician genealogies and oriental geographies: Joyce, language and race', in Derek Attridge and Marjorie Howe (eds), *Semicolonial Joyce* (Cambridge University Press, 2000), pp. 219–239 (221).

14   Joseph Kelly, *Our Joyce: From Outcast to Icon* (Austin: University of Texas Press, 1998), pp. 63–4.

15   K. K. Ruthven, *Ezra Pound as Literary Critic* (London: Routledge, 1990), p. 170.

16   Attridge and Howe, *Semicolonial Joyce*, p. 13.

17   Howard J. Booth and Nigel Rigby (eds), *Modernism and Empire* (Manchester: Manchester University Press, 2000), p. 3.

18   Elleke Boehmer, '"Immeasurable Strangeness" in imperial times: Leonard Woolf and W. B. Yeats', *Modernism and Empire*, pp. 93–111 (103–4).

19   W. B. Yeats, 'Gitanjali', *Essays and Introductions* (London: Macmillan, 1961), pp. 387–95 (392).

20   R. F. Foster, review of Declan Kiberd, *Inventing Ireland*, *The Times*, Thursday 14 December 1995, 38.

21   C. L. Innes, 'Modernism, Ireland and empire: Yeats, Joyce and their implied audience', *Modernism and Empire*, pp. 137–55 (154).

22   Helen Carr, 'Imagism and empire', *Modernism and Empire*, pp. 64–92 (75).

23   Máire ní Fhlathúin, 'The anti-colonial modernism of Patrick Pearse', *Modernism and Empire*, pp. 156–74 (171).

24   Attridge and Howe, *Semicolonial Joyce*, p. 11.

25   Lawrence Rainey, *Institutions of Modernism: Literary Elites and Public Culture* (New Haven and London: Yale University Press, 1998), p. 100.

26   Michael North, *Reading 1922: A Return to the Scene of the Modern* (Oxford: Oxford University Press, 1999), p. 209.

27   Interviewed by Clive Wilmer, in Wilmer's *Poets Talking: Poet of the Month Interviews from BBC Radio 3* (Manchester: Carcanet Press, 1994), pp. 36–42 (41).

28   Marjorie Perloff, 'What We Don't Talk About When We Talk About Poetry: Some Aporias of Literary Journalism', in Jeremy Treglown and Bridget Bennett (eds), *Grub Street and the Ivory Tower* (Oxford: Clarendon Press, 1998), pp. 224–49 (224, 229).

29   Andrew Crozier and Tim Longville (eds), *A Various Art* (Manchester: Carcanet Press, 1987), p. 13.

30   Patricia Coughlan and Alex Davis (eds), *Modernism and Ireland: The Poetry of the 1930s* (Cork University Press, 1995), pp. 18, 20, 2.

31   Perloff, *Grub Street and the Ivory Tower*, p. 229.

32 Robert Crawford, *Devolving English Literature* (Oxford: Clarendon Press, 1992), p. 270.

33 See Thom Gunn, *Shelf Life: Essays, Memoirs and an Interview* (London: Faber and Faber, 1993), pp. 228, 223; Clive Wilmer, Interview with Thom Gunn, *Poets Talking*, pp. 1–7 (5).

34 See Edna Longley, "'Something Wrong Somewhere?" Louis MacNeice as Critic', in Longley, *Poetry & Posterity* (Tarset, Northumberland: Bloodaxe Books, 2000), pp. 134–166.

35 Louis MacNeice, 'Poetry Today', in Alan Heuser (ed.), *Selected Literary Criticism of Louis MacNeice* (Oxford: Clarendon Press, 1987), pp. 10–44 (37).

36 Louis MacNeice, *The Poetry of W. B. Yeats* (Oxford: Oxford University Press, 1941; London: Faber and Faber, 1967), p. 191.

37 See Paul Morrison, *The Poetics of Fascism: Ezra Pound, T. S. Eliot, Paul de Man* (Oxford: Oxford University Press, 1996), pp. 122–3.

38 MacNeice, *The Poetry of W. B. Yeats*, p. 157.

39 Louis MacNeice, *Varieties of Parable* (Cambridge: Cambridge University Press, 1965), p. 16.

40 *The Collected Poems of Louis MacNeice*, ed. E. R. Dodds (London: Faber and Faber, 1966), pp. 502–3.

41 *Ibid.*, p. 503.

42 Paul Muldoon, *To Ireland, I* (Oxford: Oxford University Press, 2000), p. 125.

43 Peter Nicholls, *Modernisms: A Literary Guide* (Berkeley: University of California Press, 1995), p. 277.

44 Ciaran Carson, *Belfast Confetti* (Loughcrew, Co. Meath: Gallery Books, 1989), p. 46.

45 Paul Muldoon, *Meeting the British* (London: Faber and Faber, 1987), pp. 34–5.

46 See Peter McDonald, 'Yeats, Form and Northern Irish Poetry', in Warwick Gould and Edna Longley (eds), *Yeats Annual 12: That Accusing Eye: Yeats and His Irish Readers* (London: Macmillan, 1996), pp. 213–42.

47 Ruthven, *Ezra Pound as Literary Critic*, p. 41.

48 Berman, *All That Is Solid Melts into Air*, p. 346.

49 *Yeats's Poems*, ed. A. N. Jeffares (London: Macmillan, 1989), p. 315.

50 *Ibid.*, pp. 317–18.

51 Rainer Emig, *Modernism in Poetry*, pp. 52–3.

52 J. Hillis Miller, 'Yeats: The Linguistic Moment', in Harold Bloom (ed.), *W. B. Yeats* (New York, New Haven, Philadelphia: Chelsea House, 1986), pp. 189–210 (191–2).

11
The Disconsolate Chimera: T. S. Eliot and the Fixation of Modernism

Stan Smith

Entre deux gares

In July 1941, C. Day Lewis and L. A. G. Strong published, under the auspices of Methuen and Co, *A New Anthology of Modern Verse 1920-1940*, simultaneously in a School Edition and in one for the general reader. Their commission, as they indicate in an introduction constructed as a dialogue between the two editors, was 'to make a new anthology from the point at which Sir Algernon Methuen left off, in 1920':

> Thus we cover a period of twenty years: the space between two wars. Though I don't know that we have found that fact significant.[1]

That is Strong. Day Lewis responds with what is already a substantively revisionary question: 'Why should there be any poetic significance in a period between two wars? English poetry seems to have made one of its many new starts in 1930 rather than in 1920.' Strong's response in turn is cast as another question, aimed ostensibly at Day Lewis, but actually, rhetorically, at the reader:

> Might not that be the point at which a new generation became articulate - a generation looking forward to the next instead of looking backward to the last? A generation whose Muses were Cassandra and the Goddess of the Machine? (1941: p.xiii)

The anthology, which went through ten editions between 1941 and 1945 (four of them specifically for schools), was widely influential in shaping public perception of what was subsequently categorized as the era of 'high' modernism – a period T. S. Eliot himself famously dismissed, in 'East Coker' in 1940, as 'Twenty years largely wasted, the years of *l'entre deux guerres*'.[2]

For the editors, Eliot's own status is an area of primary contestation. Day Lewis casts his work as 'the start of a new movement in poetry, although his influence on poetry did not begin to make itself felt till about 1930'; while the older Strong claims to 'have always regarded Eliot as a traditional poet, not as a revolutionary ... a poet anxious to continue in the tradition, and indignant because it had obviously broken down'. 'He proceeded to cast about', Strong continues, 'and was not happy until he had found a tradition within which to work.' Day Lewis insists, however, that 'For all that, I still think Eliot's influence on younger poets was a revolutionary one; it was through him chiefly that the technique of the French Symbolist poets was communicated to them'. Strong concedes that 'Certainly his influence was revolutionary – for he showed beyond all doubt that the tradition had collapsed, and they must break new ground for themselves', but seeks to distinguish this 'influence' on the 'new movement' from the actual, 'traditional' body of his work (1941: p. xx).

This dispute is a symptomatic one, apparent everywhere in the critical accounts of 'modern' or (less frequently) 'modernist' writing published in the 1920s and 30s. In all these debates, the desire to produce a definitive account of what Eliot represents is repeatedly entangled with the need to characterize that 'new movement in poetry' which Day Lewis saw emerging 'about 1930'. Eliot's modernity, that is, can be defined, apparently, only in its relation to that 'new generation' of poets who have absorbed his influence. From the start, 'modernism', and in particular Eliot's contribution to it, can be figured only in a configuration of generations, as a genealogical lineage.

Eliot was himself keenly alert to the property dispute conducted over his name throughout this period, fostering a younger 'revolutionary' generation of writers, both by publishing them and by oblique critical approval, in such works as *The Use of Poetry and the Use of Criticism* (1933), while moving insistently, here and in such texts as *After Strange Gods* (1934), towards increasingly 'orthodox' definitions of the literary and philosophical tradition which dissociate him from this lineage.

I have found only one usage of the term 'modernist' in Eliot's writings. His introduction to Baudelaire's *Intimate Journals* in 1930 speaks of Baudelaire's 'recognition of the reality of Sin' as something 'which separates him from the modernist Protestantism of Byron and Shelley'.[3] Significantly, he deploys the word not to speak of the specific literary movement initiated by himself and Ezra Pound, but to identify a generic, transhistorical sensibility, focused by that earlier cultural moment from which his criticism had repeatedly dissociated itself. In the iconography of the time, however, this can be read as a coded, or implied, reference to W. H. Auden and Stephen Spender, both of whom Eliot was shortly to publish at Faber and Faber. In the thirties, Spender was regularly equated with Shelley, while Auden, the satirist of *The Orators* (a volume which draws on Baudelaire's *Journals*), was in a few years' time to acknowledge the analogy by publishing his own 'Letter to Lord Byron', in a volume specifically commissioned by Faber. By implication, likewise, Eliot can be seen here identifying his own modernity – a quality distinct from 'modernism' – with that of Baudelaire, whom he describes as 'the greatest exemplar in *modern* poetry in any language, for his verse and language is the nearest to a complete renovation that we have experienced' (pp.191–2; Eliot's italics).

Eliot was himself in two minds about whether twentieth-century modern-ism really constituted a literary 'revolution'. Pound wrote in 1932 of this 'movement to which no name has ever been given' as a 'revolution of the word', effected 'In the dim mainly forgotten backward of 1908 and 1910 [by] a few men in London'.[4] In 1928, however, Eliot had already penned a dis-missive and self-extricating obituary notice in the *Dial*: 'We can now see that there was no movement, no revolution, and there is no formula. The only revolution was that Ezra Pound was born with a fine ear for verse'.[5] The very title of Eliot's piece, 'Isolated Superiority', insists on the egregiousness of this achievement.[6]

In a preface, exactly contemporary with Day Lewis and Strong's introduc-tion, to *A Little Book of Modern Verse* which he had commissioned from Anne Ridler, Eliot wrestled with what might constitute a specifically 'modern' poet-ic.[7] Apart from Yeats and Hopkins, he says,

> we may take as within the term of 'modern poetry' the work of those writers who had arrived at individual form and idiom during the four or five years immediate-ly preceding the last war. Those who first found their speech during that war – whether we call them 'war poets' or not – form a second age group; and since 1918 at least two other poetic generations can be distinguished.

The generational insistence is symptomatic. Eliot notes, over 'the last twenty years ... the rapidity with which one literary generation has followed another'. The cause of 'this acceleration of change', he says, lies not in individual talents, but 'is to be found, if at all, in the history of a changing and bewildered world, the mutations of which have given it a different appearance to poets no more than ten years apart in age':

> Among so much variety, people are still found to ask, and to give an answer to, the question: what is it that makes modern poetry modern? Those who think that they can define modern poetry, are more often found among its detractors than among its admirers – for while it is easy to attribute a common quality to every-thing we like, it is still easier to attribute a common vice to what repels us ... But the definition of 'modern poetry' cannot be made more than partially by the intelligence. It cannot be explained in terms of influences: we can only explain a poet by the influences he has experienced, when he is not really a poet at all.

Through a series of negative refinings, Eliot seems determined to dissolve into a plethora of autonomous and incompatible impulses the whole idea of a specifically modernist poetic:

> It cannot be explained in terms of what the poets are consciously trying to do; for, apart from the fact that no two are trying to do quite the same thing, their aware-ness of purpose is only part of the situation. It certainly ... cannot be explained in

terms of a common idiom, vocabulary, or metric. Modern poets do not all write in what is called *vers libre*; they do not unanimously, or even predominantly, adopt the words and imagery of an urban, industrialised and mechanised civilisation; they do not all share the same political or religious views, and in much of their work there is no evidence of any political bias or religious conviction at all. Finally, however, he shrinks back from such categorical dismissal, to offer a positive definition which is not so much textual as contextual, transgressing merely literary parameters:

> Yet they have something in common, though every definition of what it is will be mostly wrong or inadequate; what they have in common can be perceived by the sensibility, but not defined in words. For an explanation of what makes modern poetry would have to be an explanation of the whole modern world; to understand the poet we should have to understand ourselves – we should have, in fact, to reach a degree of self-consciousness of which mankind has never been capable, and of which, if attained, it might perish.

The faint recollection, here, of 'Burnt Norton''s 'human kind / Cannot bear very much reality', is not, I think, gratuitous, for the developing sequence of *Four Quartets* can be seen to constitute at one level a sustained and self-conscious meditation on a modernism which is, in the words of 'Little Gidding', 'Both intimate and unidentifiable', fixated perpetually 'Between two worlds become much like each other', isolated *'entre deux guerres'* but also *entre deux gares*, like that 'underground train, in the tube' in 'East Coker', which 'stops too long between stations / And the conversation rises and slowly fades into silence / And you see behind every face the mental emptiness deepen'.

Noticeably, the analogies Eliot deploys in the preface to Ridler's anthology are political and quasi-juridical, not literary, in a classic Eliotic evasion which defers such questions to a domain beyond the legitimate boundaries of criticism (compare, for example, the last paragraph of 'Tradition and the Individual Talent' and the closing peroration of *The Use of Poetry and the Use of Criticism*):

> [J]ust as every people is ready, on occasion, to find political scapegoats for its own delinquencies (and a democratic people differs from others only in having to find more at once) so it is sometimes inclined to find scapegoats in its men of letters, in an outcry which exceeds the ordinary dislike of everything new. To say that this or that writer is a fraud may be legitimate literary criticism: to arraign a generation of writers is merely bad sociology. The answer is not to insist on the merits of that whole generation ... The answer is in a more thorough and scientific examination of the state of society: an answer which, being outside of literary criticism, is as far beyond the terms of reference of this preface as it is beyond the space which it should occupy.

Eliot's final advice to the reader is purely pragmatic: 'I believe a reading of all the poems together will give a feeling of what "modern poetry" is: even though he does not find himself able to make a definition of "modernness", it will help to put him on guard against other people's definitions'. All attempts to define the modern are, he says, 'a blackboard exercise, to be erased as soon as completed'.

A blackboard exercise

Let me, however, undertake that exercise. For 'other people's definitions' are of central importance in understanding how Eliot himself came to construe his own relation to the movement subsequently known as 'modernism', and critical accounts of his impact throughout the interwar years repeatedly evince the same conflicted ambiguity apparent in Day Lewis and Strong's assessment.[8]

The epithet 'modernist' is usually credited to Robert Graves and Laura Riding in their 1927 study *A Survey of Modernist Poetry*, in which Eliot is deployed as a touchstone, specifically in a brilliant extended analysis of 'Burbank with a Baedeker' which offers the poem as a definitive example of 'modernist poetry'.[9] Their conclusion is, perhaps, premature, but nonetheless unequivocal in fingering Eliot as the leading figure of a generation of modernists:

> the modernist generation is already over before its time, having counted itself out and swallowed itself up by its very efficiency – a true 'lost generation'. Already, its most 'correct' writers, such as T. S. Eliot, have become classics over the heads of the plain reader. (pp. 265–6)

Nevertheless, they contrast 'the highly organized nature of Mr Eliot's criticism in its present stage with the gradual disintegration of his poetry since the *Waste Land.*'

Graves and Riding in turn derived the 'modernist' epithet from that fleeting little magazine published out of Nashville, Tennessee, with which they were intimately involved, the *Fugitive*, whose editors, Donald Davidson, Allen Tate and John Crowe Ransom, variously use the word in the columns of the journal and in their correspondence. Ransom in particular continued to use the terms in essays of the 1930s in such quasi-academic journals as the *Southern Review*, several of which were collected in *The World's Body* (1938), and it is probably via this route that the words enter academic discourse in the period after the Second World War. In this early phase, 'modern' and 'modernist' are interchangeable terms, but it is clear with whom they are associated. In the final issue of the *Fugitive* for 1922, for example, an essay on 'Modern Art' argues that 'Perhaps T. S. Eliot has already pointed the way for this and the next generation,' adding, confidently, 'However, the Moderns have adequately arrived'.

1928 saw two further attempts to define a specifically 'modernist' poetry, both influenced by Graves and Riding and each deploying Eliot as a touchstone, though to different ends. The then fashionable poet Humbert Wolfe's *Dialogues and Monologues*[10] devotes a whole chapter to 'Modernism in Verse' (pp.197–253), in the form of an unequal dialogue between pro- and anti-voices, cites Graves and Riding, and identifies 'the Modernist school of thought' 'as illustrated in Great Britain by the Sitwells and Herbert Read, and in the United States by T. S. Eliot, Conrad Aiken, John Gould Fletcher, and Archibald Macleish' (p.197). This odd assortment, which puts up a quietly snobbish resistance to Eliot's anglicization, casts Modernism as primarily a movement of 'Transatlantic innovators' (p. 224) and correlates '*Waste-Land* and the true Modernist movement' (p. 226).[11]

The same year, however, the young and rather better poet Roy Campbell, writing on 'Contemporary Poetry' in Edgell Rickword's collection *Scrutinies*,[12] deployed the epithet as a term of abuse held at arms' length by scare quotes, indicting 'The most formidable innovations with which the more conscious "modernists" have threatened poetry so far' (pp. 177–9). Campbell, however, applies the term not to Eliot, whom he praises as the author of 'the one outstanding poem of our time', but to 'his most unconditional imitators of to-day', 'the younger university poets' – in 1928, the coteries around W. H. Auden in an Oxford abuzz with modern attitude.

For these allegedly 'modernist' poets Campbell has little but contempt, observing that their 'technical innovations, which are invested with such importance by contemporary critics, are about as likely to influence poetry as the invention of a new style of hairpin would be to revolutionise engineering.' The immediate Oxford butt of Campbell's contempt here is probably the young Tom Driberg, later a Labour MP and British/Soviet double or even triple agent. It was Driberg who in 1926 had introduced his fellow undergraduate Auden to *The Waste Land*. Driberg can also be credited with fostering in Oxford circles the idea of specifically modernist movement. According to Geoffrey Grigson,[13] in June 1927 Driberg invited Edith Sitwell to speak in Oxford, as part of a series of talks at the new English club involving several 'eminent and curious ladies', Woolf, Riding, and Gertrude Stein. Holding up a copy of Eliot's journal *The Criterion*, Grigson says, 'He had spoken gracefully, at a small table, of the delights of intellectualism and modernism'. Grigson suggests a relation between this whole sequence of events and the Auden gang:

> There were poets in the university who were to dominate letters before very long, W. H. Auden, for example, and Louis MacNeice.... But it was Thomas Driberg who now appeared to dominate the obvious and outer and smarter intellectuations of the university, who wrote poems in the blend of Eliotese and Edith-Sitwellese which appeared week by week in *Cherwell.*

And he records of Stephen Spender that by the time he left Oxford he was 'almost exclusively interested in … the "experimental" modernism of Eliot and Joyce and Ezra Pound and Virginia Woolf and Laura Riding', adding '"Modernism," then, was working like a mole in spring under the smooth beds of the garden', and 'what was alive in this modernism was kicking hard with life' (pp.121–2). Significantly, Spender's *The Struggle of the Modern* was in 1963 one of the first postwar academic attempts to distinguish 'modern' from 'modernist', contrasting traditional writing about 'modern subject matter' and the object of his study, in which 'I am only discussing obvious examples of modernism or anti-modernism', and, in a chapter on 'Moderns and Contemporaries' distinguishing 'art which is modern … from several movements grouped approximately under the heading "modernism"'.[14]

'Modernism' if used at all in the early 1930s is usually a pejorative term, as in J. C. Squire's caustic remark, in his introduction to Eric Gillett's 1932 anthology *Poets of Our Time*, that 'Nothing, in every age, stales more rapidly than Modernism'.[15] In 1933, however, R. D. Charques's timely study *Contemporary Literature and Social Revolution*[16] has an approving chapter entitled 'Echoes in the Waste Land' which carries further the equation of 'the disintegrations of Mr. Joyce and the modernism of Mr. Eliot' (p. 9) with a new generation of socialist poets, foremost of whom are Auden and Spender (pp. 71–3). By contrast, Percy Wyndham Lewis in *Men Without Art* in 1934 uses both 'modernist' and 'modernism' in a concerted assault on the 'critical standpoint we associate today with the name of Mr. T. S. Eliot and his school.' Significantly, a key chapter, called 'T. S. Eliot (Pseudoist)', moves beyond the men of 1914 to praise the true modernity of Auden's *The Orators*, which, he says, has finally 'really given the coup de grace to Mr Eliot's spell' over the younger generation: 'at last the spell has been broken. And Mr. Auden has done it'.[17]

The same ambivalence about Eliot's status can be seen in Louis MacNeice's critical writings of the period. In 1935 he contributed an essay on 'Poetry To-day' to Geoffrey Grigson's collection *The Arts To-day* in which the idea of 'modernism' is conspicuous by its absence. Though MacNeice refers to such well-established 'isms' as Imagism, Futurism, Surrealism and post-Impressionism, he merely observes that 'in 1922 appeared the classic English test-pieces of modern prose and verse – *Ulysses* by James Joyce and *The Waste Land* by T. S. Eliot.' If Eliot provided 'a bridge between the dominant poetry of the early nineteen-twenties and the dominant poetry of the early nineteen-thirties', MacNeice says, it is largely through his admiration for Dryden ('there is undoubtedly a Drydenism in the air'): 'Eliot's influence has been towards classicism' and under it 'Auden, who to start with was very difficult, is grinding his verse into simplicity'.[18]

MacNeice's book *Modern Poetry*[19] in 1938, however, uses the word 'modernist' to make a key distinction. Much of the book, like its title, still speaks of 'modern poetry'. But it reserves the Graves/Riding epithet for discussions which focus on the disjunctive lineage running from Eliot, through the 1920s, to MacNeice's own generation. It is as an historical and changing dynamic that 'modernism' *per se* is here constituted: 'Modernist poetry, as introduced to England by Eliot, inherited its use of imagery both from recent French poets and, among English poets, from the late Elizabethans and the Metaphysicals' (p.103). It is not Eliot and Co., that is, but what MacNeice speaks of as the generation *affected by* the methods of *The Waste Land* who spring to mind when he discusses modernism.

In *The Poetry of W. B. Yeats* three years later[20] MacNeice notes that Yeats's later work 'made such an impression on the younger English poets of the time, who had been brought up on *The Waste Land*', and admits to 'a certain snobbery in our new admiration, a snobbery paralleled in Yeats's own remark: "I too have tried to be modern"'. 'The word "modern,"' he continues, 'is always relative. What did Yeats's modernity – a quality which in his youth he had violently repudiated – consist in?' (p.178). His penultimate chapter in this book, 'Some Comparisons', however, pits this generation *against* Eliot, in defining their modernity. It even attempts what he admits at once to be a 'fallacious' distinction between a school of Eliot and a school of Yeats (among whom he specifically numbers Auden and Spender): 'In England about 1930 a school of poets appeared who mark more or less of a reaction against the influence of Eliot. Curiously, in spite of their violently "modern" content, they were not so much in reaction against Yeats' (pp. 223–4). So 'modernism' here is associated both with Eliot and with the reaction against Eliot, in a complex, not to say contradictory tangle which only a Freudian analysis could unravel.

To complicate matters, in a discussion with Yeats's protégé, the Irish nationalist F. R. Higgins, in July 1939, MacNeice – responding to Higgins's distinction between 'modern Irish poetry. Modern poetry, mark you, as distinct from modernist' – provokes an exchange which prefigures that between Day Lewis and Strong a couple of years later:

> MacNeice: When you say modernist, I would like to know what poets you are referring to. Would you say Eliot?
>
> Higgins: No, I would not say that Eliot is a modernist; I rather consider him an American Victorian. I could mention E. E. Cummings, with his mathematical designs in word arrangement; for him poetry is merely a matter of typography. In substance, in expression, Yeats, for instance, was a Traditionalist. He 'scorned the sort now growing up, all out of shape from toe to top'. Yeats was most modern without being modernist.
>
> MacNeice: So in my opinion is W. H. Auden.[21]

This is a symptomatic elision. The attempt to distinguish the two words, 'modern' and 'modernist', automatically suggests the name of Eliot, who is then withdrawn from the contest, but only after his name provokes an almost equally automatic invocation of the name of his most obvious successor and heir, Auden.

The association of Eliot's poetic revolution with a cultural and political one of which Auden was the cutting edge is endemic in the 1930s. The much reprinted anthology first published in 1935, *Modern Poetry 1922–1934* – selected and edited by Maurice Wollman, MA, billed as Senior English Master, Barking Abbey School – is unequivocal in its identifications, in the opening words of its introduction:[22]

> In 1798 appeared Wordsworth's and Coleridge's *Lyrical Ballads*, which is usually regarded as the starting-point of that new movement in poetry called the Romantic Movement. In 1922 appeared Mr T. S. Eliot's *The Waste Land*, which many poets and critics of to-day regard as the most significant landmark in post-War literature.

'Mr Eliot', Wollman observes, 'has had many imitators, including himself', and a biographical note adds that 'He has greatly influenced the younger generation of writers, in both England and America'. For Wollman, Eliot is inextricably linked with his successor generation:

> Foremost of the defeatist poets in this Anthology is Mr. T. S. Eliot, with the bleak *Journey of the Magi* and *The Hollow Men*, the hollow men being those who have lived neither in life nor in death, whose existence has been a negation of life, and who are taken by the poet as a symbol of many of this generation. Then come other defeatist poets: Mr. W. H. Auden, another poet of the 'nerves' rather than of the 'brain' or 'soul,' who, in imagery much of which is recondite and more of which is personal, and in language which is sometimes deliberately nonsensical, reveals the temper of to-day as he sees and feels it.[23]

By the time Eliot began to compose the poems that finally constituted *Four Quartets*, starting with 'Burnt Norton' (1936) and proceeding through 'East Coker' (1940) to 'The Dry Salvages' (1941) and 'Little Gidding' (1942), the whole debate about modernism was focused on the configuration which his and Pound's hitherto nameless movement had come to assume with the Auden generation. As Babette Deutsch concluded in 1936, in her shrewd assessment of 'The Post-War Scene' in *This Modern Poetry*, a book published by Eliot's own publishing house and almost certainly commissioned by Eliot: 'The depression did not suddenly breed a new race of poets, speaking a strange tongue. The impress of Pound and Eliot has not been erased. But a new temper is evident in current verse.' If '[a] new generation is looking at life with the aggressive eyes of the young', this is a generation which associates the modernist impulse with 'the muse of Marx'.[24] It is in this light that we should examine Eliot's own troubled and anxious relation with the idea of modernism, a light which, I would suggest, also elucidates one of the key themes of *Four Quartets*.

Between Two Words

Eliot's reluctance to be identified as a 'modernist' is not unrelated to the paternal obligation regularly foisted upon him, by critics, for a generation of younger poets in political and social revolt. Such, at least, is implied in a contribution to the symposium in 1935 on *Faith that Illuminates*, which he took seriously enough to have reprinted in full in his *Selected Prose*:[25]

> And I say that while individual modern writers of eminence can be improving, contemporary literature as a whole tends to be degrading. And that even the effect of the better writers, in an age like ours, may be degrading to some readers; for we must remember that what a writer does to people is not necessarily what he intends to do. It may be only what people are capable of having done to them. A writer like D. H. Lawrence may be in his effect either beneficial or pernicious. I am not sure that I have not had some pernicious influence myself (p.40).

He expects, he says, a 'rejoinder from the liberal-minded' towards these sentiments. Significantly, it is a preoccupation with the idea of literary generations which underpins his case:

> This argument might have some value, if we were always the same generation upon earth; or if, as we know to be not the case, people ever learned much from the experience of their elders. These liberals are convinced that only by what is called unrestrained individualism will truth ever emerge ... Anyone who dissents from this view must be either a medievalist, or else a fascist, and probably both.

But

> The reader of contemporary literature is not, like the reader of the established great of all time, exposing himself to the influence of divers and contradictory personalities; he is exposing himself to a mass movement of writers who, each of them, think that they have something individually to offer, but are really all working together in the same direction ... What I do wish to affirm is that the whole of modern literature is corrupted by what I call Secularism, that it is simply unaware of, simply cannot understand, the meaning of the primacy of the supernatural over the natural life: of something which I assume to be our primary concern. (pp. 41–2)

This casts significant light on the disquisition about the 'quiet-voiced elders' in 'East Coker', who may have been lying to us, or to themselves, as we too may be doing in our turn. For the generation corrupted by Eliot's own 'pernicious' influence, for which he here disclaims responsibility, is one comprised of that 'very large number of people in the world to-day who believe that all ills are fundamentally economic' (p. 43) on both left and right:

My complaint against modern literature is not that modern literature is in the ordinary sense 'immoral' or even 'amoral' ... It is simply that it repudiates, or is wholly ignorant of, our most fundamental and important beliefs; and that in consequence its tendency is to encourage its readers to get what they can out of life while it lasts, to miss no 'experience' that presents itself, and to sacrifice themselves, if they make any sacrifice at all, only for the sake of tangible benefits to others in this world either now or in the future. (p. 44)

In a passage from *The Use of Poetry and the Use of Criticism* excerpted in his 1953 *Selected Prose*,[26] Eliot writes of Johnson's *Lives of the Poets* as a major contribution to literary history, not just empirically but as exemplifying a perpetual responsibility of criticism, for 'every generation must make its own appraisal of the poetry of the past, in the light of the performance of its contemporaries and immediate predecessors'. Eliot certainly sees it as a model for his own activity, in words which faintly prefigure the image, in 'Burnt Norton' two years later, of 'The Word in the desert ... attacked by voices of temptation':

Considering all the temptations to which one is exposed in judging contemporary writing, all the prejudices which one is tempted to indulge in judging writers of the immediately preceding generation, I view Johnson's *Lives of the Poets* as a masterpiece of the judicial bench (pp. 51–2).

Elsewhere in the *Selected Prose* the parallel is driven home by the recruitment of Johnson under the banner of modernity. Johnson, Eliot says, in his revisionary comments on Milton delivered as a British Academy lecture in 1947, 'was, in his day, very much a modern ... concerned with how poetry should be written in his own time'.[27]

The *Selected Prose* is an important but neglected volume. Published in 1953, at a significant moment in Eliot's critical institutionalization, it has some of the status of a manifesto. The Penguin edition of 1958 describes it as 'a comprehensive introduction to one of the finest and most original critical minds of our time', 'Edited and introduced with his approval by Mr. John Hayward'. Hayward, Eliot's friend and confidant – indeed, his flatmate from 1946 to 1957 – is acknowledged at the start of *Four Quartets* as a friend to whom the poet has a particular 'obligation ... for improvements of phrase and construction'. This is not an accidental concurrence, for the passages Hayward selects for this volume contain many semes and themes, literary and political, which we can find formulated more obliquely in the poetry of the *Quartets*.

Hayward's introduction begins by calling attention to Eliot's essay on Arnold, 'from which the first extract in this book is taken', under the heading 'The Function of Criticism'. It is, Hayward says, 'an important statement about the purpose of literary criticism, which throws light on T. S. Eliot's own critical method and achievement', and he quotes its first sentence: '"From time to time," it runs, "every hundred years or so, it is desirable that some critic shall appear to review the past of our literature, and set the poets and the poems in a new order." Such critics are rare', Hayward continues, 'for they must possess, in addition to an unusual capacity for judgement, an independence of mind powerful enough to recognise and to interpret for their generation its own values and categories of appreciation', and he goes on to cite Arnold, Coleridge, Johnson, Dryden, concluding, 'and such, in our own day, is Mr. Eliot himself.'[28]

What I want to focus on here is that generational model at the heart of the extract placed first in Hayward's selection. The 'task' of the critic, Eliot says in the passage excerpted as 'The Function of Criticism' (pp.17–18), in setting poets and poetry in 'a new order', 'is not one of revolution but of readjustment'. After the critic has intervened, 'What we observe is partly the same scene, but in a different and more distant perspective', with 'new and strange objects in the foreground', while 'the more familiar ones ... now approach the horizon', enabling the discerning reader 'to gauge nicely the position and proportion of the objects surrounding us, in the whole of the vast panorama'.

Faced by 'the tendency of a nimble but myopic minority to progenerate heterodoxies', and the tendency of majorities uncritically to accept the opinions of others, we must be alert to the fact that

> no generation is interested in Art in quite the same way as any other; each generation, like each individual, brings to the contemplation of art its own categories of appreciation, makes its own demands upon art, and has its own uses for art. 'Pure' artistic appreciation is to my thinking only an ideal, when not merely a figment, and must be, so long as the appreciation of art is an affair of limited and transient human beings existing in space and time. Both artist and audience are limited. There is for each time, for each artist, a kind of alloy required to make the metal workable into art; and each generation prefers its own alloy to any other.

The image of the alloy recalls earlier chemical analogies, such as that of the inert catalyst in 'Tradition and the Individual Talent'; but it also adds an interesting gloss to that play in *Quartets* between the merely contingent present and the 'pattern of timeless moments' which transcends it. Similarly, the metaphor of the 'vast panorama' points in two directions: back ten years, in 1933, to that description of Joyce's *Ulysses* as a work making 'the modern world possible for art', transmuting, via 'the mythical method', the 'immense panorama of futility and anarchy which is contemporary history'; and forwards almost a decade, to that lament for dying generations in 'East Coker' in the first year of the Second World War, which begins 'O dark dark dark. They all go into the dark, / The vacant interstellar spaces, the vacant into the vacant', whether captains, merchant bankers, statesmen, civil servants, or 'eminent men of letters', and its culminating evocation of 'the darkness of God':

> As, in a theatre,
> The lights are extinguished, for the scene to be changed,
> With a hollow rumble of wings, with a movement of darkness on darkness,
> And we know that the hills and the trees, the distant panorama
> And the bold imposing façade are all being rolled away ...

– a passage immediately followed by the image of the underground train stopped between stations.

Four Quartets is many things, a religious meditation on time and eternity, an attempt to emulate the musical structures of Beethoven and Bartók in poetry, a Symbolist poem, and so on, but it is also a discursus on the nature of poetic generations. 'East Coker' makes this clear in its opening assertion, 'In my beginning is my end', a reflection, in part, on that supersession which all innovatory artists inevitably experience, as 'In succession, / Houses rise and fall, crumble, are extended, / Are removed, destroyed, restored, or in their place, / Is an open field, or a factory, or a by-pass' (the stage effects of the 1930s 'Pylon Poets') – all idioms which can be seen to translate into cultural-historical allegory, via the mythical method, those remarks about tradition and innovation in *The Use of Poetry*, or, more than a decade before that, in 'Tradition and the Individual Talent'. It is, indeed, as much the reinvention of the literary past – its reconstruction in a new configuration – as its destruction which 'East Coker' records, and enacts in its own reprise of *Ecclesiastes*.

The fear of supersession is latent in every twist of the poem's plot, even in the image of the poet leaning against a bank while the van passes, the promise of the early owl, and dawn pointing to another day. And supersession is then cast explicitly in terms of literary generations in that disquisition on the 'periphrastic study in a worn-out poetical fashion' which recalls those astronomical passages from Chapman's *Bussy D'Ambois* which haunt Eliot's early criticism. All particular styles of writing succumb to becoming merely fashionable, and in the process prepare their own supersession, the poem suggests. No style of writing is absolute. Every 'way of putting it' is ultimately 'not very satisfactory', 'Leaving one still with the intolerable wrestle / With words and meanings'. But if 'The poetry does not matter / It was not (to start again) what one had expected', the ambiguity of that parenthesis enacts the duplicity of poetry's relations to time and in time. Is the poet saying that he will now rephrase what he has just said, in a new, more direct, less periphrastic way of putting it? (He says, a little later, echoing Walt Whitman, 'You say I am repeating / Something I have said before. I shall say it again, / Shall I say it again?') Or is he saying that 'it' – i.e., having 'to start again' - was not what one expected?

Generations here, too, participate in the general deceit: the quiet-voiced elders deceived us, or themselves, bequeathing a wisdom which was 'only the knowledge of dead secrets', that is, of a tradition that is not reborn but merely stifles. That Eliot has his own early, 'revolutionary' writings in mind here is suggested by the echoic repetition of moments from that earlier work. In particular, is not that parenthetical 'to start again' simply a reprise of one of *The Waste Land*'s most desolate moments: 'After the event / .... He promised "a new start"'; and is not that 'knowledge of dead secrets' which frustrates the enquirer – that 'knowledge derived from experience' which is of 'limited value', because it imposes a pattern, and thus falsifies – a reiteration of the knowledge spoken of in 'Gerontion', after which there is no forgiveness, a knowledge which also 'deceives with whispering ambitions / Guides us by vanities'? Gerontion's tense, anxious antitheses are likewise recalled in 'East Coker':

For the pattern is new in every moment
And every moment is a new and shocking
Valuation of all we have been. We are only undeceived
Of that which, deceiving, could no longer harm.

Eliot is concerned in 1940, that is, as in 1933, with his own poetic supersession, his supplanting by a new generation of poets, who have taken his literary revolution and rewritten it into a new pattern, in the process leading him to revise his own estimation of himself, and to cast himself, derogatorily, among the deceitful quiet-voiced elders who were themselves deceived. He too shrinks now, like those old men, in fear of being possessed by the tradition he inaugurated, 'Of belonging to another, or to others, or to God'. But he shrinks fastidiously, too, from that 'fools' approval' which only stings, from the honour, and honours, that merely stain, seeking to be 'restored' – a significant word, in context – in 'that refining fire / Where you must move in measure, like a dancer.'

Which brings me to my last section.

The disconsolate chimera

In his British Academy lecture in March 1947 Eliot offered a major revaluation of Milton, that poet who had been anathema to his younger self. The likelihood, he says, 'that the development of poetry in the next fifty years will take quite different directions from those which seem to me desirable to explore' does not deter him from asking the questions that Johnson implied:

How should poetry be written now? And what place does the answer to this question give to Milton? And I think that the answers to these questions may be different now from the answers that were correct twenty-five years ago. (Hayward, p. 134)

(That is, in 1922.) Eliot's answer, at the end of the worst winter of the century, which had reduced to desperation, in its second year, a Labour Government returned in 1945 with a massive majority and high popular expectations of a social revolution, is unexpectedly politico-historical, with a sharp contemporary relevance:

The fact is simply that the Civil War of the seventeenth century, in which Milton is a symbolic figure, has never been concluded. The Civil War is not ended: I question whether any serious civil war ever does end. Throughout that period English society was so convulsed and divided that the effects are still felt. (p.134)

The English Civil War had already bulked large, on the three-hundredth anniversary of its commencement, in 'Little Gidding', published separately in October 1942, as the Second World War began to turn in Britain's favour.[29]

Unlike many of his conservative contemporaries, Eliot was prescient enough to recognize that some social transformation would of necessity have to follow any successful outcome to the war. Reading Johnson's life of Milton, he says in 1947, 'one is always aware that Johnson was obstinately and passionately of another party'; but 'No other English poet, not Wordsworth, or Shelley, lived through or took sides in such momentous events as did Milton' (p. 134). Such partisanship in part accounts, Eliot confesses, for his own 'antipathy towards Milton the man'. But at this point, in a characteristic swerve, Eliot turns away from political considerations, to 'the charge that he [Milton] is an unwholesome influence' on the development of poetic language. And here, surprisingly, Eliot recants, rejecting that younger self who was the author of 'A Note on the Verse of John Milton' in 1936 and the even younger one who was the coiner in 1921 of the phrase 'a dissociation of sensibility'.[30]

Milton, he now believes, is 'a great poet and one whom poets to-day might study with profit' (p. 135). And he finds Mallarmé '[o]f all modern writers of verse, the nearest analogy' to Milton – 'a much smaller poet, though still a great one', because both men write a 'poetry at the farthest possible remove from prose', distinguished by its 'remoteness ... from ordinary speech' (pp. 141–2). The Mallarméan desire 'To purify the dialect of the tribe' in 'Little Gidding', by this token, suggests that Milton too may be an element in that poem's familiar compound ghost.

Coming at last, he says, 'to compare my own attitude, as that of a poetical practitioner perhaps typical of a generation twenty-five years ago, with my attitude to-day' (p. 147), Eliot speaks at unusual length about his own part in what almost for the first time he does not deny was a poetic revolution, in the lineage of Dryden and Wordsworth:

> By the beginning of the present century another revolution in idiom – and such revolutions bring with them an alteration of metric, a new appeal to the ear – was due. It inevitably happens that the young poets engaged in such a revolution will exalt the merits of those poets of the past who offer them example and stimulation, and depreciate the merits of poets who do not stand for the qualities which they are zealous to realize. (p.147)

Milton, he reminds us, was 'at the extreme limit' from contemporary speech, and from a poetic like that of the moderns which sought to make poetry from 'the non-poetic', from 'material refractory to transmutation into poetry' (p. 148). But, he says, 'We cannot, in literature, any more than in the rest of life, live in a perpetual state of revolution'. English culture, and the language in which it is realized, now face 'a progressive deterioration'. To avert this, the poetry of the rest of the century should 'discover new and more elaborate patterns of a diction now established', which would 'avoid the danger of a *servitude* to colloquial speech and to current jargon' (p. 148). 'History may be servitude, / History may be freedom', as 'Little Gidding' reminds us, but 'liberation' requires that the faces and the places, and the self that loved them, must now vanish, 'To become renewed, transfigured, in another pattern'. And it is in the deliberate artifice and musically cadenced syntax of Milton's verse that he finds the pattern of a new, post-War poetic.

The 'antique drum' which the poet evokes only to renounce in the third section of 'Little Gidding', and all the circumstantial references to the English Civil War, reinforce the idea that Milton is also a secret sharer in that 'familiar compound ghost' which accosted the poet in the previous section. Babette Deutsch wrote in 1936 that 'Eliot is a poet who welcomes ghosts, and who knows both how to entertain and how, courteously, to dismiss them', quoting him on how 'the ghost of some simple metre should lurk behind the arras in even the "freest" verse, to advance menacingly as we doze, and withdraw as we rouse;'[31] and one thinks of how Dante's encounters with the ghosts of his dead masters, from Virgil to Arnaut Daniel, haunt both the poetry and the prose, of how Stetson is hailed among the ghosts flowing over London Bridge in *The Waste Land*, and of how, in 'What Dante Means to Me' (1950), Eliot calls up Baudelaire's *'spectre en plein jour'* who accosts the passer-by (*'raccroche le passant'*) like a common prostitute. One recalls, too, that 'sad ghost of Coleridge' that 'beckons to me from the shadows', at the very end of *The Use of Poetry and the Use of Criticism*. Accosting seems to be a common feature of all these ghostly transactions, and it suggests too a constellation which links the merely contemporary poet, hailed by another's voice in 'Little Gidding', to the scolding, mocking and chattering voices that 'assail' the transcendent

Word in the modernist desert of 'Burnt Norton', in a passage which begins by
equating words and music ('Words move, music moves / Only in time') but
then disintegrates into a threnody on how

> Words strain,
> Crack and sometimes break, under the burden,
> Under the tension, slip, slide, perish,
> Decay with imprecision, will not stay in place,
> Will not stay still ...
> ... The Word in the desert
> Is most attacked by voices of temptation,
> The crying shadow in the funeral dance,
> The loud lament of the disconsolate chimera.

A chimera is, of course, a mythical beast, but it is also, like that 'compound
ghost', a composite and miscegenated one. Of its many occurrences in classical and English literature, three in particular stand out.[32] One occurs in that
play which Eliot repeatedly cites in his criticism, and echoes in his verse,
Chapman's *Bussy D'Ambois* (Act IV, sc. I, ll. 182–8). Two others are to be
found in Milton: in *Comus* (ll. 515–7), where poets tell stories of 'dire Chime-
ras' at the entrance to Hell; and in *Paradise Lost* (Book II, ll. 626–8), which
describes an underworld where, as in the darkest recesses of the *Quartets*, 'all
life dies, death lives' and nature breeds 'inutterable' things 'worse / Then Fables yet have feignd'.[33]

Eliot's ghostly interlocutor, called on, like Hamlet's father's ghost, to 'speak',
claims '"I am not eager to rehearse / My thought and theory which you have
forgotten. / These things have served their purpose: let them be"', for, as he
says in words which echo Eliot's dismissal of the poetic revolution he and
Pound had effected: '"last year's words belong to last year's language / And
next year's words await another voice"'.

What that alternative voice might be is suggested in an essay published in
the same year as 'Little Gidding', and also reprinted in *Selected Prose* (pp. 56–
67). 'The Music of Poetry' prefigures some of the argument of the 1947 Milton lecture, but also utters, in the tones of a 'quiet-voiced elder', a claim which,
if spelt out, would constitute 'a new and shocking / Valuation of all we have
been'. The essay observes that 'Every revolution in poetry is apt to be, and
sometimes to announce itself as, a return to common speech'. Wordsworth,
he says, had been preceded a century before by Oldham, Waller, Denham,
and Dryden, and he places himself and Pound in the same lineage by adding that 'the same revolution was due again something over a century
later'. But, he goes on, in terms which clearly allude to that successor genera-

tion represented by Auden, 'The followers of a revolution develop the new poetic idiom in one direction or another; they polish or perfect it; meanwhile the spoken language goes on changing, and the poetic idiom goes out of date' (p. 58). Eliot here dissociates himself from this successor generation and its revolutionary posturing, whether literary or political:

> I have said enough, I think, to make clear that I do not believe the task of the poet is primarily and always to effect a revolution in language. It would not be desirable, even if it were possible, to live in a state of perpetual revolution: the craving for continual novelty of diction and metric is as unwholesome as the obstinate adherence to the idiom of our grandfathers. There are times for exploration and times for the development of the territory acquired. (p. 63)

But 'Old men ought to be explorers', he had said at the end of 'East Coker', and, in disclaiming the 'revolution of the word' which Eugene Jolas had associated with the first generation of modernists, Eliot lives up to this premise by performing a remarkable double-take.

Shakespeare's 'dual achievement', he argues, is that he effected two transformations of language: 'During the first, he was slowly adapting his form to colloquial speech' (as Eliot had done in the 1910s). The second transformation lay in taking poetic language, in the last plays, as close as he could to the condition of music, 'experimenting to see how elaborate, how complicated, the music could be made without losing touch with colloquial speech altogether'(p. 64). Poetry, Eliot says, 'quickly loses contact with the changing colloquial speech, being possessed by the mental outlook of a past generation'. It turns, that is, into 'a worn-out poetical fashion'. 'Forms have to be broken and remade' (p. 66), the essay argues, just as in 'East Coker' he had written about 'Twenty years largely wasted', 'Trying to learn to use words', where 'every attempt / Is a wholly new start' ('to start again') but also 'a different kind of failure',

> Because one has only learnt to get the better of words
> For the thing one no longer has to say, or the way in which
> One is no longer disposed to say it,

so that 'each venture' is 'a raid on the inarticulate / With shabby equipment always deteriorating …' This, one might note, is the 'progressive deterioration' of language of which he was to speak in his 1947 Milton lecture. When Eliot in the poem speaks of 'the fight to recover what has been lost / And found and lost again and again' he is situating himself, that is, within that lineage of linguistic 'perpetual revolution' which reaches back through Wordsworth and Johnson to Dryden, in the very moment that he denies the possibility of such a thing.

It is here that Eliot makes his most ambitious claim, but so surreptitiously that, like the transformation of the literary landscape described in 'Tradition and the Individual Talent', it is hardly noticed. If the work of the last twenty years is worthy of being classified at all, he says, it is one 'belonging to a period of search for a modern colloquial idiom'. But when the poetic idiom has been 'stabilized', 'a period of musical elaboration can follow. I think that a poet may gain much from the study of music: how much technical knowledge of musical form is desirable I do not know':

> The use of recurrent themes is as natural to poetry as to music. There are possibilities for verse which bear some analogy to the development of a theme by different groups of instruments; there are possibilities of transitions in a poem comparable to the different movements of a symphony or a quartet; there are possibilities of contrapuntal arrangements of subject-matter ... poetry has always before it ... an 'endless adventure'. (p. 67)

Here Eliot is writing a manifesto for *Four Quartets*, shortly to be published in its entirety. 'Little Gidding' draws to a conclusion with a similar undertaking:

> We shall not cease from exploration
> And the end of all our exploring
> Will be to arrive where we started
> And know the place for the first time.

'The Music of Poetry' in 1941 lays claim to a lineage that links Eliot directly to Shakespeare, for, like Shakespeare alone, he has accomplished two poetic revolutions in one lifetime. The first, that 'modernist' transformation, he had seen played out in the bagpipe music of the thirties. The second, aspiring to the condition of music, beginning perhaps with that variation on late Shakespearean themes, 'Marina', and ascending through *Ash-Wednesday*, culminates in *Four Quartets*, with its desire to be 'restored' by the refining fire of art, 'Where you must move in measure, like a dancer'.

Having in his early essays constructed a critical tradition which sought to fix the contours of an emerging modernist poetic, Eliot then, in the 1930s and 40s, quietly sought a new start: a second revolution, or counter-revolution, or, most appositely, perhaps, opening up the political resonances of 're-stored', a restoration. This restoration matches that which in 1660 returned the Stuart dynasty to the throne, and, ironically, freed a previously insurgent Milton, nameless but unmistakable at the end of 'Little Gidding', from the servitude of history, to write an epic poem about War in Heaven distinguished by its 'remoteness ... from ordinary speech'. There is a certain poetic justice in the process by which the rebellious regicide comes to figure, with Shakespeare, as the patron of this (poetic and political) restoration. At the end of 'Little Gidding', 'a king at nightfall', 'three men, and more, on the scaffold', 'a few who died forgotten ... here and abroad', and 'one who died blind and quiet', are all, finally, 'United in the strife which divided them'. Poetic and political restorations converge in a postwar settlement where, then as now, the poem affirms, 'History is now and England'. Like Johnson before him, 'obstinately and passionately of another party', Eliot seeks to assume the partisan radicalism Milton represents into a unifying 'constitution of silence' where 'All shall be well', and – the oxymoronic politics refiguring, in 1943, the contradictory nature of that mythical compound beast, the 'disconsolate chimera' – tradition and revolution will be reconciled, 'folded in a single party'.

Notes

1 C. Day Lewis and L. A. G. Strong, *A New Anthology of Modern Verse 1920–1940* (London: Methuen and Co, 1941) p.xiii. Hereafter, page numbers are supplied in the text.
   The volume to which they refer is *An Anthology of Modern Verse*, 'Chosen by A. Methuen, With an Introduction by Robert Lynd' (London: Methuen, 1921). From first publication on 12 May 1921, Methuen's collection went through a further six editions that year, including an enlargement in its fourth edition, in September 1921. By April 1923 it had entered its twelfth edition. In addition, the school edition, presumably a much larger print run, was reprinted once in 1921 and twice in 1922. The book is dedicated to 'Thomas Hardy, O.M. Greatest of the Moderns'. Lynd's belletristic introduction, 'On Poetry and the Modern Man', finds a certain metaphysical 'home-sickness' at the heart of modernity, and concludes that 'What is most important in modern poetry is not that which distinguishes it from the poetry of yesterday, but that which makes it in its degree one with the poetry of Homer and Sappho, of Shakespeare and Shelley' (p. xxxii). The anthology prints only one poem by Eliot, 'La Figlia Che Piange', none by Pound, and nine by Yeats, all from his early phase.
2 T. S. Eliot, *Four Quartets* (London: Faber and Faber, 1943).
3 Reprinted in T. S. Eliot, *Selected Prose*, ed. John Hayward (London: Penguin Books in association with Faber and Faber, 1953 & 1958), pp. 185–196; this quotation, p.193. Except where otherwise indicated, quotations from Eliot's prose are taken from this volume, which offers an authoritative and judiciously chosen exposition of his views as he redefined them in the period immediately after the Second World War.
4 Ezra Pound, 'Harold Monro', *Criterion*, July 1932, p. 590; reprinted in Ezra Pound, *Polite Essays* (London: Faber and Faber, 1937). Ezra Pound, 'We Have Had No Battles But We Have All Joined In And Made Roads', *Polite Essays*, pp. 49–50.
5 T. S. Eliot, 'Isolated Superiority', *Dial* 84 (January 1928), 4.
6 Eliot always evinced a congenital dislike for labelling literary movements, seeing

this as a product of the academic rather than the poetic or – even – critical imagination. Thus in *After Strange Gods* (1934), in a passage which, despite his suppression of this volume after Munich, he felt worthy of excerpt in Hayward's *Selected Prose*, he wrote of the concepts 'romanticism' and 'classicism' in words that have equal, and probably intended, application to the emerging idea of a 'modernist' movement: 'It is true that from time to time writers have labelled themselves "romanticists" or "classicists", just as they have from time to time banded themselves together under other names. These names which groups of writers and artists give themselves are the delight of professors and historians of literature, but should not be taken very seriously; their chief value is temporary and political – that, simply, of helping to make the authors known to a contemporary public ... No sensible author, in the midst of something that he is trying to write, can stop to consider whether he is going to be romantic or the opposite. At the moment when one writes, what one is, and the damage of a lifetime, and of having been born into an unsettled society, cannot be repaired at the moment of composition.'

The slack sentence construction, in which that closing 'at the moment of composition' reiterates anxiously and redundantly the opening 'At the moment when one writes', only serves to emphasize how overdetermined was this 'moment' in Eliot's thought, here gathering to it, perhaps, all the 'damage of a lifetime'.

7 Anne Ridler (ed.), *A Little Book of Modern Verse* (London: Faber and Faber, 1941), pp. 5–9 *passim.*

8 The next few paragraphs summarize and extend conclusions reported elsewhere. See Stan Smith, 'Lineages of Modernism, or, How they brought the good news from Nashville to Oxford', in *Miscelánea: A Journal of English and American Studies*, vol. 20, ed. Stan Smith and Jennifer Birkett (Zaragoza: Zaragoza University Press, 1999).

9 Laura Riding and Robert Graves, *A Survey of Modernist Poetry* (London: William Heinemann, 1927). The account of 'Burbank' can be found on pp. 235–242.

10 Humbert Wolfe, *Dialogues and Monologues* (London: Victor Gollancz, 1928).

11 The Sitwells' contribution to the ethos of 'modernism' is now largely ignored. But as the recollections of Geoffrey Grigson below indicate, they were a powerful force in 1920s definitions of the beast. A publisher's advertisement in the end-papers of Harold Monro's 1920 critical study, *Some Contemporary Poets (1920)* (London: Leonard Parsons, 1920), describes their anthology *Wheels*, then punningly in its 'Fifth Cycle', as 'this annual anthology of ultra-modern poetry, which has been described by *The Saturday Review* as "The vanguard of British poetry."'

12 Roy Campbell, 'Contemporary Poetry', in Edgell Rickword (ed.), *Scrutinies by Various Writers* (London: Wishart & Co, 1928).

13 Geoffrey Grigson, *The Crest on the Silver* (London: The Cresset Press, 1950), pp.114–15.

14 Stephen Spender, *The Struggle of the Modern* (London: Hamish Hamilton, 1963), pp.xi–xii, 71ff.

15 Eric Gillett, *Poets of Our Time: Poems by Contemporary Poets* (London: Thomas Nelson and Sons, 1932, repr. 1938 and three times in 1939), p.xiv. Gillett is described on the title page as Johore Professor of English Language and Literature, Raffles College, Singapore. Squire's 'Modernism', though capitalized, is used, as by Eliot, as a term for a generic, transhistorical sensibility, to be distinguished from 'most good modern English verse', though when he comes describe its characteristics, he is historically precise: 'To some the collection, doubtless, will be like a red

rag to a bull, as most of the poets drawn from have felt no inclination to join in the clamour for The New, topical subjects, novel doctrines, deliberately strange forms, or no forms, for their own sakes ... [R]eal poets who merely let themselves alone, however simple their songs, must (without pains) take tinge from their age just by living in it. To some, all this is obstinate "traditionalism." Let them think so ... There are many in England and America who angrily throw missiles at each other's Muses. It seems a waste of time; in any event the eternal truths about Art and Beauty are not going to be destroyed by mud-slinging' (pp. xiv–xv).

16 R. D. Charques, *Contemporary Literature and Social Revolution* (London: Martin Secker, n.d., publ. 1933).

17 Percy Wyndham Lewis, *Men Without Art* (London: Chatto and Windus, 1934), pp. 200, 66.

18 Louis MacNeice, 'Poetry To-day', in Geoffrey Grigson (ed.) *The Arts To-day* (London: John Lane The Bodley Head, 1935), pp. 32–62 *passim.*

19 Louis MacNeice, *Modern Poetry: A Personal Essay* (London: Oxford University Press, 1938).

20 Louis MacNeice, *The Poetry of W. B. Yeats* (London: Oxford University Press, 1941).

21 'Tendencies in Modern Poetry: Discussion between F. R. Higgins and Louis Mac-Neice, broadcast from Northern Ireland', *The Listener*, 27 July 1939. I am grateful to Antony Shuttleworth for calling this exchange to my attention.

22 Maurice Wollman (ed.), *Modern Poetry 1922–1934* (London: Macmillan, 1935), pp. vii–xii *passim.*

23 A decade later, a more sympathetic note is sounded by another schoolmaster anthologist, W. G. Bebbington, in his Faber collection *Introducing Modern Poetry* in 1944. All the poems in his anthology, he says, 'are modern in the strictest literary sense of the word, but not one of them is – at least as far as I can see – either occult or incomprehensible'. 'By "modern" poetry', he continues, 'is not meant contemporary poetry in general. "Modern" when used to describe any art-form has never connoted mere contemporaneity but has always served as a comprehensive term for the ideas contained in such words as "different" and "experimental". All those artists, therefore, whose expression continues merely to maintain traditions of manner and matter which they themselves have done nothing to create but which are legacies from the past are not considered "modern" and it is of no relevance to this point that they believe that past to be right in contrast with present standards and ideas' (pp. 5–6). The 'separable groups of artists who have earned for themselves the right to be called "modern" and to be adversely criticised by those contemporary critics who always do adversely criticise them just because they are "modern" (and especially if they are young)' include, he says, Stephen Spender and W. H. Auden but not de la Mare and Edmund Blunden.

Bebbington shies away from definitions, like Eliot a couple of years earlier: 'It does not seem to me to be my duty here to analyse in detail the meaning of the word "modern" thus applied, for this has been done elsewhere by poets themselves. Obvious difference exist between the poetry of John Masefield and Alfred Noyes, both contemporary poets, on the one hand and that of T. S. Eliot and Michael Roberts, both modern poets, on the other'. Unfortunately, however, the poems of Eliot's which Bebbington includes are hardly test-cases of what constitutes 'modernism': 'Mungojerrie and Rumpelteazer' and 'Macavity', 'Morning at the Window' and 'Cousin Nancy' (with its eloquent non-definition: 'And her aunts were not quite sure how they felt about it, / But they knew that it was modern'), 'Conversation Galante', 'The Journey of the Magi', the third of the 'Five–finger Exercises', the sixth chorus from *The Rock*, and two choruses from *Murder in the Cathedral*.

24 Babette Deutsch, *This Modern Poetry* (London: Faber and Faber, 1936), p. 255.

25 Hayward (ed.), *op. cit.*, pp. 32–44.

26 See n.3 above.

27 *Ibid.*, p. 133. Headed simply 'Milton II', the text is that of Eliot's Henriette Hertz Lecture at the British Academy, 26 March 1947.

28 *Ibid.*, p. 7. The generational emphasis here is important, and picks up Eliot's own preoccupation with the idea. The *Selected Prose* also reprints the full text of Eliot's Yeats Lecture at the Abbey Theatre in Dublin in 1940, a lecture which looks both backwards and forwards in generational terms, beginning: 'The generations of poetry in our age seem to cover a span of about twenty years. I do not mean that the best work of any poet is limited to twenty years: I mean that it is about that length of time before a new school or style of poetry appears. By the time, that is to say, that a man is fifty [Eliot was 52 when he wrote this] he has behind him a kind of poetry written by men of seventy, and before him another kind written by men of thirty. [Auden was 33.] That is my position at present, and if I live another twenty years I shall expect to see still another younger school of poetry' (p.197). He goes on to say that his relation to Yeats does not fit this scheme. When he was a young man beginning to write in America, 'Yeats was already a considerable figure in the world of poetry'. He does not recall Yeats making any impression, for a young poet is 'looking for masters who will elicit his consciousness of what he wants to say himself', and this did not exist in English but in French poetry. Early Yeats did not exist for him 'until after my enthusiasm had been won by the poetry of the older Yeats' (p.198) from 1919 on, by which time 'my own course of evolution was already determined'. 'Hence, I find myself regarding him, from one point of view, as a contemporary and not a predecessor; and from another point of view, I can share the feelings of younger men, who came to know and admire him by that work from 1919 on, which was produced while they were adolescent'. That phrase 'looking for masters' is telling, for it points towards the 'familiar compound ghost' of 'Little Gidding', encountered in the uncertain hour before the morning after a bombing raid:

> I caught the sudden look of some dead master
> Whom I had known, forgotten, half recalled
> Both one and many ...

Yeats, in Eliot's prose account, is, like the ghost, transfixed 'Between two worlds become much like each other', 'a contemporary and not a predecessor', and the 'dead patrol' of the poem, recalling the night-walking of Yeats's Byzantium poems and his 'All Souls' Night', also calls up the Yeatsian trope of poetry as '"that refining fire / Where you must move in measure, like a dancer"'. This ghostly figure is, of course, 'both one and many', and his '"thought and theory which you have forgotten"' encompasses not only Pound (punningly lurking in that 'compound ghost') but the French Symbolists represented by the Mallarméan desire 'To purify the dialect of the tribe'. But I shall return to this matter later.

29 There is immense historical resonance here. In his Mansion House speech on 10

November 1942, Winston Churchill observed, of the successful outcome to the Battle of Egypt, 'Now this is not the end. It is not even the beginning of the end. But it is, perhaps, the end of the beginning'. A mere month after the publication of this poem of the Blitz by Britain's most famous poet, the Prime Minister is surely recalling the words which open the last section of 'Little Gidding': 'What we call the beginning is often the end / And to make an end is to make a beginning. / The end is where we start from', with its reprise of the opening of 'East Coker', first published separately on 21 March 1940, at the darkest moment of the war, 'In my beginning is my end'. Lyndall Gordon reports that 'Helen Gardner recalled the extraordinary impact of this poem' at the time, so that it had to be reprinted in May and June, and had sold nearly 12,000 copies within a year. (*Eliot's New Life* (Oxford: Oxford University Press, 1988), p.110.)

30 This latter is 'one of the two or three phrases of my coinage', he adds a little later, 'which have had a success in the world astonishing to their author' (Hayward, p. 139).

31 *Op. cit.*, p. 71.

32 A fourth, possibly the most relevant, but which I cannot go into here, is to be found in Flaubert's *Temptation of St Anthony*, where Chimera and Sphinx are contrasted as figuring the rebuses of imagination and reason. Other instances can be found in Spenser's *Faerie Queen* (VI: I, 7–8), where it is associated with the 'Blatant Beast'; in Browning's 'Old Pictures in Florence' (ll. 270–2); in Cowley's *Orinda* (4), Denham's 'Progress of Learning' (ll.161 ff), Hesiod's *Theogony* (ll.321–5), the *Iliad* (VI, ll.178–82), and Apollodorus (II, iii).

33 Eliot's 1936 essay on Milton adds a further association, quoting, with the comment that 'for the single effect of grandeur of sound, there is nothing finer in poetry' (Hayward, p.131), the passage about Lycidas's drowned body 'beyond the stormy Hebrides', visiting 'the bottom of the monstrous world', surely recalled by 'Little Gidding''s ghostly interlocutor, who 'left my body on a distant shore'.

12

Shifting the Frame – Modernism in the Theatre

Christopher Innes

Standard books like Peter Faulkner's *Modernism* ignore drama almost altogether, dismissing the whole genre as intrinsically unsuited to 'the complexities of modernism'[1] – yet the list of people at the forefront of the Modernist movement who wrote plays is long. These include, among others, Yeats, Eliot, Auden, Wyndham Lewis, Lawrence, even Joyce, as well as continental artists like Kokoschka. So looking at theatre might bring a new perspective.

Modernism in poetry, the novel, or painting has fairly clearly identifiable qualities: the rejection of mimesis, and of the narrative method; aesthetic revolt and primitivism; abstraction, and a focus on inner experience; the transcendence of politics; art as an autonomous sphere; and an inherent elitism. In the theatre things are different, which is why so few studies of Modernism deal with drama. 'Impure' in mixing different arts, it is almost by definition a populist medium (although Yeats did attempt, as he said, 'to create for myself an unpopular theatre and an audience like a secret society'), and any performance is transitory. Yet the crossover from poetry and painting to the stage is so common among Modernists that it suggests we need to redefine Modernism to take theatre into account.

How different? For a start, even the way 'Modernism' is defined varies widely. For ten years I edited one of the major scholarly journals in the field – indeed with typical academic arrogance, we like to think of it as THE leading journal. Its title is *Modern Drama*: simple, direct, and you might think specifically on target. However, what the journal defines as 'modern' is ANY play written after about 1850; and that includes every sort of stylistic approach – the poetic drama of Cocteau or T. S. Eliot, the deconstructionist performance pieces of Dada during World War I or contemporary Americans like Spaulding Gray, Strindberg and the Expressionists, the mind-games and open theatricality of Pirandello or the minimalism of Beckett – but also the great figures of naturalism like Ibsen and Chekhov, social documentaries, political and epic theatre, even the Well Made Plays of Pinero.

What this points to, of course, is the confusion between the different usages of the term 'modern', which refers both to a chronological period in general and to a specific type of art. However, this association is one Modernists themselves fostered, in declaring that their 'unflinching aim' (as Ford Madox Ford put it) was 'to register my own times in terms of my own time'.

The journal's 1850 start-date for *Modern Drama* may sound ridiculously early – it is over 30 years before the founding of the Société des Artistes, 40 years before the first date given in the Chronology that prefaces the *Cambridge Companion to Modernism* (1890: the publication of the first volumes of *The Golden Bough*) and 60 years before the 1910 exhibition of post-Impressionists in London, which is sometimes seen as the origin of Anglo-American Modernism. But in fact it is by no means arbitrary, or simply a period-designator. 1850 is the date of Ibsen's first play; and Ibsen (as Bernard Shaw so powerfully articulated in 1891) is generally seen as the very first 'modern dramatist. For Shaw, Ibsen's Modernism was marked by two main characteristics: an attack on the conventions of 19th-century drama in substituting discussion for action in a play's climax; and the undermining of idealism that made Ibsen 'a mighty destroyer of idols' – and at least in thematic terms these are qualities that would become typical of the Modernist movement.

That stress on 'Discussion' (Nora does not kill herself, but has a long talk with her husband before simply walking out of the Victorian doll's house) leads to Shaw's creation of a 'drama of ideas', which is picked up by Brecht's development of a 'rational theatre' and followed through by one of the leading British playwrights of the 70s, Edward Bond, who calls for a 'drama of reason'. This intellectual line, associated with socialism (both Shaw's Fabian brand and Marxism), parallels some of the Modernist concerns of writers in other genres. Yet it is given very different expression, by privileging logic and conscious thought.

At the same time, the revolutionary aspect in Ibsen's and Shaw's attack on tradition and both literary as well as social idealism – summed up by Shaw as Sardoodledom and Bardolatry – is the same urge that motivates Gertrude Stein's stylistic radicalism, or James Joyce's 'scorching' of culture. It links up with Wyndham Lewis's principle that 'Revolution is the normal state of things' (expressed through the Ezra Pound-like protagonist of his play, *The Ideal Giant*) or Antonin Artaud's howl of 'No More Masterpieces!'[2] Yet again, on the stage this translates into a sharp contrast with one of the key principles generally used to define the Modernist movement as a whole: that art should be hermetically distinct from the political. While the revolutionary drive in drama certainly has a stylistic aspect, plays almost automatically retain a strong social dimension – perhaps simply because the dramatic medium itself is the interaction between actors, they are never free from social reality – and even the plays written by Modernists, who in other fields reject any political involvement, contain this element. So for example in his poetry W. H. Auden categorically states:

Art is not life and cannot be
A midwife to society.

Yet the plays he wrote with Christopher Isherwood are all explicitly political. *The Dog Beneath the Skin* deals with Fascism; *On the Frontier* ends with the young hero declaring:

Believing it was wrong to kill,
I went to prison, seeing myself
As the sane and innocent student
Aloof among practical and violent madmen,
But I was wrong. We cannot choose our world ...
This much I learned in prison. This struggle
Was my struggle. Even if I would
I could not stand apart.[3]

Even *The Ascent of F6*, which is the most experimental and symbolic of their plays, with an action largely outside time (on mountain tops, in a highly figurative Tibetan monastery, through visions), contains a newspaper-reading chorus who stand for suburban society.

There are, of course, apparent exceptions – the most obvious being W. B. Yeats's 'Plays for Dancers'. Designed to hold their distance from 'a pushing world', these drew on the alien and archaic Noh drama, which from a European perspective incorporated key Modernist qualities of internal unity and anti-realism; and when *At the Hawk's Well* was performed at Lady Cunard's house in London a famous Japanese dancer called Michio Ito appeared as the bird-spirit. As Fenellosa, the first translator of Noh plays, described the form, 'All elements – costume, motion, verse and music – unite to produce a single clarified impression ... elevated to the plane of a universality by the intensity and purity of treatment.' And in the Noh Yeats found his ideal of a theatre 'close to pure music ... that would free [the stage] from imitation, and ally [dramatic] art to decoration and the dance.'[4] Action is reduced in each of the 'dance plays' to a single event, framed by the ritual unfolding of a cloth with an invocation 'to the eye of the mind' and culminating in a formal dance diametrically opposed to 'the disordered passion of nature.'[5] Scenery is pared down to a single blank screen at the back of the acting area, a square of blue fabric on the floor for the well. This is drama at its most abstract. Yet these 'Plays for Dancers' still had clear political overtones. Even aiming at private performance, whether in Cavendish Square or in the country mansions of the Anglo-Irish aristocracy like Coole, they were making an implicit statement about the elitist place of culture in society while drawing mythic subjects from Irish legend. Still more directly, these plays were contributing to the Irish Literary Revival that Yeats was involved with, and furthering the cause of Irish nationalism. Yeats's plays are also, in their own way, a highly intellectualized form of drama, though appealing through symbols to the imagination rather than (like Shaw) promoting ideas through argument.

Of course, it might be objected that the politicization of Auden and Isherwood's plays, written between 1936 and 1938, only shows that Modernism had been overwhelmed by world events and the threat of war with Hitler's Germany. And indeed by some definitions the period of high Modernism at least is bounded by the outbreak of World War II in 1939 (the date when the Chronology in the *Cambridge Companion to Modernism* closes). However there is an equally Marxist line in Auden's poetry during the 1920s and early 30s. Class-consciousness and the social effects of the First World War are very much present even in a landmark of high Modernism like Virginia Woolf's *To the Lighthouse*. Then there is Ezra Pound's notorious brand of ideological radicalism. Even the Modernist withdrawal from politics *per se* could be seen as taking a political position – so perhaps we need to rethink the meaning of at least one key principle of Modernism: the autonomy of art as a superior order of inner experience.

Two further plays illustrate other aspects of theatrical Modernism. The first, by Wyndham Lewis, was published in the opening issue of *Blast* in 1914, as part of the Vorticist manifesto. The second, Eliot's earliest play, was published in 1928 and performed initially in America in 1933, then a year later by the Group Theatre (which also produced Auden's plays).

As a close associate of Joyce, Eliot, and above all Ezra Pound – who extolled him as 'a born revolutionary, a Trotsky of the written word and the painted shape' – Wyndham Lewis was a key figure of the Modernist movement in England. He had of course already made a reputation for his painting, and *The Enemy of the Stars* was his first attempt to translate his Vorticist visual art into words. It is striking that, although almost all the rest of his literary output was in poetry or novels, Lewis chose a dramatic form for this composite of fragmented Cubist 'visions from within'. In addition to serving as an exemplar of Modernist art, the play is an explicit discussion of the philosophy behind the movement. Stirner appears, together with his book *The Ego and Its Own* which Pound had adopted as a key text of Modernism, and the action illustrates that 'Self, sacred act of violence, is like murder on my face and hands. The stain won't come out.' The titanic and perpetual conflict of the twin characters, Arghol and Hanp (representing mind and body: 'humility and perverse asceticism opposed to vigorous animal glorification of self'), ends with one murdering his alter-ego then leaping off a bridge to drown himself, 'his heart a sagging weight of stagnant hatred.'[6] These inseparable, antagonistic figures are progenitors of Joyce's Daedalus/Bloom duo in *Ulysses*, and – being presented as circus clowns, one of whom is attacked by anonymous booted figures every night – even more clearly foreshadow Samuel Beckett's double pairings of Didi and Gogo (clowns), as well as Pozzo and Lucky (physical versus intellectual existence) in *Waiting for Godot*.

Although film was still in its infancy at the time, *The Enemy of the Stars* calls for cinematic effects. It breaks out of all theatrical conventions, being not only a 'dream of action', but a dream specifically within a dream, which is itself a circus performance where the spectators are 'POSTERITY ... SILENT, LIKE THE DEAD, AND MORE PATHETIC'. The perspective is deliberately impossible: 'AUDIENCE LOOKS DOWN INTO SCENE, AS THOUGH IT WERE A HUT ROLLED HALF ON ITS BACK, DOOR UPWARDS, CHARACTERS MOUNTING GIDDILY IN ITS OPENING'. The scale is superhuman, with stars as 'machines of prey' and the whole world as a projection of emotional states, as in

> The night plunged gleaming nervous arms down into the wood, to wrench it up by the roots. Restless and rhythmical, beyond the staring red-rimmed doorway, giddy and expanding in drunken walls, its heavy drastic lights shifted.
>
> Arghol could see only ponderous arabesques of red cloud, whose lines did not stop at the door's frame, but pressed on into shadows within the hut ...[7]

Violent, subliminal, and primitive, *The Enemy of the Stars* directly embodies many of the main elements of Modernism. Never produced on stage, it is a drama of the mind in more than one sense; and even if Eliot's imagery is very different, *Sweeney Agonistes* is clearly following the same line. It is the most unequivocally Modernist of his plays.

Here again narrative structure is consciously avoided, with the play being arbitrarily split into two halves, both incomplete, 'Fragment of a Prologue' and a 'Fragment of an Agon': an expressionistic montage which the 1934 London production emphasized by blackouts between each small segment of action. It too is presented as a dream. All the other characters are seen as projections of the title figure's agonized consciousness, and indeed an early title had been *The Marriage of Life and Death: A Dream*. Specifically Sweeney's dream is a grotesque nightmare of murder, with Sweeney himself as the notorious wife-murderer Dr Crippen (with whom Eliot might have identified, since Crippen was an American from St. Louis – Eliot's birthplace – transplanted to England, like Eliot, who had buried his wife's dismembered body in his London basement). In the text Sweeney, for whom 'life is death', merely expresses the desire to 'do a girl in', telling the story of a man – perhaps himself – who kept his butchered female victim's body for months in a bathtub, preserved in lysol, while he goes about his daily routine.

As blind (in moral terms) as Samson Agonistes, Sweeney is the modern equivalent of Milton's biblical hero, who has been degraded to Jack the Ripper under the corrosive pressures of the twentieth-century world. This is rendered by jazz rhythms in the dialogue and a parody of a Bob Cole's hit 'Under the Bamboo Tree' – and the 1934 London production ended with Sweeney brandishing a cut-throat razor as he chases a prostitute, a police whistle, then pounding on the door and a girl's scream in the final blackout: a gruesome dance of death. Following Yeats, Eliot wanted performances of the play to be stylized, as in Noh drama. There is also a certain primitivism, with one of the gangster figures being taken from Negro minstrel shows – 'Snow as Bones' (a double death-figure) – and the play's short 'turns' and songs coming from music hall, which was in Eliot's eyes 'one of the few surviving rituals in modern life'.[8] The play is a literal transcription of his principle that 'the music of poetry ... must be a music latent in the common speech of its time.'[9] In his notes for the director of the 1933 American production Eliot suggested that the chorus should sound like a street drill; and unlike his other dramas, this play deals with unsavoury lower-class, even underworld 'furnished flat sort of people'. It was intended as an explicit attack on 'the conventionalities of modern behaviour with its empty code and heartiness – immoral, but never immoral enough – decaying, but so long in dying.'[10] And in the 1934 London production, with which Eliot was directly involved, the gap between performers and audience was broken down, by setting the acting-area in the middle of the spectators. With the actors seated among the spectators when 'off-stage', the latter were implicitly cast as a chorus of accomplices.

Sweeney Agonistes is in many ways central to Eliot's work. The figure of 'apeneck Sweeney' surfaces recurrently in Eliot's poems, representing degraded and aggressive sexuality. Found 'Among the Nightingales' (a slang term for prostitutes), in 'Sweeney Erect' he is reduced to little more than a phallus, as the title of the poem indicates. He reappears in *The Waste Land,* perverting the life-giving urges of spring by resorting to a brothel, while one of the whores from the play also carries over into the poetry, giving her name to 'Doris's Dream Songs' (published in 1924, with one of the poems becoming Part III of 'The Hollow Men'). Eliot recognized drama as the logical development of his poetic aims, since in his view 'The most useful poetry, socially, would be one which could cut across all the present stratifications of public taste – stratifications which are perhaps a sign of social disintegration. The ideal medium for poetry ... and the most direct means of social "usefulness" for poetry, is the theatre.'[11]

Even if the continuum between his poetry and his plays is nowhere clearer than in *Sweeney Agonistes,* it was an experiment Eliot never repeated. Yet of all his drama, *Sweeney Agonistes* has been perhaps the most influential. Yeats saw the performance – and elements of it appear in his last play, *The Death of*

Cuchulain, with its elements of self-parody in the figure of a music-hall Presenter, and its attack on the materialism of a 'vile age' which reduces myth to a 'tale that the harlot / Sang to the beggar-man'.[12] Another who saw the Group Theatre production was Bertolt Brecht – greatly impressed, he borrowed both its episodic structure and the half-masks of Eliot's characters for his Epic Theatre. And *Sweeney Agonistes* was picked up by the American avant-garde after the Second World War in an early Living Theatre production that also featured Picasso's *Desire* and Gertrude Stein's *Ladies' Voices.* As this indicates, Modernism remained alive and well on the stage, long after the movement is generally assumed to have died or metamorphosed into something else.

Brecht's Epic Theatre in turn influenced a great deal of British drama in the 1950s and 60s. But possibly the most significant dramatist of the whole post-war period is Sam Beckett; and Beckett's connections with the Modernist movement are direct. Although his first play was only performed in 1953, he acted as Joyce's amanuensis for *Finnegans Wake* and his literary career began in the 1920s, one of his early works being a study of Proust. So although from a younger generation, Beckett overlapped with the period of high Modernism. His starting point was a rejection of 'the grotesque fallacy of realistic art', and his drama can be seen as the most complete realization of Modernist principles in the theatre. [13]

Quite apart from specific details – like the paired figures of *Waiting for Godot,* which have their analogues in *The Enemy of the Stars;* the appreciation of the music hall that he shares with Eliot; or the consistent theme of time, which draws on his appreciation of Proust – Beckett's increasingly minimalist plays follow Yeats's example, with appropriate homage being paid in the quotations from Yeats in *Happy Days.* Although there is no musical accompaniment, while dancing is vestigial at best in the capering of *Waiting for Godot* and eliminated entirely from his subsequent plays, there is the same reduction of scene and action to essentials. Indeed the core of Fenellosa's description of Noh drama as creating a 'single clarified impression ... elevated to the plane of universality by the intensity and purity of treatment' applies just as much, if not more, to Beckett as to Yeats's 'Plays for Dancers'. Yeats expressed the wish to rehearse his actors in barrels, ruling out gesture to restore the sovereignty of words; and in one of his pieces Beckett encases his characters completely in urns, with only their faces sticking out of the tops. Despite Beckett's highly decorated part in the French Resistance during World War II, the whole world of politics is excluded. His plays are divorced from specific time and place, abandoning mimesis – at least in terms of scenery, which is sometimes (as in *Footfalls* or *Rockabye*) completely absent, with the background reduced to a grey void – and with characters who approach total immobility, and action replaced by repetitive activity. Some are externalizations of psychological states, as in long stream-of-consciousness monologues like *Not I,* where the only thing that can be seen is a mouth, speaking to a barely visible cloaked figure. Highly poetic, though written in a pared-down prose, Beckett's plays are mental images. Increasingly short and non-representational, these pieces exemplify autonomous art at its purest. Indeed in some cases they achieve true abstraction, as with *Breath* where there are no human figures or dialogue at all, only:

1 Faint light on stage littered with miscellaneous unidentified rubbish. Hold about 5 seconds.

2 Faint cry and immediate inspiration and slow increase of light together reaching maximum in about 10 seconds. Silence and hold about 5 seconds.

3 Expiration and slow decrease of light together reaching minimum (light as in 1) in about 10 seconds. Silence and hold about 5 seconds. [14]

That is the complete play. All human life – birth to death – distilled to essentials.

Such pieces are quintessentially Modernist (the only element missing is primitivism, though that is hardly universal to the movement). And Beckett, whose Nobel Prize was awarded largely for his drama, has had an immense impact. As far as I know, Lewis' *The Enemy of the Stars* has never been performed. Only experimental groups with small audiences have staged Eliot's *Sweeney Agonistes.* Although several of Yeats's plays were initially performed at the Abbey Theatre, they have attracted mainly academic interest. By contrast, Beckett has been one of the most frequently performed playwrights over the last forty years; and one should note that even *Breath* was part of a highly popular revue, *Oh! Calcutta!* – though a highly ironic contribution, given the shockingly erotic nature of the show as a whole.

In a sense Beckett can be seen as a holdover, a misplaced Modernist. However, his work has changed the whole context of theatre today. As Tom Stoppard put it, responding to the London premiere of *Waiting for Godot* in 1956: before Beckett, drama was X; after Beckett it was minus-X. The question is whether this means that theatre still remains in a Modernist mode, or if Beckett's work pushes the principles of Modernism to such an extreme that what emerges is a different form of art. Does he mark a continuum, or a new Post-Modernist phase? Or perhaps the whole issue should be phrased in quite a different way: Do Beckett's example and influence show that there is in fact no real distinction between Modernism and Post-Modernism? Does theatre demonstrate that Modernism is still a vital force that spans the whole twentieth century?

Notes

1 Peter Faulkner, *Modernism* (London: Methuen, 1977), p. 21.
2 Wyndham Lewis, *A Soldier of Humour and Selected Writings*, ed. Raymond Rosenthal (New York: New American Library, 1966), p. 122; the title of a chapter in Antonin Artaud's *The Theatre and Its Double*, trans. Mary Richards (New York: Grove Press, 1958).
3 W. H. Auden and Christopher Isherwood, *The Ascent of F6 and On the Frontier* (London: Faber and Faber, 1958), p. 189.
4 'Fenellosa on the Noh', in *The Translations of Ezra Pound* (London: Faber and Faber, 1953), pp. 279-80, and W. B. Yeats, *Explorations* (London: Macmillan, 1962), p. 178.
5 *The Variorum Edition of the Plays of W. B. Yeats* (London: Macmillan, 1966), p. 400, and W. B. Yeats, *Essays and Introductions* (London: Macmillan, 1961), p. 230.
6 *Blasting and Bombardiering* (London: Eyre and Spottiswoode, 1937), p. 285; *A Soldier of Humour*, pp. 86, 83.
7 *A Soldier of Humour*, pp. 101, 105, 104, 74, 76, 84.
8 T. S. Eliot, in the *Dial* (London; December 1922), 659.
9 T. S. Eliot, *On Poetry and Poets* (London: Faber and Faber, 1957), p. 31. For a full description of the 1934 and 1935 Group Theatre productions of *Sweeney Agonistes*, see Michael Sidnell, *Dances of Death: The Group Theatre of London in the Thirties* (London: Faber, 1984), pp. 100ff.
10 Eliot, cited in *The Journals of Arnold Bennett, 1921–29* (London: Cassell & Co., 1933), p. 52, and Richard Doone, Producer's Note in the programme for the Westminster Theatre production, 1 October 1935.
11 T. S. Eliot, *The Use of Poetry and the Use of Criticism* (London: Faber and Faber, 1933), pp. 152–3.
12 W. B. Yeats, *Selected Plays*, ed. Norman Jeffares (London: Macmillan, 1964), pp. 232, 242.
13 Samuel Beckett, *Proust* (1931) (New York, 1970), p. 57.
14 Beckett, *Breath, and Other Shorts* (London: Faber and Faber, 1971), p. 11.

13
Political Modernism and the Quest for Film Studies

Erik Hedling

Towards the end of his seminal 1985 book *Narration in the Fiction Film*, one of the most thorough studies of the various narrative modes typical for the art of cinema, leading American film scholar David Bordwell concludes: 'Throughout this book I have refrained from using the term "modernism"'.[1]

The reason for this avoidance – or even, one could say, dismissal – of the most powerful term employed within the histories of art, literature, and theatre of the latter half of the 20th century is, claims Bordwell indirectly, that it is not good enough.

'Modernism' in the traditional sense of Joyce, Kafka, and Camus would find its equivalent in what Bordwell simply labels 'the European art cinema', that is, a decisive part of European film history – from the Italian neo-realists of the 1940s and the French new wave of the 1950s and 60s to the highly stylized, anti-realist, visually oriented cinema of, for instance, Peter Greenaway and Derek Jarman in 1980s Britain. The art cinema worked in what could be called a modernist opposition to the classic narrative structure of Hollywood cinema. It tried to achieve more profound levels of describing the real world than traditional narrative realism, objectively as in the temporal and spatial verisimiltude in Vittorio de Sica's *Bicycle Thieves* (1948) or subjectively as in the highly symbolic employment of film style in Ingmar Bergman's *Persona* (1966).

But the term 'modernism', continues Bordwell – now more in the sense of explicitly political artists like Brecht, Meyerhold, and Eisenstein – could also find its cinematic equivalent in what Bordwell himself labels 'historical materialist narration', that is, the constructivist, formalist, highly self-conscious, openly rhetorical Soviet cinema of the 1920s. A late representative of this mode could be found in the British cinema of the 1970s in the shape of Kevin Brownlow and Andrew Mollo's film *Winstanley* (1975), a film about the 17th-century 'Digger movement'.

There is also a third tradition in modern cinema where the term 'modernism' could, according to Bordwell, apply as well. That is a cinematic 'modernism' in the tradition of the serial music of Boulez, or Stockhausen, or the 'nouveau roman' of, for instance, Robbe-Grillet. Here Bordwell finds his examples in the extremely stylized and formally programmatic cinema of Carl-Theodor Dreyer, Robert Bresson, and Jean-Luc Godard.

Thus one might conclude with Bordwell – at least as he writes at the time of *Narration in the Fiction Film* – that the term 'modernism' really is too semantically blurred for effective scholarly use within film studies.

This dismissal of the concept of 'modernism', I will claim, was closely tied to the institutionalization of academic film studies and should be seen in the historical context that is sketched in the following pages.

The *Screen* debate and political modernism

When Bordwell wrote his influential book, the term 'modernism' was in fact already well established in film studies, although it obviously meant different things to different theorists. When film began seriously to enter academia as a discipline in its own right in the early 1970s, the main theoretical impetus came from the British journal *Screen*. Influenced by Althusserian Marxism, Barthesian semiotics, and later also Lacanian psychoanalysis, *Screen* favoured an experimental form of cinema, particularly European films employing 'Brechtian' devices borrowed from 1960s theatre. The films – often directed by Godard, Makavejev, or Straub and Huillet – were much admired for the challenge they posed against what was labelled as bourgeois modes of realist narration, like the classic Hollywood cinema. What the form of these admired films should actually be called became a debated issue at quite an early stage.

The distinction initially made by *Screen* could somewhat crudely be described as located between on the one hand 'modernism' – that is, Brechtian techniques, political radicalism, deconstruction of the signified – and on the other 'realism' – classic realist narrative as in Hollywood movies, unity, illusionism, and a strong emphasis on the signified. A famous and often quoted essay by the *Screen* contributor, film-maker, and film theorist Peter Wollen, 'The Two Avant-Gardes', originally published in 1975,[2] sought to establish some distinctions within the radical strand in film production.

In his essay Wollen traced cinematic modernism in terms of its antecedents in art, literature, and theatre. One trend in modernism, one of what he called the avant-gardes, was the experimental, non-narrative film-making represented by, for instance, the Anglo-American Co-op movement, with film-makers like Peter Gidal and Malcolm Le Grice. The influence of this avant-garde, Wollen writes, mostly

> comes from painting, bringing with it a tendency to abstraction – pure light or colour; and non-figurative design – or deformation of conventional photographic imagery, involving prismatic fragmentation and splintering, the use of filters or

stippled glass, mirror-shots, extreme and microscopic close-ups, bizarre angles, negative images, all of which are to be found in twenties films. Editing tended to follow principles of association (related to poetry or dream) or analogies with music – shots of fixed length, repetition and variation, attempts at synestethic effects, theories of counterpoint.[3]

Significant for this version of the avant-garde, Wollen claims, was the lack of verbal narrative and verbal language. It also focused on essentialist notions of the purely cinematic, on film as distinctively film, on film about film, on the old concept *le cinéma pur*, not leaning on any other means of communication, thus establishing film as a modern art in a manner comparable to modernist trends in the other arts.

The other modernist avant-garde, Wollen continues, derives from narrative traditions, and hence (one might add) more from literature or the theatre. Wollen's prime example here is the cinema of Godard, which he claims is more modest in its break with traditional narrative illusionism but still as innovative and radical, or possibly even more so. Regarding Godard's film *Le Gai Savoir* (1968), a film made in the wake of the Paris events of that year, Wollen compares Godard to a famous painting by Picasso, to which he attributes certain signifying structures:

> In a sense, Godard's work goes back to the original breaking-point at which the modern avant-garde began – neither realist or expressionist, on the one hand, nor abstractionist, on the other. In the same way, the Demoiselles d'Avignon is neither realist, expressionist or abstractionist. It dislocates signifier from signified, asserting – as such a dislocation must – the primacy of the first, without in any way dissolving the second. It is not a portrait group or a study of nudes in the representational tradition, but on the other hand, to see it simply as an investigation of painterly or formal problems or possibilities is to forget its original title, Le Bordel Philosophique.[4]

Accordingly, Wollen emphasizes the narrative dimension or semantic meaning, the signified, in a more traditional sense, while at the same time exposing Godard's and Picasso's awareness of how form inevitably shapes meaning. Besides these characterizations of the two avant-gardes, Wollen gives some thought to the at the time highly fashionable topic of 'intertextuality', according to his line of reasoning one 'of the main characteristics of modernism'.[5] 'Quotation', he concludes, plays a similar role in both Le Grice's and Godard's work, which can thus both be encompassed by the term 'modernism'. Finally, of course, Wollen stresses the politics of the two avant-gardes, both of which he claims for radicalism and anti-bourgeois Marxism.

I think one needs to contextualize Wollen's argument historically. Most of the *Screen* writers were academically trained in English literature – in Wollen's case at Oxford – and since Wollen and others also represented a serious study of film on the brink of academic institutionalization in the mid-70s, they needed strong links to traditional academia (not least because of their politics). The dominant film production of Hollywood was, of course, generally despised by humanities scholars and radical Marxists alike, in spite of its enormous cultural influence. Consequently one had to turn to other cinematic expressions – in fact, to those referred to as 'modernism' – in order formally to establish a new academic subject, dealing with 'serious art' as well as with radical politics. Or, as Wollen would himself claim much later in one of his many discussions of the issue:

> Part of the problem facing the cinema, from an aesthetic point of view, was the total dominance of Modernism in the other arts. In literature or painting or music, Modernism had become, so to speak, the guarantor of 'Art-ness'– as Roland Barthes might have said, Modernism connoted 'Art-ness'. But Modernism had made very little headway in Hollywood.[6]

I would claim, however, that Wollen's essay 'The Two Avant-Gardes' indirectly marked a kind of turn within film studies. It expressed a slight preference, in spite of Wollen's painstaking line of argument, for the kind of 'modernism' represented by narrative – as in the Godard case, strongly characterized by experimentalism, overt political radicalism, and precisely 'art-ness' – instead of the painterly, essentialist, non-narrative aesthetics represented by the other avant-garde.

The argument about 'modernism' and 'avant-garde', particularly taking into consideration the *Screen*-writers' adherence to Marxist principles, was further elaborated by *Screen*-collaborator Paul Willemen. In response to Wollen, although with a similar political outlook, Willemen made a clear distinction between the terms 'avant-garde' and 'modernism'. In the essay 'An Avant-Garde for the 90s',[7] his most refined version of this argument, Willemen states that the terms 'modernism' and 'the avant-garde' describe two entirely different artistic ventures, though they can sometimes co-exist in such artistic movements as surrealism or in the work of single artists, for example Pound or Blanchot, or, from a cinema point of view, Godard. Modernism, according to Willemen, is

> a set of formal characteristics, a set of procedures frozen into a specific generic practice ... suggesting that modernism is a period style, as was impressionism or expressionism, or any other historically circumscribed style. ... [M]odernism is most definitely used as a normative category, distinguishing between objects on the grounds of attributes such as self-reflexiveness ..., immanence and indeterminancy. Modernism insists that these features be present in the form of experiments with visual perspective, narrative structure, temporal logic, and so on. The theoretical shadows of modernist procedures are concepts such as undecidability, deconstruction, decentring and specificity.[8]

Identical with Wollen's first avant-garde – the painterly experimentalism of the Co-op film-makers – modernism was hence, according to Willemen, an aesthetic like any other. Its cultural object was to preserve notions of 'art-ness', or even high art, and thus, as Willemen quotes from Andreas Huyssen, 'to salvage the purity of high art from the encroachments of modern mass culture'.[9]

The avant-garde proper, on the other hand – in Willemen's terms identical with Wollen's second avant-garde, the narrative type – is still a political movement, trying to free art from its institutional and cultural constraints. It can take any shape, use any aesthetic form, as long as it breaks the ruling norms of established art – in the 20th century synonymous with 'modernism' – as in the narrative films of Godard, or, as Willemen states in an obvious *hommage* to his *Screen*-adversary Wollen, in Peter Wollen's and Laura Mulvey's film *Crystal Gazing* (1982).

Willemen's essay constitutes a kind of conclusion to the 'modernism-realism debate' within the *Screen* project, and thus also a step forward to a more sociological approach to the academic study of narrative, and indeed also of popular films. 'Modernist' film, in the sense of essentialist, experimental, visually oriented film, was after all not really a part of the Marxist radical film-studies project – Modernist specificity was even characterized by Willemen as a Freudian 'fetish'.

Traditional narrative, although not in the Hollywood sense as it would become somewhat later, was the issue at stake. In this way, film studies at the time – I am speaking of the early 1980s – overcame the problematic issue of 'modernism' within the established arts[10] and developed its own cultural approach, which would eventually lead to serious study and reappraisal also of the previously despised Hollywood cinema.

In the context of the present discussion, it is necessary to point out that Willemen's political critique of 'modernism' as a basically reactionary mode of expression complements David Bordwell's initial linguistic dismissal of the term. That is, we now have two rejections of the concept of 'modernism' in film studies, albeit on completely different grounds.

The crisis of modernism

These rejections of 'modernism' are both representative of the end of what could be called the first phase of academic film studies: that is, from the beginning of the 1970s to the early 1980s. They also represent the initial institutionalization of film studies and its handling of a particularly difficult problem complex in a manner which obviously has something to do with the social status of the discipline itself in the academic world. Initially, the established arts had been necessary; now the time had come to break away from them.

Film studies was in fact initiated in a moment of crisis for modernism. 'Modernism', as Colin MacCabe claims in his 'Preface' to Fredric Jameson's highly influential book *The Geopolitical Aesthetic*,

> is the attempt, after a loss of innocence about representation, to invent forms which will determine their own audiences, to project an interiority onto a future unmediated by any form of commodity. It is for this reason that the history of modernism is marked by new forms of sponsorship and above all an avant-garde ethic which, be it of an aesthetic or political form, looks into the future for an ideal Joycean or proletarian reader. Modernism thus constitutes itself, well before the cultural analyses of an Adorno, as an area of art constitutively opposed to commerce. The effort to project the self onto reality is premissed on a perfect future man who will become the ideal audience for ideal art.[11]

Modernism, however, MacCabe continues, became the topic of much criticism in the 1970s, particularly in the area of architecture where the shortcomings of modernist aesthetics, like those of for instance Le Corbusier, became the target; we are all aware of the present drab realities of 1960s cityscapes. The cinema, like architecture, was an inherently commercial venture – at least from a historical point of view, since cinema itself was a product of capitalist industrial production. Thus its status of commodity was inescapable.

In the light of this, the modernist *Screen* project, which came to dominate film studies during its inception, can – in MacCabe's words – be regarded as 'a terribly belated last gasp of modernism in which a figure like Godard promised to articulate the relation between art and politics prefigured by Mayakovsky and the Formalists in the Soviet 20s or Brecht and Benjamin in the German 30s'.[12]

But as far as I can see, this must also have been related to a striving for academic status, an attempt to find oneself on equal terms with English literature and art history. Once that was in any sense achieved, at least reasonably so, one could revolt against the somewhat alien concept of modernism and instead focus on cinema in its entirety: that is, on cinema as popular culture, as commodity, and as art. Hence the need at the time for both Willemen and Bordwell, albeit on somewhat different grounds, to free film studies from the constraints of a politics of 'modernism'.

Apolitical modernism in contemporary film studies

In our post-modern age – whatever precise meaning we attach to that term – film studies address the notion of 'modernism' in a much more unproblematic manner, liberated from the political and institutional associations of the term in the 1970s and early 80s. In his book *On the History of Film Style*, for example, David Bordwell, who had dismissed the term 12 years earlier, even indulges in a marked use of it. Without referring to his 1985 statement, Bordwell employs 'modernism' in a general common-sense-orientated way, as an aesthetic practice describing different avant-gardes as well as the European art cinema: 'The world's conception of cinematic modernism', Bordwell thus claims, 'was largely founded upon that body of work running from late Neo-realism and early Bergman through the films of Antonioni, Bresson, Fellini, and Buñuel, to all the "Young Cinemas" of the 1960s, most notably France's nouvelle vague'.[13] This description is germane to the concept of 'modernism' as employed in most standard modern film histories, where, as in Maureen Turim's study of the cinematic flashback, European art films – for instance Alain Resnais' *Hiroshima, Mon Amour* (1959) and *L'année dernière à Marienbad* (1961, the latter scripted by Robbe-Grillet) – are explicitly compared to the great modernist novels of the times.[14]

In Robert Stam's recent book on film theory the argument goes even further, also incorporating the notion of modernism into mainstream cinema and vice versa, claiming that in 'the cinema this realist/modernist dichotomy can easily be overdrawn. When Hitchcock collaborates with Salvador Dalí on the dream sequence in *Spellbound* is he still pre-modernist? Was Hitchcock ever pre-modernist? When Buñuel makes genre films within the Mexican industry, does he remain an avant-gardist?'[15]

We have thus approached a position where the concept of 'modernism' has been depoliticized, deprived first of its former political implications, and second of its sociological function of legitimizing film studies in terms of 'art-ness'. 'Modernism' in the 1970s was, in the Wollen sense, a political strategy; in the 90s it is, in the Willemen sense, a textual strategy, even though traces of 'political modernism' can still have some impact.[16]

There are, of course, many other concepts of 'modernism' flourishing in film studies; but the preceding reflections should go some way towards indicating how the term functions in relation to some of the most notable 20th-century trends in the discipline.

Notes

1 David Bordwell, *Narration in the Fiction Film* (London: Methuen, 1985), p. 310.
2 Peter Wollen, 'The Two Avant-Gardes' [1975], *Readings and Writings: Semiotic Counter-Strategies* (London: Verso, 1982, pp. 92–104). (The article was originally published not in *Screen*, but in *Studio International*, Dec. 1975.)
3 *Ibid.*, p. 96.
4 *Ibid.*, p. 100.
5 *Ibid.*, p. 102.
6 Peter Wollen, *Signs and Meaning in the Cinema* [1969], third ed. (London: BFI, 1998), pp. 156–7.

7   Paul Willemen, *Looks and Frictions: Essays in Cultural Studies and Film Theory* (Bloomington and London: Indiana University Press and British Film Institute, 1994), pp. 141–60.

8   *Ibid.*, p. 143.

9   *Ibid*, s. 146.

10 On the topic of film semiotics at the time, film theoretician Dudley Andrew writes: '[T]he issue in cinema is not so easy, for this is an art born in, and as part of, the age of realism. It has known no other norm. Even today, despite the struggle of modernist filmmakers, realist cinema dominates our screens. Semiotics of cinema has, then, felt obliged to deal with the issue over and over. Film semiotics is virtually synonymous with the study of codes of illusion.' See Dudley Andrew, *Concepts in Film Theory* (Oxford etc.: Oxford University Press, 1984), p. 63.

11 Colin MacCabe, 'Preface', *The Geopolitical Aesthetic: Cinema and Space in the World System* (Bloomington and London: Indiana University Press/British Film Institute, 1992), p. xiii.

12 *Ibid.*, p. xv.

13 David Bordwell, *On the History of Film Style* (Cambridge/Mass. and London: Harvard University Press, 1997), p. 87.

14 Maureen Turim, *Flashbacks in Film: Memory & History* (London and New York: Routledge, 1989), especially the chapter 'Memory Flashes and the Modernist Literary Conjunctions', pp. 210–26.

15 Robert Stam, *Film Theory: An Introduction* (Oxford: Blackwell, 2000), p. 16.

16 As, for instance, in Christopher Ames's 1997 study of American movies about the movies – Brechtian self-referentiality was once considered one of the cornerstones of 'modernist aesthetics' – where the author claims himself uninterested in 'measuring cinematic self-referentiality against a modernist yardstick', that is, he links to the term 'modernism' connotations of avant-gardism, anti-commercialism, and high-art qualities. Christopher Ames, *Movies about the Movies: Hollywood Reflected* (Lexington: The University of Kentucky Press, 1997), p. 11.

14

Between Categories: Modernist and Post-modernist Appropriations of Wallace Stevens

Stefan Holander

In one of Wallace Stevens' proverbs, the so-called *Adagia*, we read that 'progress in any aspect is a movement through changes in terminology'.[1] Stevens' adagium already seems to establish a connection between the poet and the linguistic turn, but it should be kept in mind that his statement is not primarily a piece of epistemological theory (although in a sense, as Kenneth Burke suggests in *A Grammar of Motives*, it is this as well).[2] Instead it refers, in the context of Stevens' poetics, to the strong poet's imaginative capacity to unmake obsolete but still oppressive fictions in order to create new forms to believe in. 'Progress' in Stevens criticism could of course itself be understood in terms of the capacity of his work, of which the history of his receptions gives a great deal of evidence, to be re-formulated – or, in his own terms, re-imagined – from within the terminological frameworks of different, and often apparently incompatible, paradigms.

In a fairly selective but, I hope, illustrative account I will try not only to describe, but also implicitly criticize, a few acts of 'appropriations' of 'Stevens', paying special attention to the ways in which a number of critics claiming allegiance to postmodern ideas tried to wrest 'Stevens' from the grip of conservative critics and make his modernism 'radical'. These critical interventions exemplify what Melita Schaum has called, in a book dedicated to Stevens' criticism, the way in which the critical debate around Wallace Stevens' work has had the shape of 'a redefinition of the concept of literary modernism itself'.[3] Schaum's definition of the institution of literary criticism in Foucauldian terms as a 'play of power and knowledge'[4] raises the question whether the postmodern reinterpretations, made by critics belonging to the paradigm that enables us to understand the nature of 'paradigms', can be essentially different: arguably, they should – although this is also strictly forbidden – know better than to be just another paradigm. 'Paradigm' is here used in its very common, 'looser' sense, derived from Thomas Kuhn's radically pessimistic theory on human knowledge, yet quite contrary to its most radical implications, roughly designating the main beliefs and convictions embraced by a particular faction involved in the struggle for dominance in the scientific and cultural spheres.[5] Before dealing with critical radicalizations of Stevens' work, I will briefly discuss a text that explicitly formulates an idea of modernism as a radical artistic and critical practice, Astradur Eysteinsson's *The Concept of Modernism*.

Although Eysteinsson's comprehensive discussion is stimulated by the essential indeterminacy of the concept, he takes a hostile stance towards what he sees as 'powerful critical attempts at fixing modernism into an unquestionable, and unquestioning, aesthetic practice'.[6] Eysteinsson's idea that a fully known and safely classified modernism no longer has the power to be challenging or disturbing makes him redirect his query from a concern with referential stability towards a discussion of modernism's value or significance as a 'cultural force'. Eysteinsson produces a kind of resistance to theory, a 'modernism' if you will, in the very opacity of the concept itself whose purpose, instead of being helpful in an instrumental sense, is to continue generating a debate over (or perhaps better 'within' or 'of') modernism, rather than putting an end to it. Eysteinsson's analyses could be called *post*modernist insofar as they take place 'after the fact'. The prefix 'post', however, does not suggest the distance accessible from a viewpoint 'beyond', 'outside', or 'after' the event of modernism. Instead the emphasis is on the critic's involvement in a modernist legacy, a heritage which ultimately depends on what we make of it. By admitting to, even stressing, the implication of his own discourse in a modernist tradition, Eysteinsson defines the often lamented confusion of knowledge and value as one of the main sources of relevance of literary scholarship.[7]

As far as Eysteinsson's modernism 'is' something, it is conceived of as an unremittingly critical force whose only power lies in a willed refusal 'to communicate according to established socio-semiotic contracts', constantly able to 'question', 'interrupt', 'disrupt', 'undermine', and, in even more violent terms, 'subvert', 'break', 'fracture', and 'rupture', our comfortable perception of 'naturalized' orders of signification. This capacity is itself always situational, context-bound, and has no other essence than this negative power to thwart and unsettle received modes of communication. The fierce and noisy imagery Eysteinsson uses to embody the idea of modernism's disruptive potential does not primarily pretend to illustrate the way actual readers are disturbed or 'defamiliarized' by radical art, something which, as Eysteinsson admits, has become increasingly difficult to argue. More importantly, it can be understood to mime the modernist break of 'literature' out of its institutionalized boundaries, a questioning of the borders between literature and what is not literature. A condition for this capacity is a self-reflexive questioning of the limits and possibilities of critical language: Eysteinsson's injunction that 'modernism must reach beyond a purely aesthetic function if its "destructive" practices are to be a critical and potentially subversive force' is clearly directed to literary critics rather than to artists.[8] In response to the idea that academe's ultimate effect on art is to domesticate it, Eysteinsson proposes that 'if modernism proved prey to institutionalization, the institution has embraced a force that has the potential to rupture its totalized order.'[9] This 'embrace', however, is not to be understood simply in terms of the propensity of critical language to assimilate, close or forestall the potential 'rupture'. Instead, criticism is asked to perform a self-willed exposure to a questioning of one's own legitimacy, as productive of a critical attitude. Modernism can, Eysteinsson suggests, even be conceived of as a pedagogic project with an emancipatory potential. 'Is it not possible', he asks, 'to think of modernism as helping us to resist "innocent" reception and possible subjugation as we confront the rhetorical powers of various channels of communication?'[10] Here, the word *modernism* has ceased to refer directly to the historical event of revolutionary changes in artistic perception and become an idea – or an ideal (albeit modelled on the historical event) – of permanent vigilance, to be maintained as the very possibility of cultural criticism.

Stevens' place in Eysteinsson's book is not very prominent, and his first appearance is anything but flattering. The phrase 'O Blessed rage for order' from his early poem 'The Idea of Order at Key West'[11] serves as the heading for a subchapter in which Eysteinsson criticizes the view of modernism as 'a kind of aesthetic heroism, which in the face of the chaos of the modern world (very much a "fallen" world) sees art as the only dependable reality and as an ordering principle of a quasi-religious kind.'[12] In view of several of Stevens' statements this placement seems quite apt: for Stevens, the poet's imaginative agency is called for in a post-lapsarian world where a 'pressure of reality', as exercised by the mass media, urban life, the vulgarization of culture, and the Second World War, demands a 'pressing back' of the imagination, which, as in 'The Noble Rider and the Sound of Words',[13] must achieve a new 'nobility' of the modern time. The success of poetic response, which relies on the poet's power 'to abstract himself and also to abstract reality, which he does by placing it in his imagination'[14] (and, as Stevens provocatively admits, means 'strictly speaking, escapism'), can only be accomplished by a poet who seeks 'those purposes that are purely the purposes of the pure poet'[15] and who, in affirming that 'there is a life apart from politics',[16] claims recourse to a sphere of art untainted by ideology, where an 'alternative view of life' becomes possible. Even if the imagination, in order to be viable and true, has to 'adhere' to reality, it is clear that reality, although it 'is the base', is 'only the base', to reverse another of Stevens' *Adagia*.[17]

Rather than exposing the real for 'what it is', then, the moment of insight into true reality is indistinguishable from the moment of creativity: in 'Notes toward a Supreme Fiction' it is said that 'a fictive covering weaves always glistening from the heart and mind',[18] meaning that 'The Plain Sense of Things', as in the poem with the same name,[19] is finally inaccessible, since 'the absence of the imagination had itself to be imagined'.[20] The destructive, 'decreationist' powers of the intellect thus always tend toward, even fuse with, imaginative affirmation. To this may be added the creation, in the course of Stevens' career, of 'Ideas of Order', 'Major Men', and 'Supreme Fictions' in which we might believe 'beyond belief'.[21] Although Stevens believed that 'the poem must resist the intelligence almost successfully',[22] and found it essential to eliminate 'from the romantic what people speak of as the romantic',[23] thus talking about a form of 'defamiliarization', his language on aesthetic issues tends to employ an imagery of pleasure.

This intentionally simplified account seems to legitimate placing Eysteinsson's use of Stevens to exemplify the kind of modernism which celebrates art as a secular religion, and which Frank Lentricchia called a 'conservative fictionalism'.[24] Such a conclusion, however, is based on the assumption that it is the poet's intention, or, more sophisticatedly, his 'project' within a history of ideas, that is the locus of modernism, an idea that is questioned by Eysteinsson's argument.

Two significant attempts to reinterpret Stevens from a postmodernist point of view were made by the American deconstructors J. Hillis Miller and Joseph Riddel, whose re-readings of Stevens were openly connected to the larger project of enforcing a paradigm-shift in literary criticism. Miller's double article 'Stevens' Rock and Criticism as Cure' was simultaneously an exploration of the never-ending etymological branchings of Stevens' words in 'The Rock' and a promotion of Jacques Derrida and the Yale Deconstructors, the so-called 'uncanny critics'.[25] In his book-length study *The Linguistic Moment,* where the article reappeared, the analysis paved the way for a definition of 'the perennial task of criticism' as the persistent, but always frustrated effort to follow the blind alleys of language that only lead to more language,[26] an idea of criticism that appears to find its perfect match in Stevens' poem, which 'calls forth potentially endless commentaries, each one of which, like this essay, can only formulate and reformulate the poem's receding abysses.'[27] In *After the New Criticism,* Frank Lentricchia indicted American deconstruction for squandering the potential for a genuinely historical critique in Derrida's philosophy, and perpetuating a kind of aestheticist hedonism by merely reformulating the intra-literary, textualist and ahistorical formalism of the New Critics. This failure, Lentricchia argued, was due to a conception of poetic language – and, as Miller appears to say, of criticism – with *one perennial* task, precisely to affirm the kind of autonomous sphere that is questioned by Eysteinsson. The constant 'questioning of the ground,' which Miller claims 'Stevens pursued',[28] can only lead on to more words in a dynamic, but never-ending and therefore ultimately pointless activity, producing the gratifica-tions of a kind of vertigo of the bottomless textual abyss. The critic, although provided with an eternal duty (and, one could imagine, a 'steady job'), loses all ground to stand on. Freed from any obligation to address the world out-side the institution, the critic is also deprived of the possibility of maintaining a position from which to be 'critical' in a fundamental sense.

Joseph Riddel's reinterpretations of Stevens, like Miller's, explicitly func-tioned as revisions of his own earlier theoretical positions, and perhaps more clearly demonstrate certain dilemmas involved in Stevens' postmodernization in particular and theoretical 'appropriations' in general. In 1972, reviewing Helen Vendler's prize-winning book on Stevens' long poems from three years earlier, *On Extended Wings*, Riddel asked: 'Have our poets really made a rad-ical departure into the modern? That is, are our central poets, to use Stevens' phrase, really postmodern?'[29] For Riddel, Helen Vendler epitomizes 'mod-ernism' insofar as she is a representative of 'the so-called New Criticism, born of modernism', which now, he announces, needs to be reassessed. Since Rid-del's argument draws its energy from its polemics with Helen Vendler, it is instructive to review briefly her version of Stevens' poetry and poetics.

The moral and epistemological frame for Vendler's criticism is the need for a deep congeniality with Stevens: she does not just take his ideas about poetry as the object of study, as an unknown which needs to be interpreted, but as the already authorized – and unquestionable – way to approach his work. The formalist idea that a poem is an independent unit of expression finds its anal-ogy on a larger scale in Vendler's way of pressing the notion that Stevens' *Collected Poems* is a consummated *oeuvre*, a fully achieved 'Whole of Harmo-nium', as he planned to call it at an early stage of his career. This alleged unity demands that 'we keep, in reading Stevens, a double attitude, seeing the ma-jor poems both as things in themselves and as steps in a long progress toward his most complete incarnations of his sense of the world.'[30] Such an idea could well be interpreted as primordially ethical: it should at least in principle be the duty of any interpreter to regard any work of art as an individual expression that needs to be understood, and whose integrity needs to be respected. The assumption of integrity which functions as an ethically required starting-point for the interpretation of an utterance could not, however, in principle, be demonstrated by interpretation itself: or if it could, these two assertions would be of different orders altogether. It is notable, however, that Vendler apparently *does* feel the need to anchor her argument empirically by suggest-ing that Stevens' achievement *in fact* reached its actual completion in a very late poem, 'The Course of a Particular', of which I will quote the last two stanzas:

The leaves cry. It is not a cry of divine attention,
Nor the smoke-drift of puffed out heroes, nor human cry.
It is the cry of the leaves themselves that do not transcend themselves,

In the absence of fantasia, without meaning more
Than they are in the final finding of the ear, in the thing
Itself, until, at last, the cry concerns no one at all.[31]

'One can hardly doubt', Vendler writes, 'that the leaves, as well as being leaves, are Stevens too.'[32] Hence, the poem tells the story of Stevens' failed efforts up to this very point where he 'has gone beyond crying out to Jerusalem, beyond crying out even to a living name or place or thing, beyond directed cries at all.'[33] In this cry, all the poetic 'trials of device' reach their end and attain their full meaning in an ecstatically imploding schwa which, although apparently meaningless (as a 'pure directionless, sound', which 'concerns no one at all'), incarnates the entire life of a poet, whose trials receive their final remuneration in the form of poetic success. Vendler's very 'literary' introduction may perhaps be seen as the least serious part of her book, and this eccentric framing of her work as a mere rhetorical flourish, or even, as is often said about Vendler's style, an example of 'good writing'. Critical language, however, may be at its most powerful, simultaneously assuming and enforcing an interpretative community, at its most casual. Vendler's suggestion of the unassailable presence of a poem written at the end of life (and, as it were, writing the end of life) describes a point where the literary and the biographical, art and life, are indistinguishable; it both *forces* and *enables* her to repudiate the violence of subjective interpretation altogether. This makes her limit her critical act to a description of the structure of Stevens' rhetoric, supposing, of course, that description can be something essentially different from interpretation. The imperative to treat Stevens' poems as empirical objects, whose interpretation is to be annulled by the identity of the objects themselves, is motivated by the belief that they are expressions of an individual, and very fragile, personality.

From a perspective which I would cautiously call postmodern, Vendler's interpretative ethics are highly questionable. Such a way of thinking would imply that the total separation between the work and its interpreter, which is meant to preserve and respect a certain inviolable otherness (and identity) of the singular artistic utterance, is conditioned upon a prior act of equally total identification. The humility implicit in Vendler's submission to 'Stevens' can thus be seen as the very opposite of humility: the presumed respect for absolute integrity is made possible only by the utmost (because essentially silent, hidden) interpretative violence. Vendler in fact admits to exerting a 'necessary' violence, but absolves herself by claiming that her critical acts leave the poems just as they are (which raises the question as to why criticism was called for in the first place): 'To make Stevens' poetic arrangements clear to the eye I have not hesitated to realign certain poems according to their rhetorical rather than metrical shape, to reprint others to show their *true* rhythmic form rather than their *putative* one, and in general to *violate*, for a purpose, Stevens' own lineation, assuming always a *Collected Poems* near at hand for the reader where the *true* poem can be found.' [34]

Rather than focusing on the way in which Vendler's assumptions arbitrarily close off a reading of Stevens, Riddel's main interest is to show that her interpretations are not properly 'authorized' by his texts. 'Mrs. Vendler's whole point', Riddel complains, 'is that Stevens' poetry progresses beyond any effort to create "divinities, heroes and human beings," or to evoke "self-transcendence" in order to become purely itself. She is, I think, right, but for the wrong reason.' [35] Riddel compares the cry in 'The Course of a Particular' with other cries in Stevens' work and concludes that 'it is not a cry of', but 'a cry towards', the 'history of language itself, of utterance as violence, as a departure, and as a regathering into a new place (topos) – or, in Heidegger's terms, as a coming into being, a standing there.' [36]

Riddel's main focus, however, is on Vendler's valorization of what she, relying on Stevens' own terms, calls Stevens' 'poem of words' over his 'poem of the idea', [37] a distinction roughly between poetry considered as a 'purposive form without purpose', art that is powerful enough to separate itself from the contingencies of ordinary, historical language, and the poetry of falsifiable philosophical argument, of incomplete, failed language. For Vendler, Riddel argues, Stevens' poetry 'is separated from life in order to reconstitute an order once held in the presence of religion or culture', [8] and thus turned into 'mere being' rather than problematic meaning. Of course, Vendler herself denies this purity as soon as she uses this idea as a criterion for distinguishing between *degrees* of success *within* Stevens' *oeuvre*. Instead of simply stressing this inconsistency, however, Riddel responds by reversing the priority. Stevens' virtues, he argues, lie in his 'discursive, philosophizing, rhetorical manner' which is 'invariably undercut by eloquence, verbal play, deliberate and innocent self-contradiction', [9] that is, in its (both self-reflexive and naïve) exposure of philosophical error. Significantly, these qualities are to be found precisely in poems that Vendler does not value, a notion that actually makes him concede an important part of her argument.

Vendler's and Riddel's respective versions of Stevens' poetry both describe meanings that do not quite reach the state of fully formulated sense, that are cancelled out before making concrete assertions. Vendler's idea that Stevens' rhetoric is saved, or absolved, from the contingencies of interpretation by an endless 'qualification' of assertions is based on the model of musical language. The persistently qualified, musically modulated language, 'a few words tuned and tuned and tuned', as Stevens says in 'Gallant Chateau',[40] is unified, brought to an end, in the *telos* of a harmonious musical structure whose end is contained in its beginning. This way of understanding a poem also makes it possible to see its temporal unfolding as a solid (and self-identical) object extended in space: a structure. The deconstructive Riddel, however, hears instead the noisy shortcomings of a short-circuited philosophical language that fails to ground itself, although he is not out to criticize Vendler's interpretation by deconstructing Stevens' texts or her interpretations of them. Rather, he confides in the notion that the deconstruction of Vendler is already there 'in the text itself' which, then, *actively* (from one or other ground somehow proper to itself) undermines its own assertions. The impression that it is nearly impossible to distinguish Riddel's critique of Vendler's theoretical assumptions from his critique of her misinterpretation of Wallace Stevens' poetry can be further illustrated by Riddel's portentous redescription of Stevens' imaginative project (italics are mine):

> It is precisely because Stevens is so insistent on decentering or interpreting the myth of the center, even as he moves toward *the poet's necessity of totalization*, that he is the ideal poet for exposing the blindness of a formalist criticism. He is postmodern.[41]

The imagination, which is here synonymous with 'interpretation', is understood only in its negative aspect, as a 'decentering' activity rather than the affirmative 'recentering', however provisional, that the historical Stevens to all appearances desired. At the same time as Riddel implicitly recognizes Stevens' contradictory gestures as belonging to one complex poetic moment (the de- in de-centering does not entirely annul the rest of the word) he relies both on their separability and the possibility of rhetorically emphasizing one of them. What Riddel calls 'a poet's necessity' – the 'totalization', a violent adequation of otherness into the same by a synthetic imagination – is tucked away in a subordinate clause. Stevens (no longer exactly the historical Stevens, but still, at least, the proper name and its pseudo-personal agency) *needs* to totalize, but to do so only *in order* to expose.

The problem with this choice 'between and not of' can be further exemplified by a discussion of Stevens' proverb that 'The final belief is to believe in a fiction, which you know to be a fiction, there being nothing else. The exquisite truth is to know that it is a fiction and that you believe in it willingly.'[42] Regardless of what one sees as called for – the creation of new beliefs or an incessant demythologizing – this statement will permit 'appropriations' of people from both camps. Stevens' emphasis, however, seems to be on 'the exquisite truth' of the simultaneous existence, rather than mutual exclusiveness, of belief with its nemesis, the destructive powers of the mind. Rather than merely to believe or disbelieve, the difficult challenge is henceforth to maintain a knowledge of the fictionality of that in which one believes while not cancelling out the good of belief itself. Of course, this can be seen as an old problem, although such a difficult effort at double vision could in many ways be seen as a veritable challenge in a postmodern and post-colonial world, where non-essentialist and non-fundamentalist ways of affirming cultural and religious identity are badly needed.[43] Regardless of whether one puts the emphasis on knowledge or belief, however, there is a hierarchy of interpreters implied, and political possibilities hidden, in Stevens' adagium: there is still the difference between those who believe naively as in a myth, and those who, since they are empowered to know that they believe in something inessential, are able to create new fictions for themselves, and myths for others.

As Stevens' formulation 'the exquisite truth' suggests, it is possible to understand this dilemma in terms of pleasure and pain, with the gratifications of belief in antagonistic tension with self-critical knowledge. Fred Hoerner has redescribed Stevens' poetics of sensuous enjoyment – 'It Must Give Pleasure' – as a 'politically chastening' aesthetics, calling attention to the ways in which his poems are counter-epiphanies that 'hollow out' the core of their own creations, preventing the reader from 'lunging forward' into affirmative enjoyment. Hoerner is not only interesting as a reincarnation of the 'High-toned Old Christian Woman' mocked in Stevens' poem with the same name, but his tortuous language exemplifies, in a way similar to Riddel's, the difficulties for critical discourse to formulate the complexity of this tension. The 'hollowing' effect of Stevens' poetry, Hoerner explains, 'occurs because its verbal and aesthetic form reconstructs the process whereby interested abstractions infect transparent descriptions at the moment time slips our notice and the awareness of structuring is deadened.'[44]

Like Hoerner's, Riddel's effort at redescribing 'Stevens'' poetic project as 'postmodern' is based on the idea that Stevens, although he was not quite aware of this, did (or perhaps more appropriately *does* – a difficult tension between historicism and synchronicity is visible in this choice of tense, although Stevens, for Riddel, *is* postmodern) no longer desire to 'recover a logos' or create new satisfactions of our will to believe, but to partake in the never-resting critical activity of deconstruction. Understandably, Riddel disclaims any reliance on what 'Stevens' 'says': 'it is not Stevens' thematic, his "ideas," which need emphasizing', but what instead brings the reader fully into the meaning of Stevens' poem as an 'act of the mind' is his 'interpretation of interpretation', something that must not be wholly conscious – to be deduced simply from the poet's 'ideas' – nor violently imposed by the theoretical grid of the interpreter. It must, however, still be possible to ascribe it to 'Stevens'. As I will try to show, this can be accomplished by placing his work in a movement of history somehow stronger than his own conscience of it.

As Eysteinsson points out, the crisis of language and subjectivity, which we could either see as *reflected in* or *brought about by* modernist art (Eysteinsson is intentionally ambiguous in this respect), has close parallels in much post-structuralist thinking.[45] Poststructuralist theorists have not only drawn inspiration from, and exemplified their ideas by references to, modernist art; insofar as their own texts 'perform' the radical practice of questioning official truths they too could be said to participate in modernism's 'interruption of modernity', which may also suggest that radical modernism was a precursor, an *avant-garde* whose culmination is postmodern philosophy. By appropriating Stevens for the postmodern 'paradigm', Riddel is simultaneously inscribing Stevens into a history of progress, in something as problematic as a postmodern teleology. At the end of the essay, however, Riddel semi-capitulates by qualifying his former statement, conceding that 'Stevens and the [now] *modernist-postmodernist* poet *may have desired* to fulfill the Platonic project, but that they could only fulfill it by bringing it into question.'[46] There is still a nostalgia for the old ordering fictions, but their recuperation, in the modern world, can only be achieved through a hard-boiled process of radical doubt.

Apparently dissatisfied with this result, Riddel gives it another try eight years later, with a more flamboyant strategy. In close readings of two of Stevens' long poems, 'Esthétique du Mal' and 'Notes toward a Supreme Fiction' (the last of which was one of Vendler's favored 'pure' poems), Riddel finds coincidences between words in Stevens' poems and key concepts in Derrida's *Of Grammatology* which are striking enough to allow him to suggest a strong affiliation between the projects of the two writers. At the quite novelistic beginning of 'Esthétique du Mal', somebody – '(a poet?)', Riddel suggestively asks – sits by a table in a café 'at Naples, writing letters home / And, between his letters, reading paragraphs / On the sublime' while in the ominous background 'Vesuvius had groaned / For a month'.[47] The fact that the somebody, who is already taken to be a poet, is writing letters home is taken to mean that he is homeless. This, in turn, means that he is not only eccentric (as poets in cafés are) but 'ex-centric'[48] and the scene (since he is writing letters home) is a scene of writing, which in turn is understood as 'the problematic scenario of representation',[9] which is also 'a scene of violence'. That is, Riddel explains, 'not a scene of nature but a text'.[50] This is supported by the fact that 'the poet' in the café 'could describe the terror of the sound, [of Vesuvius] because the sound / Was ancient',[51] that is, since it is already written in the logocentric script of the 'book' which, as we read further on in the poem, 'makes sure of the most correct catastrophe'. In only a few paragraphs, Riddel has thus already had Stevens use, and, in a postmodernist historical narrative, *prefigure*, several of the early Derrida's most important terms: 'writing', 'text', 'the book', 'ex-centricity'.

My intention here is not simply to accuse Riddel of anachronism, nor of letting Stevens' words be usurped by a foreign vocabulary. His essay does make important points about Stevens' poems that are actually linked to many thought-provoking coincidences between Derrida's *brisures* and Stevens' texts. The problem is that Riddel wants to do much more than just suggest interesting parallels, or illuminate Stevens' poem by juxtaposition. This is evident in Riddel's interpretation of Stevens' statement, in the essay 'Imagination as Value',[52] on the imagination as 'the irrepressible revolutionist':

> Writing destroys the nostalgia for a 'chief image,' a center, by exposing its fictionality. The 'chief image,' like a 'first idea,' is a belatedly produced fiction, an imaginary construct. It is neither original nor central but the mark of the imagination as nothing in itself, as a negation, a negating or revolutionary force. To displace the notion of a 'chief image' is to destroy the 'book.'[53]

The last line here echoes Derrida's proclamation of 'The End of the Book and the Beginning of Writing', at the beginning *Of Grammatology*. Above, 'writing' refers both to Derrida's concept of 'writing' and 'writing' as 'modern poetry'. Riddel, however, extends the powers of 'writing', not only to destroy the belief in a 'chief image' but even to do away with the 'nostalgia' for such belief. How 'nostalgia' is 'destroyed' by exposing the fictionality of its object is an open question, but in any event it is clear that Derrida's anti-concept, which is meant to unsettle and challenge the ways we perceive the relations between language, subjectivity and reality, has here acquired the status of a magic word that not only absolves 'Stevens' from all remnants of logocentrism, but of the troublesome nostalgia of the biographical Stevens that Riddel ran up against in his previous interpretation. By ascribing this unambiguous power to writing, Riddel pretends to have rooted out any doubt about Stevens' role in the postmodern project, a role inseparable from the insertion of his work into a postmodern historical narrative.

In an essay from 1985, 'The Impasse of the Modernist Lyric', Riddel's attempt to make Stevens radical by association was characterized as mere 'wishful thinking' by Marjorie Perloff, another critic whose radicality is based on poststructuralist ideas. The essay was published at the same time as 'Stevens/Pound, Whose Era?', one of the chapters of *The Dance of the Intellect*, in which she signalled a paradigmatic divide in modernism between the aesthetics of Wallace Stevens and Ezra Pound, visible in the split in literary criticism between so-called 'Stevensians' and 'Poundians'.[54] Perloff's argument is particularly interesting in that it defines Stevens' aesthetics, and the criticism derived from it, as fundamentally Romantic, belonging to the tradition of lyrical poetry, a 'belated' form of expression which is not only out of tune with, but somehow outside, history.[55] Perloff very efficiently points out the hopelessness in Riddel's rhetorical exorcism of Stevens' nostalgia by listing, as

I did earlier, the 'conservative' features of his poetics along with his personal characteristics: his provinciality, his reluctance towards political involvement, his 'escapism'. Fundamental to her argument is the analogy between Stevens' personality and political standpoints on the one hand and his choice of poetic form on the other, analogies that are much more than suggestive parallels. The indictment of Stevens' unreality is underpinned theoretically by Mikhail Bakhtin's idea (or, should we say, a strong interpretation of it) that lyrical poetry is an *inherently* speech-based, 'monologic' form of discourse, which represses other voices in totalitarian fashion. Stevens' ahistoricality and belatedness thus inhere in the very ahistoricality of his poetic genre itself, which is ontologically closed to history. At the outset of her essay, Perloff provides the reader with a list of historical events around the time when Stevens wrote 'Notes toward a Supreme Fiction', events which never made it into his poems, unless transformed beyond recognition.

'Totalization', or the synthetic agency of the imagination, now equated with monologue and lyric poetry, is for Perloff not a 'poet's necessity', as Riddel suggested, but a matter of historical choice. To the Stevensian version of modernism Perloff opposes the road not taken before of an authentically modern 'open', 'impure', and 'writerly' poetics interested in radical formal change, exemplified by Ezra Pound. While Stevens' closed poetic form is defined negatively as the objective correlative of his pathological escapism, Poundian aesthetics has a larger claim to reality since the 'freedom' or 'openness' of its expressive mode allows for a more colloquial diction, the inclusion of subject matter formerly seen as unpoetic, and the allowance, in a Bakhtinian aesthetics, of foreign, mutually incompatible voices. Strangely enough, Perloff's relegation of Stevens to a state of utter isolation from history, in spite of her avowed wish to introduce politics and history into the discussion, depends entirely on the possibility that Helen Vendler could actually be right, although maybe, as Riddel said, 'for the wrong reasons'. Stevens' poetic form becomes a verbal icon of repressive consciousness whereas Pound's 'open' 'dialogic' form incarnates the very democratic virtues that its inventor vitiated in his Italian radio speeches. Perloff's utopian formalism, a confessed continuation of Pound's thinking, according to which changes in literary form have the capacity to accomplish radical changes in the world, indicates, in several senses, a continuity with a Platonist 'fear of literature', 'fear' meaning both 'fright' and 'reverence'. Her faith in the power of poetry has its obverse in a terror not so much of the danger of lyrical seduction, but of the possible unreality, the unjust (and unauthorized) distortion of the real that Stevens' poetry threatens to bring about, in its unjust reflection of historical reality. This is visible in the fact that for all her championing of radical form through emphasizing 'defamiliarizing' strategies such as conspicuous breaks in syntax, graphic experimentation, and collage techniques by which pieces of reality are wrested from their 'proper' or naturalized context into foreign territory, she simultaneously relies heavily on the ethics of mimetic and expressive theory.

One of the purposes of this essay has been to bring out certain problems with the impact of postmodern thinking on the inherited functions of literary criticism, a topic which, although much discussed elsewhere, has not lost its urgency. For the evaluating and canonizing functions of literary studies to be powerful the realms of knowledge and value need to be kept separate, but only in order for their union to be consummated, for value, as it were, to be known (and for knowledge to be valuable). The separation accomplished by an understanding of critical discourse as transparent, and the restriction of the 'literary' – narrative, metaphorics, and 'value' – to the literary 'itself', is evident in Helen Vendler's discussion of Stevens, where instrumental rationality and pure subjectivity appear as two sides of the same coin. This ontology, however, also affects the practices, if not the theories, of all the other critics I have referred to. In his preface to a book on William Carlos Williams, Joseph Riddel himself formulated a postmodern critique of this model:

> Criticism is an act of interpretation, and thus, to use Heidegger's terms, an act of violence, of translating, or carrying over. It is a carrying over of language by language into language – an interpretation (the poem) by interpretation (criticism) into interpretation (poetics). There is no unmediated criticism; none that leaves the work as it was, as *itself*, and thus none which is itself a final *word* on the work. No matter the objective or scientific ideals of the critic, what he is after is a poetics (the structure of poetry), though he may desire, anxiously or desperately, to know or possess or worship the 'work' (sacred object, art) without transgression. One of the motives, and one of the illusions, of criticism has been that the critic can 'know' the work, that criticism can be transparent. And this depends, in turn, on the illusion that there is a work itself (like the philosopher's *thing itself*).[56]

Riddel's critique of the idea that there can be a 'work itself' has not, as I have tried to show, kept him from participating in the same interpretative game as Vendler, producing a different but equally determinate Stevens. In fact, the several versions of Stevens we see emerge in this essay, all ready to be enlisted for the enforcement of paradigmatic dominance, have it in common that they are all equally unambiguous. The particular violence of Riddel's own appropriation of 'Stevens' suggests an aspect he does not discuss above, that interpretation is guided by larger interests of a political and strategic sort, in which conveying a determinate message is a condition for discursive power. This is so even if (since Stevens' 'interpretation of interpretation' coincides so remarkably with his own) this message is itself that interpretative discourse is necessarily situated, limited, and inconclusive.

One of the most striking things about the miniature culture war I have tried to describe here is that it is largely an interdisciplinary affair, confirming in its practice (although, again, not *in theory*) the inherited purposes and methods of literary criticism. The strength of postmodern criticism could be (although this possibility is never to be taken for granted) to try to take half a step back from the heroic writing of competing canons, and criticize the very assumptions of the game, precisely by not denying one's implication in it. The 'idealism' implicit in this statement is not the same as that of Helen Vendler who, we saw, was not only 'both in and out of the game at the same time' – but both totally in and totally out, which is different. Unlike 'cultural studies' in which literary criticism threatens to dissolve (many would claim because of arguments such as mine), the very existence of a discipline called 'Stevens criticism' suggests that much literary criticism is motivated in its structure by the task of bringing out the artistic achievements of individual talents: Stevens criticism, then, is not simply a subsection of modernist studies. Critical discourse, as soon as it acknowledges a particular potential to verbal art and participates in its realization, to some extent fulfils the function of Plato's rhapsode Ion, serving as a mouthpiece for literary expression, and, on a larger scale of course, for literature. In Plato's dialogue, Socrates criticizes Ion because his interpretations of Homer's poetry (in his case closer to the sense of 'performance', or, say, the 'interpretation' of a piece of music) are not essentially based on knowledge, but have the form of a blind, possessed, and irrational acting out of their signifying potential. While reason for Plato resided in the capability of seeing truths beyond the devious chimera of phenomena, a postmodern rationality needs to acknowledge the dimension of subjective involvement and a certain 'blindness' as a necessary condition for one's understanding. According to this way of thinking, any effort at transcending Ion's blindness and the irrationality of the medium for poetic expression needs to be understood as an itself unverifiable effort not so much to secure firm knowledge as to think the conditions of one's own discourse.

If we are to believe Astradur Eysteinsson, modernism is not just something we may look at to find out what it is or was, but something which looks at us, makes demands, and refuses as yet to be nailed down. Also, if modernism (in Eysteinsson's strangely disembodied but powerful formulation of the concept) makes us question the fundaments of the relationship between criticism and literature, modernism and the traditional functions of literary criticism could be seen as two contrary, but equally indispensable and mutually productive, forces. Perhaps, then, since Stevens' elusive poetry, like the concept of modernism, seems to baffle final determination in a persistent way, and continues producing critical discussions, we could talk about it in similar terms; which is to suggest, perhaps, that it is 'its' modernism that both arouses and resists our efforts at definition. Although an undercurrent in this essay has been the intimation that Stevens' texts elude the appropriations made by the critics reviewed here, I have not primarily gone to the texts themselves to prove why this is so. My excuse for this refusal to play the game, withdrawing into the supposedly disinterested and safe sphere of meta-criticism, may be that such a resistance to theory cannot itself simply be a property of a particular text, but is always itself produced as a positive formulation, something that requires a different argument, which I hope to be able to make elsewhere. Instead, I will end by mentioning a couple of recent studies that I believe have made an important difference in changing the way we are capable of approaching Stevens.

For Wallace Stevens' poetry, which, to a large extent owing to his own statements, has been dissociated from the world of history and politics, the drive to historicize has been instrumental in opening for a new critical discussion of his poetry. Even if historicism will not finally resolve questions about literature and aesthetics, since the whole point with literary works may be that they can signify differently and validly outside of their original context, its introduction into Stevens criticism has been a very salutary alternative to the absolutisms we have seen here. In two books[57] Alan Filreis narrates in almost provocatively minute detail how Stevens in fact lived in reality, and how his poems, instead of simply being filled with artifice (nor, as some forms of historicism may suggest, filled only with reality in the form of discourse or ideology), resist, and, of course, *cannot* and *will not* resist the pressure of reality. The recent work of Beverly Maeder,[58] whose study of how Stevens' poetry wrestles with the inherited syntactical patterns and founding metaphors of the English language as a *historical* language, may exemplify the emergence of a new formalism, congruent both with historicist research such as Filreis' and the most important implications of poststructuralist theory. While allowing poetry the possibility of expressive renovation, Maeder's formalism does not grant it the privilege of a pure idiom; Stevens' modernist transcendence of inherited and oppressive language is never formulated as a literary fact, an accomplished achievement whose absolute value can simply be proclaimed, but emerges as a possibility in the text which is brought out in critical practice. Finally, Maeder manages to let the question whether the main significance of Stevens' experimental language is to negate preceding fictions or to achieve a new affirmative language remain unsolved, displaying a 'negative capability' that in itself helps us to comprehend the complexity of the discourses of modernism in which we are involved.

Notes

1 Wallace Stevens, *Collected Poetry and Prose* (New York: Library of America, 1997), p. 900.
2 Kenneth Burke, *A Grammar of Motives* (Berkeley: University of California Press, 1969), pp. 212–13.
3 Melita Schaum, *Wallace Stevens and the Critical Schools* (Tuscaloosa: University of Alabama Press, 1988), p. 129.
4 Melita Schaum, '"Preferring Text to Gloss": From Decreation to Deconstruction in Wallace Stevens Criticism', *The Wallace Stevens Journal: A Publication of the Wallace Stevens Society* 10.2 (1986), 84–99, pp. 98–9.
5 As far as the postmodernist wager in those wars is concerned, the attraction of Kuhn's concept may in fact be the powerful rhetorical possibility of combining Kuhn's dark theory with the more hopeful understanding that a 'better' paradigm may actually succeed in overthrowing a less respectable one. In practice, the idea that a new 'paradigm' does not grow organically from knowledge accumulated in other paradigms, but constitutes a violent refutation of earlier forms of knowledge, can be used as evidence of the solidity of one's own beliefs and as a justification for refusing to engage in communication with one's opponents. This can be accomplished by combining the 'argument is war' metaphor, which makes us see intellectual endeavour as strategy or discursive intervention, with the idea, strictly disallowed by Kuhn's theory, that since one's own paradigm is on the side of historical developments, it represents progress. For an interesting version of this argument see David Kellogg's 'Perloff's Wittgenstein: W(h)ither Poetic Theory?' in *Diacritics: A Review of Contemporary Criticism* (Fall–Winter 1996), 67–85, pp. 78–9.
6 Astradur Eysteinsson, *The Concept of Modernism* (Ithaca: Cornell University Press, 1990), p. 4.
7 This idea recalls Andrew Bowie's recent argument that the fact that there are no stable conceptual definitions of 'literature' or 'art' could actually be seen as the strength of the concepts, and of literary criticism. See Andrew Bowie, *From Romanticism to Critical Theory: The Philosophy of German Literary Theory* (New York: Routledge, 1997), p. 9.
8 Eysteinsson, *The Concept of Modernism*, p. 240.
9 *Ibid.*, p. 223.
10 *Ibid.*, p. 228.
11 Stevens, *Collected Poetry and Prose*, pp. 105–106.
12 Eysteinsson, *The Concept of Modernism*, p. 9.
13 Stevens, *Collected Poetry and Prose*, pp. 643–55.
14 *Ibid.*, p. 657.
15 *Ibid.*, p. 900.
16 *Ibid.*, p. 7.
17 *Ibid.*, p. 917.
18 *Ibid.*, p. 342.
19 *Ibid.*, p. 428.
20 *Ibid.*, p. 428.
21 *Ibid.*, p. 295.
22 *Ibid.*, p. 910.
23 Holly Stevens and Richard Howard, eds, *Letters of Wallace Stevens* (Berkeley: University of California Press, 1996), p. 277.

24 Frank Lentricchia, *After the New Criticism* (Chicago: University of Chicago Press, 1980), p. 30.

25 J. Hillis Miller, 'Stevens' Rock and Criticism as Cure', *Georgia Review*, Athens, Georgia (1976), 5–31, 330–48.

26 J. Hillis Miller, *The Linguistic Moment: From Wordsworth to Stevens* (Princeton: Princeton University Press, 1985), p. 423.

27 *Ibid.*, p. 422.

28 *Ibid.*, p. 423.

29 Joseph N. Riddel, 'Interpreting Stevens: An Essay on Poetry and Thinking', *Boundary 2: A Journal of Postmodern Literature*, Binghamton, NY (1972), p. 80.

30 Helen Vendler, *On Extended Wings: Wallace Stevens' Longer Poems* (Cambridge/Mass.: Harvard University Press, 1969), p. 6.

31 Stevens, *Collected Poetry and Prose*, p. 460.

32 Vendler, *On Extended Wings*, p. 5.

33 *Ibid.*

34 *Ibid.*, p. 8. The emphases are mine.

35 Riddel, 'Interpreting Stevens', p. 87.

36 *Ibid.*

37 Stevens, *Collected Poetry and Prose*, p. 912.

38 Vendler, *On Extended Wings*, p. 82.

39 Riddel, 'Interpreting Stevens', p. 80.

40 Stevens, *Collected Poetry and Prose*, p. 130.

41 Riddel, 'Interpreting Stevens', p. 94.

42 Stevens, *Collected Poetry and Prose*, p. 903.

43 An analogous challenge, I believe, is suggested by Eysteinsson's image of the 'embrace' on behalf of the academic institution of its own potential rupture.

44 Fred Hoerner, 'Gratification and Its Discontents: The Politics of Stevens' Chastening Aesthetics', *The Wallace Stevens Journal: A Publication of the Wallace Stevens Society* 18.1 (1994), 104.

45 Cf. Eysteinsson, *The Concept of Modernism*, pp. 133–5. This idea has also been formulated by Paul de Man: 'Certain forces that could legitimately be called modern and that were at work in lyric poetry, in the novel, and the theatre have also now become operative in the field of literary theory and criticism … This development has by itself complicated and changed the texture of our literary modernity a great deal and brought to the fore difficulties inherent in the term itself as soon as it is used historically and reflectively.' Paul de Man, 'Literary History and Literary Modernity', in *Blindness and Insight: Essays in the Rhetoric of Contemporary Criticism* (Minneapolis: University of Minnesota Press, 1983), pp. 143–4.

46 Riddel, 'Interpreting Stevens', p. 95. Emphases are mine.

47 Joseph Riddel, 'Metaphoric Staging: Stevens' Beginning Again of the "End of the Book"' in *Wallace Stevens: A Celebration*, eds Frank Dogget and Robert Buttell (Princeton: Princeton University Press, 1980), pp. 303–38 (308).

48 Riddel, 'Metaphoric Staging', p. 310.

49 *Ibid.*, p. 309.

50 *Ibid.*, p. 314.

51 *Ibid.*, p. 309.

52 Stevens, *Collected Poetry and Prose*, pp. 724–39.

53 Riddel, 'Metaphoric Staging', p. 314.

54 On Perloff's use of the concept of the 'paradigm' see David Kellogg's article 'Per-
    loff's Wittgenstein', 79.
55 A similar argument is made by Gerald Bruns in his essay 'Stevens without Episte-
    mology' from the same year in *Wallace Stevens: The Poetics of Modernism*, ed. Albert
    Gelpi (Cambridge: Cambridge University Press, 1985), pp. 24–40.
56 Joseph Riddel, *The Inverted Bell: Modernism and the Counterpoetics of William Car-
    los Williams* (Baton Rouge: Louisiana State University Press, 1974), p. xvii.
57 Alan Filreis, *Wallace Stevens and the Actual World* (Princeton: Princeton University
    Press, 1991), and Alan Filreis, *Modernism from Right to Left: Wallace Stevens, the
    Thirties & Literary Radicalism* (Cambridge: Cambridge University Press, 1994).
58 Beverly Maeder, *Wallace Stevens' Experimental Language: The Lion in the Lute* (New
    York: St. Martin's Press, 1999).

15

Postscript: So what about Postmodernism? Fredric Jameson vs Linda Hutcheon

Gunilla Florby

The revision/ing of modernism as a classifying concept, the central concern of this volume, leads naturally over to a scrutiny of its ungrateful heir, its discontinuous continuation, postmodernism. The American poet David Antin's often quoted words, referring to the interrelationship between the two critical paradigms, 'From the modernism you choose you get the post-modernism you deserve',[1] can be made to serve as well in the present context where the stability of the construct of modernism is questioned. Even more unstable, both in terms of periodization[2] and the set of criteria it puts into play, postmodernism provides the focus of this postscript, which addresses its culturally conditioned relativity as a mode of perception. The different ways in which the concept is used in different cultural frameworks gives rise to a number of questions which are directly connected with the issue of stability.

Coming like Shakespeare's epilogue, in the wake of great doings, I am conscious of constraints of scope, and I can here only suggest the direction my investigation is taking. The object of this essay is to chart some of the sometimes diverging, sometimes intersecting borderlines of postmodernism as presented in the discourse of two major North American critics. The focus will be on the claims staked by the American Fredric Jameson and the Canadian Linda Hutcheon, but an attempt will also be made to touch on the force fields surrounding them.[3] What Fredric Jameson has called 'this whole global, yet American, postmodern culture'[4] seems to look different from the Canadian side of the border, at least if you see it with the eyes of Linda Hutcheon. It is often claimed that Canadian postmodernism is related to American,[5] but how related is 'related' in the case of Hutcheon and Jameson? What does the American theorist see when he describes certain cultural circumstances, or certain strategies of writing, as postmodern? How does this differ from the perceptions of his Canadian counterpart? Sometimes the discrepancies of vision are marked enough to make it seem as if we are dealing with different epistemes.

Every choice can be challenged, and an explanation why these two have been selected to illustrate the lack of consensus about the nature of postmodernism may be in order. Jameson and Hutcheon both belong to the second generation of theorists of postmodernism that emerged after 1980; they have roughly the same status in their respective countries and have set the tone of subsequent studies.[6] Both have repeatedly reviewed their definitions of postmodernism, both offer a pragmatic combination of ideology, theory, and criticism; moreover, both are very much aware of each other's interventions and have repeatedly commented on them. Both Jameson and Hutcheon aim for all-inclusiveness, discussing such diverse manifestations of postmodernism as architecture, photography, writing, film, music, and Pop Art. Admittedly, their emphases differ. Hutcheon privileges literature; Jameson favours video, film, and television, quite in line with his focus on postmodern visibility and spatiality. Neither addresses the problem of definition as merely a matter of style. Jameson's formulation of his field of enquiry is illuminating: '"postmodernism" not as a style, but rather as a cultural dominant ... the force field in which very different kinds of cultural impulses ... must make their way' (56–7). These cultural impulses are dialectically related to what Jameson, following Ernest Mandel,[7] sees as capitalism's third stage, or 'late capitalism'. Hutcheon takes Jameson to task for not distinguishing between postmodernity and postmodernism, between the general socio-cultural formation on the one hand and its manifestations in the arts and in literature on the other. She writes:

> My exhortation to keep the two separate is conditioned by my desire to show that critique is as important as complicity in the response of cultural postmodernism to the philosophical and socio-economic realities of postmodernity: postmodernism here is not so much what Jameson sees as a systemic form of capitalism as the name given to cultural practices which acknowledge their inevitable implication in capitalism, without relinquishing the power or will to intervene critically in it.[8]

My preamble ends here. The protagonists have been introduced. After two quotations we know as much about them as we will perhaps ever know. On the one hand Jameson's resolutely Marxist approach with late capitalism as the sole determining factor, on the other Janus-faced Hutcheon always taking in the situation from two directions, keeping her binarisms balanced: critique versus complicity, inevitable implication versus critical intervention.[9] But let us go on and see how these positions condition their views on arts and history, on society and politics, on the blurring of the borderlines between high culture and mass culture. What do their different conceptual frameworks allow them to make of postmodernism? With what kind of nuance do they treat its various manifestations?

I shall start by tracing the two critics' perceptions – sometimes diverging, sometimes partly overlapping – as they emerge in two seminal analyses of postmodern culture, Jameson's 'Postmodernism, or, The Cultural Logic of

Late Capitalism' and Hutcheon's *A Poetics of Postmodernism*, complementing these with occasional references to other works and comments on the larger theoretical and ideological frameworks in which they write.

To Jameson postmodernism represents a clean break with modernism. He refers to a belief in 'some radical break or *coupure* generally traced back to the end of the 1950s or the early 1960s' (53). He contends that the two paradigms 'remain utterly distinct in their meaning and social function, owing to the very different positioning of postmodernism in the economic system of late capital' (57), the point being that while modernism upheld a critical stance[10] postmodernism happily plays along with the capitalist system. Hutcheon disagrees with this view of placid complicity. She speaks of a postmodernist practice which is both 'a challenging *and* an exploiting of the commodification of art by our consumer culture'. Jameson, she says, sees only the second half of this paradox.[11] For his initial definition Jameson relies on an inventory of representative postmodern phenomena, as does Ihab Hassan in *The Postmodern Turn* (1987), only Jameson's list is more limited and quite idiosyncratic. 'Often the theory is just based on too partial a sampling of the various discourses available to it', writes Hutcheon in *A Poetics of Postmodernism* (xi), without any specific address. In a review article Victor Li amplifies this criticism: '[Jameson's] choice of cultural materials is limited mainly … to what Dana Polan has called "that sort of upper-West-side-New-York-culture that is a source of clichéd parody in the films of Woody Allen" … We can also sense a theoretical deficiency in Jameson's assertion that "yuppies" are the leading class or class-fraction of postmodernism.'[12] The only visual artist mentioned by name in Jameson's inventory is Andy Warhol, the only filmmaker Godard, while music is represented by John Cage, Philip Glass, and Terry Riley. Burroughs, Pynchon, Ishmael Reed, and the French new novel stand for writing, 'along with alarming new kinds of literary criticism, based on some new aesthetic of textuality or *écriture* …' (54). A page or so later Jameson's sense of alarm is superseded by moral repudiation as he touches on the 'offensive features' of the postmodern revolt (56), on 'this whole "degraded" landscape of schlock and kitsch' (55).

For Linda Hutcheon the break with modernism is not absolute. While Jameson keeps reminding his readers of the difference in almost formulaic, antithetical phrases in his cultural analyses – it seems as if no description were complete until either of the labels 'modern' or 'postmodern' has been plastered[13] – Hutcheon often points to interrelations, to features that are shared or inherited. She questions the much-favoured technique of setting up parallel columns, pitting modernist traits against their allegedly postmodern opposites, as this leads to a disregard of the mixed and plural nature of postmodernism (20). The opening of the border between high culture and mass culture – if indeed this is what has happened – presents less of a problem for her: 'the crossing of such borders does not necessarily mean … an increasing de-humanization of life, as Jameson seems to believe.'[14]

When looking at the contemporary cultural scene Jameson sees depthless-ness, as illustrated by two contrasting examples from the visual arts. Juxtapos-ing Van Gogh's peasant shoes with Warhol's *Diamond Dust Shoes* in 'Post-modernism, or, The Cultural Logic of Late Capitalism' is, as Jameson himself implies, a move that is neither innocent nor random (58), especially as Van Gogh's painting is introduced as being a statement about 'the whole object world of agricultural misery, of stark rural poverty, and the whole rudimenta-ry human world of backbreaking peasant toil, a world reduced to its most brutal and menaced, primitive and marginalized state' (58). A quotation from Heidegger's *Der Ursprung des Kunstwerkes* adds to the emotional charge. 'In them' intones Heidegger resonantly, looking at the shoes, 'there vibrates the silent call of the earth, its quiet gift of ripening corn and its enigmatic self-refusal in the fallow desolation of the wintry field. … Van Gogh's painting is the disclosure of what the equipment, the pair of peasant shoes, *is* in truth …'[15] No similar special treatment is lavished on Warhol's footgear,[16] the assumption being that peasants are tragic victims of oppression, dancers are not. Hutcheon tentatively offers another Warhol, ironic and critical, whose work may be seen as a comment on the commodification of contemporary life (204). Instead of being symptomatic of an ongoing process of reification, Warhol's mundane shoes can be interpreted as a criticism of reification.

The replacing of depth by surface, experienced by Jameson, is linked to what he labels 'the waning of affect' in postmodern culture (61). Again Andy Warhol is invoked to supply the negative pole, this time with his Marilyn, while the modernist touchstone is *The Scream* by Edvard Munch, 'a canonical expression of the great modernist thematics of alienation, anomie, solitude and social fragmentation and isolation' (61). We have here a strange slippage of association. Jameson will have picked out the image of Marilyn because she, if anyone, was acquainted with 'alienation, anomie, sol-itude and social fragmentation and isolation'. But of course Warhol's picture was created in another context, which makes the comparison problematic. Skewed as it may be, the comparison is mainly used to open up a critique of contemporary theory which, according to Jameson, insists on surface, or multi-ple surfaces,[17] while repudiating not only 'the hermeneutic model of inside and outside which Munch's painting develops' but also other depth models, the dialectical one of essence and appearance, the Freudian of latent and manifest, the existential of authenticity and inauthenticity, and the semiotic opposition between signifier and signified (61–2). Exactly what he means by this very gen-eral statement is not clear, as exemplification and argumentation are lacking.

In Jameson's schema the waning of affect is a result of the decentring of the subject, a displacement that in its turn results in the disappearance of an individual style. Hutcheon counters: 'While *theorists* like Jameson[18] see this loss of the modernist unique, individual style as a negative ... it has been seen by postmodern *artists* as a liberating challenge to a definition of subjectivity and creativity that has for too long ignored the role of history in art and thought' (11). To which can be added a question. Do not modernist works like *Finnegans Wake* or *Endgame* mark the end of a road? Make it two questions. Would not contemporary readers be able to distinguish between the individual voices of authors like John Fowles and Graham Swift, J. M. Coetzee and Toni Morrison, Salman Rushdie and Angela Carter, much as older readers no doubt enjoyed the difference between, say, Joseph Conrad and D. H. Lawrence, and can we not hear the individual sound of music by Philip Glass and R. Murray Schafer, or poetry by Elizabeth Bishop and John Ashbery?

While Hutcheon observes a new awareness of history Jameson diagnoses a weakening of historicity. Jameson posits a marked ahistorical drive, Hutcheon argues that postmodernism is not ahistorical or dehistoricized, neither is it nostalgic (xii), and this reads like a reply to Jameson's complaint about what he calls 'the nostalgia mode' (67). She claims to see 'a new engagement with the social and the historical world.'[19] Hutcheon argues that while postmodernism 'reinstalls historical contexts as significant and even determining ... it problematizes the entire notion of historical knowledge' (89). What is problematic, more specifically, according to Hutcheon, is Jameson's 'History' as 'uninterrupted narrative', and her example of an opposing postmodern approach is the plural 'chutnified' historiography of novels such as Salman Rushdie's *Midnight's Children*.[20] To Hutcheon, the characteristic postmodernist fiction is historiographic metafiction, and part of the debate between her and Jameson has turned on a novel that can be seen as paradigmatic of this genre, E. L. Doctorow's *Ragtime*. To illustrate what he sees as a crisis in historicity Jameson refers to *Ragtime* whose decentred narrative, he claims, vitiates any possibility of a 'solid historiographic formation on the reader's part' (70). *Ragtime* is 'the most peculiar and stunning monument to the aesthetic situation engendered by the disappearance of the historical referent', exclaims Jameson (71), rousing Hutcheon to respond that what he objects to is the mixing of fiction and history, 'the major means to making the reader aware of the particular nature of the historical referent' (89). If Jameson takes no cognizance of the historical-political consciousness that pervades the novel, is it because it is not realized as a linear narrative along the lines of good old bourgeois realism but as discrete and disparate episodes? Leery of such features of postmodernism as fragmentation and collage, he describes the contemporary cultural productions as 'heaps of fragments' (71), as characterized by discontinuity and disjunction (75). The disagreement over *Ragtime* has a sequel, however. As 'Postmodernism, or, The Cultural Logic of Late Capitalism' was reprinted in 1991 as the first chapter of the massive book bearing the same title, minor modifications were added, among them an answer to Linda Hutcheon. After quoting at length from her explication of the political content of Doctorow's book, Jameson adds in a strangely conflicted sentence : 'Hutcheon is, of course, absolutely right, and this is what the novel would have meant had it not been a postmodern artifact'. And he explains the point: '[*Ragtime*] not only resists interpretation, it is organized systematically and formally to short-circuit an older type of social and historical interpretation.'[21]

Turning to architecture for further examples of postmodernism's repudiation of history, Jameson speaks of its 'random cannibalization of all the styles of the past, the play of random stylistic allusion' (65–66) and the replacement of historicity by a sense of nostalgia. 'This is not a nostalgic return; it is a critical revisiting', counters Hutcheon, apropos of a specific work of architecture, the 'Strada Novissima.'[22] Other verdicts are directly addressed to Jameson: 'Postmodernist ironic recall of history is neither nostalgia nor aesthetic cannibalization' (24) and 'There is absolutely nothing random or "without principle" in the parodic recall and re-examination of the past by architects like Charles Moore or Ricardo Bofill. To include irony and play is *never* necessarily to exclude seriousness and purpose in postmodernist art' (27). But it is not only among architects that Jameson senses nostalgia. Nostalgia film is another target of his vitriol. Hutcheon acknowledges the existence of a nostalgic strain in contemporary culture but draws a firm line between the nostalgic appropriation of past meaning and postmodernist ironic and parodic strategies.[23] The nostalgic filter that blurs the focus of certain films is dismissed by Jameson as 'an alarming and pathological symptom of a society that has become incapable of dealing with time and history.'[24] Hutcheon, who quotes this statement, has an answer at the ready; postmodern film certainly takes on history but not in the positive utopian way that Jameson would like. Speaking of the obsession with history and with the question of how we can know the past, which she feels characterizes postmodern film and fiction, she again reacts to one of Jameson's pronouncements: 'How can this be an "enfeeblement of history"?'[25]

In Jameson's world of late consumer capitalism, effective political action is no longer possible. Immobilized by 'spatial as well as … social confusion' (92) the individual subject is reduced to passivity. According to Hutcheon it is not hard to find political commitment in postmodernist art, perhaps not of a radical or revolutionary kind, but certainly with a subversive potential: 'in its very contradictions, postmodernist art … might be able to dramatize and even provoke change from within'.[26] She sees 'a literature which, while asserting its modernist autonomy as art, also manages simultaneously to investigate its intricate and intimate relations with the social world in which it is written and read' (45), which is a far cry from unquestioning acceptance. While Hutcheon points to the impact feminism and other minoritarian movements have had on postmodernism, Jameson appears largely to disregard the processes of decolonization and democratization and the emancipation of previously suppressed groups. In his review of *Postmodernism* Victor Li notes, '[i]n a book 430 pages long, feminism as a topic appears only four times in the index and an examination of those instances reveals very little'.[27] It is true that Jameson touches on the democratization of culture in postmodernism in a 1986 interview with Anders Stephanson. However, his comment on the increased accessibility of culture ('that cannot be altogether bad') is not enthusiastic.[28]

Jameson maintains that pastiche, not parody, is the privileged mode of postmodernism. Pastiche is 'without any of parody's ulterior motives', claims Jameson, 'amputated of the satiric impulse, devoid of laughter and of any conviction that alongside the abnormal tongue you have momentarily borrowed, some healthy linguistic normality still exists' (65). Modernist parody presupposes a unique style that can be mocked but also a norm that resonates in the background. In postmodernism there is a blurring of styles, collapsing the difference between high culture and mass culture. Hutcheon, on the other hand, sees parody as the central rhetorical strategy of postmodernism as it 'paradoxically both incorporates and challenges that which it parodies' (11). It is precisely parody, she argues, that enables postmodernism's confrontation between on the one hand art, and on the other the political and historical world (22). Parody is one of the ways in which the representational process is foregrounded and problematized.[29] 'The paradox of postmodernist parody', writes Hutcheon, 'is that it is *not* essentially depthless, trivial kitsch, as ... Jameson ... believe[s], but rather that it can and does lead to a vision of interconnectedness' (24). She suggests that Marxist critics (her examples are Jameson and Eagleton) are blind to postmodernism's basic seriousness, misreading its ironic intertextuality for triviality (134).

To Jameson the postmodern has brought 'a repudiation of representation, a "revolutionary" break with the (repressive) ideology of storytelling generally.'[30] 'This misconception', says Hutcheon, 'shows the danger of defining the postmodern in terms of (French or American) anti-representational late modernism'.[31] Jameson's 1987 essay 'Reading without Interpretation: Postmodernism and the Video-text' is even more explicit: 'If interpretation is understood ... as the disengagement of a fundamental theme or "meaning", then it seems to me that the postmodernist text ... is from that perspective defined as a structure or a sign-flow which resists meaning.'[32]

While Jameson gives voice to a sense of a loss of connection between discourse and reality, Hutcheon sees a productive problematizing (141). To Hutcheon the reading act is an allegory of coming to terms with reality – even if it is a postmodern work the reader engages with. Following Benveniste she emphasizes the importance of enunciation, of the communicative moment, which, she claims, 'Jameson wrongly reduces to … "an unstable exchange between … speakers, whose utterances are now seen less as a process of the transmission of information or messages, or in terms of some network of signs or even signifying systems, than as … an essentially conflictual relationship between tricksters"' (82).

Attempting to conceptualize a virtually global postmodernism and its relation to a virtually global capitalism Jameson casts a wide net. What comes up is consistently challenging and sometimes problematic. For one thing, insisting on a decisive break between modernism and postmodernism he disregards important continuities. Many of the tendencies that according to Jameson are constitutive of postmodernism can be traced in modernist and avant-gardist art as well. Thus, for instance, while leading analysts of architecture such as Charles Jencks see the Bonaventure Hotel in Los Angeles as an example of late modernism,[33] to Jameson it is paradigmatic of postmodernism. Jameson includes the French *nouveau roman* in his catalogue of postmodernist culture; to Hutcheon it is a manifestation of modernism. Similarly, Margaret Rose notes that Jameson's definition of postmodern pastiche echoes Jean Baudrillard's description of modernism.[34] On a more formal level, collage techniques, discontinuity, and fragmentation, to Jameson defining features of postmodernism, are frequent in modernism and in avant-gardist art as well.

The confusion bedevilling Jameson's modernism/postmodernism dichotomy is compounded by the sudden intrusion of realism. What Jameson describes as the ahistorical drive of postmodernism (and Hutcheon sees as a fruitful problematization of history) is a continuation of modernist tendencies. The opposite pole here is clearly the 19th-century historical novel, and not, as Jameson intimates, modernism.

Jameson's conflation of postmodernism and poststructuralism is also unfortunate, as is his linking of poststructuralist theory with the privileging of surface over depth which he diagnoses in contemporary culture. Reacting to Jameson's statement that modernist depth relationships (essence–appearance, latent–manifest, authentic–inauthentic, signifier–signified) have been flattened out in contemporary culture, David Shumway writes: 'Poststructuralism does not deny the latent or the signified, it just argues that the manifest and the signifier will invariably mislead us.'[35]

'Dialectic' is for obvious reasons a key term in Jameson's works. His exegetes like to stress his dialectical thought, 'his sustained dialectical reflection' (Hayden White). In 'Postmodernism' the dialectical approach consists mainly in the relating of various postmodern phenomena to the system of late capitalism. There is no room for the utopian vision which is usually seen as an important dimension of Jameson's theory, nor are there any signs of the type of dialectical analysis which encompasses conflicting forces, which thinks 'positively *and* negatively all at once' (86). Jameson's analysis of postmodernism is predominately negative.

Ironically, what is often seen as a defining trait of the Marxist dialectic, the ability to see contradictory aspects and accept the resulting complexity, to incorporate opposing positions into a comprehensive theory, is better represented by Hutcheon, in her analysis of postmodern culture. Throughout she points to the contradictions and the tension, to the 'both–and' or 'yet also' of postmodernism, to its inscribing and subverting, installing and problematizing, using and abusing. The setting-up of contrasts, the coupling of opposites is her characteristic method of coming to grips with the postmodern, whether she engages with realist narrative conventions, subject-formation, self-reflexivity, history, the canon, the authority of the text, or the autonomy of art. It is true that she claims, 'There is no dialectic in the postmodern: the self-reflexive remains distinct from its traditionally accepted contrary – the historico-political context in which it is embedded' (x), but it is a statement that is perhaps more ideological than descriptive. 'Embeddedness' certainly does not exclude co-existence and cooperation within a dualistic frame. At least as regards some of its applications her dictum seems to go against the grain of her own analyses. Her readings of postmodernist texts manage not infrequently to demonstrate a creative complexity rather than a war of opposites or an immobilizing conflict between the self-reflexive and a historical consciousness. Self-reflexivity is not intrinsically incompatible with a historico-political framework – they can be equally informed by a critical spirit, a problematizing of the act of representation. However, her insistence on there being no dialectic in postmodernism becomes more pertinent if we focus on the problematics of representation from another angle and shift the dichotomy to complicity versus contestation. Here is a contradiction that cannot be resolved. Derrida tells us that 'the authority of representation constrains us, imposing itself on our thought through a whole dense, enigmatic, and heavily stultified history. It programs us and precedes us'.[36] Contestation will of necessity be from within the system. Criticism will be coloured by complicity, by its dependence both on the dominant discourse and on the dominant ideology, but there can be no unification of opposites here, no reconciliation.

The best guess I have about why Hutcheon keeps stressing the contradictory nature of postmodernism[37] is that it is a reaction to Jameson's insistence on totalization,[38] his view of social life as a whole and (capitalized) History as a single story with class struggle and production as the constant leitmotifs. Says Hutcheon: 'Jameson ... is calling for the opposite of the postmodern as I have defined it. He does not want the contradictions and paradoxes; he does not want questioning. Instead he wants answers, totalizing replies – which postmodernism cannot and will not offer' (214).[39] Under her somewhat petulant summing up of their respective positions resounds the rumble of the mighty clash between Marxist totalization and post-structuralist valorization of difference and particularity.[40] Again and again she reacts against over-generalizations in his grandiose overviews, to a blindness to tendencies that run counter to his project. However, if my conjecture is correct she is beaten at her own game by Jameson. In 'The Antinomies of Postmodernity', the essay that opens *The Seeds of Time,* published in 1994, Jameson discusses the difference between antinomy and contradiction, a difference that can be summed up as follows: the antinomy consists of two propositions that are irreconcilable while the contradiction turns on matter that can be resolved or reconciled. As regards postmodern culture, antinomy is more applicable than is dialectic, he suggests.[41]

I am coming to the end of my postscript, which is perhaps after all a post-mortem. Hans Bertens speaks of a general feeling that postmodernism is moribund.[42] Fredric Jameson sums up his articulations on the postmodern from two decades,[43] Ihab Hassan tours the world with a lecture entitled 'What Was Postmodernism,'[44] Mark A. Cheetham and Linda Hutcheon publish a book entitled *Remembering Postmodernism,*[45] and the Danish literary historian Johan Fjord Jensen writes *Tomrum. Efter det postmoderne.*[46] Jameson's 'antinomy' helps strike the closing note. Antinomy, an opposition which is irreconcilable, can also serve as a description of the relation between Jameson's postmodernism and Hutcheon's. Jameson constructs postmodernism as the opposite of modernism, while Hutcheon sees a dialogue between the two paradigms. To Jameson postmodernism is a politically immobilized period of decadence, to Hutcheon it is a fruitful development, the logical sequel of the radical student protests of 1968. Their definitions of postmodernism are unremedially conflicted, marking an instability surpassing that relating to modernism.

Is it not time to lay these unquiet spirits to rest and see what we can make of the opposing positions on postmodernism taken by our two theorists? Instability is inherent in any hermeneutics, but is it enough to say with Peter Abelard that 'Since ... some statements, even those of the saints, appear not only to differ from one another, but even to be mutually opposed, one should not judge them rashly'?[47] I think that the time has come to judge the opposing statements. We have gained some distance from the heated debates of the eighties and can discern a number of truly important postmodern works of art towering above the detritus of the consumer culture, the bilge of schlock and kitsch that sloshes around their feet. These are works that allow space for difference and particularity, for plurality and heterogeneity, works that investigate the production of meaning and 'truth' and question an unthinking acceptance of historical, social, political, and ethnic assumptions. With all his brilliance, encyclopaedic knowledge, and political pathos Fredric Jameson has contributed to a trivialization of the postmodern enterprise that obscures the importance of its critique of homogenizing systems and totalizing master narratives. His articulation of contemporary culture as schizophrenic, depthless amnesia is a caricature.

Notes

1 As quoted by Henry M. Sayre in *The Object of Performance: The American Avant-Garde since 1970* (Chicago and London: University of Chicago Press, 1989), p. xi.

2 The term 'postmodern' first appeared in 1870 in connection with painting, reappeared in 1917 in the collocation 'postmoderner Mensch', was used in 1934 to distinguish stages of Spanish and Hispanic–American poetry, and was applied in 1947 to political theory. Only in the late 1950s was the term consolidated, more or less. See Wolfgang Welsch and Mike Sandbothe, 'Postmodernity as a Philosophical Concept', in *International Postmodernism*, eds Hans Bertens and Douwe Fokkema (Amsterdam: John Benjamins B. V., 1997), pp. 76–7.

3 I am not concerned here with Jameson's contributions to Marxian cultural theory in works such as *Marxism and Form* (Princeton: Princeton University Press, 1971) and *The Prison House of Language* (Princeton: Princeton University Press, 1972) or his launching of a narrative theory inspired by Marxism in *The Political Unconscious* (London: Methuen, 1981). My focus is on his studies on postmodernism from the 1980s, especially 'Postmodernism, or, The Cultural Logic of Late Capitalism', which builds on two previous essays, 'The Politics of Theory: Ideological Positions in the Postmodern Debate' in *New German Critique*, 33 (1984), 53–65, and 'Postmodernism and Consumer Society' in *The Anti-Aesthetic*, ed. Hal Foster (Port Townsend, Wash.: Bay Press, 1983), pp. 111–125, and leads up his magnum opus, *Postmodernism, or, The Cultural Logic of Late Capitalism* (Durham: Duke University Press, 1991). The works by Linda Hutcheon that have formed the basis of this study are *A Poetics of Postmodernism: History, Theory, Fiction* (New York and London: Routledge, 1988), *The Canadian Postmodern: A Study of Contemporary English-Canadian Fiction* (Toronto and Oxford: Oxford University Press, 1988), and *The Politics of Postmodernism* (London: Routledge, 1989).

4 Fredric Jameson, 'Postmodernism, or, The Cultural Logic of Late Capitalism', *New Left Review*, 146 (1984), 57. Further references to this article will appear in parentheses in the text.

5 See for instance Walter Pache, '"The Fiction Makes Us Real": Aspects of Postmodernism in Canada' in *Gaining Ground: European Critics on Canadian Literature*, edited by R. Kroetsch and R. Nischik (Edmonton, Alberta: NeWest Press, 1985), pp. 64–78.

6 Alison Lee's *Realism and Power: Postmodern British Fiction* (London and New York: Routledge, 1990) and Brenda K. Marshall's *Teaching the Postmodern: Fiction and Theory* (New York and London: Routledge, 1992) are indebted to Hutcheon's post-

structuralist brand of postmodernism. In 1989 Douglas Kellner proclaimed Jameson's 'Postmodernism, or, The Cultural Logic of Late Capitalism' 'probably the most quoted, discussed, and debated article of the past decade'. See *Postmodernism/ Jameson/Critique*, ed. Douglas Kellner (Washington: Maisonneuve Press), p. 2.

7 Like Ernest Mandel in *Late Capitalism* (London: Verso, 1975) Jameson posits three stages of capitalism: market capitalism, monopoly capitalism, and late, multinational, or consumer capitalism. For Jameson these moments correspond to realism, modernism, and postmodernism respectively. Mandel, however, claims that late capitalism started after the Second World War, i.e. circa 1945.

8 Linda Hutcheon, *The Politics of Postmodernism*, p. 26.

9 Hutcheon marks her distance to Marxism's master narrative even in the first paragraph of *A Poetics of Postmodernism*: 'You will not find here... any apocalyptic wailing about the decline of the west under late capitalism'.

10 This notion finds somewhat guarded expression in the Introduction to Jameson's book, *Postmodernism, or, The Cultural Logic of Late Capitalism*: 'modernism was still minimally and tendentially the critique of the commodity' (p. x), to become more assertive in the Conclusion, where Jameson claims that 'the deepest and most fundamental feature shared by all the modernisms is ... their hostility to the market' (pp. 304–5).

11 *A Poetics of Postmodernism*, 207–8. Further references to this book will appear in parentheses in the text.

12 Victor Li, 'Naming the System: Fredric Jameson's "Postmodernism"', *Ariel* 22: 4 (October 1991), 138.

13 I am thinking not least of *Signatures of the Visible* (London and New York: Routledge, 1990) and *The Geopolitical Aesthetic* (Bloomington: Indiana University Press, 1992).

14 *The Politics of Postmodernism*, p. 28.

15 As quoted by Jameson, p. 59.

16 '[I]f this copiously reproduced image [by Van Gogh] is not to sink to the level of sheer decoration, it requires us to reconstruct some initial situation out of which the finished work emerges', says Jameson (58). No 'initial situation' is sketched in the case of Warhol.

17 Cf. 'what is often called intertextuality is ... no longer a matter of depth' (62).

18 She refers here to Jameson's article, 'Postmodernism and Consumer Society' in Hal Foster's *The Anti-Aesthetic*, pp. 114–19.

19 Linda Hutcheon, *The Canadian Postmodern*, p. 1.

20 *The Politics*, p. 65.

21 *Postmodernism*, pp. 22 and 23.

22 *The Politics*, p. 4.

23 *Ibid.*, p. 98.

24 'Postmodernism and Consumer Society', p. 117.

25 *The Politics*, pp. 113–14. The reference is to Jameson's 'On magic realism in film', *Critical Inquiry* 12. 2 (1986), 303.

26 *The Politics*, p. 7.

27 Li, 'Naming the System', 139.

28 Anders Stephanson, 'Regarding Postmodernism: A Conversation with Fredric Jameson', *Postmodernism/Jameson/Critique*, p. 53.

29 See also pp. 35 and 39.

30 'Fredric Jameson, The politics of theory: ideological positions in the post-modernism debate', *New German Critique* 33 (1984), 54.

31 *The Politics*, p. 50.

32 In *The Linguistics of Writing: Arguments between Language and Literature*, eds Nigel Fabb *et al.* (Manchester: Manchester University Press, 1987), p. 212.

33 'Why has Jameson collapsed the categories of late modern and postmodern, which Venturi, Jencks, and others have carefully and persuasively articulated?' asks David R. Shumway in 'Jameson/Hermeneutics/Postmodernism' (Douglas Kellner, ed., *Postmodernism/Jameson/Critique*, p. 194).

34 See Margaret A. Rose, 'Post–Modern Pastiche', *British Journal of Aesthetics*, 31. 1 (1991), 28–9.

35 Shumway, 'Jameson/Hermeneutics/Postmodernism', p. 200.

36 Jacques Derrida, 'Sending: on representation', trans. Peter and Mary Ann Caws, *Social Research* 49.2 (1982), 304.

37 See also for example p. 100: 'the formalist and the historical live side by side, but there is no dialectic. The unresolved tensions of postmodern aesthetic practice remain paradoxes, or perhaps more accurately, contradictions'.

38 The frequency of phrases like 'a whole new economic world system', 'the whole object world of agricultural misery', 'the whole rudimentary human world of backbreaking peasant toil' (58) can be seen as lexical symptoms of Jameson's totalizing stance and of his repudiation of the postmodernist ideology of difference and its challenging of all master narratives. Says Hutcheon: '"to totalize" does not just mean to unify, but rather means to unify with an eye to power and control ...' (xi). See also Hutcheon's section '"Total History" de-totalized' in *The Politics of Postmodernism*, pp. 62–70.

39 See also p. 101: 'To operate paradoxically (to install and then subvert) may be less satisfying than to offer resolved dialectic, but it may be the only non-totalizing response possible'.

40 J. F. Lyotard does not mince words as he repudiates totality in the concluding part of his essay 'Answering the Question: What is Postmodernism ?': 'Let us wage a war on totality; let us be witnesses to the unpresentable; let us activate the differences and save the honor of the name' (*The Postmodern Condition*, Minneapolis: Minnesota University Press, 1984, pp. 71–82).

41 Fredric Jameson, *The Seeds of Time* (New York: Columbia University Press, 1994), pp. 1–2.

42 Hans Bertens, 'The Debate on Postmodernism', *International Postmodernism*, eds Hans Bertens and Douwe Fokkema, p. 3.

43 Fredric Jameson, *The Cultural Turn* (London: Verso, 1998).

44 The title of a lecture given at Lund University in the spring of 2000 playfully echoes that of Harry Levin's essay, 'What Was Modernism?' in *The Massachusetts Review* 1.4 (1960), 609–30. Other, earlier echoes were rung in William V. Spanos's 'What Was Postmodernism?', *Contemporary Literature* 31 (1990), 108–15 and in John Frow's 'What Was Post–Modernism?' in *Past the Last Post: Theorizing Post-Colonialism and Post-Modernism*, eds Ian Adam and Helen Tiffin (New York and London: Harvester Wheatsheaf, 1991), pp. 139–52.

45 Mark A. Cheetham with Linda Hutcheon, *Remembering Postmodernism. Trends in Recent Canadian Art* (Toronto: Oxford University Press, 1991).

46 Århus: Klim, 1999. ['Vacuum. After the Postmodern'. *Ed.*]

47 In his exegetical workbook *Sic et Non*. Translation by Catherine Brown in *Contrary Things: Exegesis, Dialectic, and the Poetics of Didacticism* (Stanford: Stanford University Press, 1998), p. 4.

A Bibliography of Modernism

Marianne Thormählen

As anyone who has worked on literary modernism knows, the literature on the subject is vast and only a small selection can be offered here by way of a concluding bibliography. Nevertheless, it seemed worthwhile to attempt such a selection as a service to readers. The first part summarizes ten different categories of relevant material: bibliographical guides; compilations of sources/primary texts; general explanatory studies whose main emphasis is on the English-speaking countries; works with a European outlook and an orientation towards the arts in general; studies of historical context in a wide sense; discussions that problematize modernism and the modernism concept; works whose specific orientation is towards the link between Romanticism and modernism; enquiries into the relationship between modernism and postmodernism; feminist studies of modernism; and works whose main emphasis is on modernist texts as physical entities and commercial goods. Part II lists a selection of works on modernism not mentioned in Part I. Most have reasonably self-explanatory titles, but brief descriptive comments are supplied where deemed appropriate.

Part I

Bibliographies of modernism have been compiled in the past, but much has happened since: it is twenty years since Alistair Davies' *An Annotated Critical Bibliography of Modernism* (Brighton: Harvester, 1982) appeared, and thirty since Maurice Beebe listed works on modernism as an appendix to a seminal article entitled 'What Was Modernism?' in *Journal of Modern Literature*, 3.5 (1973–4). More recent bibliographical assistance is provided by, for instance, Michael Levenson's *Cambridge Companion to Modernism* and Peter Nicholls' *Modernisms* (see below).

Cyril Connolly's *The Modern Movement: One Hundred Key Books from England, France and America, 1880–1950* (London: A. Deutsch, 1965) offers bibliographical assistance of another, source-orientated, kind. Where **sources** are concerned, the present-day student of modernism is greatly helped by the **anthologies of primary texts** – some of them with instructive introductions and annotations attached – that are available today. Peter Faulkner's *A Modernist Reader: Modernism in England 1910–1930* (London: B. T. Batsford, 1986) is a good place to start, with basic and indispensable texts and a lucid

introduction. In 1998 Edinburgh University Press published a far more ambitious selection, *Modernism: An Anthology of Sources and Documents*, edited
by Vassiliki Kolocotroni, Jane Goldman, and Olga Taxidou. This anthology
of over 600 pages goes back to Marx, Darwin, and Wagner and extends up to
the year 1940. The selection edited by Todd Bender *et al.*, *Modernism in
Literature* (New York: Holt, Rinehart, and Winston, 1977), remains helpful.
Peter Brooker (ed.) *Modernism/Postmodernism* (London: Longman, 1992)
begins the balancing of modernism and postmodernism with a highly informative discussion of 'the modern'. A wide-ranging volume edited by Lawrence Cahoone, *From Modernism to Postmodernism: An Anthology* (Oxford:
Blackwell, 1996), goes back to Descartes, Rousseau, and Kant but is predominantly geared towards situating the postmodern. Two earlier books should be
mentioned: David Lodge included an important essay by the great anti-mod-
ernist Georg Lukács in his generally useful collection of *20th Century Literary
Criticism* (London: Longman, 1972), and Cyrena N. Pondrom performed a
great service to students of modernism in the English-speaking world by
compiling relevant source texts (the French ones with translations) in *The
Road from Paris: French Influence on English Poetry 1900–1920* (Cambridge:
Cambridge University Press, 1972).

So what was/is modernism? Among the many **generally expository** works
on modernism, here is a selection, arranged in roughly chronological order. It
makes sense to begin with Harry Levin's classic lecture/essay, 'What Was
Modernism?', frequently reprinted, *inter alia* in *Refractions: Essays in Contemporary Literature* (Oxford: Oxford University Press, 1966). Levin's piece is a
glowing eulogy on the achievement of the great modernists, whom he regards
as a giant race before the flood: the 'Post-Modern Period' is immeasurably
inferior; '[w]e have fallen among epigones' (p. 273). Irving Howe edited an
early volume of criticism called *Literary Modernism* (Greenwich, Conn.:
Fawcett, 1967); on Howe, see further below under problematizing works. In
1976 appeared Malcolm Bradbury and James McFarlane's landmark volume
Modernism 1890-1930. A Pelican Guide to European Literature, this classic,
still in print from Penguin, adopts a pan-European perspective. 1977 saw the
publication of another standard work, Peter Faulkner's *Modernism* (London:
Methuen, 1977). Faulkner, who is particularly good on the discontents of
modernism (such as Yvor Winters) and on Americanness versus Englishness,
situates the term in mid-twentieth-century debates on literature, culture, and
society on both sides of the Atlantic. David Lodge's *The Modes of Modern
Writing: Metaphor, Metonymy, and the Typology of Modern Literature* (London:
Edward Arnold, 1977) is illuminating on 'modernity' in general.

For three decades, Frank Kermode has discussed the nature and status of
modern(ist) literature in print, from *Romantic Image* (first published by

Routledge and Kegan Paul in 1957) via *The Sense of an Ending: Studies in the Theory of Fiction* (first published by Oxford University Press in 1967) to *History and Value: The Clarendon Lectures and the Northcliffe Lectures 1987* (Oxford: Clarendon Press, 1988). While modernism as such has not been his chief subject, his insights into modern literature are of an explanatory as well as evaluative character. A more deliberately expository work is Stan Smith's *The Origins of Modernism: Eliot, Pound, Yeats, and the Rhetoric of Renewal* (New York: Harvester Wheatsheaf, 1984), which applies political perspectives and stresses the retrospectiveness of modernism. Ricardo J. Quinones' *Mapping Literary Modernism: Time and Development* (Princeton: Princeton University Press, 1985) regards modernism as a dynamic force which evolved in stages, paying special attention to temporal aspects and looking towards period terms such as 'Renaissance' and 'Romanticism'. C. K. Stead is also interested in, and rather clearer in his treatment of, the relationship between Romanticism and modernism; his *Pound, Yeats, Eliot and the Modernist Movement* (New Brunswick: Rutgers University Press, 1986) is a perceptive and readable book.

By the mid-1980s a considerable mass of secondary literature on modernism had appeared, and Stanley Sultan's *Eliot, Joyce and Company* (New York and Oxford: Oxford University Press, 1987) takes most of it on board while being especially good on early modernism. A standard work on the latter subject was published a few years earlier: Michael H. Levenson's *A Genealogy of Modernism: A Study of English Literary Doctrine 1908-1922* (Cambridge: Cambridge University Press, 1984), whose consideration of modernism's roots in the nineteenth century introduces a masterful study. Another important book soon followed: Perry Meisel's *The Myth of the Modern: A Study in British Literature and Criticism after 1850* (New Haven and London: Yale University Press, 1987), which (unlike many books with the word 'modernism' in their titles) discusses the major modern writers in a way that consistently addresses their 'modernist' qualities. With Norman F. Cantor's *Twentieth-Century Culture: Modernism to Deconstruction* (New York: Peter Lang, 1988) the focus shifts towards another transition, the one from modernism to postmodernism. Cantor usefully catalogues modernist characteristics, emphasizing the centrality of art.

1990 saw the publication of another landmark, Astradur Eysteinsson's *The Concept of Modernism* (Ithaca and London: Cornell University Press, 1990). For the first time, the academic term 'modernism' was subjected to extended scrutiny in a full-length monograph, and the book presents the life of that term in the academy from a variety of perspectives. Like many writers on modernism, including a large proportion of the ones mentioned under 'context' and 'material(ist) aspects' below, Eysteinsson wrote with a left-wing bias. In his discussions he was able to engage with exponents of postmodernism, and so do contributors in Steve Giles (ed.), *Theorizing Modernism: Essays in Critical Theory* (London and New York: Routledge, 1993), including the editor himself. Art Berman's *Preface to Modernism* (Urbana and Chicago: University of Illinois Press, 1994) emphasizes the position of the modernist in capitalist society. *The Cambridge Companion to Modernism* edited by Michael Levenson (Cambridge: Cambridge University Press, 1999) covers a great deal of ground, in the other arts and culture/ society as well as in literature proper, in its modest 232 pages which are followed by an excellent bibliography.

Among the earlier works on modernism which **deal with the arts in general, adopt a pan-European outlook,** and are available in English, three are especially noteworthy. Joseph Frank's *The Widening Gyre: Crisis and Mastery in Modern Literature* (Bloomington: Indiana University Press, 1963) engages – like many of its successors – with Ortega y Gasset's ground-breaking work *The Dehumanization of Art* (1925). Peter Bürger's *Theory of the Avant-Garde* (the German original, *Theorie der Avantgarde*, had appeared from Suhrkamp/ Frankfurt am Main in 1974), translated by Michael Shaw (Manchester: Manchester University Press, 1984), has had a considerable impact on theoretical discussions on modernism and postmodernism in the English-speaking countries as well. Among Matei Calinescu's works on modernism, *Faces of Modernity: Avant-garde, Decadence, Kitsch* (Bloomington: Indiana University Press, 1977; a later version, issued in 1987, is entitled *Five Faces of Modernity*) has become especially prominent in Anglo-American discussions of modernism, and with reason: the book is extremely helpful on the international history of modernism and on the meaning of the concept in general.

Another ambitious study by Continental modernism experts is Douwe Fokkema and Elrud Ibsch's *Modernist Conjectures: A Mainstream in European Literature 1910–1940* (London: C. Hurst & Co., 1987; an earlier Dutch version was entitled *Het Modernisme in de Europese Letterkunde*, Amsterdam 1984). The book's main emphasis is on intellectual/epistemological aspects of modernism. A contemporary volume edited by Monique Chefdor, Ricardo Quinones, and Albert Wachtel, *Modernism: Challenges and Perspectives* (Urbana: University of Illinois Press, 1986), incorporates all the arts in its searching reconsiderations of modernism. So does another important book which did not originate in Anglo-American academe: Christian Berg, Frank Durieux, and Gert Lernout (eds), *The Turn of the Century: Modernism and Modernity in Literature and the Arts* (Berlin and New York: Walter de Gruyter, 1995; it is vol. 3 in Walter Pape (ed.), European Cultures: Studies in Literature and the Arts). This copious collection of papers in English and French begins with a section called 'Terminological and Theoretical Issues' which is especially pertinent in the present context; see, for instance, the contributions by Walter Gobbers and Matei Calinescu.

Peter Nicholls' *Modernisms: A Literary Guide* (Basingstoke: Macmillan, 1995) is an excellent introduction to international modernism in literature and the arts, starting with French symbolism and according plenty of space to Futurism (in Russia as well as Italy) and Expressionism. A generous bibliography adds to its value. Anna Balakian's *The Snowflake on the Belfry: Dogma and Disquietude in the Critical Arena* (Bloomington and Indianapolis: Indiana University Press, 1994) is only partly relevant to a discussion of modernism, but its fearless outlook on issues that had perhaps been allowed to 'settle' rather too comfortably is refreshing. Christopher Butler's *Early Modernism: Literature, Music, and Painting in Europe, 1900–1916* (Oxford: Clarendon Press, 1994) is another standard work in the field, and Michael Bell's *Literature, Modernism and Myth: Belief and Responsibility in the Twentieth Century* (Cambridge: Cambridge University Press, 1997) is a fine study of the international scene which includes an insightful chapter on Eliot and Pound.

Michael Bell is also the author of a comparatively early work on **modernism in a sociocultural context**, *The Context of English Literature, 1900–1930* (London: Methuen, 1980). Bell's book is more solidly informative in design and execution than Marshall Berman's ideologically charged and influential *All That Is Solid Melts into Air: The Experience of Modernity* (New York: Simon and Schuster, 1982; reissued by Penguin in 1988). Nobody who is interested in this aspect of modern literature can avoid engaging with Lionel Trilling's classic *Beyond Culture: Essays on Literature and Learning* (New York: Viking Press, 1965; several reprints). Trilling's book applies far broader perspectives than another study of modernism and society, James F. Knapp's *Literary Modernism and the Transformation of Work* (Evanston, Ill.: Northwestern University Press, 1988); but Knapp offers sidelights on political and cultural history which anticipate some of the analyses of material aspects of modernism that appeared in the 1990s (see below). Like Michael Bell's *Context of English Literature* mentioned above, *Literature and Culture in Modern Britain. Volume One: 1900–1929*, edited by Clive Bloom (London and New York: Longman, 1993), is a wide-ranging historically/socially contextualizing work. It is especially helpful in combination with Gary Day and Brian Docherty (eds), *British Poetry 1900–1950: Aspects of Tradition* (London: Macmillan, 1995).

In three important books, Michael North has examined various aspects of the cultural/social/political context of modernism: *The Political Aesthetic of Yeats, Pound and Eliot* (Cambridge: Cambridge University Press, 1991); *The Dialect of Modernism: Race, Language, and Twentieth-Century Literature* (New York: Oxford University Press, 1994); and *Reading 1922: A Return to the Scene of the Modern* (Oxford: Oxford University Press, 1999). The latter is a particularly intriguing work, giving space to phenomena which have very little to do with the flowering of literary modernism.

More 'context', in a somewhat different sense, is offered by the TLS Companion volume called *The Modern Movement* which John Gross edited for Harvill in 1992 – an instructive, entertaining, and sometimes illuminating book. Two recent works by John Jervis apply challenging perspectives to a broad reconsideration of international modernism in a cultural context, *Exploring the Modern: Patterns of Western Culture and Civilization* and *Transgressing the Modern: Explorations in the Western Experience of Otherness* (Oxford: Blackwell, 1998 and 1999 respectively). Postcolonial ideas predominate in a book edited by Howard J. Booth and Nigel Rigby, *Modernism and Empire* (Manchester: Manchester University Press, 2000). Finally, Charles Ferrall has investigated the politics of the leading Anglo-American writers in *Modernist Writing and Reactionary Politics* (Cambridge: Cambridge University Press, 2001).

As this book was in press, a volume appeared which looks likely to become another landmark in modernism studies: David Bradshaw (ed.), *A Concise Companion to Modernism* (Oxford: Blackwell, 2002). This collection of specially commissioned essays presents the intellectual matrix of Anglo-American modernism by discussing ideas and cultural/scientific phenomena such as eugenics, Nietzscheanism, psychoanalysis, technology, and publishing.

Most of the works listed above as 'generally expository' in character contain reservations about the term 'modernism', but some academic writers have been more aware of its problematic aspects than others. Among the **works that include a problematizing dimension,** the following selection affords some idea of where people who have been troubled by the concept have felt that their troubles lay.

A suitable opening note is sounded by Monroe K. Spears's *Dionysus and the City: Modernism in Twentieth-Century Poetry* (New York and Oxford: Oxford University Press, 1970). Its very first sentence runs, 'Modernism is, of course, an impossible subject'. Spears goes on to look at such difficult areas as the 'modern' versus the 'contemporary' in what constitutes a valuable summing-up of the situation on the brink of the 1970s, that decisive decade in modernism scholarship. Irving Howe's *Decline of the New* (London: V. Gollancz, 1971) raises a number of conceptual issues, arguing that modernism was/is 'a dynamism of asking and of learning not to reply' and stressing the 'devotion to discomfort' (pp. 8–9). Worries about the term 'modernism' crop up towards the end of an article by Robert Adams, unoriginally entitled 'What Was Modernism?', in *Hudson Review* 31 (1978), 20–33; it adopts a pan-European/arts-in-general approach.

As the concept of modernism became fully established in Academe and had done a solid amount of work there, the repercussions of that work began to bother a number of scholars, and the 1980s saw a considerable degree of scepticism about the term and what it stood for. Roger Shattuck's criticism – under the guise of fiction –in *The Innocent Eye* ('The Poverty of Modernism'; New York: Farrar etc., 1984) is referred to in the introduction to this book (as is that of a subsequent critic who has drawn on Shattuck, John Harwood in *Eliot to Derrida: The Poverty of Interpretation* (London: Macmillan, 1995)). Another voice of radical discontent was that of Robert Conquest, in an entertaining piece of polemics called 'But What Good Came of It at Last? An Inquest on Modernism', in *Essays by Divers Hands*, ed. Michael Holroyd, vol. XLII (1982). Arguing that the best writers of the twentieth century were those who while not modernists had learnt from them, Conquest decided that the modernists had actually failed to be fresh, lively, and new.

Other writers voiced their reservations in less uncompromising terms than Conquest and located their uneasiness in Academe rather than in modernist literature itself. Ever urbane, Bernard Bergonzi – author of what remains the best life-and-works introduction to Eliot (*T. S. Eliot*, first published in 1972) – articulated his unhappiness about some of the effects of 'modernism' in the academy, for instance in the introduction to *The Myth of Modernism and Twentieth-Century Literature* (Brighton: Harvester, 1986). An important volume edited by Robert Kiely with John Hildebidle, *Modernism Reconsidered* (Cambridge/Mass.: Harvard University Press, 1983), contains several contributions in which problematic aspects of modernism are analysed. At much the same time, in *The Failure of Modernism: Symptoms of American Poetry* (New York: Columbia University Press, 1986), Andrew Ross argued that modernism had failed in that it had not managed to do away with subjectivity.

One of the troubles with the term 'modernism' (as the present book has repeatedly pointed out) is that its valorizing properties have tended to detract from the respect and interest that are due to other kinds of writing, and several of modernism's discontents have drawn attention to that problem. In the 1980s, Carol T. Christ argued that the anti-Victorianism of the modernists had obscured their own roots in Romanticism, the common ground from which both they and the Victorians had sprung; see her *Victorian and Modern Poetics* (Chicago and London: University of Chicago Press, 1984), ch. 5. A dozen years later, *Seeing Double: Revisioning Edwardian and Modernist Literature*, a book with a social orientation edited by Carola M. Kaplan and Anne B. Simpson (Basingstoke: Macmillan, 1996), made a similar point, questioning the posited dichotomy between Edwardian and 'Modernist' work. Even more recently, the problems inherent in not being a modernist have been raised in Lynne Hapgood and Nancy L. Paxton (eds), *Outside Modernism: In Pursuit of the English Novel, 1900– 1930* (Basingstoke: Macmillan, 2000).

About ten years after Kiely and Hildebidle *et al.* had 'reconsidered' modernism, Kevin J. H. Dettmar (ed.) and the scholars who participated in his volume *Rereading the New: A Backward Glance at Modernism* (Ann Arbor: University of Michigan Press, 1992) also applied a retrospective approach to the subject. The book covers both America and Britain and all literary genres, using postmodernism as a starting-point. Several of the contributors problematize the modernism concept, among them Morton P. Levitt who involves it in an attack on postmodernism. Another 1990s expository writer on modernism, Rainer Emig, admits that the 'modernism' term is 'both too general and too ill-defined to be of much use' (p. 3 in his *Modernism in Poetry: Motivations, Structures and Limits*, London and New York: Longman, 1995). Similar reservations are expressed by some of the contributors to Martin Klapper and Joseph C. Schöpp, *Transatlantic Modernism* (Heidelberg: C. Winter, 2001), vol. 89 of American Studies, a wide ranging collection which includes photography, architecture, philosophy, and painting.

An issue that has interested a good many writers on modernism, including some mentioned above (see, for instance, Quinones and Stead), is the relationship between Romanticism and modernism. John Bayley's *The Romantic Survival: A Study in Poetic Evolution* (London: Constable, 1957) appeared in the same year as Kermode's *Romantic Image* (see above). In *Yeats* (New York and Oxford: Oxford University Press, 1970), Harold Bloom maintained – along lines similar to the ones adopted by most scholars who have worked on this topic – that modernism is a belated version of Romanticism. Albert Gelpi saw modernism as continuing the Romantic quest for imaginative transcendence in *A Coherent Splendor: The American Poetic Renaissance, 1900–1950* (Cambridge: Cambridge University Press, 1987). Bruce E. Fleming's *Modernism and Its Discontents: Philosophical Problems of Twentieth-Century Literary Theory* (New York etc.: Peter Lang, 1995) problematizes the relationship between Romanticism and modernism, situating the latter in the context of recent literary theory.

Other scholars/critics have looked not at what went before modernism but at what came after, and there is no shortage of studies on modernism in relation to postmodernism. David Lodge was one of the first to contemplate modernism from such an angle, in *Modernism, Antimodernism and Postmodernism* (Birmingham: University of Birmingham Press, 1977). In the 1980s, a number of books and articles on the subject appeared, among them Douwe W. Fokkema's *Literary History, Modernism and Postmodernism* (Amsterdam: Benjamins, 1984). Andreas Huyssen's influential book *After the Great Divide: Modernism, Mass Culture and Postmodernism* (London: Macmillan, 1986) discerns two periods of postmodernism, which is presented as predominantly an American phenomenon. An appendix entitled 'Postmodern Poetics Unfair to Modernist Poetry' in Charles Altieri's *Painterly Abstraction in Modernist*

American Poetry: The Contemporaneity of Modernism (Cambridge: Cambridge University Press, 1989) is a vigorous and amusing onslaught on certain manifestations of postmodernism.

A different tone and 'message' characterize David B. Downing and Susan Bazargan (eds), *Image and Ideology in Modern/Postmodern Discourse* (New York: State of New York University Press, 1991), which argues that there is no clear distinction between modernism and postmodernism. Patricia Waugh's *Practising Postmodernism/Reading Modernism* (London: Edward Arnold, 1992) is especially interesting in what it has to say about autonomy and expressiveness. Hugh Witemeyer (ed.), *The Future of Modernism* (Ann Arbor: University of Michigan Press, 1997) contains a number of valuable contributions, among them an essay by Sanford Schwartz on 'The Postmodernity of Modernism'. Richard Murphy applies perspectives gathered from many more or less recent literary theorists in his *Theorizing the Avant-Garde: Modernism, Expressionism, and the Problem of Postmodernity* (Cambridge: Cambridge University Press, 1999). Emphasizing the energy, scepticism, and anarchic humour that characterized the Dada movement, Richard Sheppard sees Dada as a link between modernism and postmodernism in *Modernism – Dada – Postmodernism* (Evanston, Ill.: Northwestern University Press, 2000); the book's extensive bibliography, with many entries related to Europe and the arts in general, is an extra bonus.

At about the same time as the modernism/postmodernism debate was building up steam, **the status of the woman writer in the context of modernism** became a hot topic, and the work of leading male exponents of modernism was subjected to **feminist** criticism. A landmark volume which combines both features is Bonnie Kime Scott (ed.), *The Gender of Modernism: A Critical Anthology* (Bloomington: Indiana University Press, 1990). Here the case for the addition of new women writers to the modernist canon is made alongside 'feminist introductions' to, for instance, T. S. Eliot. Two subsequent books by Kime Scott deal with women writers only. *Refiguring Modernism: Volume 1 The Women of 1928* and *Volume 2 Postmodern Feminist Readings of Woolf, West, and Barnes* appeared from Indiana University Press in 1995.

A similar focus on women predominates in Sandra Gilbert and Susan Gubar, *No Man's Land: The Place of the Woman Writer in the Twentieth Century* (three vols., New Haven: Yale University Press, 1988–94). This is also the case with Alice Jardine, *Gynesis: Configurations of Women and Modernity* (Ithaca: Cornell University Press, 1985); Suzanne Clark, *Sentimental Modernism: Women Writers and the Revolution of the Word* (Bloomington: Indiana University Press, 1991); and Gabriele Griffin (ed.), *Difference in View: Women and Modernism* (London: Taylor & Francis, 1994).

Other feminist books on modernism apply gender perspectives to the writings of both sexes; see, for instance, Lisa Rado's two books *Rereading*

Modernism: New Directions in Feminist Criticism (New York and London: Garland, 1994) and *Modernism, Gender, and Culture: A Cultural Studies Approach* (New York and London: Garland, 1997), as well as Rita Felski, *The Gender of Modernity* (Cambridge/Mass.: Harvard University Press, 1996). Women writers are usually foregrounded by feminist writers, though, as in Elizabeth Harrison and Shirley Peterson (eds), *Unmanning Modernism: Gendered Re-Readings* (Knoxville: University of Tennessee Press, 1997). However, it is noteworthy that one of the most influential feminist books on modernism, Marianne DeKoven's *Rich and Strange: Gender, History, Modernism* (Princeton: Princeton University Press, 1991), concentrates on male writers (among them James and Conrad); DeKoven is especially interested in narrative.

Among other works on women modernists, Shari Benstock's groundbreaking book *Women of the Left Bank: Paris, 1900–1940* (London: Virago, 1987) holds a special place. Three further feminist studies concentrate on individual women writers: Susan Stratford Friedman's *Penelope's Web: Gender, Modernity, H. D.'s Fiction* (Cambridge: Cambridge University Press, 1990), Kristin Bluemel's *Experimenting on the Borders of Modernism: Dorothy Richardson's Pilgrimage* (Athens etc.: University of Georgia Press, 1997), and Georgina Taylor's *H. D. and the Public Sphere of Modernist Women Writers, 1913–1946: Talking Women* (Oxford: Clarendon Press, 2001).

The 1990s witnessed the emergence of a new sub-speciality as scholars began to examine **modernist writings as physical/material phenomena**. A book edited by George Bornstein, *Representing Modernist Texts: Editing as Interpretation* (Ann Arbor: University of Michigan Press, 1991) combines textual scholarship with editorial considerations of a 'critical' kind. Similar concerns are addressed in Douglas Mao's *Solid Objects: Modernism and the Test of Production* (Princeton: Princeton University Press, 1998) and Michael Kaufmann, *Textual Bodies: Modernism, Postmodernism, and Print* (Lewisburg: Bucknell University Press and London etc.: Associated University Presses, 1994). Several scholars have contributed much-needed information about the modernists and the marketplace. In addition to Lawrence Rainey's *Institutions of Modernism: Literary Elites and Public Culture* (New Haven: Yale University Press, 1998), the following works should be mentioned: Joseph McAleer, *Popular Reading and Publishing in Britain, 1914–1950* (Oxford: Clarendon Press, 1992); Richard Ohmann, *Selling Culture: Magazines, Markets, and Class at the Turn of the Century* (London and New York: Verso, 1996); Ian Willison, Warwick Gould, and Warren Chernaik (eds), *Modernist Writers and the Marketplace* (Basingstoke: Macmillan, 1996); and Joyce Piell Wexler, *Who Paid for Modernism? Art, Money, and the Fiction of Conrad, Joyce, and Lawrence* (Fayetteville: University of Arkansas Press, 1997). Kate Campbell (ed.), *Journalism, Literature and Modernity: From*

Hazlitt to Modernism (Edinburgh: Edinburgh University Press, 2000), contains chapters on Dora Marsden, Rebecca West, Virginia Woolf, and Laura Riding as journalists. George Bornstein's recent *Material Modernism: The Politics of the Page* (Cambridge: Cambridge University Press, 2001) historicizes modernism from the point of view of production and dissemination.

Part II

Most of the works listed below are, at least in part, specifically concerned with literary modernism in the Anglo-American sphere. The exceptions – such as the occasional biography – were included because they have something to offer the student of modernism along the lines of what used to be called 'background'. Space considerations made it impossible to list more than a couple of works predominantly concerned with the Continent and with the arts in general, and even fewer articles could be admitted. There are thousands of books about the individual modernist writers, and only works which explicitly address the relevant writer's position in relation to modernism could be included here.

Some classic critical/scholarly works on early twentieth-century literature published during the first half of the century are listed, but key texts by modernist writers (e.g. Eliot, Pound, and Woolf) were omitted since no student of modernism can fail to encounter them; see, for instance, the anthologies of primary texts mentioned above.

NB: Works mentioned in Part I above are not listed here.

Albright, Daniel. *Quantum Poetics: Yeats, Pound, Eliot, and the Science of Modernism.* Cambridge University Press, 1997. [Accent on natural science.]

– *Untwisting the Serpent: Modernism in Music, Literature, and Other Arts.* Chicago and London: University of Chicago Press, 2000. [European in outlook.]

Alldritt, Keith. *Modernism in the Second World War: The Later Poetry of Ezra Pound, T. S. Eliot, Basil Bunting, and Hugh MacDiarmid.* New York: Peter Lang, 1989.

Ardis, Ann. *New Women, New Novels: Feminism and Early Modernism.* New Brunswick and London: Rutgers University Press, 1990. [Emphasis on the 'New Woman' of the late 19th century.]

Ayers, David. *English Literature of the 1920s.* Edinburgh University Press, 1999.

Beer, Gillian. *Open Fields: Science in Cultural Encounter.* Oxford: Clarendon Press, 1996. [Addresses modernism in relation to scientific developments in the Victorian age.]

Begam, Richard. *Samuel Beckett and the End of Modernity.* Cambridge

University Press, 1997.

Behler, Ernst. *Irony and the Discourse of Modernity.* Seattle and London: University of Washington Press, 1990. [Orientated towards literary theory.]

Bennett, Deborah Tyler. *Edith Sitwell: The Forgotten Modernist.* Sheffield: PAVIC Publications, 1996. [A short book; no extensive analyses of S.'s modernism.]

Berman, Jessica. *Modernist Fiction, Cosmopolitanism, and the Politics of Community.* Cambridge University Press, 2001. [Orientated towards theory and politics.]

Boone, Joseph Allen. *Libidinal Currents: Sexuality and the Shaping of Modernism.* Chicago and London: University of Chicago Press, 1998.

Bornstein, Daniel. *The Postromantic Consciousness of Ezra Pound.* Victoria BC, English Literary Studies, University of Victoria, 1977.

Bornstein, George. *Transformations of Romanticism in Yeats, Eliot, and Stevens.* Chicago: University of Chicago Press, 1976.

Bradbury, Malcolm. *The Modern World: Ten Great Writers.* Harmondsworth: Penguin, 1989.

Brooker, Jewel Spears. *Mastery and Escape: T. S. Eliot and the Dialectic of Modernism.* Amherst: University of Massachusetts Press, 1994.

– With Joseph Bentley. *Reading* The Waste Land: *Modernism and the Limits of Interpretation.* Amherst: University of Massachusetts Press, 1990.

Brooks, Cleanth. *Modern Poetry and the Tradition.* Chapel Hill: University of North Carolina Press, 1939.

Brown, Dennis. *The Modernist Self in Twentieth-Century English Literature: A Study in Self-Fragmentation.* Basingstoke: Macmillan, 1989.

– *Intertextual Dynamics within the Literary Group – Joyce, Lewis, Pound and Eliot: The Men of 1914.* Basingstoke: Macmillan, 1990.

Bush, Ronald, ed. *T. S. Eliot: The Modernist in History.* Cambridge University Press, 1991.

Carey, John. *The Intellectuals and the Masses: Pride and Prejudice among the Literary Intelligentsia 1880-1939.* London: Faber and Faber, 1992.

Castle, Gregory. *Modernism and the Celtic Revival.* Cambridge University Press, 2001.

Childs, Donald J. *Modernism and Eugenics: Woolf, Eliot, Yeats, and the Culture of Degeneration.* Cambridge University Press, 2001.

Childs, John Steven. *Modernist Form: Pound's Style in the Early Cantos.* Selinsgrove: Susquehanna University Press; London and Toronto: Associated University Presses, 1986.

Childs, Peter. *Modernism.* London: Routledge, 2000. [A good general handbook by the author of the equally readable *The Twentieth Century in Poetry* (Routledge 1998); both books include useful bibliographies.]

Clark, T. J. *Farewell to an Idea: Episodes from a History of Modernism*. New Haven: Yale University Press, 1999.

Clearfield, Andrew M. *These Fragments I Have Shored: Collage and Montage in Early Modernist Poetry*. Ann Arbor: UMI Research Press 1984. [A lucid study of experimental techniques, also good on the history of modernism.]

Coughlan, Patricia, and Alex Davis, eds. *Modernism and Ireland: The Poetry of the 1930s*. Cork University Press, 1995. [Irish poetry only.]

Crawford, Robert. *The Savage and the City in the Work of T. S. Eliot*. Oxford: Clarendon Press, 1987.

Daiches, David. *Poetry and the Modern World*. Chicago: University of Chicago Press, 1940, reprinted in 1978.

Daly, Nicholas. *Modernism, Romance and the Fin de Siècle: Popular Fiction and British Culture, 1880-1914*. Cambridge University Press, 1999.

Davis, Alex and Lee M. Jenkins, eds. *Locations of Literary Modernism: Region and Nation in British and American Modernist Poetry*. Cambridge University Press, 2000.

DiBattista, Maria, and Lucy McDiarmid, eds. *High and Low Moderns: Literature and Culture, 1889–1939*. New York and Oxford: Oxford University Press, 1996.

Donoghue, Denis. *The Old Moderns: Essays on Literature and Theory*. New York: Alfred A. Knopf, 1994.

Dubnick, Randa. *The Structure of Obscurity: Gertrude Stein, Language, and Cubism*. Urbana and Chicago: University of Illinois Press, 1984.

DuPlessis, Rachel Blau. *H. D.: The Career of That Struggle*. Brighton: Harvester, 1986.

Ehrlich, Heyward, ed. *Light Rays: James Joyce and Modernism*. New York: New Horizon, 1984.

Ellison, David. *Ethics and Aesthetics in European Literature: From the Sublime to the Uncanny*. Cambridge University Press, 2001. [Emphasis on the nineteenth-century origins of modernist engagement with beauty and morality.]

Ellmann, Richard, and Charles Feidelson, eds. *The Modern Tradition: Backgrounds of Modern Literature*. Oxford University Press, 1965.

Erdinast-Vulcan, Daphna. *Joseph Conrad and the Modern Temper*. Oxford University Press, 1991.

– *The Strange Short Fiction of Joseph Conrad: Writing, Culture, and Subjectivity*. Oxford University Press, 1999.

Filreis, Alan. *Modernism from Right to Left: Wallace Stevens, the Thirties & Literary Radicalism*. Cambridge University Press, 1994.

Fitzgerald, Penelope. *Charlotte Mew and Her Friends*. London: Collins, 1984.

Fokkema, Douwe W., and Hans Bertens, eds. *Approaching Postmodernism.* Amsterdam and Philadelphia: Benjamins, 1986.

Foshay, Toby Avard. *Wyndham Lewis and the Avant-Garde: The Politics of the Intellect.* Montreal etc.: McGill-Queen's University Press, 1992.

Foster, John Burt, Jr. *Heirs to Dionysus: A Nietzschean Current in Literary Modernism.* Princeton University Press, 1981.

Fraser, G. S. *The Modern Writer and His World.* Originally published in 1953 by D. Verschoyle; reprinted by Penguin in 1970. [Still an informative, and very readable, introduction to 20th-century poetry in general.]

Furbank, P. N., and Arnold Kettle, eds. *Modernism and Its Origins.* Milton Keynes: Open University Press, 1973. [Basic but useful.]

Gambrell, Alice. *Women Intellectuals, Modernism, and Difference: Transatlantic Culture 1919–1945.* Cambridge University Press, 1997. [Emphasis on culture in a wide sense; deals with *i.a.* Carrington and Kahlo.]

Garvin, Harry R., ed. *Romanticism, Modernism, Postmodernism.* Lewisburg: Bucknell University Press, 1980.

Gelpi, Albert, ed. *Wallace Stevens: The Poetics of Modernism.* Cambridge University Press, 1985.

Gillie, Christopher. *Movements in English Literature 1900–1940.* Cambridge University Press, 1975.

Glover, Philip, ed. *Ezra Pound The London Years: 1908–1920.* New York: AMS Press, 1987.

Grant, Joy. *Harold Monro and the Poetry Bookshop.* London: Routledge and Kegan Paul, 1967.

Graves, Robert, and Laura Riding. *A Survey of Modernist Poetry.* London: William Heinemann, 1927.

Greaves, Richard. *Transition, Reception and Modernism in W. B. Yeats.* Basingstoke: Palgrave, 2002. [This brief monograph problematizes the term 'modernism' in a spirited attempt to 'see Yeats as Yeats, and not as a partial example – or failed example – of modernism in literature'.]

Habermas, Jürgen. *Der philosophische Diskurs der Moderne*; translated by Frederick Lawrence as *The Philosophical Discourse of Modernity: Twelve Lectures.* Cambridge/Mass.: MIT Press, 1987.

Haefner, Gerhard. *Klassiker des englischen Romans im 20. Jahrhundert: Joseph Conrad, D. H. Lawrence, James Joyce, Virginia Woolf, Samuel Beckett. Begründung der Moderne und Abrechnung mit der Moderne.* Heidelberg: C. Winter, 1990.

Hamburger, Michael. *The Truth of Poetry: Tensions in Modernist Poetry since Baudelaire.* London: Weidenfeld and Nicolson, 1968; reprinted, most recently by Anvil Press (London) in 1996. [Emphasis on Europe.]

Hammer, Langdon. *Hart Crane and Allen Tate: Janus-Faced Modernism.* Princeton University Press, 1993. [Useful American orientation and a thoughtful introduction on modernism as cultural/political response.]

Hanscombe, Gillian E., and Virginia L. Smyers. *Writing for Their Lives: The Modernist Women, 1910–1940.* London: Women's Press, 1987. [Mostly biographical.]

Harmer, J. B. *Victory in Limbo: Imagism 1908–1917.* London: Secker & Warburg, 1975.

Harvey, David. *The Condition of Postmodernity: An Enquiry into the Origins of Cultural Change.* Oxford: Blackwell, 1989.

Hassan, Ihab. *The Dismemberment of Orpheus: Toward a Postmodern Literature.* New York: Oxford University Press, 1971. 2nd ed., Madison: University of Wisconsin Press, 1982.

Hayman, David. *Re-forming the Narrative: Toward a Mechanics of Modernist Fiction.* Ithaca: Cornell University Press, 1987.

Head, Dominic. *The Modernist Short Story: A Study in Theory and Practice.* Cambridge University Press, 1992.

Hermans, Theo. *The Structure of Modernist Poetry.* London and Canberra: Croom Helm, 1982. [One chapter on Pound, rest on Continent.]

Hewitt, Andrew. *Fascist Modernism: Aesthetics, Politics and the Avant-Garde.* Stanford University Press, 1993.

– *Political Inversions: Homosexuality, Fascism and the Modernist Imaginary.* Stanford University Press, 1996. [Focus on male homosexuality.]

Hewitt, Douglas. *English Fiction of the Early Modern Period 1890–1940.* London: Longman, 1988.

Hoffman, Frederic J. *The Twenties: American Writing in the Postwar Decade.* First publ. 1963, rev.ed. 1965, from the Free Press in New York.

Hoffpauir, Richard. *The Art of Restraint: English Poetry from Hardy to Larkin.* Newark: University of Delaware Press; London and Toronto: Associated University Presses, 1991.

Hughes, Glenn. *Imagism and the Imagists: A Study of Modern Poetry.* Stanford University Press, 1931; reprinted in 1960 and 1973.

Hughes, Robert. *The Shock of the New: Art and the Century of Change.* London: Thames and Hudson, 1980.

Hutcheon, Linda. *A Poetics of Postmodernism: History, Theory, Fiction.* New York and London: Routledge, 1988.

Innes, Christopher. *Modern British Drama: 1890–1990.* Cambridge University Press, 1992.

– *Avant-Garde Theatre: 1892–1992.* London: Routledge, 1993.

– With Frederick Marker, eds. *Modernism in European Drama.* UTP 1998.

Jackson, Tony E. *The Subject of Modernism: Narrative Alterations in the*

Fiction of Eliot, Conrad, Woolf, and Joyce. Ann Arbor: The University of Michigan Press, 1994.

Jameson, Fredric. *Fables of Aggression: Wyndham Lewis, the Modernist as Fascist*. Berkeley: University of California Press, 1979.

– *Postmodernism, or, The Cultural Logic of Late Capitalism*. Durham: Duke University Press, 1991.

Johnson-Roullier, Cyraina E. *Reading on the Edge: Exiles, Modernities, and Cultural Transformation in Proust, Joyce, and Baldwin*. New York: State University of New York Press, 2000.

Jones, Alun R. *The Life and Opinions of T. E. Hulme*. London: Victor Gollancz, 1960.

Josipovici, Gabriel. *The Lessons of Modernism and Other Essays*. London: Macmillan, 1977.

Journal of Modern Literature. The whole fifth number of Vol. 3 is devoted to modernism (July 1974).

Kaplan, Sydney J. *Katherine Mansfield and the Origins of Modernist Fiction*. Ithaca: Cornell University Press, 1991.

Kenner, Hugh. *The Pound Era*. Berkeley and Los Angeles: University of California Press, 1971, and London: Faber and Faber, 1972.

Kouidis, Virginia. *Mina Loy: American Modernist Poet*. Baton Rouge: Louisiana State University Press, 1980.

Krauss, Rosalind E. *The Originality of the Avant-Garde and Other Modernist Myths*. Cambridge/Mass. and London: MIT Press, 1987.

Laity, Cassandra. *H. D. and the Victorian Fin de Siècle: Gender, Modernism, Decadence*. Cambridge University Press, 1996.

Lamos, Colleen, *Deviant Modernism: Sexual and Textual Errancy in T. S. Eliot, James Joyce, and Marcel Proust*. Cambridge University Press, 1998. [Gender emphasis, social implications.]

Langbaum, Robert W. *The Mysteries of Identity: A Theme in Modern Literature*. New York: Oxford University Press, 1977.

Larrissy, Edward. *Reading Twentieth-Century Poetry: The Language of Gender and Objects*. Oxford: Blackwell, 1990.

Leavis, F. R. *New Bearings in English Poetry: A Study of the Contemporary Situation*. First published in 1932; repr. by Chatto and Windus in 1961.

Lentricchia, Frank. *Modernist Quartet*. Cambridge University Press, 1994. [On Frost, Stevens, Pound, and Eliot.]

Levenson, Michael. *Modernism and the Fate of Individuality: Character and Novelistic Form from Conrad to Woolf*. Cambridge University Press, 1991.

Levitt, Morton P. *James Joyce and Modernism: Beyond Dublin*. Lewiston, New York, and Lampeter: Edwin Mellen, 2000.

Lewis, Pericles. *Modernism, Nationalism, and the Novel.* Cambridge University Press, 2000.

Lidderdale, Jane, and Mary Nicholson. *Dear Miss Weaver: Harriet Shaw Weaver, 1876–1961.* London: Faber, 1970.

Lindberg, Kathryne. *Reading Pound Reading: Modernism after Nietzsche.* New York and Oxford: Oxford University Press, 1987.

Longenbach, James. *Modernist Poetics of History: Pound, Eliot and the Sense of the Past.* Princeton University Press, 1987.

– *Stone Cottage: Pound, Yeats, and Modernism.* New York and Oxford: Oxford University Press, 1988.

Lucas, John. *Modern English Poetry from Hardy to Hughes.* London: Batsford, 1986.

Lukács, Georg. *The Meaning of Contemporary Realism.* London: Merlin Press, 1963.

Luthersson, Peter. *Modernism och individualitet: en studie i den litterära modernismens kvalitativa egenart.* Stehag: Symposion, 1986; subsequently reprinted.

Lyotard, Jean-François. *The Post-Modern Condition: A Report on Knowledge* (trans. G. Bennington and B. Massumi). Minneapolis: University of Minnesota Press, 1984. First published as *La Condition postmoderne: rapport sur le savoir,* Paris: Les Éditions de Minuit, 1979.

Malamud, Randy. *The Language of Modernism.* Ann Arbor: UMI Research Press, 1989.

de Man, Paul. *Blindness and Insight: Essays in the Rhetoric of Contemporary Criticism.* New York and Oxford: Oxford University Press, 1971.

Martin, Graham, and P. N. Furbank, eds. *Twentieth Century Poetry: Critical Essays and Documents.* Milton Keynes: The Open University Press, 1975. [Basic, as the handbook it is, but useful.]

Martin, Taffy. *Marianne Moore: Subversive Modernist.* Austin: University of Texas Press, 1986.

Martz, Louis L. *Many Gods and Many Voices: The Role of the Prophet in English and American Modernism.* Columbia and London: University of Missouri Press, 1998. [A useful bibliography adds to the value of this fine study.]

Materer, Timothy. *Modernist Alchemy: Poetry and the Occult.* Ithaca: Cornell University Press, 1995. [See also Surette below.]

Matz, Jesse. *Literary Impressionism and Modern Aesthetics.* Cambridge University Press, 2001. [Emphasis on fiction, notably James, Conrad, and Woolf.]

McCartney, George. *Confused Roaring: Evelyn Waugh and the Modernist Tradition.* Bloomington: Indiana University Press, 1987. [Interesting sidelights on the modernist heritage through the work of a 'non-modernist' author.]

McGann, Jerome. *Black Riders: The Visible Language of Modernism.* Princeton University Press, 1993.

McGrath, F. C. *The Sensible Spirit: Walter Pater and the Modernist Paradigm.* Tampa: University of South Florida Press, 1986. ['Genealogical' suggestions.]

Melaney, William D. *After Ontology: Literary Theory and Modernist Poetics.* New York: State University of New York Press, 2001. [Relates modernist literature to postmodern theory.]

Menand, Louis. *Discovering Modernism: T. S. Eliot and His Context.* New York and Oxford: Oxford University Press, 1987.

– 'Lost Faculties'. *The New Republic,* 9 and 16 July 1990, 36-40.

Miller, Jane E. *Rebel Women: Feminism, Modernism and the Edwardian Novel.* London: Virago, 1994.

Minow-Pinkney, Makiko. *Virginia Woolf & the Problem of the Subject.* Brighton: Harvester, 1987.

Modernity and Modernism, Postmodernity and Postmodernism. A periodical published by Telos Press since 1986.

Monro, Harold. *Some Contemporary Poets (1920).* London: Leonard Parsons, 1920.

Montefiore, Jan. *Men and Women Writers of the 1930s: The Dangerous Flood of History.* London: Routledge, 1996.

Müller, Harro. *Gifipfeile: zu Theorie und Literatur der Moderne.* Bielefeld: Aisthesis, 1994.

Muir, Edwin. *We Moderns: Enigmas and Guesses.* New York: Alfred A. Knopf, 1920.

Norris, Margot. *Joyce's Web: The Social Unraveling of Modernism.* Austin: University of Texas Press, 1992.

O'Keefe, Paul. *Some Sort of Genius: A Life of Wyndham Lewis.* London: Jonathan Cape, 2000.

Osterwalder, Hans. *British Poetry between The Movement and Modernism.* Heidelberg: C. Winter, 1991. [An inclusive study with useful bibliographical components.]

Parisi, Joseph, ed. *Marianne Moore: The Art of a Modernist.* Ann Arbor: University of Michigan Research Press, 1990.

Pease, Allison. *Modernism, Mass Culture, and the Aesthetics of Obscenity.* Cambridge University Press, 2000. [Going back to the eighteenth century, this book discusses the modernists' appropriation of pornography for high art.]

Perkins, David. *A History of Modern Poetry: From the 1890s to the High Modernist Mode.* Cambridge/Mass. and London: Belknap Press (Harvard), 1976. [This is the first volume of a two-volume work which provides excellent surveys and a surprising amount of in-depth consideration of individual poets, not least 'non-modernist' ones. An indispensable guide.]

Perl, Jeffrey M. *The Tradition of Return: The Implicit History of Modern Literature*. Princeton University Press, 1984.

– *Skepticism and Modern Enmity: Before and After Eliot*. Baltimore: Johns Hopkins University Press, 1981.

Perloff, Marjorie. *The Poetics of Indeterminacy: Rimbaud to Cage*. Princeton University Press, 1981.

– *The Futurist Moment: Avant-Garde, Avant-Guerre, and the Language of Rupture*. Chicago and London: University of Chicago Press, 1986.

– *Poetic License: Essays on Modernist and Postmodernist Lyric*. Evanston: Northwestern University Press, 1990.

Pinkney, Tony. *D. H. Lawrence and Modernism*. Iowa City: University of Iowa Press, 1990.

Poggioli, Renato. *The Theory of the Avant-Garde*. Cambridge/Mass.: Belknap Press, 1968.

Press, John. *The Chequer'd Shade: Reflections on Obscurity in Poetry*. London and New York: Oxford University Press, 1958, reprinted in 1963.

– *A Map of Modern English Verse*. Oxford University Press, 1969.

Rabaté, Jean-Michel. *The Ghosts of Modernity*. Gainesville etc.: University Press of Florida, 1996.

Raitt, Suzanne. *May Sinclair: A Modern Victorian*. Oxford: Clarendon Press, 2000.

Richardson, Brian. *Unlikely Stories: Causality and the Nature of Modern Narrative*. Newark: University of Delaware Press; London: Associated University Presses, 1997.

Riddel, Joseph. *The Inverted Bell: Modernism and the Counterpoetics of William Carlos Williams*. Baton Rouge: Louisiana State University Press, 1974.

– *The Turning World: American Literary Modernism and Continental Theory*. Ed. Mark Bauerlein. Philadelphia; University of Pennsylvania Press, 1996. [Ch. 5, 'The Anomalies of Literary (Post) Modernism', is of particular interest in the present context.]

Rieke, Alison. *The Senses of Nonsense*. Iowa City: University of Iowa Press, 1992. [Addresses writing 'beyond the limits of conventional sense' by Joyce, Stein, Stevens, and Louis Zukofsky.]

Rogers, Timothy, ed. *Georgian Poetry 1911–1922: The Critical Heritage*. London: Routledge, 1972.

Ross, Robert H. *The Georgian Revolt: Rise and Fall of a Poetic Ideal 1910–1922*. London: Faber, 1967. [Rogers' and Ross's books provide a healthy counterweight to the massive literature on modernist writers, as well as fascinating sidelights on the 'modernists'' position on the literary scene.]

Roston, Murray. *Modernist Patterns in Literature and the Visual Arts*. Basingstoke: Macmillan, 2000.

Ryan, Judith. *The Vanishing Subject: Early Psychology and Literary Modernism.* Chicago and London: University of Chicago Press, 1991.

Sass, Louis A. *Madness and Modernism: Insanity in the Light of Modern Art, Literature, and Thought.* Cambridge/Mass. and London: Harvard University Press, 1994.

Schleifer, Ronald. *Rhetoric and Death: The Language of Modernism and Postmodern Discourse Theory.* Urbana: University of Illinois Press, 1990.

– *Modernism and Time: The Logic of Abundance in Literature.* Cambridge University Press, 2000. [Emphasis on science, politics, and culture and society in general; heavily theorized.]

Schneidau, Herbert N. *Waking Giants: The Presence of the Past in Modernism.* New York and Oxford: Oxford University Press, 1991.

Schwab, Gabriele. *Subjects without Selves: Transitional Texts in Modern Fiction.* Cambridge/Mass. and London: Harvard University Press, 1994.

Schwartz, Nina. *Dead Fathers: The Logic of Transference in Modern Narrative.* Ann Arbor: University of Michigan Press, 1994.

Schwartz, Sanford. *The Matrix of Modernism: Pound, Eliot, and Early Twentieth-Century Thought.* Princeton University Press, 1985.

Schwarz, Daniel R. *Reconfiguring Modernism: Explorations in the Relationship between Modern Art and Modern Literature.* Basingstoke: Macmillan, 1997.

Sherry, Vincent B. *Ezra Pound, Wyndham Lewis, and Radical Modernism.* Oxford University Press, 1993. [Mostly political in orientation.]

Simon, Myron. *The Georgian Poetic.* Berkeley etc.: University of California Press, 1975. [A short but insightful and elegant monograph along lines similar to those found in Robert Ross's book; see above.]

Smith, Andrew, and Jeff Wallace, eds. *Gothic Modernisms.* Basingstoke: Palgrave, 2001. [Picks up Gothic elements in, *inter alia*, Woolf, Barnes, Lawrence, and Lewis. Two contributions on film, including Lang's *Metropolis.*]

Spender, Stephen. *The Struggle of the Modern.* London: Hamish Hamilton, 1963. Subsequently reprinted by Methuen.

Stevens, Hugh, and Caroline Howlett, eds. *Modernist Sexualities.* Manchester University Press, 2000. [A lively collection of essays exploring the margins of modernism, sometimes from gender/queer perspectives. Introduction by Hugh Stevens problematizes the modernism concept.]

Stevenson, Randall. *Modernist Fiction.* Hemel Hempstead: Harvester, 1993.

Strychacz, Thomas F. *Modernism, Mass Culture, and Professionalism.* Cambridge University Press, 1993.

Sumner, Rosemary. *A Route to Modernism: Hardy, Lawrence, Woolf.* Basingstoke: Macmillan, 2000.

Surette, Leon. *The Birth of Modernism: Ezra Pound, T. S. Eliot, W. B. Yeats, and the Occult.* Montreal etc.: McGill-Queen's University Press, 1993. [See also Materer above.]

Sussman, Henry. *Afterimages of Modernity: Structure and Indifference in Twentieth Century Literature.* Baltimore: Johns Hopkins University Press, 1990.

Svarny, Erik. *'The Men of 1914': T. S. Eliot and Early Modernism.* Milton Keynes: Open University Press, 1988.

Tate, Trudi. *Modernism, History and the First World War.* Manchester University Press, 1998.

Tratner, Michael. *Modernism and Mass Politics: Joyce, Woolf, Eliot, Yeats.* Stanford University Press, 1995.

Treichel, Hans Ulrich. *Auslöschungsverfahren: Exemplarische Untersuchungen zur Literatur und Poetik der Moderne.* Munich: W. Fink, 1995.

Trotter, David. *The Making of the Reader: Language and Subjectivity in Modern American, English, and Irish Poetry.* London: Macmillan, 1984.

–*The English Novel in History 1895-1920.* London: Routledge, 1993.

– *Paranoid Modernism: Literary Experiment, Psychosis, and the Professionalization of English Society.* Oxford University Press, 2000.

Vargish, Thomas, and Delo E. Mook. *Inside Modernism: Relativity Theory, Cubism, Narrative.* New Haven and London: Yale University Press, 1999.

Walker, Jayne L. *The Making of a Modernist: Gertrude Stein from Three Lives to Tender Buttons.* Amherst: University of Massachusetts Press, 1984.

Wees, William C. *Vorticism and the English Avant-Garde.* Manchester University Press, 1972.

Weinstein, Philip M. *The Semantics of Desire: Changing Models of Identity from Dickens to Joyce.* Princeton University Press, 1984.

Weir, David. *Decadence and the Making of Modernism.* Amherst: University of Massachusetts Press, 1995. [Emphasis on France and on the turn of the century; one chapter deals with Joyce and Gide.]

Weisberg, David. *Chronicles of Disorder: Samuel Beckett and the Cultural Politics of the Modern World.* New York: State University of New York Press, 2000.

Welsch, Wolfgang. *Unsere postmoderne Moderne.* Weinheim: Acta Humaniora, 1988.

Wheeler, Kathleen. *'Modernist' Women Writers and Narrative Art.* London: Macmillan, 1994. New York: New York University Press, 1994.

White, Allon. *The Uses of Obscurity: The Fiction of Early Modernism.* London: Routledge, 1981.

White, John H. *Literary Futurism: Aspects of the First Avant-Garde.* Oxford:

Clarendon Press, 1990.

Whitworth, Michael H. *Einstein's Wake: Relativity, Metaphor, and Modernist Literature.* Oxford University Press, 2001.

Widmer, Kingsley. *Edges of Extremity: Some Problems of Literary Modernism.* Tulsa, Oklahoma: University of Tulsa, 1980. [A short book which deals with modernist fiction and problematizes the concept of modernism.]

Wilde, Alan. *Horizons of Assent: Modernism, Postmodernism and the Ironic Imagination.* Baltimore: Johns Hopkins University Press, 1981.

Williams, Keith, and Steven Matthews, eds. *Rewriting the Thirties: Modernism and After.* Harlow, Essex: Longman, 1997.

Williams, Raymond. *Culture and Society: 1780-1950.* Harmondsworth: Penguin, 1958.

– *The Politics of Modernism: Against the New Conformists.* Ed. Tony Pinkney. London: Verso, 1989.

Wilson, Edmund. *Axel's Castle: A Study in the Imaginative Literature of 1870–1930.* New York: Scribner, 1931; reprinted in 1959.

Wright, Anne. *The Literature of Crisis, 1910-22.* London: Macmillan, 1984.

Index

The index lists names (including those of editors and translators at the first occurrence), selected titles, and a few concepts of special relevance to the book's subject. The bibliographical section has not been indexed.